THE CALLED SHOT

The Called Shot

BABE RUTH, THE CHICAGO CUBS, AND
THE UNFORGETTABLE MAJOR LEAGUE
BASEBALL SEASON OF 1932

THOMAS WOLF

University of Nebraska Press | Lincoln

Portions of chapter 16 previously appeared in "The Warden
Takes a Murderer to the World Series," *Cooperstown
Symposium on Baseball and American Culture* (2005–2006):
201–13, and "The Golden Era of Prison Baseball and the
Revenge of Casey Coburn," *Cooperstown Symposium on
Baseball and American Culture* (2017–2018): 116–25.

Library of Congress Cataloging-in-Publication Data
Names: Wolf, Thomas, 1947–, author.
Title: The called shot: Babe Ruth, the Chicago Cubs, and
the unforgettable major league baseball season of 1932 /
Thomas Wolf.
Description: Lincoln: University of Nebraska Press, 2020. |
Includes bibliographical references and index. | Summary:
"The story of the 1932 baseball season and Babe Ruth's
called shot"—Provided by publisher.
Identifiers: LCCN 2019035338
ISBN 9780803255241 (hardback)
ISBN 9781496221681 (epub)
ISBN 9781496221698 (mobi)
ISBN 9781496221704 (pdf)
Subjects: LCSH: Baseball—United States—History—20th
century. | Ruth, Babe, 1895–1948. | New York Yankees
(Baseball team)—History—20th century. | Chicago Cubs
(Baseball team)—History—20th century.
Classification: LCC GV863.A1 W648 2020 | DDC
796.3570973—dc23
LC record available at https://lccn.loc.gov/2019035338

Set in Whitman by Laura Ebbeka.

For Patricia Lee Bryan

CONTENTS

ACKNOWLEDGMENTS

I started work on this book many years ago, and I've benefitted greatly from other writers, researchers, friends, and readers who have offered advice and constructive criticism. I am grateful to an entire team of collaborators on this project.

Thanks to Steve Wendl and the late Richard Snavely who first told me the tale of Snap Hortman and generated my interest in telling a story about the 1932 baseball season and Babe Ruth's called shot.

I am especially fortunate to have a superb agent, Stacey Glick, who has been persistent, insightful, prodding, and supportive during the years this book took shape. I greatly appreciate Rob Taylor, Ann Baker, Courtney Ochsner, and the team at the University of Nebraska Press for their patience, editorial expertise, belief in this project, and enthusiasm for the rich history of baseball. I also want to acknowledge Amanda Jackson for copyediting this manuscript in preparation for publication.

I received valuable assistance from all of those at the National Baseball Hall of Fame with whom I've worked: Tim Wiles, Jim Gates, Matt Rothenberg, John Horne, and Cassidy Link. They listened to my frequent questions and queries and responded promptly with useful information.

I have participated in many sessions of the Cooperstown Symposium on Baseball and American Culture and wish to thank the people I've met in connection with those programs, especially William Simons, William Steele, Paul Hensler, Lee Lowenfish, and Charles DeMotte.

Dave Shaw, Marjorie Hudson, and Marko Fong all read significant portions of this manuscript in progress and contributed intelligent baseball-infused guidance that made this a much better book. And thanks also to fellow baseball researcher Jack Bales for his thoughtful commentary on my project, as he worked on his own books and articles about the history of the Chicago Cubs. Thanks to Kirk Griffin and Don Knefel for their friendship and support over the years. Thanks also to Carol and Des Runyan, Carol and Ted Ballou, Julie Bosworth, and Grace Dolfi for their encouragement and interest in this project. Amelia Melching, Lauren Brown, and Evonna Sampedro deserve credit for helping me with baseball stadium research.

For information about Charles Ireland and his family, I am indebted to his grandchildren, Nancy Tschorn and John Schweitzer, who shared family stories, photos, letters, and memorabilia that enhanced my knowledge and understanding of life at the Men's Reformatory in the 1930s.

Thanks to Curt Smith for sharing his insights and thoughts on Tom Manning and the announcers who called the World Series games of 1932.

Jody Hanshew and Charles Sydnor at Emory and Henry College assisted with research into the fascinating life and exploits of Monte Weaver. Dick DeCourcy shared anecdotes about Joe Sewell and provided an introduction to the world of sports memorabilia. Taylor Browne provided research help.

I wish to acknowledge my three sons—John, Michael, and David—who have patiently waited for the completion of this book. At last, here it is.

Most important, thanks to my wife, Patricia Bryan, who has cheered me on since I first started working on this book. I deeply appreciate Patricia's enthusiasm and encouragement. Without her support, this book wouldn't exist.

INTRODUCTION

In the summer of 1932, at the beginning of the decade that would remake America, baseball fans were treated to one of the most remarkable seasons in the history of the sport. This book tells the story of that season.

It was a pivotal time in the nation's history. After a decade of unparalleled ambition, greed, affluence, and self-indulgence, America was suffering from what historian William Leuchtenberg called "the perils of prosperity."[1] Unemployment rose; one in four Americans seeking work couldn't find a job. Wages dropped. Banks and privately owned businesses failed. The value of farm property plummeted. Construction of new homes declined.[2]

By the middle of the summer, more than 15,000 angry World War I veterans, calling themselves the Bonus Army, had marched into the nation's capital demanding an early payment of their veterans' bonuses.

Abroad, there were similar economic problems and social disruption. In Europe a rising young politician named Adolph Hitler placed second in the German presidential elections, receiving 37 percent of the vote.

In this critical year—a presidential election year, no less—Americans turned to baseball as a diversion. While other sporting events—horse races, boxing matches, tennis and golf tournaments—attracted attention, baseball was the national pastime, the only team sport that mattered. Many of the greats of the game were in their prime or nearing the end of their careers. The names of baseball luminaries like Ruth, Gehrig, Foxx, Hornsby, Grove, McGraw, and McCarthy dominated the sports pages.

Five young pitchers—Dizzy Dean, Johnny Allen, Van Lingle Mungo, Lon Warneke, and Monte Weaver—would make dramatic contributions in their first full year in the big leagues. A former Major League star named Mark Koenig, toiling in the Minor Leagues, would be summoned back to the Majors in August and play a key and controversial role in the heat of a pennant race.

The Major Leagues consisted of sixteen teams located in just ten cities—none farther south than Washington DC; none farther west than St. Louis. Five of those teams—the Yankees, Giants, Dodgers, Cubs, and White Sox—played in America's two biggest cities: New York and Chicago. The World Series would feature a clash between two iconic franchises: the New York Yankees and the Chicago Cubs.

The city of Chicago would play an outsized role in the major events of 1932. Both presidential nominating conventions would be held in the city. Baseball's commissioner, Judge Kenesaw Mountain Landis, would investigate and arbitrate from his offices in downtown Chicago. A pretty brunette, in love with a rookie shortstop, would shoot her lover in the Hotel Carlos, just a few blocks from Wrigley Field. And in October, Wrigley Field would be the setting for Babe Ruth's most famous home run.

You didn't have to live in a big league city to be a fan or follow a favorite team. Ballpark attendance, which had slumped from 10.1 million in 1930 to 8.5 million in 1931, would fall again in 1932, to just under seven million.[3] Increasingly fans relied on the radio to bring the game into their homes. The immediacy of radio broadcasts—more than summaries in the sports pages of daily newspapers—had the capacity to deliver the drama of each pitch, each at bat, to those who could not attend games in person: the men and women who lived too far from Major League cities to travel to games; the unemployed and poor who couldn't afford tickets; urban dwellers and rural farm families; the elderly, the sick, the young; even inmates in prisons.

In the National League, the defending champion St. Louis Cardinals and runner-up New York Giants would be challenged by the Brooklyn Dodgers, the Pittsburgh Pirates, and the Chicago Cubs. The Philadelphia Athletics in the American League, paced by the young slugger Jimmie Foxx, were the odds-on favorite to win a fourth consecutive pennant, though Connie Mack expected his team to be challenged by the New York Yankees and the Washington Senators.

The season did not lack for drama, on or off the field: a challenge to Babe Ruth's home run record, fistfights involving players and umpires, managerial dismissals, allegations of gambling, and judicial proceedings impacted the outcome of heated pennant races.

This book begins by going back to another time when the nation was in crisis—the fall of 1918 when the baseball season was shortened by one month and the United States had become deeply involved in the war that raged in Europe. In 1918 the Boston Red Sox were playing the Chicago Cubs for the world championship, and a young Red Sox pitcher was considered to be the key to the series. The pitcher's name was Babe Ruth.

CAST OF CHARACTERS

CHICAGO CUBS

Guy Bush	Rogers Hornsby
Kiki Cuyler	Billy Jurges
Woody English	Mark Koenig
Charlie Grimm	Pat Malone
Gabby Hartnett	Charlie Root
Billy Herman	Lon Warneke

NEW YORK YANKEES

Sammy Byrd	Lefty Gomez
Ben Chapman	Tony Lazzeri
Earle Combs	Joe McCarthy
Frank Crosetti	Red Ruffing
Bill Dickey	Babe Ruth
Lou Gehrig	Joe Sewell

PLAYERS, MANAGERS, COMMISSIONER

Dizzy Dean	Walter Johnson
Jimmie Foxx	Connie Mack
Kenesaw Mountain Landis	Joe McCarthy

CAST OF CHARACTERS

UMPIRES AND ANNOUNCERS

Bill Dinneen	George Moriarty
Bill Klem	Beans Reardon
Tom Manning	Quin Ryan

FANS IN THE STANDS

Herbert Hoover, president	Bill "Bojangles" Robinson, entertainer
Harry "Snap" Hortman, prison inmate	Franklin Roosevelt, governor
Charlie Ireland, prison warden	John Sbarbaro, judge
Matt Kandle, videographer	Harold Warp, videographer
Violet Popovich, showgirl	

CAMEOS

Lucius Barnett, hustler	Alabama Pitts, Minor League player
Al Capone, criminal	Sparky Rubenstein, hustler
John Dillinger, criminal	Piggy Sands, Negro Leagues player

THE SEVEN BOYS OF SUMMER

Lowell Blaisdell	John Paul Stevens
Irving "Pro" Boim	Sam Sciullo
Charles Ireland	Paul Warhola
Bernard Malamud	

THE CALLED SHOT

Prologue

A Broken Umbrella in a Rainstorm

In all of baseball, there was nobody else like him.

Babe Ruth was twenty-three years old, a young man with thick black hair, a large flat nose, and small eyes set in a round face. He was not handsome or especially graceful, but he was tall and husky, his strength packed into his torso and hips. Standing six foot two and weighing more than two hundred pounds, he was taller and bigger than most players of his era.

He was engaging, boastful, and unknowable in the way that great public figures are often as inscrutable as their accomplishments. He gulped life like it was oxygen. He ate and drank with gusto. He smoked expensive cigars and bought fancy suits. Fans stood in line to buy tickets so they could watch him throw and hit a baseball. Reporters reveled in his company and wrote unabashedly about his prowess on the field. He exuded a distinctive boyish charm and innocence. Women adored him.

This was Babe Ruth in the early fall of 1918: a young man who had mastered the art of living in the present. He didn't think about the past or worry about the future. For Ruth, life was an endless succession of glimmering moments, each to be indulged to the fullest. He was already the human embodiment of a decade that had not yet roared into existence.

He was a man ahead of his time.

On Monday evening, September 2, 1918, a train carrying Ruth and his Boston Red Sox teammates rolled out of New York City and tunneled into the darkness, moving west toward Chicago. Two days after clinching the American League pennant, and just hours after a season-ending doubleheader against the Yankees at the Polo Grounds, the Red Sox players were exhausted and preoccupied. The Red Sox had played 6 games—three doubleheaders—over the previous four days of the regular season. The first game of the 1918 World Series against the Chicago Cubs was to be played in less than forty-eight hours.

As the train rocked along on steel rails, Ruth played cards with his teammates. Everyone on the team knew that Ruth was a lousy card player, but even as he lost money, he was carefree. He laughed and joked with his teammates, predicting that his losses at the card table would bring the team good luck.

His teammates didn't know much about Ruth's past. His boyhood was shrouded in mystery—the troubled early years on the streets of Baltimore; his removal from the family home at the age of seven to go to St. Mary's Industrial School for Boys; the extent of his boyhood under the guidance of Brother Mathias; the death of his mother; then his discovery by the scout Jack Dunn and his rapid rise to the Major Leagues.[1]

Near the end of the season, Ruth had suffered a personal loss. His father, George Ruth, had died in a brawl outside of the bar he owned in Baltimore. On Saturday afternoon August 24, the Babe had pitched the Red Sox to a 3–1 win over the St. Louis Browns at Fenway Park, his twelfth win of the season. That evening, the elder Ruth had been knocked down in an altercation with his wife's brother-in-law, striking his head on a curb. While the details were never clear, Ruth's father died a few hours later in a Baltimore hospital. When Ruth got the news on Sunday morning, he rushed to Baltimore. The funeral was held on Tuesday, and Ruth wept at the service.[2] He had a younger sister, but he was not close to his blood relatives. Except for his teammates and his young first wife, Helen, who was barely twenty, he was alone. A few days after his father's funeral, Ruth rejoined the Red Sox. If he was still grieving from the emotional trauma of his father's death, it wasn't evident to his teammates.

What his teammates did know was this: Ruth was an extraordinary baseball player. Although he was not yet a legend, he stood out among his peers. In 1915, his first full season in the Major Leagues, Ruth established himself as the best young pitcher in baseball. At age twenty, he won 18 games and lost only 8. A year later, in 1916, he was 23–12, leading the league with an earned run average of 1.75 and setting a modern record for left-handed pitchers by hurling nine shutouts. That season, Ruth faced Walter Johnson—the era's greatest pitcher—head-to-head on five occasions, winning the first four meetings and giving up only 2 runs in 37 innings of work.

In addition to his pitching brilliance, Ruth was a menacing presence at the plate, especially against right-handed pitching. Ruth loved to hit the baseball. Prior to the 1918 season, Ruth made it clear to team owner Harry Frazee and new Red Sox manager Ed Barrow that he wanted to play every day in the outfield so he could hit more regularly.[3] But when the season started, Barrow used him strictly as a pitcher. Finally, on May 6 the manager inserted Ruth into the lineup as an outfielder to take advantage of his offensive talents. It was the first time in Ruth's Major League career that he had played any position other than pitcher. Through the rest of the season, Barrow began to use Ruth more sparingly as a pitcher and to employ him occasionally both as an outfielder and first baseman. Ruth finished the regular season with a record of 13–7, and despite having just 317 at bats, he tied for the league lead in home runs, with 11. The power hitting was a harbinger of things to come.

Ruth and his teammates had concerns that went beyond baseball. The entire season had been played under the cloud of World War I as American doughboys fought in the trenches of Europe—a war the nation entered a year earlier amid much public opposition and protest. Strict new laws had been enacted to ensure support for the war. Eugene Debs, a three-time presidential candidate of the Socialist Party of America, was imprisoned for preaching his pacifist views and urging resistance to the draft.

Baseball had been deeply affected by the conflict. Due to the war, the 1918 season was shortened by five weeks. Attendance at Major League games declined 40 percent, from 5.2 million in 1917 to 3 million. Work or Fight rules had been in effect since July 1, requiring ballplayers between the ages of twenty-one and thirty to register for the draft. Gen. Enoch Crowder, the provost marshal of the army, was responsible for making sure that the selective service system operated smoothly and that young men of draft age were registered and ready to be called. Slacker raids rounded up draft dodgers. Teams in both leagues had been decimated as players had to choose either possible conscription or employment in vital war industries. Career Minor Leaguers were promoted to fill the roster spots vacated by players who were forced to take other jobs or join the military. Shipyards, munitions plants, and steel-producing factories actively recruited ballplayers to play for their company teams and signed them to contracts.

Even Babe Ruth was forced to consider his options. In July he flirted briefly with the notion of leaving the Red Sox to play in the Delaware River Shipbuilding League. He disappeared from Boston for a few days, saying that he would play in Pennsylvania for the Chester Ship-yards team on July 4. Ruth knew that other players were signing up with company teams to avoid being drafted, but his midseason rebellion was primarily aimed at Boston's management, a reaction against its insistence that he continue in a primary role as a pitcher. Ruth's one-man strike was short lived. Eventually the Red Sox threatened legal action, and Ruth returned to Boston, agreeing to pitch whenever needed through the rest of the pennant race.[4]

Due to the abbreviated season, the World Series would be played a month earlier than usual. Wartime travel restrictions also impacted the scheduling of games. The first 3 games of the series were set for Chicago; the remaining games were to be played in Boston. Oddly enough, the Cubs' owner, Charles Weeghman, had arranged for the Chicago games to be played at Comiskey Park—the home of Chicago's American League team, the White Sox—because Comiskey Park had twice the seating capacity of Weeghman Park. Weeghman was willing to give away home field advantage for the chance to sell more tickets.

The Red Sox train arrived in Chicago on a damp Tuesday afternoon. Manager Ed Barrow had scheduled a workout but changed his mind and decided to let the players go directly to their hotel so they would have the remainder of the day to relax before playing the first game of the series on Wednesday afternoon. A line of cabs appeared to transport the Red Sox players through the streets of Chicago to the Hotel Metropole, a seven-story red brick and terra cotta building located on the corner of Michigan Avenue and 23rd Street. The hotel had been designed by Chicago architect Clinton J. Warren in 1891, and in a few years, it would become a famous Chicago landmark: notable as the headquarters for Al Capone, who kept a suite of offices in the hotel until 1928.[5]

On Wednesday, it rained. All morning a steady drizzle fell, and a chilling breeze blew the rain off Lake Michigan and into the city, threatening the start of Game One. At mid-morning, Garry Herrmann, the president of the National Commission, called White Sox owner Charles Comiskey to inquire about the condition of the playing field.

After Herrmann called to check on the field, Comiskey contacted the umpires and instructed them to go out to the park to take a look. A crowd of a hundred or so hopeful fans stood outside the park, waiting in the rain for the ticket booths to open so they could purchase admission to the bleachers. Inside the structure, the infield was covered with a tarpaulin. Water pooled on the tarp and in the outfield. It was impossible to imagine the field would be ready for play by that afternoon.

Comiskey and Herrmann conferred and decided the field was unplayable. The game was canceled. Posters were printed and tacked to buildings and poles in downtown Chicago announcing the postponement. The new schedule called for games to be played on Thursday, Friday, and Saturday.

The players were notified of the cancellation and had all day to kill time. Most of the Cubs players stayed home with their wives and families and drifted into regular routines. The Red Sox players, still drained from the long train ride, looked for something to do. Some of them napped in the hotel. Others played cards. A few went to the movies or braved the weather to go sightseeing in Chicago.

For Babe Ruth, the postponement of the game was a window of opportunity. He liked Chicago. Ruth called local sports writer Harry Hochstadter and asked if he wanted to go out on the town. Hochstadter was a good-natured man, a perfect companion for the young ballplayer. Hochstadter had an interest in all sports but mainly covered boxing and horse racing for the *Chicago Evening Post*.[6] In particular, Hochstadter liked to drink and gamble. A dozen years later, on his deathbed in a Chicago hospital, Hochstadter would beg a nurse to do him a favor; as a last request, he asked the nurse to go out and make a wager for him on a horse race.

Hochstadter was more than happy to spend a rainy day carousing and drinking with Ruth. The two men made plans to meet.

At 3:11 p.m. on that wet and quiet afternoon, a bomb exploded outside the Federal Building in downtown Chicago, at the corner of Adams and Dearborn. The blast ripped a hole in an eighteen-inch thick wall, spewing bricks, mortar, wood, marble, and glass in all directions. Windows were blown out in the nearby Edison building. A flying radiator struck and killed a horse in the street.[7]

Ambulances and police vans screamed down Dearborn Street. A crowd gathered and discovered four mangled bodies in the wreckage. One of the victims was a young woman named Ella Miehlke, the daughter of a wealthy contractor; she was on her way into the post office to mail a letter. A young sailor, who worked as a messenger at the Navy Intelligence Bureau, died on the steps outside the Federal Building. Two postal employees, one inside the building and one outside, died instantly when the bomb detonated. A sixteen-year-old postal worker, Walt Disney, was in the lobby of the building when the blast occurred and barely escaped serious injury.[8] More than thirty other people were injured by the flying debris.

Eyewitness accounts varied. A woman claimed that she saw a man run up the steps of the building carrying a cigar box with a fuse. According to her, the man was smoking a cigar and touched the cigar to the end of the fuse, then kicked the box under a circular radiator and raced back down the steps. Another witness reported seeing two men drive up in a red Stutz automobile. One of the men wore a brown felt hat, the other a panama hat. Just before the explosion, one man scampered up the steps of the building then rushed back down and jumped into a car that zoomed off down Clark Street.

The police suspected that the attack was the work of someone associated with the Industrial Workers of the World (iww), or its sympathizers. More than one hundred members of that organization had been tried in the sixth floor courtroom of the Federal Building during the spring and summer, accused under the Espionage Act of interfering with the war effort and conspiring to hinder draft registration. A white-haired federal judge named Kenesaw Mountain Landis, a native of Indiana, had been on the bench for the trial. Landis, appointed to the federal judiciary by Pres. Theodore Roosevelt in 1905, had a reputation as a tough judge with fortitude and uncompromising integrity. In less than two years Landis would be appointed to an even more prestigious position. In 1920 he would become the first Commissioner of Major League Baseball, replacing Garry Herrmann as the administrative boss of the game. Landis would be the man entrusted with overseeing the investigation into the alleged plot to fix the 1919 World Series and restoring trust in the fairness of the national pastime.

The iww trial had ended in August with convictions of all the defendants, including iww leader Big Bill Hayward. Judge Landis sentenced Hayward, and other top leaders of the organization, to twenty years in Leavenworth, the stiffest possible penalty. On the day of the bombing, most of the iww leaders were in the Cook County jail awaiting transfer to the federal facility, but Hayward happened to be in the Federal Building, just two floors above Judge Landis's courtroom. He was dictating to his secretary, Mary Service, in the United States Marshall's office. Hayward had little response to the explosion except to say, "I suppose the IWW will be blamed. We have been blamed for many things."[9]

Given the timing of the bombing and the location, the police speculated that perhaps it was an assassination attempt on Judge Landis.

As it turned out, the judge was on vacation in Alanson, Michigan. Landis responded with characteristic calm. "The news of the explosion comes as a surprise," he said. "I have no reason to suspect an IWW plot or to blame the organization or any of its members for the outrage."[10]

That evening the Chicago police and United States secret service agents went into action. More than fifteen hundred law enforcement officials combed through the city of Chicago, knocking on doors, asking questions, and making arrests. Witnesses were interviewed. Dozens of people were dragged out of their houses and apartments, shoved into police vans, and escorted to police stations for interrogation.

At the corner of Dearborn and Adams, laborers worked to remove the rubble. The rain finally ended. Shovels clicked against the street throughout the night.

Although a swarm of reporters descended on downtown Chicago after the bombing at the Federal Building, it is unlikely that Hochstadter or Ruth heard the news until that evening. Even if they had known, it is doubtful that the explosion would have derailed their plans.

Hochstadter and Ruth celebrated all day. Full-fledged Prohibition was less than a year away, and more than half of the counties in Illinois were already dry, but no law was going to force the closure of drinking establishments in Chicago. That evening the two men rolled into a crowded party at a hotel suite. Ruth was alert and apparently unfazed by the day's adventure. Hochstadter was too drunk to stand up. He collapsed onto a couch.[11]

A motley collection of writers and professional gamblers clustered around a steel washtub filled with ice and bottles of wine.[12] One of the writers was Gene Fowler, a tall, loose-limbed man with big features, who had been hired by the *New York American* to report on the World

Series. Fowler had grown up on the streets of Denver and found a home in newspaper work, rising to the position of city editor of the *Rocky Mountain News* by his mid-twenties. Like many of the reporters of his era, he worked hard, wrote fast, and liked to hang out with athletes and eccentrics of any type. He pushed his way across the room to Hochstadter's couch.

Fowler had been trying to locate Hochstadter and Ruth earlier in the day. Failing to do so, he dropped by Comiskey Park in the afternoon—it must have been around the time the bomb went off at Dearborn and Adams—and visited with Charles Comiskey in his private quarters. Comiskey offered the reporter a drink and something to eat. They watched the rain fall on the sodden field. Comiskey told Fowler stories about his youth and his experiences driving a brick wagon.[13]

Hochstadter was too inebriated for meaningful dialogue, so Fowler struck up conversation with Ruth. He asked Ruth if he thought he'd be able to pitch the next day. Ruth smacked Fowler on the back, a blow strong enough to knock a lesser man to the floor. "I'll pitch'em all if they say the word," Ruth bellowed.[14]

If Ruth knew he was going to be the Red Sox starting pitcher in Game One, he didn't let on. His thoughts were elsewhere. Ruth told Fowler he had an appointment later that evening with a young woman, and the reporter surmised that the pitcher would spend the rest of the night drinking and socializing.[15] A few minutes later, Ruth left the party and disappeared into the night.

The skies finally cleared. Thursday morning was cool and sunny. At Comiskey Park, fans began lining up outside ticket windows early in the morning. A police wagon appeared a short while later, and officers jumped out to arrest six men involved in a craps game.[16]

Red Sox players were on the field two hours before game time to warm up and take batting practice. Ruth stepped into the batter's box to take his swings. He couldn't have slept more than a few hours the night before, if at all, but Ruth stroked the first batting practice pitch into the right-field bleachers. He showed no signs of fatigue from the previous day's activities.

Neither manager tipped his hand about who would be his starting pitcher. The Cubs' manager was Fred Mitchell. Oddly enough, Mitchell had stronger ties to Boston than to Chicago. Born and raised in Massachusetts, Mitchell had started his career with the Boston Americans and appeared in the franchise's first game, coming in to relieve the starter, Cy Young. In the off-season Mitchell lived just outside of Boston on a small farm with an apple orchard. He was reserved, studious, and intelligent, a keen observer of the game. He was confident the Cubs were the better ball club and that his team would win the series. Mitchell was worried about Babe Ruth's bat, but Ruth was supposedly vulnerable to left-handed pitching, and Mitchell had two good left-handers to use against the Red Sox: Hippo Vaughn and Lefty Tyler. Mitchell did not tell the press which of the two pitchers would start Game One. He had both Vaughn and Tyler warm up prior to the game.

Ed Barrow was also coy about his strategy. About thirty minutes before game time, Barrow sent Joe Bush to the bullpen to warm up for the Red Sox, but a couple minutes later Ruth joined him and started throwing, too. It wasn't until the managers exchanged scorecards at home plate that the lineups were set. Vaughn was designated as the Cubs' starter. Barrow listed Ruth as his starting pitcher, batting him in the number nine spot in the order.

The official attendance was announced as 19,274, a disappointing crowd for the opening game of the series. Vaughn retired the Red Sox easily in the top half of the first inning. When Babe Ruth walked to the mound to warm up, he glanced at the half-filled stands. Ruth noticed rows of empty seats in the upper decks; most fans were quietly scattered throughout the lower deck. Many of the men wore white straw hats, a fashion statement indicating that it was still summer.

The Red Sox team that took the field behind Ruth was one of the weakest in World Series history. Of the infielders—Fred Thomas at third, Everett Scott at shortstop, Dave Shean at second, and Stuffy McInnis at first—only McInnis was a reliable batter. Thomas was a rookie with only 147 Major League at bats; Shean was a lifetime .230 hitter; Scott had batted .221 during the season. In the outfield, Harry Hooper was a solid hitter and destined for the Hall of Fame, but Amos Strunk, in center field, had batted a career low .257 in 1918.

At this point in his career, Ruth thought of left field as his natural position, but Barrow wanted him to pitch and that meant George Whiteman was in the lineup as the left fielder. Whiteman was thirty-five years old, a career Minor Leaguer. Before the 1918 season, he had a total of 43 Major League at bats. If not for the war and the Work or Fight rules, Whiteman would have had to pay admission to get into a Major League ballpark. He was slow in the outfield and ineffective at the plate. In 71 games he had collected just 57 hits.

In the bottom of the first inning, Ruth quickly retired the first two Cubs batters. Then Les Mann, the Cubs' left fielder, hit a ball that bounced off a small stone and scooted into the outfield; a couple of pitches later, Mann stole second. Dode Paskert hit a line drive to left that dropped in front of Whiteman and caromed off his leg. By the time Whiteman got the ball back to the infield, Paskert had advanced to second and Mann stood on third. Ruth worked carefully to Fred Merkle, the fifth hitter of the inning, and walked him to load the bases.

The next batter was Charlie Pick. He was a journeyman and not feared as a power hitter. In 512 lifetime at bats, Pick had never homered, but he was adept at making contact, capable of driving the ball into outfield gaps, and a hard man to strike out. Pick settled into the batter's box, arranged his feet, and stared out at the mound.

On the fourth pitch of the at bat, Pick saw a pitch he liked and swung, driving the ball over Everett Scott's head in a soft arc toward left-center field. The smack of the bat was followed by a hopeful roar from the fans.

Ruth watched the ball float toward the outfield. George Whiteman got a slow start then drifted to his left, stuck his glove out and caught the ball about knee-high. The collective gasp of the crowd collapsed to a murmur. A jolt of adrenaline cleared Ruth's head. He left the mound and headed for the dugout.

After the first inning, Ruth was masterful. He shut out the Cubs. He allowed just 6 hits, walked one batter, hit another batter, and pitched a complete game. The Red Sox scored their only run on a two-out single by Stuffy McInnis in the fourth inning. The 1–0 win by the Red Sox set the tone for the series. All of the games would be low-scoring. Every hit, every opportunity, would be vital.

The game was not without other memorable moments. In the middle of the seventh inning a brass band played the "Star Spangled Banner," one of the first times the song had been played at a Major League game.[17] Players turned to face the flag, and the crowd gave out a loud cheer when the band finished. In the eighth inning six biplanes flew over the park in formation, a recognition that more serious events were occurring overseas.[18]

A curious thing happened before the start of Game Two. Chicago fans taunted Ruth during batting practice, chanting insults as he took his swings before the game. Ruth addressed the fans and boasted, "Watch this one." He hit the next pitch into the bleachers, turned back to the fans, and said, "I told you so."[19]

It wasn't the first time that season that Ruth had called his shot. On May 5, in a game against the Yankees at the Polo Grounds, Ruth had blasted a long foul ball. He turned around and spoke to home plate umpire Billy Evans and predicted, "I'll hit this one right back and there'll be no doubt about it."[20] Ruth smacked the next pitch into the upper deck for a home run.

But Ruth was on the bench when Game Two started. Manager Barrow had decided that George Whiteman, who had 2 hits in the game, would be his regular left fielder against the left-handed pitching of the Cubs. With Ruth watching from the dugout, Lefty Tyler pitched the Cubs to a 3–1 win. Ruth didn't play the next day either, as Carl Mays out pitched Hippo Vaughn, and the Red Sox won 2–1.

In Boston, the series followed the same course as in Chicago. Before an enthusiastic crowd in Boston, Ruth was back on the mound in Game Four, matched up against Lefty Tyler. Once again, Ruth dominated the game. He tripled in 2 runs in the fourth inning and shut the Cubs out until the eighth inning, stretching his streak of consecutive scoreless innings in the World Series to 29⅔ innings. It was a record that would stand for forty-three years, lasting longer than Ruth's single-season record of home runs. It was, Ruth would later claim, his greatest accomplishment as a player.

Hippo Vaughn shut out Boston in Game Five, but the Red Sox won Game Six, 2–1, once again behind Carl Mays; then the series was over. Ruth played the last two innings of the final game as a defensive replacement for George Whiteman, who injured himself in the seventh inning making an acrobatic catch.

And so the Major League baseball season was over—the date was September 11, 1918—and whether there would be a season in 1919 was anybody's guess. There were more than two million American soldiers on the ground in Europe. No one knew what the future held for the country.

Ruth had been the pitching star of the series, finishing with an ERA of 1.06, and now at the youthful age of twenty-three, Ruth had been a part of three World Championship teams with Boston. He expected to play in many more World Series as a member of the Red Sox.

First he had to get through the off-season and see what lay ahead for the national pastime. But Ruth was restless—and the public wanted to see more of him. He made an appearance as an honorary starter at a motorcycle race and officiated in a local boxing tournament. He joined some of his teammates for a few postseason events, playing in several exhibition games to the delight of fans in New Haven, Hartford, and Baltimore.

Soon his teammates scattered. Many went to work in war-related industries. Carl Mays got married, enjoyed a short honeymoon, and joined the army. Harry Hooper contemplated retirement. Ruth and his then-wife, Helen, rented an apartment in Lebanon, Pennsylvania, where Babe intended to go to work for the Bethlehem Steel Company until the war ended. Other ballplayers were also signing up to work for

Bethlehem Steel so they could avoid going overseas and continue playing baseball.

Playing baseball—and hitting a baseball—was what Babe Ruth wanted to do more than anything else. It must have bruised his ego to read what one *Boston Globe* reporter wrote after the end of the 1918 series. Noting that the triple Ruth banged out in Game Four was the only hit Ruth managed in five at bats, the journalist observed that Ruth as a hitter was "about as useful as a broken umbrella in a rainstorm."[21]

Fourteen years would pass before Ruth would play another game in Chicago against the Cubs. By that year—1932—no one would dare refer to Babe Ruth's bat as a "broken umbrella."

1

Rogers Hornsby

In early July of 1918, Rogers Hornsby received a notice from his draft board in Fort Worth, Texas. It was not good news. Under the recently enacted Work or Fight rules, Hornsby was required to either find employment in an industry deemed essential to the war effort or face enlistment in the army.

It had been a difficult season for both the twenty-two-year-old shortstop and his St. Louis Cardinals team. The Cardinals would finish dead last, 27 games under .500, and 33 games behind the pennant winning Chicago Cubs. Hornsby was in his third full season in the majors, and he, too, was struggling. After batting .313 in his rookie season in 1916, and then hitting .327 in 1917—a year in which he led the National League in both slugging average and triples—Hornsby had slumped both in the field and at the plate in the war-shortened 1918 season. He had been slowed by a series of minor but nagging injuries, and he had quarreled with his manager, Jack Hendricks, a man he considered incompetent to run a Major League team.[1] It would not be the last time that Hornsby battled with a manager or general manager.

After the Cardinals completed their season by losing both ends of a doubleheader to the Cincinnati Reds on Labor Day, Hornsby arranged to go to work for the Harlan Shipyards in Wilmington, Delaware. Officially, he was hired as a plate setter; unofficially, he was expected to concentrate on his role as the new shortstop on the company baseball team. He was to be paid $400 a month, a slightly higher rate of pay than what he had earned that year as a Major League baseball player.[2]

Hornsby cleaned out his locker in the Cardinals' clubhouse and relocated to Delaware. He married his fiancé and went to work.

Less than two months later, the war in Europe turned dramatically in favor of the Allied Forces. On November 11, 1918, the fighting and dying stopped.[3] An armistice was declared, the guns were silenced, and negotiations soon began to arrange the terms of peace. By the end of the process, national borders would be redrawn and hopes would rise—at least in the hearts of the most optimistic citizens of the world—that this would be the last great armed conflict between nations.

After the armistice was signed, Hornsby played a few more games for the shipyard team, but by the end of November, he and his new wife had moved back to his hometown of Fort Worth, Texas, where he would turn his attention to the 1919 season.

Born in 1896 on the edge of the western frontier, Hornsby had been raised on the windswept plains of west Texas. After Hornsby's father died, his mother moved the family to the rough meatpacking city of Fort Worth, where Hornsby's older brothers supported the family by working in the stockyards. The city was named for a U.S. Army general but became famous in the early 1900s for its saloons, dance halls, gambling establishments, prostitutes, drunken cowboys, violent crime, and pervasive wickedness.[4] In 1911, a passionate Baptist minister, J. Frank Norris—some called him the "Texas Cyclone" for his reformist zeal—took a public stand against racetrack gambling, vice, and prostitution.[5] On February 4, 1912, arsonists set fire to his church; a month later, they burned down his parsonage.

Baseball was Hornsby's first memory. His brothers, aspiring semi-pros, introduced him to the game. "I can't remember anything that happened before I had a baseball in my hand," he said.[6] As Hornsby learned to play on the Texas sandlots, baseball was just edging its way into the American consciousness as the national game. The first World Series was played in the fall of 1903, the year Hornsby turned seven. For a boy in Fort Worth at that time, the distance from west Texas to the Major Leagues must have seemed immeasurable. Except for the railroad and a few dirt roads, there seemed to be no way out of the city. The nearest Major League team was in St. Louis, nearly six hundred miles to the east.

But baseball flourished in the Fort Worth area, and for those with talent and ambition, baseball offered opportunity, something more glamorous and appealing than working in the slaughterhouses.

As a youth, Hornsby was gangly and rawboned with hard blue eyes and an aloofness that masked his fierce determination. Education didn't appeal to Hornsby. He dropped out of high school at the age of fifteen and went to work as an office boy at Swift and Company, playing baseball in his spare time on city teams.

Hornsby did not immediately exhibit the skills that would enable him to reach the top echelon of his profession. He did not hit with power and, at best, he was mediocre in the field. Nevertheless, he was good enough so that at eighteen he began his professional career by signing with the Dallas Steers of the Texas League, for a salary of seventy-five dollars a month. In the spring of 1915 he earned a roster spot with another Texas-based team, the Denison Railroaders, a Class D team that played in the Western Association. The Railroaders boosted Hornsby's pay to ninety dollars a month. He played well enough to be noticed by Major League scouts.[7]

In September, Hornsby's contract was purchased by the St. Louis Cardinals, and he was invited to join the ball club for the final 18 games of the 1915 Major League season. Hornsby stuffed his clothes and baseball gear into a small carpet bag and took the train from Denison to Cincinnati to join his big league teammates—a two-day trip that covered twelve hundred miles. He arrived in Cincinnati with three dollars in his pocket.[8]

When baseball resumed after World War I, Hornsby got a new manager. Branch Rickey, who already served as team president and part owner, agreed to take over from Jack Hendricks. Rickey, a thoughtful and sophisticated man with a college degree from Ohio Wesleyan

University, was a devout Christian who observed the Sabbath, even when his team was playing a game on Sunday. As a baseball executive, Rickey was the first in his profession to establish and develop a farm system to identify and cultivate young talent.

Over time Rickey proved to be an astute judge of baseball talent, and he regarded Hornsby as the best player in the Major Leagues. Before the start of the 1918 season, Charles Weeghman, owner of the Chicago Cubs, scheduled a lunch with Rickey for the express purpose of offering to buy Hornsby's contract. Weeghman offered $60,000, but Rickey turned him down.[9]

Under Rickey's leadership, the Cardinals improved modestly in 1919, winning 54 games and losing 83, climbing out of the cellar to finish in seventh place. Hornsby's contribution was significantly better than the previous season. He batted .318 and placed second in the league in batting average, hits, runs batted in, and total bases. Once again, the Cardinals were approached about selling their young star. This time it was the New York Giants who came calling. John McGraw, who had managed the Giants since 1902, had had his eye on Hornsby for a long time, and McGraw convinced Giants owner Charles Stoneham to make an offer that Rickey could not possibly refuse. In the summer of 1919 McGraw and Stoneham met with Rickey at a tavern in New York. Stoneham offered Rickey $175,000 for Hornsby's contract. Again, Rickey refused. Stoneham upped the offer to $300,000, plus a $50,000 bonus if the Giants won the pennant with Hornsby in their lineup. Rickey still refused. A year later, the Giants would try again—this time offering cash plus five players—but Rickey stood firm and continued to reject Stoneham's attempt to acquire Hornsby.[10]

In 1920, the Cardinals nearly made it to .500 with a record of 75-79, good for a tie for fifth place in the league. Hornsby, now twenty-four and with his best years still ahead of him, was outstanding, hitting a robust .370 and leading the league in five offensive categories: batting average, hits, doubles, runs batted in, and slugging average. Over the next five years, no one in the National League would come close to his level of production.

From 1921 through 1925 Hornsby averaged an astounding .402, hitting over .400 in three seasons and twice leading the league in home runs. He hit for average, and he hit for power. Over the course of his career he would win seven batting titles, including six in a row from 1920 through 1925, and lead the league at least twice in every major offensive statistical category: hits, doubles, triples, runs scored, runs batted in, bases on balls, on-base percentage, and slugging average.

Only one player in baseball matched Hornsby's production during the 1920s. That was Babe Ruth. Ruth's power numbers—home runs, runs batted in, slugging average—were superior to Hornsby's, but his batting average for the decade was slightly lower than Hornsby's, and Ruth never led the league in hits, doubles, or triples. Hornsby won the Triple Crown twice—in 1922 and 1925; Ruth won it just once—in 1924.

Through the first four seasons that the Cardinals were managed by Branch Rickey, the manager and his star player generally got along. But in 1923 Hornsby, who was dealing with a variety of off-field personal issues, clashed with both Rickey and Cardinals management.[11] After a game in August, Hornsby questioned Rickey's strategy and the two men—the volatile Hornsby and the mild-mannered Rickey—were pulled apart in the locker room before either could land a punch. The rest of the season was a tense standoff between Hornsby and management. Hornsby sat out a number of games with a knee injury and developed a skin rash. Although the team physician indicated that Hornsby was capable of competing, Hornsby refused to play on the grounds that he hadn't fully recovered. Eventually Cardinals owner Sam Breadon lost patience with his recalcitrant star, suspended Hornsby for the last 5 games of the season, and fined him $500.[12] Hornsby left the team and went into the off-season making it clear that he didn't want to play for Rickey.

Hornsby's discontent with the Cardinals manager and management was no secret around the league. Once again the Cubs expressed interest in acquiring Hornsby's services. By 1923 the Cubs had a new owner, William Wrigley, the chewing gum magnate, and Wrigley desperately wanted to build a winning team. In particular, he wanted to build his team around

Hornsby, a player he greatly admired, despite Hornsby's well-known reputation as an irritant to managers and owners. Wrigley's general manager, a former newspaper man named William Veeck, approached Breadon with an offer. But the Cardinals rejected the proposed deal.[13]

Hornsby didn't have much choice but to return to the Cardinals in 1924. Although he batted .424, it was another difficult year for the franchise. After third place finishes in 1921 and 1922, and a fifth place finish in 1923, the team dropped to sixth in 1924.

Another off-season passed. Then, two months into the 1925 season, Sam Breadon made the decision to switch managers. Breadon was unhappy both with the performance of the team and the attendance at home games. Branch Rickey was removed as manager but retained his position as club president.[14] Breadon asked Hornsby, at age twenty-nine, to accept the responsibility of also managing the team. At first, Hornsby was reluctant to give up his total focus on his own on-field performance. The transition from Rickey to Hornsby as field manager was also complicated by the fact that Rickey, a minority stockholder in the team, wanted to divest himself of the stock he owned. Eventually a deal was worked out. Hornsby would take over as manager and buy Rickey's shares, with the share purchase financed by Breadon. It was to be one of the many legal and financial entanglements that Hornsby would need to deal with in future years.

When Hornsby took over, the Cardinals had a record of 13-25, last place in the National League, 13 games out of first. For the rest of the season, Hornsby not only managed the team but bashed National League pitching, capturing the Triple Crown by hitting .403, driving in 143 runs, and hammering 39 home runs. It was the third time in the past four seasons that Hornsby had batted over .400. Unsurprisingly, he was also selected the league's most valuable player. The Cardinals went 64-51 with Hornsby as the manager and finished the season in fourth place in the standings.

Meanwhile, Branch Rickey silently fumed. He was unhappy about being ousted as manager and believed that Hornsby's success was due to two main factors: first, that the early season schedule, when Rickey was the manager, had the Cardinals playing mostly on the road, while during Hornsby's months as manager the Cardinals played the majority of their games at home; second, the team was young and composed mostly of players that Rickey had signed and brought along through his farm system.

Hornsby went into the 1926 season knowing that he still had to prove himself as a manager. Already the best player in the National League, Hornsby was now ready to claim the mantle of the best player in either league. The greatest players of early twentieth century baseball—Ty Cobb, Tris Speaker, Eddie Collins, Walter Johnson—all played in the American League, and they were all in their late thirties, in the twilight of their careers. The only challenge to Hornsby's attaining recognition as the premier player in all of baseball was his contemporary: Babe Ruth.

But Ruth had slumped badly in 1925, plagued with injuries and playing in only 98 games, hitting 25 home runs, and driving in a paltry 66 runs. He batted only .290, the first time in a decade he hadn't hit .300 or better. Not only did Ruth fail to lead the league in any offensive category, he didn't even lead his own team in any offensive statistic, except for one: Ruth led the team in strikeouts. Many observers felt that Ruth's decline was permanent, that his inability to train properly or preserve his body was the result of years of reckless behavior and overindulgence. It was suggested that the once-great Ruth, now in his early thirties, would never again attain the prowess of his younger years.

In spring training, Hornsby's Cardinals feasted on the competition— mostly Minor League teams—and by the time the Cardinals had returned to St. Louis to begin the season, Hornsby had established a winning attitude, boldly declaring, "If there's anybody in this room who doesn't think we're going to win the pennant, go upstairs now and get your money and go on home because we don't want you around here."[15] The 1926 Cardinals team was built around young players: a trio of youthful outfielders; a twenty-four year old third baseman, Les Bell; a power-hitting first baseman, Jim Bottomley; a twenty-two-year-old rookie shortstop, Tommy Thevenow; a physically gifted pitcher, Flint Rhem. A few older players, like Bob O'Farrell, the catcher, provided leadership. At the age of thirty, Hornsby was the oldest position player on the roster.

The Cardinals opened by winning 5 of their first 6 games and then regressed to playing .500 ball for most of April and May. In June the Cardinals began to perform the way that Hornsby had predicted, winning 16 of 22 games and moving within 3½ games of first place. More importantly, two key veteran players were added to the roster: Billy Southworth, an outfielder, via a trade with the New York Giants, and Grover Cleveland Alexander, the future Hall of Famer, who was acquired for $4,000 after being waived by the Chicago Cubs. Southworth was installed as the Cardinals right fielder and batted .317 for the team. Alexander, who suffered from both epilepsy and alcoholism, was thirty-nine years old and well past his prime, but the Cardinals guessed he had a bit of life remaining in his right arm and could help stabilize a shaky starting rotation.

By early August, Hornsby had the Cardinals in the thick of a pennant race. A 6-game winning streak, all on the road in early August, and an 8-game winning streak, during a home stand in mid-August, allowed the Cardinals to climb into first place. They entered the last month of the season with a slim lead over the Pirates and Reds.

The schedule, however, favored Pittsburgh and Cincinnati. From September 2 to the end of season, the Cardinals would play their last 24 games on the road. Hornsby remained confident in his players, though he was increasingly frustrated and angry with Rickey and Breadon. Hornsby didn't like Rickey hanging around the team, talking to his players, and he was furious that Breadon had tried to squeeze in 3 exhibition games during the road trip—games in Syracuse, Buffalo, and New Haven. Breadon and Rickey saw the exhibition games as a way to earn a few extra dollars and generate positive publicity. Hornsby viewed the games as unnecessary and counterproductive to his efforts to keep his team rested and focused during the pennant stretch run.[16] Hornsby confronted Breadon after a loss to Pittsburgh, cursing at the owner and shouting, "Now get the hell out of my clubhouse."[17]

The key series in the road trip turned out to be in Philadelphia. The teams played 6 games in four days: single games on Wednesday and Friday, doubleheaders on Thursday and Saturday. The Cardinals crushed Philly pitching, scoring 61 runs in the series, taking 1 game by a score of 23–3, and winning the first 5 games. Flint Rhem pitched and won 2 of the games. Six days later the Cardinals clinched the pennant with a 6–4 win over the Giants at the Polo Grounds. It was the first time a Major League team from St. Louis had achieved the dream of reaching the World Series.

The Yankees, like the Cardinals, had been in a tough down-to-the-wire battle for the pennant. Babe Ruth had rebounded from his disappointing 1925 year by slugging 47 home runs and knocking in 145 runs.[18] The series shaped up as a battle of Hornsby's Cardinals versus Ruth's Yankees.

If Hornsby wanted proof or vindication that he was the best player in the game, he'd get a chance to prove it on the game's biggest stage. But a personal tragedy struck Hornsby as he practiced with his team in Yankee Stadium prior to Game One. Hornsby received a telegram bearing the news that his mother had died in Austin, Texas. The death was not totally unexpected; Mary Dallas Hornsby, age sixty-two, had been ill for years. Her last wish, as conveyed by her sister, was that, whatever happened to her, Rogers should be told to stay with his team and participate in the World Series. Hornsby remained in New York.

The series opened on October 2 in Yankee Stadium, and the Yankees took the first game, 2–1, with Ruth scoring the winning run on a clutch single by Lou Gehrig. The Cardinals came back to take Game Two behind Grover Alexander who gave up 2 early runs but settled down to retire the last 21 Yankees hitters in a row.

Game Three was back in St. Louis on a wet, gloomy Tuesday. Rain showers delayed play in the top of the fourth inning with the game scoreless. The teams retreated to the shelter of their dugouts. During the interruption, two policemen entered the dugouts of the Yankees and the Cardinals and asked the players to sign baseballs for Johnnie Sylvester, a sick child in Essex Falls, New Jersey. Rogers Hornsby and 14 of his Cardinals' players signed one ball. Five Yankees, including Babe Ruth, signed the other ball. On one side of the ball, Ruth added a message for Johnnie: "I'll knock a homer for you in Wednesday's game."[19]

Play resumed. In the bottom of the fourth inning, the Cardinals' pitcher, Jesse Haines, provided all the runs he would need when he knocked a 2-run homer off Yankees starter Dutch Ruether. Haines pitched a 5-hit shutout, and the Cardinals won again, 4–0, to take the lead in the series.[20]

On Wednesday, the Yankees walloped the Cardinals by a score of 10–5. Ruth delivered on his promise to Johnnie Sylvester by homering not once, but three times. It was not the first time, nor would it be the last time, that Ruth had accurately predicted a home run. The Yankees would also win Game Five in St. Louis by a score of 3–2, taking a 3-games-to-2 lead in the series.

The teams returned to New York with the Yankees needing just 1 win to claim the World Series championship, but St. Louis won Game Six in Yankee Stadium pounding out 13 hits and winning 10–2. The Cards got another strong pitching performance by Grover Alexander, who pitched a complete game 8-hitter.

The weather on the day for the deciding game was problematic. There was rain in the morning, and a light fog, which kept many fans away from the stadium. A crowd of 38,100 hardy fans eventually showed up, along with dignitaries like New York mayor Jimmy Walker and Commissioner Landis. The conditions were not perfect, but the game itself proved to be a classic.

Waite Hoyt pitched for the Yankees, and Jesse Haines started for the Cardinals. Ruth homered in the bottom of the third to give the Yankees a 1-run lead. Thanks to errors by Mark Koenig and Bob Meusel, the Cardinals were able to score 3 unearned runs in the top of the fourth. The Yankees scored in the sixth to cut the lead to 3–2.

In the bottom of the seventh, the Yankees threatened again, loading the bases with 2 outs and Tony Lazzeri coming to the plate. Lazzeri had hammered the ball off Haines all afternoon, blasting long foul balls and flying out to deep center. Hornsby was also aware that Haines was pitching with a damaged finger, and when Hornsby jogged in from second base to check on his starting pitcher, Haines showed his manager the bloody finger and admitted that he couldn't pitch any more. The Cardinals had a 1-run lead and needed 6 more outs for the team's first world championship.

Throughout the game, Flint Rhem and Grover Alexander had been sitting side by side in the Cardinals' bullpen, trying to stay warm. Alexander was wearing a red sweater over his uniform. Now Hornsby signaled from the mound that he wanted Alexander to pitch to Lazzeri.[21]

Alexander ambled in from the bullpen. When he reached the mound, he stripped off the sweater and Hornsby handed him the ball. Alexander threw 3 warm-up pitches and said he was ready. Lazzeri stepped to the plate.

Lazzeri was a rookie. In the Pacific Coast League he had hit 60 home runs in a single season. That kind of power hitting got the attention of Major League teams and led to his signing by the Yankees. In 1932 he had hit .300 with 15 homers and 113 RBIS.

Alexander's first pitch to Lazzeri was inside for ball one. The second pitch was a strike. Lazzeri was ready for the next offering and connected solidly, driving the ball deep toward the left field fence; at the last moment, the ball hooked foul and landed in the stands. Lazzeri had missed a grand slam by about ten feet. On the next pitch, Lazzeri struck out on a ball that was low and outside.

Alexander retired the Yankees in the eighth, then faced the top of the order in the bottom of the ninth, still protecting a 1-run lead. The first two Yankee batters, Earle Combs and Mark Koenig, both grounded out, third to first. He now faced Babe Ruth.

Hornsby trotted in from second base to have a quick conference with his pitcher. All game the strategy had been to pitch carefully to Ruth, to walk him rather than give him a good pitch to hit. Haines had put one across the plate in the third inning and paid for it when Ruth lined it into the seats. To this point, Ruth had his solo home run and 3 walks in four plate appearances.

Alexander got ahead in the count, 2 strikes and 1 ball, but then, hoping that Ruth would chase a pitch out of the strike zone, Alexander had thrown 3 balls. So Ruth was on first with his fourth walk of the game. He was the potential tying run, and the clean-up hitter, Bob Meusel, was coming to the plate.

As soon as Alexander released the first pitch to Meusel, Ruth broke for second. The pitch was a called strike, the Cardinal catcher, Bob O'Farrell, threw to Hornsby at second base who slapped a tag on the baserunner, and the umpire, Bill Dinneen, called Ruth out.[22]

Just like that the St. Louis Cardinals had won their first World Series. Years later, Hornsby would say the tag on Ruth was the greatest thrill of his baseball career.[23]

The city of St. Louis erupted into a two-day celebration. Fans were ecstatic, creating huge traffic jams as joyous crowds jammed the streets. A reception for the players was held at Sportsman's Park to honor the World Champions. Notably, one significant member of the Cardinals did not attend: Rogers Hornsby.

Hornsby traveled only as far as Union Station in St. Louis, then switched trains and continued on to Texas to attend the funeral of his mother.

It was a time of great professional achievement and personal loss for the thirty-year-old player-manager. The debate—at least in Hornsby's mind—about who was the greater player, Ruth or himself, had not been settled. Hornsby's performance on the field was adequate, but Ruth, with his 4 home runs and dominating presence in a losing cause, was the better player in the series.

For Hornsby, after twelve years in the Cardinals organization, with his accomplishments as a player, and now having guided his team to a world championship, he might think he was indispensable. That was not the case, at least in terms of how Sam Breadon saw things.

Breadon had not forgotten Hornsby's insubordination and profane dismissal of him from the clubhouse during the August road trip.

Breadon had also become increasingly irritated by Hornsby's well-known gambling habits and his many off-field legal entanglements. To make matters worse, after the season, Hornsby and Breadon became entangled in an acrimonious contract battle.[24]

It was too much for Breadon. In December the Cardinals approached John McGraw about the possibility of trading Hornsby to the New York Giants.[25] McGraw was agreeable, and a few weeks later, Breadon made a deal with Charles Stoneham, owner of the Giants. Rogers Hornsby—arguably the greatest player in the history of the National League, a man still in his prime, the man most responsible for bringing the first world championship to St. Louis—was traded for Frankie Frisch, a younger and promising infielder.[26]

The trade pleased both Hornsby and his new manager, John McGraw. For years, McGraw, among others, had tried to pry Hornsby loose from the Cardinals. The two men greatly respected each other, and they had a shared passion for the same extracurricular activity: betting on the horses. It was a marriage made in baseball heaven. And it lasted all of one season.

Hornsby performed brilliantly for the Giants. He played in every game, batting .361, hitting 26 home runs, driving in 125 runs, and scoring a league-best, 133 runs. The Giants finished second in the National League, 2 games behind the pennant-winning Pirates. By all accounts, Hornsby and McGraw got along well, and when McGraw missed a portion of the season with a respiratory ailment, Hornsby stepped in and assumed the managerial role.[27] But things were not so rosy in the clubhouse. Hornsby clashed with his teammates, who didn't like Hornsby's attitude or the rules he established: a midnight curfew, prohibition on smoking and card playing. Freddie Lindstrom, the Giants' outspoken third baseman, mocked Hornsby, saying "Once you lay aside your bat, you're a detriment to any ball club."[28] Stoneham—who Hornsby once called "that drunken bum"[29]—listened to the complaints of his players. Like his fellow owner in St. Louis, Stoneham was also disturbed by Hornsby's still unresolved legal issues, especially Hornsby's resistance to paying off his gambling debts. So

Stoneham traded Hornsby again, this time to the lowly Boston Braves. All Stoneham received in return were two marginal players—Jimmie Welsh and James Hogan—but at least he'd put down a possible rebellion from his Giants players. McGraw was not consulted about the transaction or informed until after the deal was completed.[30] The press release announcing the deal said the trade had been accomplished in "the best interests of the New York Giants."[31]

The Braves were owned by Judge Emil Fuchs, a former magistrate who had granted himself the title of judge. Fuchs owned a team that was failing in every possible way: on the field and at the box office. Fuchs hoped that Hornsby's talent and influence would rub off on his players and that his presence in the lineup would bring more customers to the ballpark. In late May, when the Braves manager, Jack Slattery, resigned, Hornsby assumed the role of player-manager. As a player, Hornsby had another stellar season: a .387 batting average, 21 home runs, 94 runs batted in. He also led the league in walks with 107. But the team finished seventh for the third year in a row, winning just 50 games and losing 103.

As dismal as the season was for the Braves, there was one bright spot for Hornsby. In midsummer he bought an eighty-seven acre farm in Missouri, fifteen miles north of St. Louis. Hornsby purchased the land from a horse breeder for $18,600 and intended to keep it as his off-season home. The farm had a spacious fourteen room house set well back from the road, numerous structures to contain cattle, hogs, and chickens, and a generous acreage allotted to the cultivation of blue grass. Hornsby expected to make a profit from his farming operation.

By the end of the season, Hornsby expected that he would be on the trading block again, and he had hopes that he might be traded back to a team in the Midwest, specifically the Chicago Cubs. In September, when the Cubs came to Boston, Hornsby spoke directly to Cubs president William Veeck and let him know that he'd be happy to wear a Cubs uniform in the future. Hornsby undoubtedly knew that Cubs owner William Wrigley would also be delighted to finally acquire the player he had pursued for many years.

Five weeks after the World Series, the deal was finalized. The Cubs sent five players and $200,000 in cash to the Braves.[32] Hornsby would be in the Cubs' lineup in 1929.

2

William Wrigley

With Rogers Hornsby in the lineup, William Wrigley almost got what he wanted in 1929. The Cubs finished the regular season with a record of 98-54, winning the pennant by 10 games over the second place Pittsburgh Pirates.

Hornsby hit .380 and tied Hack Wilson for the team lead in home runs with 39. Hornsby and Wilson combined to drive in 308 runs. The rest of the lineup produced as well, especially the other outfielders, Kiki Cuyler and Riggs Stevenson. Cuyler hit .360 with 15 home runs and 102 RBIS; Stevenson hit .362 with 17 home runs and 110 RBIS. Charlie Grimm and Woody English anchored the infield. The pitching staff was led by Pat Malone who led the league with 22 wins; Charlie Root contributed 19 wins and Guy Bush added 18 wins. The manager was Joe McCarthy, in his fourth season at the helm of the club. Under McCarthy's leadership the team had steadily improved, winning more games each year and moving up in the standings from fourth to third to first.

In September the Cubs faced the Philadelphia Athletics in the World Series. The Cubs had not won the World Series since their back-to-back triumphs in 1907 and 1908, but Cubs fans were confident and optimistic that William Wrigley had found a winning combination of players, with the right manager to guide them.

The Athletics had not played in a World Series since 1914, but they were a strong team, winners of 104 games in the regular season, and paced by sluggers Jimmie Foxx and Al Simmons.

The first two contests were in Wrigley Field, and the Athletics won both games, 3–1 and 9–3. Jimmie Foxx homered in each game to lead the offense. Howard Ehmke, the surprise starter for the Athletics in Game One, struck out a World Series record thirteen batters with a repertoire of slow curves and off-speed pitches. In Philadelphia for Game Three, the Cubs bounced back, winning 3–1 behind Guy Bush.

Though Game Four was played on a bright sunny afternoon in Philadelphia, the day would turn out to be a nightmare for the Cubs. It was a difficult day for outfielders and especially so for Hack Wilson, who struggled on fly balls hit to center field. Leading 8–0 in the bottom of the seventh inning behind a strong pitching performance by Charlie Root, the Cubs fell apart. Al Simmons led off the inning with a majestic home run that landed on the left field roof. Five more runs were scored before Pat Malone, the fourth pitcher in the inning, was able to retire anyone. Then Mule Haas hit a 2-run homer to tie the score at 8–8. Simmons, up for the second time in the inning, doubled; Jimmie Foxx was intentionally walked. Bing Miller followed with a double, bringing Simmons and Foxx home. During the inning, Hack Wilson misplayed 2 balls, losing both in the sun. When the inning ended, mercifully with a strikeout, the score was 10–8 in favor of the Athletics.

In Game Five, the Cubs crumbled once more. This time, with Malone pitching, the Cubs took a 2–0 lead to the bottom of the ninth. But Malone surrendered a 2-run homer to Haas, then a run-scoring—and series-winning—double to Miller. The Cubs had lost the series, 4-1, and the Athletics were world champions.

Disaster followed disaster. Fifteen days after the final game of the World Series, on Black Tuesday, October 29, 1929, the stock market crashed.

Still worse—at least for Cubs fans: it would be a long time, an unimaginable eighty-seven years, to be exact—before the Cubs would win another World Series.

Wrigley was exasperated and took the loss in 1929 very hard. His dream of a World Series championship for Chicago had been temporarily dashed. He was not used to failure. He was a man of accomplishment who had become one of the wealthiest men in America. By the early 1930s, his net worth was estimated at more than thirty million dollars—half a billion dollars in today's currency.[1] He owned a business that would continue to thrive in the hard times ahead. He had a loving family. He trusted his son, Philip, to manage the family business. Throughout Chicago, Wrigley was celebrated for his generosity and commitment to civic causes. He had political influence and had helped a man become president of the United States.

At age sixty-eight, he had one more goal: for his Chicago Cubs to win a World Series and become the world champions. His background suggested that Wrigley usually got what he wanted.

Born in Philadelphia a few months after the start of the Civil War, in September of 1861, Wrigley had little formal education. His father owned a small soap factory and put his son to work at an early age stirring large vats of soap. By the age of thirteen, Wrigley was on the road as a soap salesman, traveling from customer to customer in a horse-drawn wagon.

Even at this young age, Wrigley was brilliant at promotion and sales. He bragged to his father, "I am about the best salesman who ever drew a breath. I could sell pianos to the armless men of Borneo."[2] In 1891, Wrigley set out on his own, moving to Chicago with his wife, Ada, and young daughter, Dorothy. He used a $5,000 loan from his uncle to start the Wrigley Company. At first, he manufactured soap and baking soda. Before long, he was in the business of producing chewing gum, a simple product that sold in such large quantities that it would make him a fortune.[3]

Through hard work, ingenuity, and good luck, Wrigley built an empire. In addition to the Wrigley Company and his baseball team, he owned a variety of other profitable businesses, a farm in Wisconsin, a palatial estate in Arizona, and an island off the coast of California. His real estate holdings included an office building in downtown Chicago. The Wrigley Building featured four clock faces, one on each side of a four hundred foot tower. The building continues to be one of the defining features of the Chicago skyline.

At the same time Wrigley was building his business empire, he was an active civic leader and sportsman. He was generous and contributed money to worthy causes. He donated $4,000 to the Lincoln Park Zoo to buy a hippopotamus, which was named Princess Spearmint in honor of the flavor of Wrigley's gum. Wrigley played tennis and golf, and he joined the Chicago Athletic Club where he swam and boxed and socialized with some of the richest and most powerful men in the city.

In 1916—the same year that Rogers Hornsby played his first full season with the St. Louis Cardinals—Wrigley began to acquire shares in the Chicago Cubs baseball team as part of a group of investors headed by Charles Weeghman, a local restauranteur known as Lucky Charley. Weeghman, also the former owner of the defunct Chicago Feds of the short-lived Federal League, had negotiated the sale of the Cubs from its previous owner, Charles Taft, the half-brother of Pres. William Howard Taft.[4] Other investors included J. Ogden Armour, the meat packing mogul, and Albert D. Lasker, the owner of a prominent advertising agency.

In 1919, Wrigley bought Catalina Island, off the coast of California, for 3.5 million dollars. At the time of the purchase, the island had just one town—Avalon—and a large hotel named St. Catherine's. The two principal local industries were fishing and tourism. Most of the island was nothing but rocky hillside inhabited by goats. Wrigley poured money into this new project, upgrading the water and sewer systems, building a ten acre aviary, and adding a state-of-the-art theater and ballroom to the St. Catherine. He built a mansion for himself and a baseball field for the Cubs to use in spring training.

Wrigley gradually and strategically increased his investment in the Cubs by buying shares from members of the original group. By 1921, Wrigley owned a majority interest in the team. Wrigley had taken a liking to a newspaper man named William Veeck, and hired him to serve as club president and general manager. Wrigley was a man of ideas and action, and Veeck appealed to him because he had a similar gift for candor and an imagination as grand as Wrigley's. Together, they were determined to build a winning ball club and bring a world championship to the city of Chicago.

In the early 1900s, Wrigley had developed an interest in politics and joined the Republican Party. He admired Theodore Roosevelt, and in 1912, he backed Roosevelt's third party candidacy on the Progressive ticket against the Republican incumbent, William Howard Taft. When approached about making a modest donation to Roosevelt's longshot bid for the presidency, Wrigley immediately wrote out a check for $25,000.[5]

In 1920 the Democrats nominated James Cox, a three-term Ohio governor, to run for president to succeed Woodrow Wilson. The Democrat's vice presidential candidate was Franklin Delano Roosevelt, an assistant secretary of the navy, known primarily as a younger cousin of the former president, Theodore Roosevelt. Franklin Delano Roosevelt was a politician with his best years still ahead of him.

The Republicans picked Warren G. Harding, a senator from Ohio, described by one presidential historian as "a third-rater."[6] Harding was a man who lacked ambition and doubted his own capacity to serve in the office.[7] Republican politicians tried to interest Wrigley in running for vice president on the Harding ticket. Wrigley and Harding had more in common than just their shared membership in the Republican Party: they both owned baseball teams. Harding was an avid fan of the game and part owner of the Marion Diggers, of the Class D Ohio State League.[8] At the age of fifty-four Harding had taken part in a charity exhibition game, played two innings at first base and collected a base hit before jamming a finger and leaving the game.[9]

Wrigley declined the opportunity to run for elective office but played a major role in Harding's campaign. During the summer of 1920, Wrigley and his colleague, Albert Lasker, made several trips to Ohio to visit Harding at his home. Lasker and Wrigley developed a billboard advertising campaign for the fall election. Al Jolson contributed a soon-to-be-forgotten song titled "Harding, You're the Man for Us."[10] Rather than traveling to meet voters or giving speeches, Harding stayed in Marion, Ohio during most of the campaign, relying on his advertising to convince the voters that he was worthy of the presidency. The success of the so-called "front porch" campaign was due, in large part, to the work of Wrigley and Lasker.

Looking back, one imagines how history might have been different. Others in the leadership of the Republican Party would have had a say in who became Harding's running mate, but Wrigley was an immensely popular figure, highly respected, and the convention in 1920 was held in Wrigley's hometown of Chicago. As it turned out, the delegates picked Massachusetts governor Calvin Coolidge to be Harding's running mate. Coolidge was later described as "the least magnetic personality in the history of the executive office."[11] Strictly in terms of charisma and personal charm, it's safe to say that Wrigley would have been a far more attractive and dynamic candidate than Coolidge.

If Wrigley had agreed to run as Harding's vice president and been elected, he would have become the thirtieth president, on August 2, 1923, when Harding died in office.[12] The fortune of the Chicago Cubs, not to mention the history of the United States, would have taken a different course with William Wrigley in the White House.

During the years when Wrigley was establishing ownership of the Cubs, baseball in Chicago was in crisis. The Cubs had won the National League pennant in 1918, then lost in the World Series to the Boston Red Sox and their star pitcher, Babe Ruth. A year later, the Cubs' crosstown rival, the White Sox of the American League, captured the pennant and were installed as heavy favorites to defeat the National League champions Cincinnati Reds, but Cincinnati took the best-of-nine series, 5 games to 3.

Rumors that the 1919 series was fixed leaked out before the series even began.[13] The betting odds mysteriously shifted. Chicago columnist Hugh Fullerton and other writers expressed their concern that key White Sox players had conspired and deliberately underperformed in several games to ensure that the Reds won. Arnold Rothstein, a New York gambler, was reputedly involved in the scheme.[14]

Rothstein had baseball connections in both Chicago and New York. He was friends with Charles Weeghman and had business relationships with both Charles Stoneham, the owner of the New York Giants, and the Giants' manager, John McGraw. Rothstein had helped Stoneham arrange the financing of his purchase of the Giants. Rothstein and McGraw, both of whom loved to bet on horse races, co-owned a pool hall in New York.

White Sox owner Charles Comiskey went through the motions of an investigation and claimed to find nothing wrong. But during the 1920 season more reports surfaced about the integrity of the game. Eddie Collins, the White Sox captain, went directly to Comiskey to express his concern that several of his players had participated in a scheme to deliberately lose 3 straight games to Boston, late in the season. At the time, the White Sox were clinging to a half-game lead over the Cleveland Indians in the American League pennant race. It's not clear how much Comiskey knew, or suspected, or how seriously he took the warning from Collins, but he did nothing.[15]

The same weekend that Collins and his teammates were losing to the Red Sox, the Phillies and Cubs were playing a series at Wrigley Field. The Phillies were in last place; the Cubs were in fifth. Neither team had a realistic chance to win the pennant. An hour or so prior to the game, William Veeck was in his office when he received a telegram from someone in Detroit warning Veeck that the game between his Cubs and the Phillies was fixed.[16]

Veeck took action. He warned Cubs manager Fred Mitchell about the alleged fix, suggesting that his starting pitcher, Claude Hendrix, might be involved in the scheme. Mitchell replaced Hendrix with Grover Alexander, the team's best pitcher, but the Cubs lost anyway, 3–0.

There was now enough concern about the integrity of the game that both the legal system and Major League Baseball responded. A few days after the Cubs lost to the Phillies, a grand jury under the direction of

Judge Charles McDonald was impaneled in Chicago to investigate the alleged attempt to fix the Cubs' game. But that inquiry quickly refocused on the 1919 World Series. Players coming before the grand jury began to acknowledge their involvement in the scheme. Three players—Ed Cicotte, Joe Jackson, and Claude Williams—signed confessions that they had participated in fixing the series.[17]

On October 22 the grand jury returned indictments against eight members of the Chicago White Sox, plus several of the gamblers and bookmakers implicated in the plot. Notably, Arnold Rothstein was not indicted.[18]

That fall, Major League Baseball grappled with a way to improve its image. If the game was tainted, fans would stop showing up at the ballparks. The owners had their investments to protect. Notably, though not surprisingly, discussions about what to do originated in Chicago. Albert Lasker, still a minority owner of the Cubs, suggested a commission that would rule over the world of baseball. The commission, as Lasker envisioned it, would be made up of non-baseball men. William Veeck weighed in and played a significant role in the discussions.[19]

After much debate and negotiation between the leagues and club ownership, It was determined that a single authority, an independent commissioner with broad powers, could best protect and preserve the image of the national pastime. A Chicago-based federal judge named Kenesaw Mountain Landis was chosen to be the commissioner. He would define and exercise his powers as commissioner for the next twenty-five years. He was a strong-minded man who didn't hesitate to exert his influence. One writer called him "God in a three-piece suit."[20] Many years later, Leo Durocher offered a different assessment: "The legend has been spread that the owners hired the Judge off the federal bench. Don't you believe it. They got him right out of Dickens."[21]

The trial of the accused players and gamblers began in the Chicago courtroom of Judge Hugh Friend, in midsummer of 1921, less than eight months after Landis assumed his position. Mysteriously, the signed confessions of Cicotte, Jackson, and Williams, as well as other documents, had disappeared from the courthouse and could not be produced as evidence. Public sentiment seemed to side with the players. In the sweltering summer heat of Chicago the courtroom was packed every day with fans of the White Sox anxious to see their favorite players up close.

The defense argued that the state had failed to prove that a criminal conspiracy involving the players and gamblers had taken place. The case went to the jury of twelve men shortly before 8:00 on the evening of August 2, 1921. The jurors were sequestered for less than three hours and needed only one ballot to determine the guilt or innocence of the ballplayers and gamblers charged with conspiring to defraud the public and baseball owners by throwing the 1919 World Series.

Judge Friend was summoned from his quarters at the Cooper Carlton Hotel and sat on the bench as Chief Clerk Edward Myers prepared to read the jury decision. A restless and anxious crowd of spectators perched nervously on the edge of the wooden benches. Finally, the courtroom quieted as the moment of judicial decision arrived.

Chief Clerk Myers read the first verdict, pertaining to left-handed pitcher Claude Williams: "Not guilty," he announced. The crowd whistled and applauded. Spectators stomped their feet and shouted with enthusiasm for the jury's work, as Myers began reading out the remaining acquittals. Not guilty. Not guilty. Not guilty. All seven players charged with the crimes were judged to be innocent. This included the three—Eddie Cicotte, Joe Jackson, and Claude Williams—who had signed confessions.[22]

With the exception of the prosecuting attorneys, almost everyone in the courtroom joined in the midnight celebration. Players slapped each other on the back. Eddie Cicotte, the White Sox ace pitcher, hustled to the jury box to shake hands with the foreman, William Barry. "Thanks," Cicotte blurted out, "I knew you'd do it."[23]

Bailiffs smiled, Judge Friend looked on with approval, and the jurors posed with players, their attorneys, and the acquitted gamblers for a group photograph. Then the crowd adjourned to a nearby Italian restaurant and was ushered into adjoining rooms to continue the celebration.[24]

At the restaurant, the party raged on. Cigar smoke and men's voices filled the rooms. Dishes clattered and glasses clinked as waiters scurried from table to table. The raucous celebration lasted until dawn.[25]

But neither the acquittals nor the celebration could change the mind of Kenesaw Mountain Landis. The judge had been on the job for less than a year, but he recognized that he had been hired by baseball owners to clean up the game. He was quick to assert his authority and pronounce judgment. In a tersely worded and unequivocal statement Landis decreed:

> Regardless of the verdict of juries, no player that throws a game, no player that entertains proposals or promises to throw a game, no player that sits in a conference with a bunch of crooked gamblers, where the ways and means of throwing games are discussed, and does not promptly tell his club about it, will ever play professional baseball.[26]

Landis's stand was supported the next day in an editorial published in the *Chicago Tribune*:

Black Sox Acquitted, But Out

> Judge Landis says that the acquitted Black Sox are nevertheless through with organized baseball. If they were not through with it we suspect that a number of the patrons of baseball would be through with it. It would have been the end of decent interest in the game.
>
> Judge Landis took his baseball position to give organized baseball a character bath. With the Black Sox back in the game the bath would have looked worse than if it had been drawn from the Missouri river in flood time and the country would have been ready for a return to the old foot race game, the crookedest thing known in sport.[27]

The effect on the fortunes of the Chicago White Sox was devastating. The 1921 club, missing seven of its best ballplayers, won only 62 games and finished in seventh place in the American League. After assembling one of the most powerful teams in baseball—Joe Jackson, Buck Weaver, Ray Schalk, Eddie Cicotte, Claude Williams, Dickie Kerr— the White Sox failed to place in the first division for the next fifteen seasons. Only once in those years did the club win more games than they lost. It wasn't until 1936 that the White Sox, led by shortstop Luke Appling and the good-hit-no-field first baseman, Zeke "Banana Nose" Bonura, climbed back into contention. That year they won 81 games and finished third. No one from the 1919 team remained on the White Sox roster.

In the early part of the decade, the rival Cubs fared little better. From 1920 through 1924, they never finished higher than fourth. Wrigley and Veeck faced a challenging task. But together, they were determined to turn the baseball team around and bring winning baseball back to Chicago.

The Cubs started the 1925 season with Bill Killefer as manager. In July, Killefer resigned. The Cubs were in seventh place with a record of 33-42. Veeck replaced Killefer with diminutive shortstop Rabbit Maranville. It turned out to be a disastrous choice.

Maranville was thirty-three. He had played nine years with the Boston Braves and four years with the Pittsburgh Pirates. This was his first year with the Cubs. In his years with Boston he had forged a friendship with his crosstown rival, the young Babe Ruth. Maranville was a few years older than Ruth, and together they spent many nights on the town in pre-Prohibition Boston. It's safe to assume that Ruth learned a thing or two about carousing from the fun-loving shortstop.

On his tiptoes, Maranville might have stretched out to a height of five feet six inches tall, but what he lacked in size, he made up for in combativeness and eccentricity. He was just a .258 lifetime hitter, but he was an exceptionally adept fielder. As a player, he was good enough to earn a plaque in the Hall of Fame, but he was totally unsuited for the job of managing a ball club. Maranville drank heavily and sometimes played ball with a flask in his back pocket. He tormented umpires. Off the field, he was a prankster whose stunts included diving into gold-fish ponds and crawling along hotel ledges to capture pigeons. He was replaced after eight weeks as Cubs manager. The hapless Cubs ended up last, 27½ games out of first place.

William Veeck was a man who learned from his mistakes. The disaster of the 1925 season taught him a lesson. When he went looking for a new manager after the 1925 season, he made a bold choice. At the time it was considered chancy, if not downright stupid, to pick a manager who had not first established himself by reaching the Major Leagues as a player. Every big league manager at that time had competed in the league as a player.

But Veeck took a chance and picked a career Minor Leaguer to manage the Cubs, a man who had never made it to the Majors as a player but was winning games as the skipper of the Minor League Louisville Colonels of the American Association. The name of the new manager was Joe McCarthy.

McCarthy was thirty-nine years old. He had been born in a small town in Pennsylvania, and when he was three, his father died in an accident on a construction site. As a youth, McCarthy worked in the textile mills and developed a passion for baseball. Soon he was playing sandlot ball, hoping to eventually make it to the big leagues, but he didn't have the skill as a player, so he became a manager.

He was a proud Irishman who liked to drink whiskey, a private man with a prickly personality and a reputation for being strict but fair. He had deeply held beliefs about how baseball should be coached and played, and he was intensely loyal to his players. He approached the game with intelligence and a keen eye for detail. Hall of Fame catcher Gabby Hartnett, who later managed the Cubs and took them to the 1938 World Series, said, "I think McCarthy knew more baseball than any other manager I ever saw or worked for."[28]

The Cubs in 1925 were in a tailspin, a team without direction or much talent. But Veeck had faith in McCarthy and believed that the new manager could succeed at the Major League level.

For McCarthy, it was the beginning of a brilliant career. Over twenty four seasons his teams never had a losing season and never finished in the second division. When he retired in 1950, he had won 3,489 games,

9 pennants, and 7 world championships. His winning percentage of .614 in regular-season games topped all managers, as did his .698 winning mark in World Series contests.

It all began with the Cubs in 1926. Shortly after being hired by Veeck, McCarthy was asked about the prospects for his last-place team. "They tell me we don't look very good on paper," McCarthy replied. "Well, we don't play on paper."[29]

Veeck and McCarthy settled on a strategy and made plans to overhaul the roster. The 1925 Cubs had won 68 games and lost 86. The team had three good young players—the catcher Gabby Hartnett, the first baseman Charlie Grimm, the pitcher Guy Bush—who would become the core of future championship teams. The rest of the roster would soon be gone, through trades or releases or retirement.

Veeck immediately upgraded the roster by acquiring two players from the American Association, both with some Major League experience, and both recommended by McCarthy. The players were Riggs Stevenson and Hack Wilson. Veeck also purchased the contract of Charlie Root from the Los Angeles Angels of the Pacific Coast League. The acquisitions paid off in 1926. Wilson led the team in home runs and RBIs; Stevenson batted .338. Root won 18 games in the first of eight straight seasons he'd post 14 or more wins. The 1926 Cubs improved to 82–72 and finished fourth.

But Veeck and McCarthy had a few more deals to make before the Cubs would be contenders. Shortstop Woody English was added in the off-season, purchased from Toledo. Pitcher Hal Carlson was acquired in a trade with the Phillies, in June 1927. That year the Cubs again finished fourth, winning 85 games.

Two more players were added for the 1928 season: Pat Malone, another product of the American Association, and Kiki Cuyler, acquired in a trade with the Pittsburgh Pirates. The 1928 Cubs won 91 games and moved up to third place in the league, finishing just 4 games behind the pennant-winning St. Louis Cardinals.

Five weeks later, Veeck completed the deal that brought Rogers Hornsby to the Cubs. Although the 1929 Cubs team won a pennant, the goal was always the same: to build a team that could not only get to the World Series, but could win it. The disappointment of 1929 had not been forgotten.

In 1930 the Cubs came close to winning consecutive pennants, finishing second with another 90-win season, 2 games behind the Cardinals. Hobbled by bone spurs in his foot, Hornsby played in only 42 games and collected just 32 hits, the fewest since his 1915 rookie season. Even without Hornsby in the lineup, the Cubs had a potent offense, finishing first in the league in home runs and second in runs scored. Hack Wilson had one of baseball's finest seasons, slamming 56 home runs and driving in 191 runs. He led the league in errors by an outfielder, with 19—not surprising, perhaps, considering his troubles in Game Four of the 1929 World Series.

Wrigley's frustration with the team in 1930 centered on his manager. Wrigley blamed McCarthy for the team's collapse in the 1929 World Series. As the season progressed, Wrigley became convinced that what the Cubs needed was a new manager, and Wrigley believed the right man for the job was Hornsby. McCarthy was let go just before the end of the season. Hornsby managed the team in its final 4 games. McCarthy landed on his feet, switching leagues and taking the job of the manager of the New York Yankees.

In 1931 Wilson slumped badly, hitting just 13 homers, and blamed Hornsby, claiming that the new manager made him take too many pitches, especially with the count 2–0 or 3–1. Just as Wrigley had soured on McCarthy in 1930, Hornsby and Wrigley decided that Wilson was expendable. The Cubs had three good starting pitchers—Charlie Root, Pat Malone, and Guy Bush—but they needed a reliable fourth starter. So Wilson was traded in December 1931 to the St. Louis Cardinals for thirty-nine-year-old Burleigh Grimes, the pitching hero of the 1931 World Series and the winner of 257 regular-season games. Grimes was also the last pitcher in either league who was still legally allowed to throw a spitball. As for Wilson, he spent a few weeks as property of the Cardinals' organization and then was traded again, this time to Brooklyn for a Minor Leaguer named Bob Parham and $45,000 in cash.

Grimes would spend the 1932 season with the Cubs, Wilson with the Dodgers. Parham never made it to the Major Leagues.

William Wrigley spent January of 1932 at his mansion in Phoenix, Arizona, a sixteen-thousand-square-foot dwelling that cost 1.2 million dollars. The house had twenty-four rooms and twelve bathrooms. Under construction since 1929, it had just recently been completed.[30]

With a solid roster, his manager of choice in charge of the team, and the popular but troublesome Hack Wilson traded away for another starting pitcher, Wrigley must have felt good about the Cubs chances for a pennant and World Series win in 1932. He planned to join the team on Catalina Island and then come back to Chicago in April for the beginning of the season.

Wrigley loved to watch the Cubs play baseball in the ballpark that bore his name. Built in 1914 by Charles Weeghman, the Cubs began using the park when the Federal League collapsed in 1916. After being known as Cubs Park for several years, and after several renovations that increased the seating capacity from 14,000 to slightly more than 30,000, the facility was officially renamed Wrigley Field for the start of the 1927 season.[31]

By the late 1920s Wrigley Field was a splendid ballpark. Every spring the park was repainted, and before each game, a grounds crew hosed down and cleaned the seating areas. Uniformed ushers—the Andy Frain ushers—escorted ticket holders to their seats. The concessionaires sold hot dogs, popcorn, roasted peanuts, and fresh lemonade.[32] During Prohibition, nonalcoholic Prager beer, manufactured by the Atlas Brewing Company in Chicago, was available on tap under the grandstand.[33]

With Philip Wrigley in charge of the family business, William Wrigley seldom missed a home game. From the vantage point of his box seat at Wrigley Field, the team's owner expected to see a winning ball club perform in 1932.

But in late January, Wrigley fell ill. After a sudden but short illness—apparently a stroke followed by cardiac failure—Wrigley died in his home in Phoenix.[34] His death came three months to the day after White Sox owner Charles Comiskey had passed away and ten days before the death of a third owner, Barney Dreyfus of the Pittsburgh Pirates.[35]

The press eulogized Wrigley as a man of wealth, vision, business acumen, and civic devotion. Articles in the Chicago papers recounted his life story, prominently noting his various enterprises and the property he owned. John Hertz, owner of a Chicago taxi cab business, stressed that Wrigley's primary focus was his ball club: "The Cubs were the joy of his life. Money meant nothing to him."[36]

The baseball world responded with tributes. Judge Landis described Wrigley as a man "endowed with common sense, integrity, courage, and energy." National League president John Heydler called him "a fine sportsman, always optimistic and charitable." William Veeck seemed in shock, declaring that Wrigley's death was "like losing a parent."[37]

A funeral was held in Phoenix and a memorial service in Chicago. Rogers Hornsby and Gabby Hartnett represented the Cubs team in Chicago. Hartnett served as an usher. Hornsby, not usually one to speak words of praise, had nothing but good things to say about the owner: "I've worked for a lot of wonderful fellows in baseball, but I admired Mr. Wrigley more than any of my other employers."[38]

3

Spring Training

After the memorial service for William Wrigley, Rogers Hornsby returned to his farm just north of St. Louis. In Chicago, Hornsby had conferred with William Veeck about the team's prospects for the upcoming season.

Hornsby was confident in his three veteran starting pitchers: Pat Malone, Guy Bush, and Charlie Root. The trio had already earned 281 Major League wins. Burleigh Grimes, the aging spitballer who had been the star of the 1931 World Series, also figured prominently in Hornsby's plans. The fifth starter would come from one of the returning veterans—Bob Smith or Jackie May—or perhaps the rookie Bud Tinning, who had posted a 24–4 for the Des Moines Minor League team the previous year. Lon Warneke, a raw twenty-three year old, and Bobo Newsom, might also compete for a spot on the staff. Warneke had pitched briefly for the Cubs in the 1931 season, hurling 64 innings and posting a record of 2-4. Newsom had posted a 16-14 record at Little Rock in the Southern Association.

There were two good catchers on the roster—Gabby Hartnett and Rollie Hemsley—and the infield was solid with Charlie Grimm at first, Billy Herman at second, and Woody English at shortstop. Hornsby was counting on highly prized rookie Stan Hack to play third. English could play any of the infield positions, and Hornsby could fill in at second or third, so at most, he'd need to add only one more infielder to the roster.

The major roster issue facing Hornsby and Veeck was the outfield. Hornsby wanted to be able to count on Riggs Stevenson, the former Alabama football star, as his left fielder, but Stevenson was thirty-three and still recovering from a broken ankle, suffered at the end of the 1931 season. Over his career, Stevenson had been a consistent .300 hitter with some power. If healthy, Stevenson would be the Cubs left fielder.

Kiki Cuyler, the ex-Pirate, was established as Hornsby's right fielder. In his fifth full season with the Cubs the thirty-two-year-old Cuyler had hit .300 or better in 7 of his 8 Major League seasons, including a .330 mark in 1931. He was the team's most consistently productive hitter and in the prime of his career.

The big question was who could replace Hack Wilson and play center field. Hornsby was bringing several outfielders to training camp. The Canadian-born Vince Barton, who had power but hit only .238 in 1931, was one possibility. At Hornsby's suggestion, the Cubs had also purchased Lance Richbourg for $25,000 from the Boston Braves and intended to give him a chance to earn a roster spot. Richbourg was a career .300 hitter but had little power. Johnny Moore, Marv Gudat, and Danny Taylor were the other outfielders invited to spring training.

Veeck and Hornsby discussed possible trades and the availability of players who might fit into the Cubs' lineup. Outfielders Paul Waner of Pittsburgh and Chick Hafey of St. Louis were unsigned, unhappy with the contracts they had been offered, and rumored to be on the trading block. Either player would be a significant addition to the Cubs' roster, if Veeck could put together a suitable trade.

Hornsby had all of these baseball matters to ponder as he spent the last weeks of the off-season at his farm. Away from the ballpark, Hornsby had another set of headaches. For a decade, he had been cited in multiple lawsuits involving various claims, both minor and serious. Most had been settled out of court, but some lingered for years.[1] In rough chronological order, the legal entanglements had included: an automobile accident in which Hornsby was the driver of a car that seriously injured Frank Rowe, an elderly pedestrian; two other automobile accidents, one when Hornsby's wife was driving, the other when Hornsby's chauffer was driving; a suit filed by John Hine, the husband of a woman with whom Hornsby was having an affair and later married; Hornsby's divorce from his first wife; a suit filed by Hornsby's own attorney for unpaid legal fees; a claim by his wife's doctor for an unpaid medical bill; a claim by a contractor for an unpaid bill for work done on Hornsby's farm.

The most complicated and problematic suit concerned Hornsby's relationship with and legal obligations to a betting agent named Frank Moore, a man who alleged that Hornsby had welched on more $90,000 worth of racetrack wagers.[2] Although Hornsby won that case in the courtroom, the publicity from the episode contributed to his trade from the Giants to the Braves.[3]

A gambling addiction, messy relationships, unpaid bills, and bad driving were not Hornsby's only problems. In addition, there were issues with the Internal Revenue Service regarding his 1927 taxes. Hornsby had claimed that he was a resident of Texas, not Missouri, so that only half of his income should be liable for taxation. The IRS dismissed this claim and argued that Hornsby owed both back taxes and penalties for not filing on time.

If these legal entanglements weren't sufficiently perplexing, Hornsby's farm had turned out to be a business failure. As the national economy slumped, so did the demand for Hornsby's poultry and bluegrass sod. Hornsby owed interest on his loan to buy the property, as well as back taxes to the county. Foreclosure loomed. Despite Hornsby's considerable earning power as the second-highest paid player in Major League Baseball, he was close to being broke.

But Hornsby wasn't thinking about his personal problems as he spent the first weeks of February at his farm. He was thinking about spring training and would soon be immersed solely in the daily life of baseball.

When Hornsby returned to Chicago in mid-February, he once again met with William Veeck to discuss the acquisition of an outfielder to replace Hack Wilson. Veeck reported that he had made no progress in arranging a trade. Veeck also conveyed the news that the young pitching prospect, Bobo Newsom, would be unavailable for spring training. Newsom had a broken leg. He had been kicked by a mule at an auction of farm animals in South Carolina.[4]

On Saturday evening, February 13, Hornsby and the first contingent of Cubs players—mostly pitchers and catchers, including veterans Pat Malone and Gabby Hartnett, plus the coach, Charley O'Leary, and a scout, Jack Doyle—boarded the *Los Angeles Limited* for the three-day train trip to California.

The train stopped in Nebraska to pick up the Arkansas native Lon Warneke, a lanky right-handed pitcher who had been called up at the end of the 1931 season, appearing in 20 games and pitching 64 innings, mostly in relief. Warneke climbed aboard, bringing a duffle bag and a banjo. On the long train ride, Warneke entertained his teammates with music and amusing stories about the livestock he owned on his family farm.

When the *Los Angeles Limited* arrived in California, most of the Cubs boarded the cruise ship ss *Avalon* for the three-hour trip from Los Angeles to Catalina Island. Hornsby, O'Leary, and Malone decided to fly in Philip Wrigley's prop plane to avoid the choppy seas. As the plane flew over the water, Malone experienced airsickness, hung his head out the window and vomited into the Pacific Ocean.

It was an annual tradition for residents of Catalina Island to meet the Cubs when the ship docked. A light rain was falling. An individual known locally as Jimmy the Barber, attired in a white uniform and wearing a matching cap, stood in the drizzle with a small fife and drum band and greeted the players and sportswriters as they emerged from the ss *Avalon*.

It was the first time in eleven years that it rained on the day the Cubs arrived. It was also the first year that William Wrigley had not accompanied the team to Catalina. If the rain was an omen, no one mentioned it.

The Cubs were joined in California by three other teams. The Detroit Tigers trained in Palo Alto, the Pittsburgh Pirates established their camp in Paso Robles, and the New York Giants set up camp in Los Angeles, at facilities owned by William Wrigley. The relationship between the Giants and Cubs included playing a series of exhibition games, some on

Catalina Island and others in Los Angeles. Hornsby and McGraw got along well together. They both liked betting on horse races, and both were lawsuit-prone. The disgruntled and aging McGraw—he was fifty-eight years old—was suffering from a variety of medical issues. He and Charles Stoneham had also just lost a contentious lawsuit with a business partner. The two men had been ordered to pay more than $40,000 in back wages and interest to a man named Francis X. McQuade.[5]

Four teams trained at scattered locations in the Deep South: the Chicago White Sox in San Antonio, Texas; the Cleveland Indians in New Orleans, Louisiana; the Boston Red Sox in Savannah, Georgia; and the Washington Senators in Biloxi, Mississippi. The remaining eight Major League teams trained in Florida, six of them on the West Coast between Fort Meyers and Clearwater.

With the start of spring training, speculation intensified about what teams would be the favorites going into the season. In the American League it was widely acknowledged that Connie Mack's Philadelphia Athletics were the team to beat and the overwhelming favorite to win their fourth straight pennant. The Athletics had averaged 104 wins a season in claiming their three consecutive league titles. The team's best players—Foxx, Simmons, Grove, Cochrane, Earnshaw, Walberg—were still in the prime of their careers. Only the New York Yankees and Washington Senators were considered legitimate challengers to the Athletics.

The National League was a different story. The St. Louis Cardinals would go into the season as the defending World Series champions, but their roster was in flux, and at least six National League clubs had reasonable expectations that they might be able to challenge for a pennant. No one expected much from the Boston Braves and Cincinnati Reds with their anemic batting orders. In 1931 the Braves and Reds had finished seventh and eighth in the league. They were the two worst teams in the league in terms of runs scored and combined for just 55 home runs.

Each of the other national league contenders had players in the lineup who could produce runs. The Phillies had power, paced by home run and RBI leader Chuck Klein, but not much pitching. The Pirates had Pie Traynor and the Waner brothers. The Giants, led by manager John McGraw, had a balance of pitching—Carl Hubbell and Freddie Fitzsimmons—and hitting—Mel Ott and Bill Terry. Brooklyn was starting the season with a new team name—calling themselves the Dodgers instead of the Robbies—and a new manager, Max Carey, whose lineup would include recently acquired Hack Wilson as well as Lefty O'Doul and Babe Herman.

Joe McCarthy took his New York Yankees to St. Petersburg. It would be McCarthy's second season at the helm of the Yankees, his seventh as a Major League manager. His teams had never finished lower than fourth—the 1926 and 1927 Cubs—but he had taken only one team to the World Series, the 1929 Cubs, who had blown up in the seventh inning of Game Four against Connie Mack's A's.

In 1931 McCarthy had guided his team to 94 wins and a second-place finish, barely edging out the third-place Washington Senators. But the Yankees and Senators had finished far behind the pennant-winning Philadelphia Athletics, winners of 107 games.

McCarthy's 1932 roster was basically the same as his 1931 squad. All of his position players returned, as well as his top four starting pitchers. Going into camp, he had two unsigned players: Tony Lazzeri and Babe Ruth. Lazzeri had slumped badly in 1931, hitting just 8 home runs and batting .267. The Yankees had him on the trading block over the winter, hoping to trade him for another starting pitcher, but no deal developed. As for Ruth, he said he was waiting to sign until he could discuss the terms of his contract face-to-face with Yankees owner Jacob Ruppert.

Even without a contract, Ruth was happy to be in Florida, if not for the baseball then for the golf courses. To entertain local photographers, Ruth wrapped his arms around his then-wife, Claire, showing her the finer points of the golf swing as he posed for pictures.[6] While Ruth waited for Ruppert to arrive so they could argue about contract terms, he participated in several golf tournaments, competing in the amateur division. Ruth was a good golfer, scoring in the

70s. His scores were only a few strokes higher than those recorded by some of the pros—Billy Burke and Paul Runyan—who led the professional division.

While baseball teams were far away from their home cities and engaged in the routines of spring training, the nation was shocked to learn the news that the twenty-month-old son and namesake of aviator Charles Lindbergh had been kidnapped from the family's home in Hopewell, New Jersey. The toddler had been taken from his second-floor bedroom. A ransom note was found in an envelope on the windowsill of his room. The police found evidence outside the house: a crudely made wooden ladder, footprints, the child's blanket. A massive search was immediately organized. Although it was a state crime, President Hoover authorized the Department of Justice to cooperate with New Jersey authorities. A reward was offered. Al Capone even offered to help, on the condition that he was released from prison so he could assist the police.

For weeks the public followed the story as investigators searched for clues to the boy's disappearance. Thirty-one days after the abduction, a ransom of $50,000 was paid to an intermediary who claimed to know the boy's whereabouts, but the child was not returned.

Ruth's holdout was the big news in Florida, even though he was not the only prominent Major Leaguer to be holding out or disappointed with the salary offer of his team. But Ruth was not just any ballplayer. He was the financial engine of the Major Leagues.[7] In the eyes of the fans, he was baseball's number one star attraction. In his previous eighteen seasons he had never been asked to take a pay cut. Even though the nation was in the midst of unprecedented hard times, Ruth reasoned that he was a special case.

Ruth's contract demands were simple and straightforward. He wanted the most money that the Yankees would pay him. Already he was, by far, the highest paid Major Leaguer, earning a salary of $80,000 in each of the previous two seasons. Ruppert, citing the Depression and the fact that almost all Major Leaguers were taking pay cuts, offered $70,000 and said he wouldn't go any higher. Ruth countered that he only planned to play two more years before retiring and believed he was entitled to a two-year deal at his current salary of $80,000.

While Ruth waited for Ruppert to arrive in St. Petersburg, he announced that he would work out with the team and participate in intersquad games, but wouldn't play in exhibition games until he had a contract. Ruth had leverage in the negotiations. Every day Ruth was out of the lineup meant less box office revenue for the Yankees. Florida baseball fans weren't likely to pay admission to exhibition games unless Ruth was in the lineup.

Spring training started with more than two dozen unsigned players. Most of the holdouts—like Lazzeri and Ruth—showed up on time for the beginning of workouts, even though they were not under contract. Other notable holdouts included Lefty Grove and Rube Walberg of the Athletics; Frankie Frisch, Charley Gelbert, and Chick Hafey of the Cardinals; Tony Cuccinello, Joe Stripp, Joe Morrissey, and Red Lucas of the Reds; Heinie Manush of the Senators; Goose Goslin of the Browns; Wally Berger of the Braves; Heine Meine and Paul Waner of the Pirates. Baseball's other Babe—Babe Herman of Brooklyn, twenty-eight years old and one of the game's rising stars—was also unsigned. He was being asked to take a $4,000 pay cut from $19,000 to $15,000, a cut of 21 percent, despite the fact that he was coming off a season in which he produced impressive numbers: 18 HRS, 97 RBIS, .313 BA.

The players had support from one unlikely source: Westbrook Pegler, a thirty-eight-year-old writer, whose column appeared regularly in the sports pages of the *Chicago Tribune*. He had been writing the sports column since 1925 and was widely syndicated. Years later, he would be well-known for his political columns and conservative viewpoints.[8]

In early February, Pegler devoted a long column to the issue of player salaries and management's control over employees, calling the reserve clause that bound players to a single team "the baseball boycott system." Pegler also accused club owners—whom he referred to as "the magnates"—as being generous with charities and their friends, but tight-fisted when it came to salary negotiations with players. Pegler charged that the owners had colluded "to enforce their conspiracy against their employees" by agreeing to reduce salaries for the 1932 season. As an example, Pegler pointed out that a highly regarded player like Bill Terry was asked to take a 40 percent pay cut, from $22,000 to $13,200.[9]

The article concluded with Pegler arguing, "I would still believe that the ball player ought to have a free market in which to sell his work, or, anyway, some voice in the decision of his pay."[10]

Pegler's views had no observable impact on salary disputes in the spring of 1932. Few players had the influence—Ruth was the exception, of course—to actually threaten owners with a holdout. Considering the reserve clause was to remain in effect for another forty-three years, the article itself was revolutionary for its time.[11]

Spring training routines at the various camps followed a predictable pattern. While owners concentrated on contract negotiations with the unsigned players, managers focused on conditioning and drills. With roster size reduced from 25 to 23, marginal players and rookies were competing for fewer open roster spots than in past years, so even the first intersquad games were meaningful to players trying to make the final cut. In addition, players who had been traded or discarded—Hack Wilson, for example—came to their new teams with something to prove.

One ballplayer trying to make it back to the big leagues was Mark Koenig, the property of the Detroit Tigers. Koenig was a veteran, though still a young man. He was twenty-nine years old and had played five full seasons with the New York Yankees. He had been the starting shortstop on two of baseball's all-time greatest teams: the 1927 and 1928 Yankees.

In his early days with the Yankees, Koenig had a close relationship with Babe Ruth. Their lockers were next to each other in the clubhouse, and they partied together at night. On road trips, they slept in berths across the aisle from each other. But in 1927, they got into a heated exchange in the team's dugout when Ruth challenged Koenig's effort on a defensive play during an exhibition game. They shouted insults back and forth. Then Ruth pushed Koenig down the dugout steps, and the two of them scuffled before teammates broke it up. They didn't speak to each other the rest of the season.[12]

Koenig's tenure with the Yankees came to an end during the 1930 season when he lost his job to a young shortstop named Leo Durocher. Durocher was later to have his own conflict with Ruth.[13] At that point, the Yankees considered Koenig expendable, and he was traded to the Detroit Tigers. He hit poorly in Detroit: .240 in 1930 and .253 in 1931. In 1931 he had played 55 games at second base, only 35 games at short-stop. The Tigers had another shortstop, Billy Rogell, a couple of years younger than Koenig and better at the plate.

Koenig had never been an outstanding defensive shortstop. He had small hands but a powerful arm. The Tigers thought they might be able to convert him to a pitcher. At the end of the 1930 and 1931 seasons, Koenig pitched in relief a few times and started 1 game. He showed promise, though he lacked control. In 16 innings Koenig walked nine-teen batters and struck out nine.

In 1932 the Tigers were willing to give him a chance in spring training to prove that he might be able to exhibit the control and skill necessary to be a Major League pitcher. On March 9, Koenig allowed just 1 run and 2 hits in a three-inning stint against the San Francisco Seals. He had good velocity and was able to keep his pitches in the strike zone. A few days later, he had another strong outing.

On March 13, Yankees owner Jacob Ruppert arrived in St. Petersburg and went for a walk on the beach. His star player, the unsigned Babe Ruth, had a golf date with tour pro Billy Burke. "The Colonel knows where he can get me," Ruth said, "if he wants to talk." Ruth added that he'd had one of his best years in 1931—46 home runs, 163 RBIS, 149 runs scored, and a batting average of .373—and he expected to be compensated accordingly.[14] Ruth repeated his position and the terms he wanted. He said he would sign for $70,000 if it was a two-year con-tract or $80,000 for a one-year deal.

Three days later, Ruth and Ruppert met in the lavish foyer of the Rolyat Hotel, to negotiate a contract. The meeting took place in front of a large fireplace with reporters and other bystanders watching from a distance of about one hundred feet. William Brandt of the *New York Times* wrote, "The setting of today's proceedings befitted so important an episode in the career of the orphan boy who grew up to make a million dollars."[15]

After a ten minute discussion between the two men, they reached an arrangement. Ruppert and Ruth compromised, with the Babe agreeing to a one-year deal at $75,000. The two men moved outside to formalize the contract, signing at a table in front of a tropical garden. Cameras whirred as still photographers and newsreel operators captured the scene. Then the two men posed in front of a Spanish wishing well. Ruth tossed a half dollar in the water. The orphan boy told the assembled crowd that all he wished for was another pennant for the Yankees.[16]

After the signing, Ruth was in a good mood. He bragged to a reporter, "The pennant ought to be a breeze for us this season."[17]

A's manager Connie Mack wasn't ready to concede the pennant, much less front runner status to Ruth's Yankees. Speaking to the St. Petersburg Rotary Club a few days later, Mack offered his perspective on the upcoming season. He had kind words for his rivals, noting that the Yankees had improved their pitching and now had enough "speed and punch" to challenge his ball club. "I don't mind telling you," Mack said, "I am afraid of those Yankees. They were going very strong at the end of last season. They are a powerful club."[18]

It wasn't just the Yankees he was worried about. "We would very much like to make it four straight," Mack acknowledged to the Rotarians. "We may do it, if the Yankees behave and Washington, too."[19]

By the middle of March, most of the holdouts had come to terms, some more grudgingly than others, but three key players had still not signed with their clubs: Wally Berger of the Braves, Chick Hafey of the Cardinals, and Babe Herman of the Dodgers. Berger had been offered a raise of $2500, which he rejected.

Hafey was holding out for the second straight year. He remained at his home in Berkley, California. In 1931 he hadn't signed until after the season started and was docked $2,000 for his late arrival. Now he was negotiating to have that money added to his 1932 contract. The Cards were offering $12,500—and raised the bid to $13,000—but Hafey insisted he wouldn't sign unless he got $15,000, to compensate him for the money he'd forfeited the previous season. The Cardinals and their best hitter remained at a standstill.

The Dodgers and Reds figured out a way to deal with their unhappy players: they swapped them. In the major trade of the spring training season, the Reds sent Joe Stripp, Tony Cuccinello, and Clyde Sukeforth to the Dodgers for Babe Herman, Wally Gilbert, and Ernie Lombardi. A week later, Herman signed with the Reds for $16,500, a pay cut but a better deal than the one offered by his former employers in Brooklyn.

On Catalina Island, Hornsby continued to search for an outfielder. Hornsby's hope that William Veeck might be able to make a deal with the Reds to bring the newly acquired and still disgruntled Babe Herman to the Cubs was squelched in a news report: "Babe Herman is going to play with the Cincinnati Reds and not the Chicago Cubs, Manager Dan Howley said today to stifle reports the slugging outfielder would be sold or traded again."[20]

Herman would be a Cub eventually—acquired for the 1933 season—but he would play for Cincinnati in 1932.

The Cubs stayed in the St. Catherine Hotel and worked out at the ball field that William Wrigley had constructed specifically for his team's spring training regimen. The players could walk to the field from the hotel for their daily practice. A small house just beyond the left field fence was available for the players to store their gear. Hornsby's practices ran from 11:00 a.m. to 3:00 p.m. The players had the rest of the day free to roam about the island, go fishing, or play golf. They took their meals at the hotel.

After a series of intersquad games, the Giants arrived at Catalina Island for a 2-game series, the first 2 of the 8 games the teams planned to play against each other while on the West Coast. It was also an opportunity for the Giants to socialize with their rivals. As the *Chicago Tribune* reported, the visiting Giants were "treated to auto rides over the mountains, boat rides along the island's rocky coast, a barbeque at Phil K. Wrigley's fancy ranch, and free movies and dances."[21] The Cubs and Giants split the 2 games. John McGraw skipped the festivities and competition to stay on the mainland and visit the Aqua Caliente racetrack.[22]

Hornsby prided himself on his knowledge of the fundamentals of the game, and his four-hour long practices in the middle of day were focused on teaching those skills to his players, especially the younger ones. As Hornsby evaluated the rookies, Jurges and Warneke were the two who stood out. Jurges was getting a few hits; Warneke had a good outing against the Giants.

On Catalina Island, Hornsby devoted considerable time to improving the technique of both touted newcomers and marginal players. Hornsby drilled Stan Hack in the art of sliding, with repeated exercises in the sliding pit. As for his outfield problem, the manager hoped that Vince Barton, the free-swinging Canadian, might be the answer, if Hornsby could get Barton to become more disciplined at the plate, striking out less and putting more balls in play. Hornsby worked with Barton on his swing mechanics, counseling Barton to use his wrists more and not try to hit every pitch for a home run.[23] A few weeks later, the lessons seemed to pay off. In an exhibition game with Portland, Barton hit a grand slam.

On the coast of Florida, Babe Ruth was getting himself in shape for his eighteenth Major League season. He was a bit overweight and a little out of shape, suffering various minor physical discomforts, not uncommon for a player of his age. He was excused from one exhibition game with a painfully bruised toe. He skipped another with a strained neck. In one of his final Florida appearances, he played with an oilskin jacket over his uniform, in an attempt to sweat off some extra pounds. He lasted 6 innings, though he was still suffering from the neck discomfort. As reported by the *New York Times*, the Babe was "unable to turn his head to the left without wincing."[24] Then he took a couple more days off.

Fortunately for the Yankees, opening day was still thirteen days in the future. There was time for the Babe to recover.

The night before the Cubs were to leave Catalina Island, they were treated to a party at the St. Catherine Hotel. As per tradition, there was a dance contest, and as usual, the quick-footed Kiki Cuyler was the winner.

In the morning, the Cubs went to the field to collect their gear and discovered that the little house by the outfield fence had been broken into. Hornsby's shoes and Richbourg's glove had been stolen. After notifying the local police of the theft, the team went down to the dock to take the ss *Avalon* to the mainland. Jimmy the Barber conducted the locals in a farewell song: "Aloha 'Oe."[25]

One professional baseball player who was not leaving the West Coast was infielder-turned-pitcher Mark Koenig. As the spring progressed, Koenig's efforts to prove himself as a hurler had failed. In one game against the Hollywood Stars of the Pacific Coast League, the Minor Leaguers put up 14 runs.

Koenig was released by the Tigers. A few days later, he was signed to a Minor League contract with the San Francisco Missions, who planned to employ him at his old position at shortstop.

For Koenig, it would be a temporary disappointment. By midsummer, however—in approximately 100 days—he would return to the Major Leagues and play a significant role in a pennant race.

4

Opening Day

Two decades earlier, on April 14, 1910, a record opening-day crowd of 12,226 baseball fans jammed into tiny American League Park in Washington DC, to see the hometown Senators take on the visiting Philadelphia Athletics. It was sunny and warm, a near-perfect spring day.

The train carrying the Athletics had arrived in town around noon, and the team had eaten lunch at the Arlington Hotel before arriving at the ballpark. If any of the players had purchased that day's *Washington Post*, they would have read that: "The opening will not be attended by any ceremony here. There will be no parade, no speechmaking, but a battle that seems assured."[1] So the Athletics might have been surprised at the number of spectators in the stands.

In fact, it would be a day of historical significance because one of the spectators would be none other than the president of the United States.

A year earlier, William Howard Taft—a professed fan of the national game—had become the first sitting president to attend a professional baseball game since Benjamin Harrison, in 1892. Taft had been seated in a special spectator's box that had been outfitted with a large spindle-back, wooden chair for the president's comfort. Taft had enjoyed the outing and returned for other games through the summer, so Washington owner Clark Griffith had suggested that the president attend the season opener in 1911 and formally participate in the commencement of the season.

For Griffith, it served as a ploy to garner publicity and bring paying customers to the ballpark. For baseball, it was the beginning of a new tradition, linking the presidency and the national game.

The gates opened at 1:00 p.m., and when the Senators appeared on the field for warm-ups, the best seats had already been taken. Late arrivals, including some congressmen, were only able to purchase fifty-cent tickets for the bleachers.[2] The home team was attired in new white uniforms with decorative blue trim and stylish caps of "a unique shape to which spectators will have to become accustomed before they can be appreciated."[3]

Shortly before 3:45 p.m., President Taft rose from his seat and threw out the first ball of the season, which was caught by a shy twenty-two-year-old Washington pitcher named Walter Johnson. Johnson was matched up against the A's veteran Eddie Plank and won the opening day duel by a score of 3–0, no-hitting the Athletics for 7 innings and finishing with a 1-hit gem. It was the first of Johnson's 14 opening day starting assignments, during which he would compile a record of 9-5, pitching 7 shutouts and completing 12 of the starts.

The next day Johnson would send the ball to the White House with a request that the president sign it for him. Taft responded by writing "To Walter Johnson with hope that he may continue to be as formidable as in yesterday's game. William H. Taft."[4]

Although Taft's participation in the opening day ceremonies set a precedent—and expectations—for future presidents, baseball had been played in the nation's capital since the late 1850s, and Taft was just one of several presidents who had watched or expressed his appreciation for the game.[5] The two most prominent teams in the pre–Civil War era were the Washington Potomacs and the Washington Nationals. Their games were often played on what was known as "the White Lot"—today called the Ellipse—a spacious grass field, just south of the White House. President Lincoln had been a fan of the game, and even during the difficult years of the Civil War, he was occasionally spotted standing outside the White House looking down at the fields as teams played.[6] On at least one occasion Lincoln ventured down to the field with his son Tad, and watched the game from a spot along the first base line. In late August 1865, just four months after Lincoln's death, President Andrew Johnson attended a game between the Nationals and a team from Philadelphia. More than 10,000 spectators joined the new president to witness that contest.

Throughout the late nineteenth century and early twentieth century, presidents occasionally came out to the ballpark, though many were concerned that the public might see their interest in baseball as frivolous. But once Clark Griffith established the tradition by persuading President Taft to attend opening day, future presidents found it easier to justify an outing to the ballpark, and the opening day ceremonies linked the office of the president to the national pastime.

On April 11, 1932, Pres. Herbert Hoover had much more on his mind than that day's opening day baseball game. The morning newspapers carried stories about the Lindbergh kidnapping; the baby had been missing for six weeks and the $50,000 ransom paid by Charles Lindbergh had failed to bring the safe return of the baby. Political news was sprinkled throughout the paper. A revenue bill was pending. An investigation was underway in Congress to determine the extent of short selling in the stock market. Hoover had been troubled by rumors that rich investors were taking advantage of falling stock prices to make huge profits. A Texas congressman named Wright Patman was holding hearings to determine whether or not World War I veterans should be paid their bonus early. Hoover's attention was also focused on a front-page story about the German elections. The results had been tallied. Pres. Paul von Hindenburg had survived a challenge from a rising politician named Adolf Hitler, leader of the National Socialist Party. Hitler's party had garnered six million votes and finished second in the balloting.

Hoover was a man of immense talent and impressive accomplishments. He had traveled the world as a mining engineer and entrepreneur. He had been highly praised for his work during World War I as administrator of the U.S. Food Administration. After Warren Harding's election in 1920, Hoover served as secretary of commerce for the eight years before he became president. He entered the oval office with a knowledge of government, a strong work ethic, and an appreciation for organization. Unfortunately his presidency was to be marked by the disaster of the stock market crash and the beginning of the Great Depression.

After breakfast, Hoover walked to his office and took a look at his daily schedule. It was opening day, so he knew that he'd be headed out to see the Senators play in a few hours. Then he plunged into his work. An orderly stack of manila folders rested on one corner of the work-space. A telephone sat nearby. Hoover was the first president to keep a telephone on his desk.

At mid-morning, Hoover delivered a short address to the American Red Cross. He returned to the White House and sat through a series of meetings. Shortly after noon, Hoover left his office and walked outside to the South Grounds. The sky was overcast and ominous, with heavy clouds, but it was part of the president's midday routine to venture outside to greet visitors and pose for pictures. Today there was a ceremony with the commander in chief of the vfw; photographers snapped a picture. Hoover turned to shake hands with Sen. Harrison Kean of New Jersey. Kean had brought one of his constituents, a young woman who had been awarded the title South Jersey Apple Blossom Girl. The two men posed with the Apple Blossom Girl as the cameras clicked.

After a lunch, Hoover left the White House in a chauffeured car, accompanied by his wife, Lou. Various aides and cabinet officials, including the secretary of the treasury, Ogden Mills, followed in other vehicles. The caravan headed to Griffith Stadium, where Hoover was to throw out the ceremonial first pitch of the 1932 baseball season.

Built of steel and concrete in 1911 and located north of the White House at the corner of Georgia Avenue and W Street nw, Griffith Stadium had replaced American League Park and been named for the Washington Senators' owner. The stadium occupied most of a city block and contained a modest seating capacity of 32,000. The field itself was oddly shaped. The outfield fence had been constructed to preserve a large tree and several houses; the homeowners who lived just on the other side of the outfield walls had refused to sell their properties. The left field foul pole was 407 feet from home plate, but the center-field fence angled sharply around the protected tree; it was just 320 feet down the right field line.

The Senators had won back-to-back American League championships in 1924 and 1925, paced by the now legendary Walter Johnson in the twilight years of his playing career. The 1924 season had ended triumphantly for the Senators, as they defeated the New York Giants 4–3 in Game Seven of the World Series with Johnson picking up the win in relief. A year later, the Senators were matched in the series with the Pittsburgh Pirates. Despite two complete game wins early in the series, Johnson was the losing pitcher in Game Seven, a contest played mostly in the rain and partly in the dark. Four unearned runs in the seventh inning doomed the Senators. It was Johnson's last appearance in a World Series game, and it left a bitter taste in his mouth.

Now Johnson, at age forty-five, was the Senators' manager, his brilliant pitching career—416 wins, 3,508 strikeouts—a not-so-distant memory. To get his team back to the top of the league in 1932, Johnson faced stiff competition from the New York Yankees and the Philadelphia A's. The mighty Yankees of 1927 and 1928, who swept both series 4 games to none, had been replaced by Connie Mack's A's as the league's best team. The A's had won 3 straight pennants and came into the season as the team to beat. The Yankees, under second-year manager Joe McCarthy, still had the one-two combination of Babe Ruth and Lou Gehrig, but there were questions about the Babe's fitness and ability to be productive. Ruth was now thirty-seven years old, and each spring he struggled with increasing difficulty to get his body in shape for the long season. In addition, Ruth came into the season somewhat disgruntled after his off-season salary dispute.

Baseball as a business had reached a crisis point. As the national economy deteriorated, attendance sagged. Cautious owners worried about the fiscal health of their teams, and in the off-season owners had voted to make changes. Rosters were trimmed from twenty five players to twenty three. The league's crew of umpires was cut from twelve to ten. Contract negotiations between owners and players were especially contentious, foreshadowing a season during which players brawled with each other on the field, and, in one memorable incident, where an umpire challenged an entire team to a fist fight after a game.

Prior to Hoover's arrival, the comedy team of Al Schacht and Nick Altrock, former Major League pitchers turned entertainers, performed for a crowd of nearly 25,000 fans.[7] The two men had worked together as coaches with the Washington Senators and developed a popular act involving stunts, gags, and pantomimes that they performed before games across the country. Their act often concluded with a comic performance at home plate of the famous "long count" fight between Jack Dempsey and Gene Tunney. To the fans it was a hilarious scene during which the two comedians pummeled each other with oversized gloves. For the entertainers, it was an opportunity to unleash some real blows. In fact, their on-field shenanigans belied a bitter personal feud. By 1932 Schacht and Altrock were only speaking to each other when absolutely necessary.

The president's entourage arrived at Griffith Stadium shortly before game time and was seated behind first base in field level box seats. Hoover liked baseball. He had played shortstop briefly as a member of the Stanford University team, his career cut short by an injured finger and only modest skill at the game. In 1931 Hoover had attended Game Three of the World Series in Philadelphia. His popularity had already begun to falter, especially since he represented the party that continued to support Prohibition. Unruly fans in Philadelphia spotted Hoover in the stands and regaled him with a chant: "We want beer! We want beer! We want beer!"[8] But the opening day crowds at Griffith Stadium were more receptive and respectful.

As both a politician and a baseball fan, Hoover enjoyed the experience of opening day, and he had been attending season openers in Washington for more than a decade. In each of his first three years as president Hoover had participated directly in the opening day ritual, even though his presence seemed to foreshadow a loss by the home team. *The Washington Post* columnist Shirley Povich noted that the Senators had lost all of these opening day games, which Povich termed the "Hoover Jinx."

Before the start of the game, players from the two teams lined up along the first and third base lines. Then Secretary Mills joined Washington Senators owner Clark Griffith on the field, and the two men marched arm-in-arm to the flagpole in center field. The flag was raised as an army band played "The Star Spangled Banner."[9]

Hoover's ceremonial duty was to throw out the first pitch of the season. He was handed a ball and tossed it in the direction of the home plate umpire, George Hildebrand, a former Minor League pitcher and the alleged inventor of the spitball. The ball sailed over Hildebrand's head and had to be retrieved by a member of the visiting Red Sox, the first wild pitch of the season.

The opening day pitching assignment for the Senators belonged to Alvin Crowder, nicknamed General Crowder in honor of Gen. Enoch Crowder, the man responsible for originating America's draft lottery in World War I, though the pitcher and the military man were not related. A compact five foot ten right-hander, Crowder had a reputation as a tough competitor with an outstanding move to first base. He took his spot on the mound, glanced at the gray skies, and began his warm-up pitches.

Storm clouds threatened throughout the afternoon, but the skies held. Hoover stayed until the seventh inning, the game still scoreless when he left the stadium. General Crowder pitched magnificently, scattering 4 hits and stranding the few batters who reached base against him. It was an auspicious season opener for the Senators' ace. Crowder would go on to win 26 games that year and lead the American League in victories.

In the bottom of the tenth, Heinie Manush broke up the scoreless duel and doubled in the winning run for the Senators. By the time second baseman Buddy Myer crossed home plate with the game's only run, Hoover was already back at his desk in the oval office. The extra inning game had been played in a crisp two hours and eight minutes. The next day Povich would write that the Hoover Jinx was still in place since the president had left in the midst of a scoreless game.[10]

The baseball game passed from the president's mind after he returned to the White House. That evening Hoover and his wife dressed in their evening clothes and attended a dinner party at the home of Supreme Court Chief Justice Charles Evan Hughes, to celebrate Hughes's seventieth birthday. Hoover and Hughes were close friends and political allies. Hughes, who had resigned from the Supreme Court in 1916 to accept, somewhat reluctantly, the Republican nomination for president, had been appointed chief justice by Hoover in 1930.

By 10:00 p.m. the president and his wife were back in their car, rolling through the quiet streets of the nation's capital on their drive back to the White House. Outside the monuments and memorials gleamed in artificial light; cherry blossoms rested in the darkness. It was a cool evening, the temperatures settled comfortably in the low forties.

Hoover had a great deal on his mind, but he did not yet fully sense the restlessness of America. A group of agitated World War I veterans had already arrived in Washington to lobby for the passage of Congressman Wright Patman's Bonus Bill, and far across the continent a discontented vet named Walter Waters was listening to the public debate.[11] In early May, Waters and his West Coast sympathizers would climb aboard a few boxcars and ride the rails, heading east, picking up recruits along the way, gathering strength and confidence in their cause. By mid-summer, nearly twenty thousand World War I veterans, calling themselves the Bonus Expeditionary Force (BEF), would settle in makeshift camps and abandoned buildings in Washington, enduring the summer heat and demonstrating their displeasure with the government.

For America that summer, baseball would be a diversion for a troubled country, but for President Hoover there would be few opportunities to enjoy the national pastime.

5

The Math Wizard

While Hoover slept in the White House, Walter Johnson and the Washington Senators enjoyed a train ride to Boston. After the single-game series in Washington, the teams were scheduled to face each other again in the home opener at Fenway Park.

As the train curled its way northward along the Atlantic seaboard, Johnson contemplated his team's prospects. Shirley Povich, the *Washington Post* columnist who followed the team, already had expressed high hopes for the season, writing "the Washington Ball Club this season has its best chance to win the American League pennant since the post pennant era that set in in 1926."[1] By the end of the month, the Senators would play two series against the Boston Red Sox and two series against the Philadelphia Athletics. The Red Sox had finished last in 1930 and sixth in 1931; they had done little to upgrade their roster, and no one expected them to be a first division team. But the A's were the best team in baseball. The 8 games in April against Philadelphia would tell Johnson a lot about how his team might fare over the course of a season.

Johnson could count on the Senators to score runs. He didn't have a powerful duo like Babe Ruth and Lou Gehrig of the Yankees, or Jimmie Foxx and Al Simmons of Athletics, but he had a solid lineup of ballplayers who could hit for average and drive in runs. The sharp-fielding Ossie Bluege, a ten-year veteran, played third base. At shortstop, Joe Cronin, just twenty-five years old, was at the beginning of a Hall of Fame career and coming off back-to-back years of hitting over

.300. Buddy Myer at second base and the veteran Joe Judge at first, anchored the right side of the infield.

The outfield was even better, young and talented. Heinie Manush started in left field. Manush, acquired via a trade for Goose Goslin in June 1930, had hit over .300 in seven of his nine seasons. Like Cronin, Manush was destined to earn a plaque in the Hall of Fame. The center fielder was Sammy West, twenty-seven years old and a .321 lifetime hitter. In right field the Senators would deploy Carl Reynolds, acquired in the off-season from the White Sox. In four full-time seasons Reynolds had never hit lower than .290. As a backup outfielder, Johnson could use Sam Rice. At forty-two, Rice didn't have the legs or speed that produced a league-leading 63 stolen bases in 1920, but he could still hit for a high average and play adequately in the field.

Catching duties were shared by Roy Spencer, an adequate but often-injured backstop, and Moe Berg, one of the most cerebral and eccentric men to ever play the game. Casey Stengel famously remarked that Berg was "the strangest man ever to play baseball."[2] Berg had peculiar habits—he wouldn't read a newspaper if anyone else had touched it before he started reading—along with impressive intellectual credentials, including an undergraduate degree from Princeton, a law degree from Columbia University, and fluency in nearly a dozen languages. His major deficiency was that he couldn't hit Major League pitching. He had earned a spot on a Major League roster due to his defensive skills and ability to handle pitchers, qualities that Johnson appreciated.

Pitching was Johnson's main area of interest. In a preseason analysis, Shirley Povich had judged the quality of the pitching staff to be of concern, but praised the potential of the rookie Monte Weaver, "whose possibilities are as brilliant as any on the staff."[3] The mild-mannered Walter Johnson would have agreed. But if Johnson—acknowledged already as one of the game's greatest pitchers—was going to get results from his pitchers, he would be inclined to do it with gentle nudging and calm encouragement. If Johnson had a shortcoming as a manager, it was that he was too easygoing, never swearing, seldom raising his voice to criticize a player.

Johnson thought he could rely on three starters; Alvin Crowder, Firpo Marberry, and Lloyd Brown were all experienced hurlers. Marberry and Brown had multiple seasons with double-digit wins. Crowder, acquired in the same June 1930 trade that brought Manush to the Nationals, was a proven winner; at this point in his career he had won more than 18 games in just one season, with the St. Louis Browns in 1928. Johnson expected Crowder to be the ace of his staff, but he needed one more reliable hurler.

Johnson pinned his hopes on a rookie right-hander named Monte Weaver. Shirley Povich commented on Johnson's opinion of Weaver in the preseason, noting that "Johnson pronounces [Weaver] the most finished pitcher ever to make his debut in the major leagues."[4] In 1931 Weaver had a sensational year with the Baltimore Orioles in the International League, finishing with a record of 21-11. Washington owner Clark Griffith had watched him pitch and came away so impressed, he purchased Weaver's contract for $25,000. In March 1932 he was just as confident, boldly predicting, "He will win 20 games."[5]

Like his manager, Weaver was a quiet country boy who never raised his voice or cursed. He had grown up in the mountains of western North Carolina, in a small town called Lansing. Then he enrolled at Emory and Henry College, just across the border in Virginia, where he had excelled at sports and mathematics. He competed in baseball, basketball, and track, and nearly won a Rhodes scholarship.[6]

To earn money for college, Weaver pitched in the summers for a coal company team in Kentucky. When he graduated, he continued his education at the University of Virginia and pursued his pitching career during the summers with the Class C League Durham Bulls in the Piedmont League. In 1929 Weaver earned his master's degree from the University of Virginia. His thesis was a study of the geometric configuration of railroad tracks, titled "The Companion to the Litmus: The Curve Whose Vectorial Angle is Proportional to the Square of the Arc in Length."[7]

So Weaver was faced with a career choice. He could teach mathematics at the University of Virginia or follow a career in professional baseball. He was well suited for the classroom—writing formulae on a chalkboard and explaining geometry to undergraduates–so if baseball didn't work out, he would have been quite content to be a Mathematics professor. In the end, baseball offered more money, so he initially chose the mound over the classroom, but by the spring of 1932, after three years of toiling in the Minors, Weaver had decided that if he couldn't make it in the Majors, he would go back to academia.

Weaver was not particularly sociable as a teammate. He was a loner and a hypochondriac. He liked to take walks by himself and read his Bible. He was often worried about his health and picky about what he ate; in 1934 he would become a vegetarian and go on a strict diet, losing twenty-five pounds, with his weight dropping to 145 pounds.[8]

Johnson didn't care if Weaver had a few quirks. If the manager could abide Moe Berg, he would tolerate Weaver's oddities. The question was whether Weaver could pitch and win games in the big leagues. Johnson believed he could, and Johnson had the temperament to mentor Weaver and help him realize his potential. Weaver would get his first start of the 1932 season in the second game of the Boston series.

The game with Boston on April 12 was rained out, giving both teams a chance to recuperate after the overnight train ride from Washington. The home opener for the Red Sox took place the next day, on Wednesday, a mid-week game. Once again, Al Schacht and Nick Altrock were on hand to perform their comedy act before the game commenced. Fewer than five thousand paying customers turned out on that cold and gloomy afternoon, but they cheered hopefully as Boston clung to a 6–4 lead heading into the ninth inning. Then with 2 out, 2 on base, and a 2–2 count, Heinie Manush smashed a 3-run homer, his second consecutive game-winning hit. The Boston fans went home depleted, and the Nationals celebrated the come-from-behind victory.

After another rainout, Monte Weaver got his first start of the season, with Roy Spencer behind the plate. The Senators scored the only 2 runs they needed in the second inning, on a double by Ozzie Bluege and a single by Spencer. Weaver was superb, pitching like a veteran.

He hurled a complete game 4-hit shutout, walking five batters and striking out four.

It was an auspicious beginning. Walter Johnson would give Weaver 3 more starts in the next 14 days, all against the Philadelphia Athletics. On April 19—again with Spencer as his batterymate—Weaver struggled but was the winning pitcher in a 7–4 win over the A's. Five days later, Johnson started Weaver and paired him with Moe Berg, perhaps the most intellectually imposing pitcher/catcher combination in the history of baseball. Whether Weaver and Berg outsmarted the A's, or just overpowered them, the result was an 8–2 win for the Senators. In his third April start in eleven days against the World Champions, Weaver was again the winner, pitching a complete game 2–1 victory, and once again Moe Berg was behind the plate.

When the month of April ended, the Senators were tied for first place with an 11-4 record. They had won 6 of 8 games against the A's, and Crowder and Weaver owned 7 of the team's 11 wins.

For Johnson, it was an excellent start to the season and gave him some confidence that the pitching staff was adequate. Now he had to see what his club could do when they went head-to-head with the New York Yankees.

6

The Rivals

While the Washington Senators had been a perennial contender—winning the American League pennant in 1924 and 1925, and finishing second in 1930—the two best teams in the league beginning with the 1926 season had been the New York Yankees and the Philadelphia Athletics. Over the six-year span from 1926 through 1931, the Yankees compiled a record of 570-352, with a winning percentage of .618. The A's were even better with a 585-328 record and a .641 winning percentage.

The Yankees had won the pennant in 1926, 1927, and 1928; the A's had finished second in both 1927 and 1928. Then the A's won consecutive pennants in 1929, 1930, and 1931, with the Yankees finishing second in 1929 and 1931. In 1932 the A's would try to become the first team in Major League history to win 4 straight pennants.

Connie Mack, now sixty-nine years old, was starting his thirty-second year as the team's manager. No one other than John McGraw could claim such an extended tenure. Mack had experienced both highs and lows. Over that span of years, he had won more pennants—nine—than any other manager in history, and he could also claim the dubious distinction of having finished dead last in seven straight seasons, from 1915 through 1921.

In 1932 Mack would field a veteran team with holdovers from his championship years at every position except for one. The shortstop in 1932 was a rookie named Eric McNair, who replaced Joe Boley. Only five foot eight and 160 pounds, McNair would add punch to the lineup, contributing 18 home runs and 95 runs batted in during the season; in addition, McNair would lead the league in doubles, with 47.

Mack's outfield was solid. Bing Miller and Doc Cramer divided time in right field, and though neither supplied much power, together they consistently hit around .300. The center fielder was Mule Haas. Haas was not a home run hitter either, but at age twenty-eight, and in his fifth season with the A's, he was a steady performer at bat and in the field. Aloysius Harry Simmons—more commonly known as Al, or Bucketfoot Al, for his distinctive batting stance—was the A's twenty-nine-year-old left fielder. After eight seasons in the Majors, Simmons had attained a career batting average of .363. Four times he had batted .380 or higher, and he had driven in more than 100 runs in each of his Major League seasons.

Joining McNair in the infield at second base was Max "Camera Eye" Bishop, a thirty-two-year-old veteran who was entering his ninth season with the A's. Bishop's nickname reflected his ability to get on base via bases on balls. Over the six previous seasons, he had averaged 114 walks per year—against 121 hits per year. He would hit over .300 just once in a twelve-year Major League career, but in four years, from 1928 through 1931, he would never score fewer than 104 runs in a season. Jimmy Dykes, the third baseman, was coming into his fourteenth Major League season, all of them with the A's. As a player, Dykes's productive years were coming to an end—his average would drop from .273 in 1931 to .265 in 1932—but he was a reliable and shrewd veteran. He would later spend eighteen years as a big league manager. The first baseman was also the youngest of the regulars, a twenty-four-year-old power hitter named Jimmie Foxx. Over the past three seasons, Foxx had hammered exactly 100 home runs and driven in nearly 400 runs. In 1932 Foxx was destined to have the best season of his Hall of Fame career.

Connie Mack had, arguably, the best catcher in baseball behind the plate. Mickey Cochrane was a seven-year veteran and a career .326 hitter. He was the adept handler of a pitching staff that included reliable veterans George Earnshaw and Rube Walberg, as well as the undisputed ace of the staff, thirty-one-year-old Lefty Grove, a pitcher who had already claimed 156 Major League victories. Four times— including the past three seasons—Grove had led the American League in earned run average. In the pennant-winning years of 1930 and 1931 he had posted win-loss records of 28-5 and 31-4, respectively. Grove was, without much argument, the best pitcher in baseball.

The Yankees were led by Joseph McCarthy, in his second season at the helm of the Yankees. McCarthy's resume and history were considerably different from Mack's. When McCarthy was named manager of the Chicago Cubs in 1926, he was the only manager in the Majors without a history of playing in the big leagues. But he was a keen student of the game, and at Louisville and then with the Cubs in Chicago, he was noted for his eye for talent.

So McCarthy and Mack were men of different generations, different styles, different backgrounds, and contemporaries only in the sense that they both happened to be managers in the Major Leagues at the same time. In almost every other conceivable way of comparing the two men, they were dissimilar.

But their teams were comparable. McCarthy had an equally powerful cast of regulars. Babe Ruth had reached the ripe age of thirty-seven, but was not yet in decline as a hitter. Over the previous six seasons, as the Yankees and Athletics battled annually for first place in the league, Ruth had averaged 50 home runs and 154 runs batted in per year. Alongside Ruth in the outfield, McCarthy started Ben Chapman and Earle Combs. At twenty-three, Chapman was at the beginning of a solid Major League career, during which he would bat .302. He added speed to a team that was built on power. Chapman would lead the league in stolen bases four times; in 1931 he swiped a career high, 61 bases. Combs was a proven veteran, a fixture in the outfield alongside Ruth for the past seven seasons. In 1931 Combs had hit safely in 29 straight games, tying the Yankees team record set in 1919 by Roger Peckinpaugh. The record would stand for ten more years, until a youngster named Joe DiMaggio would establish the Major League record by hitting in 56 straight games.

Lou Gehrig, in the prime of his career, at age twenty-eight, anchored the infield. Gehrig had averaged 35 home runs and 151 RBIS per year over the previous six seasons, nearly matching Ruth's accomplishments. Three times he had driven in more than 170 runs, a feat still unmatched in Major League history. The second baseman was Tony Lazzeri, also a future Hall of Famer. Like the A's, the Yankees in 1932 would start a rookie at shortstop: Frankie Crosetti. The third baseman was another veteran, Joe Sewell, the hardest man in Major League history to strike out. In 1932, in nearly 650 plate appearances, Sewell would strike out just three times.

The Yankees catcher was twenty-four-year-old Bill Dickey, entering his fourth year in the big leagues. Although he was not a slugger in the mold of a Ruth or Foxx, Dickey was a steady and efficient run producer, averaging .327 at the plate and driving in close to 80 runs a year.

Another Lefty—this one named Gomez, and aptly nicknamed Goofy—had become the most reliable Yankees starter during the 1931 season. Younger than the rest of the pitchers in the Yankees' starting rotation—Red Ruffing, George Pipgras, Johnny Allen, Herb Pennock—Gomez was on the front end of a Hall of Fame career. In his first full season in 1931, he had gone 21–9 with 17 complete games and an earned run average of 2.63.

The Yankees and Athletics opened the season on April 12 with a 2-game series in Philadelphia. Joe McCarthy picked Lefty Gomez as his opening day pitcher, and Connie Mack countered with George Earnshaw, the thirty-two-year-old right-hander.

In the top of the first, the Yankees scored 4 runs to take a quick lead. The Athletics came back with 2 runs in the bottom of the inning. Earnshaw lasted until the fifth inning when the Yankees scored 5 more runs. For the day, Earnshaw had given up 10 earned runs and gotten only 12 outs. Gomez was not particularly effective either, giving up 6 runs in 8⅔ innings, but he made it to the ninth inning; and then Red Ruffing came in to get the final out. The Yankees pounded out 12 hits, including 5 home runs, 2 each by Ruth and Sammy Byrd, and 1 by Gehrig. Ruth and Gehrig combined for 6 hits and 6 RBIS. Both Al Simmons and Jimmie Foxx homered for the Athletics, but the game was essentially over after the Yankees took a 10–3 lead in the fifth.

The teams played again on Friday. Again, it was a battle of two offenses. The game see-sawed back and forth, with the Athletics scoring in the first, the Yankees tying it in the fourth, then the Athletics taking the lead again with single runs in the fourth and fifth. The Yankees came back to score 5 in the seventh, but the Yankees starter—Red Ruffing—couldn't hold the lead, and George Pipgras, in relief, gave up the tying runs in the eighth and the winning run in the bottom of the ninth. Gehrig homered for the second day in a row, as did Jimmie Foxx. For Foxx, it was an indication of things to come.

Less than a week later—after the Yankees had taken 2 out of 3 from the Red Sox, and the Athletics had split 4 games with the Senators— Connie Mack brought his team for 3 games in Yankee Stadium.

The first game of the series presented a matchup between the two best left-handers in the American League. The Wednesday afternoon game attracted a crowd of 63,000. The Yankees won 8–3 behind Lefty Gomez; Lefty Grove took the loss, removed after the sixth inning with his team trailing 4–1. Ruth homered and drove in 3 runs. The second game was also an offensive battle, but this time the A's squared the series, winning 8–6, thanks to a 5-run ninth inning rally against Red Ruffing. The A's attack featured home runs by Al Simmons and Mickey Cochrane. The rubber match of the 3-game series resulted in a one-sided 16–5 win for the Yankees. After the A's scored 5 runs on 5 singles and 2 walks in the top of the first, knocking out Yankees starter Gordon Rhodes, the Yankees came back with 6 runs in the bottom of the first. In relief for the Yankees, "Poison" Ivy Andrews pitched 8⅔ innings of 6-hit no-run baseball, in what would be the single best outing of his short career. Ruth homered—his fifth of the season in 8 games—and also tripled in the lambasting of the defending champs.

Eight games into the 1932 season, the teams seemed evenly matched and up to the challenge of a spirited fight for the pennant. They would not play head-to-head again for a month, and when they did, the Yankees would be 22-8 and in first place, leading the second place Senators by 2½ games. The A's would be in fifth with a record of 17-14.

Connie Mack understood that his team had a lot of ground to make up in their quest for a fourth straight pennant.

7

Rookie Pitchers

In the National League, the St. Louis Cardinals were odds-on favorites to win their third straight National League championship. Starting in 1926, when St. Louis had claimed the world championship under their thirty-year-old manager, Rogers Hornsby, the Cardinals had captured 4 league championships and never finished out of the first division. The powerhouse 1931 team had won 101 games, and the core of that team returned: regulars Pepper Martin, Jim Bottomley, Rip Collins, Sparky Adams, and Frankie Frisch; and pitchers Wild Bill Hallahan, Tex Carleton, Flint Rhem, and Paul Derringer.

There were three notable roster changes. Burleigh Grimes was gone, in the Hack Wilson exchange, and Chick Hafey, the league's leading hitter in 1931, had also been traded. Hafey had a history of injury problems and rankled management with annual salary demands, so Branch Rickey sent Hafey to last-place Cincinnati. Rickey got little value in return for either Grimes or Hafey, but Grimes was thirty-eight, near at the end of his big league career, and Rickey had little patience for Hafey's complaints about his salary, especially given the economic realities of the era. The third roster change was the addition of a brash and swaggering Minor League pitcher named Dizzy Dean. Rickey believed that Dean could replace Grimes in the starting rotation.

Dean was twenty-two, a garrulous rookie who said whatever came into his head and possessed a sometimes disturbing but largely entertaining degree of self-confidence. He had been born in Lucas, Arkansas, and his father named him Jay Hanna Dean, after the industrialist Jay Gould and the Republican politician Mark Hanna. Dean and his two brothers were raised on a series of small farms, where their father, a sharecropper and a skilled semi-pro player, taught them the finer points of the game of baseball.[1]

When Dean was eight, his mother died, and that's when his formal schooling ended as well. During his youth, he picked cotton with his father and older brother, and then at age sixteen, he joined the army, where he acquired his nickname and earned recognition for his pitching ability. He was signed by a scout for the St. Louis Cardinals in the fall of 1929.

He stood six feet two inches tall and weighed a solid two hundred pounds. He threw hard and worked fast, sometimes pitching complete games in less than two hours. Branch Rickey saw him pitch and followed his career with interest. For Rickey, a teetotaler and conservative businessman, it was Dean's on-field performance that showed promise. Off the field, Dean drank and partied and carried on with women. He ignored curfews and missed trains and mishandled money. On the mound, though, he was an intimidating presence with a sharp curve, a lively fastball, and excellent control for a young pitcher. Many years later, Rickey would say that the two best pitchers he'd ever seen were Christy Mathewson and Dizzy Dean.[2]

Dean spent a little over two years in the Minors, pitching for the St. Joseph Saints and the Houston Buffaloes. He was a dominating presence, often recording double-digit strikeout totals, and without regard to modesty or his opponents, he would boast about his performance after every success. As he supposedly said, "It ain't bragging, if you can back it up." Some players didn't like his attitude; others enjoyed the enthusiasm and energy that he brought to each appearance on the mound. One thing was certain: baseball fans liked to see him in action. On the days he pitched, attendance soared. Crowds—including many female admirers—flocked to the ballpark to see the show.

One of Dean's female fans was a twice-married twenty-four year old named Patricia Nash. She was a young woman with a reputation. Nash liked baseball and was a frequent spectator at the Buffaloes' games. In particular, she liked the parties after the games, especially if alcohol was available; in the idiom of the times, she was a party girl. Like the character Annie Savoy—the "Baseball Annie" of the movie *Bull Durham*—Patricia Nash dated the ballplayers who played for the Buffaloes. When Dean was going out with her, his teammates warned him that she had "screwed half the men in town."[3] Dean's response, years later—in an interview with Chicago writer Irv Kupcinet—was, typical of Dean, honest and direct: "Sure," Dean said, "I heard it. I'm one of them. That's why I want to marry her."[4]

Dean wanted the ceremony to take place at home plate during the 1931 season, but since management objected, the wedding was moved to the First Christian Church. The marriage worked, lasting forty-three years. Patricia managed the finances, improved Dizzy's social skills, and, to the extent possible, tamed the man she called "just a great big boy."[5] A year after the wedding, the partially reformed and happily married Dizzy Dean was promoted to the Major Leagues.

In spring training games Dean was hit hard, but he wasn't fazed by his inability to retire Major League batters. Although he had pledged to curb his tendency to boast, he casually told one reporter that he thought he might win 30 games in his rookie season.[6] Manager Gabby Street, though, intended to give Dean some time to adjust to big league hitters.

Street picked Flint Rhem as his opening day pitcher. Rhem was thirty-one, a right-hander who had won 10 or more games in each of the previous six seasons. A native of South Carolina, Rhem had attended Clemson University, with thoughts of earning an engineering degree when he graduated. Pitching for the Clemson Tigers, he averaged 15 strikeouts per game and earned the nickname "Big Smokey." Before he finished his degree, he signed with the Cardinals.[7]

In addition to a fine fastball, Rhem had a good curve and a knuckleball that he used on occasion. No one questioned his talent or abilities when he was on the mound. But away from the baseball field, it was a different story. Off the field, Rhem was an even more difficult and eccentric individual than the young Dizzy Dean. Also, Rhem had a serious drinking problem. It was hardly a secret that many ballplayers of the era had issues with alcohol, or that drinking negatively impacted their careers, but Rhem's drinking led to one of the more memorable and colorful stories.

During the 1930 season Rhem mysteriously vanished. Several days later, he reappeared and told Street and the media that he'd been kidnapped at gunpoint and held hostage. Rhem admitted that alcohol was involved, but in the pitcher's story, he had been forced to drink large quantities of liquor while being kept captive in a remote roadhouse. The motive for the kidnapping was never clear or articulated by Rhem.[8]

As strange and preposterous as the story was, the Cardinals welcomed Rhem back, and when he sobered up, Street put him on the mound. For the 1930 season Rhem had a respectable record of 12-8; a year later, he was 11-10 in 26 starts for the pennant-winning Cardinals. In 1932 Street had expectations that Rhem would be a key member of his pitching staff.

The Cardinals faced the Pittsburgh Pirates in the opening day game at Sportsman Park. Rhem was solid, hurling a 7-hit complete game victory. The Cardinals won easily, 10–2, banging out 13 hits. The next day, in front of a paltry crowd of just 1,500 fans, the Cardinals won again, a slugfest that ended with the Cardinals on top, 9–8. Frankie Frisch and shortstop Charley Gelbert each had 3 runs batted in.

After the first two days of the season the Cardinals were in a familiar position: first place. Then they lost 6 games in a row, 2 to the Pirates, 2 to the Cubs, then 2 more to the Pirates. By the end of April, their record was a dismal 5-10. Suddenly, they were in seventh place, 6½ games out of first.

Something was wrong. For one thing, the Cardinals lacked clutch hitting. They missed the bat of Chick Hafey, who had reported late to the Cincinnati Reds but was hitting .444 by the end of the month. More importantly, Cardinal pitchers were allowing almost 6 runs a game.

Street used Dean five times in short relief stints in April. In the first four outings Dean pitched competently, allowing just 2 hits over a combined five innings. On April 23 he relieved in the eighth inning of a 9–9 game in Pittsburg and struck out the side; in the bottom of the ninth, however, he gave up the winning run and suffered his first loss of the season. Five days later, Dean started a game against the Cubs at Wrigley Field and was knocked around for 7 hits and 6 runs in just five innings of work, though Dean didn't take the loss because the Cardinals came back to tie the score against Bob Smith. Eventually the Cubs won the game, 12–7. Charlie Root, in relief, got the win; Bennie Frey was the loser.

Street still had confidence in Dean's potential, and given the Cardinals dismal pitching during April, Dean was offered another start, on May 3, at home against the Cincinnati Reds. This time Dean lived up to his own expectations, hurling his first Major League shutout. He pitched a complete game, scattering 8 hits, walking six, and pitching out of several jams; the Reds left 11 runners stranded. In particular, Dean was pleased to hold Chick Hafey hitless in 4 at-bats.

For better or worse, Dean had earned his spot in the starting rotation. The rest of the league began to take notice of the rookie. Dizzy Dean was not about to let anyone ignore him.

Dean's success also made Flint Rhem expendable. In May, Rhem and Eddie Delker, a reserve infielder with fewer than 100 Major League at-bats, were sold to the Philadelphia Phillies.

In Chicago, Rogers Hornsby had a different combination of worries. While his personality rubbed many people the wrong way, no one questioned his desire to win or his past accomplishments as a player. Inside a Major League ballpark, Hornsby was respected as a highly focused competitor, both as a player and as a manager. Unfortunately, the death of owner William Wrigley, in January, meant that Hornsby was, once again in his career, soon to be estranged from management. Wrigley's son, Philip, had little interest in baseball matters, so decision making was now squarely in the hands of William Veeck, the general manager. Veeck, while recognizing Hornsby's reputation and accomplishments as a player, was not convinced that Hornsby was the right man to manage the Cubs.

Off the field, Hornsby continued to have an array of distracting financial problems, some of which would become more evident and troublesome as the 1932 season progressed. Despite having one of the highest salaries in baseball, he had personal solvency problems. Although he had won his court battle with Frank Moore over gambling debts, Hornsby was still betting money on horse races and losing more often than he won. In addition, his farm was going bankrupt, and he owed money to the IRS.

It was likely a relief to Hornsby to come to the ballpark and worry about nothing other than baseball. In sizing up the competition in the National League, Hornsby certainly figured he didn't have to worry about Philadelphia, Boston, or Cincinnati being contenders. The Phillies and Braves had been second division teams for more than a decade, and Cincinnati had averaged only 61 wins a year over the past three seasons. In addition to the defending champions, the Cardinals, Hornsby knew that New York and Pittsburgh had solid teams. Brooklyn was improving as well and might find a way to be in contention.

Hornsby had a veteran roster—Hartnett, Grimm, English, Cuyler, Root, Bush, Malone—and he believed that he could count on Hack and Herman to be contributors. Hornsby had approved the trade for Burleigh Grimes, though Grimes was clearly past his prime. Hornsby respected Grimes's competitive spirit and hoped he could get another good season out of the pitcher known as "old greybeard." If not Grimes, perhaps the rookie Bud Tinning could become the fifth starter.

Going into spring training, Hornsby had known the outfield was a question mark. Replacing Hack Wilson—even a subpar Hack Wilson—was harder than Hornsby anticipated. Stevenson wasn't yet back to full health, and he wasn't the only player with injury issues. Woody English broke a finger at the end of March and missed the first 18 games of the season. On April 24, Kiki Cuyler fractured his foot, just 11 games into the season, and would be lost for over six weeks.

Stan Hack had replaced English, but he hit only .205, with just 1 homer and 4 RBIs, in the weeks that English was sidelined. Billy Jurges had taken over at shortstop, and while he was excellent as a fielder, he wasn't hitting any better than Hack. With Cuyler's recent injury, the situation in the outfield had worsened. Hornsby faced a common problem for a manager over the course of a long season: the need to shuffle his lineup to adjust to player injuries and slumps and to take advantage of players who were versatile and could play multiple positions. Hornsby would be forced to rotate his outfield options—Marv Gudat, Johnnie Moore, Lance Richbourg—until Cuyler was able to play.

The one bright spot for Hornsby was the pitching staff. As it turned out, the development of Lon Warneke, not Bud Tinning, was the main reason that Hornsby had reason to feel confident about the season. Hornsby had a young pitcher who could match Dizzy Dean of the Cardinals. Like Dean, Warneke was young and raw with an exceptional arm. Unlike Dean, Warneke had a quiet demeanor and was an easier player to manage.

Though not as colorful as Dean—who was already known around the league by his appropriate nickname, Dizzy—Warneke and Dean shared similar backgrounds. The two players had been born less than a hundred miles apart in rural Arkansas, though Warneke was older by nearly two years.

Warneke's father, Luke, was a lanky six foot six farmer, and Lon spent his youth tending to the cattle and hogs on the Warneke family farm. In the summers Lon worked in the wheat fields of Oklahoma and North Dakota. His baseball career started in Mount Ida, where he played first base for the high school team. It wasn't until the summer of 1927, while playing for the Mount Ida town team, that he tried his hand at pitching. A year later, living with his sister in Houston and working as a bicycle messenger for Western Union, Warneke got a tryout with the Houston Buffaloes of the Texas League, a farm team of the St. Louis Cardinals. Warneke's audition for the Buffaloes came just two years before Dizzy Dean would begin his professional career with the same Minor League club.

It took Warneke two years to make it to the Major Leagues. Pancho Snyder, the manager of the Buffaloes, took a long look at the rail-thin, six-foot-two young man and wondered if he had the strength and stamina to be a professional athlete. Snyder thought Warneke might have the talent to eventually succeed as a ballplayer, but as a pitcher, not a first baseman. Snyder offered Warneke a contract and assigned him to a team in Laurel, Mississippi, in the Cotton States League. Snyder's hope was that Warneke would learn to control his pitches and gain some weight. Warneke lasted half a season. Though he pitched adequately, he was incapacitated midway through the season with a bout of the flu, which caused him to lose thirty pounds. Laurel released him.[9]

It is worth noting that Warneke's career had begun in the vaunted St. Louis Cardinals farm system—invented, designed, and managed by Branch Rickey. Years later, it was evident to Rickey that Warneke was one of the few future Major League stars to slip from the grasp of the Cardinal organization.[10]

Whatever disappointment Warneke suffered from being cut by Laurel didn't last long. After recovering from his illness, Warneke signed with Alexandria, also in the Cotton States League, and pitched well enough to interest the Shreveport team of the Texas League, which purchased his contract at the end of the season.[11]

Warneke went back to Mount Ida for the winter. He knew he had to get bigger and stronger, so his off-season training regimen consisted primarily of hard work on the farm and the consumption of enormous quantities of fresh milk and eggs. In March he turned twenty years old, and when he reported to spring training, he was a considerably larger and more physically mature version of the pitcher Shreveport had signed just six months earlier.

In 1929 Warneke stayed healthy, won 16 games for Shreveport, and impressed a scout for the Chicago Cubs who convinced the Cubs to buy the rights to Warneke. After spending a year with the Cubs' farm team in Reading, Pennsylvania, Warneke was ready for a promotion to the Majors. He pitched just 64 innings with the Cubs in 1931, but by the end of spring training the following year, Rogers Hornsby was ready to put him in the starting rotation.

Warneke was quiet with a good sense of humor. He didn't like his manager very much, but he got along well with teammates.[12] He had a lot in common with first baseman and captain, Charlie Grimm. Both liked music—Grimm played the banjo; Warneke kept a ukulele in his locker—and both liked to play practical jokes.[13]

Despite four well-tested veteran starters, it would be Warneke in 1932 who would emerge as the ace of the Cubs' pitching staff. In his first five starts he gave up just 9 runs. For the season, he would start 32 games, pitch four shutouts, and the Cubs would win 26 of the games he started.

Hornsby had plenty on his mind during the early weeks of the 1932 season, and he had some legitimate worries about the health and durability of his team, but he didn't have to think too hard about his starting pitchers. He thought he had the pitching to make a run for the National League pennant.

8

Brawls

For America, 1932 was a year of tragedy and conflict. The front pages of daily newspapers carried stories of social disruption and the failures of government to resolve the nation's problems. Inevitably the tensions of the era spilled over to baseball diamonds, resulting in several dramatic on-field brawls—and one notable off-field clash involving an umpire who challenged an entire team to a fight.

On May 12 the body of the Lindbergh baby was discovered in a wooded area not far from the Lindbergh home. The search for the missing boy had gone on for seventy-two days. An autopsy revealed that the child's skull had been smashed. More than two years would pass before a suspect was arrested, and during those years, the Lindbergh family was constantly in the news; in 1935 Colonel Lindbergh would move his family to Europe, seeking solace and some degree of privacy.

The experiment of Prohibition had failed, a fact that was evident just about everywhere in America during the 1920s; now it was simply a question of time, and how the nation's politicians were going to reverse course and legalize the sale of alcoholic beverages again. Both political parties would struggle to formulate and explain their positions on the issue to voters.

But the most pervasive and disturbing news concerned the state of the deteriorating economy. The calamity of the Great Depression had deepened and intensified. The economic decline rippled through cities and towns, reaching from Maine to California, from Oregon to Florida. No region of the country was spared. Only the very rich or those securely employed were not directly impacted. The decade of speculation, false hopes, and easy money had passed. For many Americans, the situation had become unfathomable, and their futures seemed bleak, at best.

As farms failed and banks closed, families lost their homes and broke apart. Shelters and soup kitchens took in and fed some of the most desperate and out of luck, but government resources were unavailable to millions of other citizens. Enclaves of plywood shacks—called Hoovervilles—appeared in major cities. The homeless lived under highway overpasses and in caves or vacant factories.[1] Many roamed the country seeking work and food, riding trains from place to place in crowded boxcars. Young boys and girls, also homeless, traveled together for safety.

The plight of the nation's downtrodden and displaced persons would be captured by a rising generation of socially conscious artists and journalists, photographers and writers.[2] In Harlan County, Kentucky, miners went on strike. The conflict arose when miners attempted to unionize and were opposed by mine owners and law enforcement. Violent clashes between miners and coal company officials resulted in the Kentucky National Guard being called out. The journalist Mary Heaton Vorse traveled to Kentucky to investigate and was threatened with physical harm or death when she tried to deliver food and supplies to the striking miners and their families.[3]

The most visible and lengthy standoff between protesting citizens and the government occurred in Washington DC, in sight of the Capitol and the White House. The demonstrations lasted nearly three months. They were widely reported and became an issue in the 1932 presidential campaign.

Veterans of World War I had been promised a bonus for their service, but the Certificates of Service they'd been issued were not redeemable by law until 1945. Because many of these former soldiers were unemployed and impoverished, they demanded an immediate payment of their bonuses. In the spring of 1932 the veterans marched on Washington, led by Walter Waters, who brought a contingent of fellow ex-soldiers across the country from Oregon to DC, sometimes on foot, sometimes on railroad cars. They called themselves the Bonus Expeditionary Force, or BEF.[4]

Waters and his men arrived in DC on May 29, joining marchers who had arrived from throughout the country. Waters immediately went to visit Wright Patman, a second-term U.S. congressman from Texas, who had introduced a bill for the release of funds to pay these bonuses.[5] Patman's bill had been defeated in late April, but President Hoover had promised to veto the bill if it had passed.

The BEF, however, was determined to stay in DC and make itself heard. Pelham Glassford, the Superintendent of the District of Columbia Police Department, helped Waters arrange accommodations in vacant government buildings and in campsites on Anacostia Flats, a park area that included a baseball field. By early June, the number of BEF vets had reached eight thousand, not counting family members and others who came to DC to join the protest.[6] The vets organized marches around the Capitol to publicize their cause, but Congress showed no inclination to change its mind on Patman's legislation. Tensions increased as the government wanted the growing BEF presence to disperse and the protesters became more determined to stay. Issues of food and sanitation worsened. Glassford and Waters tried to work together to raise funds for food and to ensure that the demonstrations remain peaceful. But no clear solution presented itself. The situation would get worse before it got better.

These multiple societal pressures spilled over onto the nation's playing fields. With rosters cut back to twenty three players, skilled former Major Leaguers toiled in the Minors, hoping for the opportunity to get back to the big leagues. Marginal players—rookies, utility infielders, aging veterans—realized they were literally playing for their jobs. And the job of a Major League baseball player, while never secure, was usually far better than the alternative for players skilled enough to have reached the Major Leagues.

While there had always been skirmishes and fights between players on the field, 1932 featured several particularly memorable battles. Small provocations would get things started: pitchers throwing at batters; words exchanged about one's competence or heritage or manhood. Often the precipitating event would be a close play at second base or home plate, a runner sliding into a base aggressively and a fielder responding.

Not all of these brawls occurred out in the open on the ball fields. Some took place under the stands—or in a few cases, in the stands. Over the years, players had physically clashed with other players, as well as sportswriters, umpires, and fans. Hecklers had been chased, and in some instances, pummeled by the players who caught up with them.[7]

Most of the umpires of the era had played the game and were as tough and combative as the players on the field. Physical confrontations between players and umpires—unthinkable today—were not uncommon. Umpires were just as ready to be combatants as they were to be peacemakers.

George Hildebrand, a relatively mild-mannered umpire, confronted George Sisler in July 1921. Sisler complained about being out in a close play at first base then shouted profanities at Hildebrand and took a swing at him. Hildebrand dodged the punch and ejected Sisler for his abusive language. A year earlier in a game at Fenway Park between the Red Sox and the Yankees, pitcher Bob Shawkey blew up at Hildebrand on a ball 4 call that walked in a run with the bases loaded. Shawkey threw a punch; Hildebrand retaliated by smacking Shawkey in the face with his mask. In a more serious escalation between a player and an arbitrator involving a disputed call, Ty Cobb challenged umpire Billy Evans to a fight, and the two men met under the stands after the game, stripped off their shirts, and battled for forty-five minutes, punching and kicking each other. Players from both teams watched the altercation and eventually broke it up. Evans went to the hospital with a broken nose and other injuries. Cobb came away less bloodied and claimed victory.[8]

It is fair to say that Cobb hated and clashed with a lot of people. But maybe he hated Babe Ruth the most—for the way he spoke, the way he played, the way he looked, for what he represented, and most importantly, how he had challenged Cobb's legacy as the game's greatest player. In 1921 Ruth had stormed into the Tigers' clubhouse after a game and challenged Cobb to a fight, but players pulled them apart.[9] A few years later in a game in Detroit, Ruth was on the bench but angry because he believed Cobb, then the player/manager of the Tigers, had ordered his pitchers to throw at Ruth. When Yankees outfielder Bob Meusel was hit in the back—in the ninth inning of a 10–6 game, apparently on instructions from Cobb—both benches emptied. Cobb raced in from center field, Ruth ran toward him. They met and briefly thrashed about near home plate before the field was overrun with a thousand fans who wanted in on the action. As both teams retreated to their locker rooms, Cobb shouted racial insults at Ruth.[10] Police and security cleared the field. The Tigers forfeited the game 9–0.[11]

Another racially charged incident involving Ruth occurred after a game in the 1922 World Series when Ruth charged into the New York Giants' locker room, intent on fighting a reserve infielder named John-nie Rawlings, who had dared to use the racial term that most enraged Ruth. Several Giants players intervened and pushed Ruth out of the room.[12]

Ruth was not much of a fighter, but he got into his fair share of altercations with both teammates and umpires. Early in the 1922 season, Ruth exchanged blows in the dugout with Wally Pipp—the issue was Ruth's criticism of Pipp's fielding. Pipp was a big man who was not afraid of Ruth's stature or reputation.[13] Ruth also had—ironically, as it turned out—two flare-ups with Mark Koenig: one in 1926, when Ruth accused the shortstop of not hustling, and the two men wrestled briefly in the dugout; again in 1929, when Ruth thought Koenig said something insulting about his then-wife, Claire.[14]

More often, Ruth's ire was ignited by something said or done by an umpire. In 1922 Ruth became furious after being called out trying to stretch a single into a double. George Hildebrand was the umpire who made the call. Ruth threw dirt in Hildebrand's face. Hildebrand ejected Ruth. A fan jeered. Ruth jumped over the fence into the crowd and chased the fan. The fan retreated as other fans began to yell at Ruth, who jumped onto the dugout roof and challenged anyone who could hear him to come down and fight. Eventually he departed for the showers.[15] Another incident found Ruth at odds with Bill Dinneen, a big man and a former big league pitcher, who threw Ruth out of a game for arguing a call. Ruth was suspended for three days. Furious at the suspension, Ruth went after Dinneen the next day, challenging him to a fight under the stands. Dinneen was happy to oblige, but two players got between them and forced a truce. Ruth got two more days of suspension for the episode. The most memorable of Ruth's conflicts with umpires occurred when he was tossed from a game after pitching to just one batter—who walked—in the top of the first. Brick Owens was the umpire. Once ejected, Ruth landed one punch while being restrained by the Washington Senators' catcher. Ruth's replacement on the mound was Ernie Shore. The base runner that Ruth walked was thrown out stealing. Shore retired the next twenty six batters in order, arguably a perfect game.[16]

Early in the 1932 baseball season, the Reds hosted the Phillies, a game that would have no great bearing on the pennant race or either team's place in the final standings. Red Lucas started for Cincinnati, opposing Phil Collins for Philadelphia. The game featured opposing shortstops Dick Bartell and Leo Durocher, both noted for their competitiveness and take-no-prisoners attitude on the diamond. Bartell, nicknamed "Rowdy Richard" and known for his aggressive base running, was one of the best shortstops of his era, an excellent fielder and reliable hitter. As a player, he never shied away from a confrontation. Durocher was also a fine fielder, but he couldn't hit. He was acknowledged more for his personality: his excessive use of profanity, his flashy clothes, and his unquestioned reputation as a ladies' man. In his later years he would make his mark as a highly successful manager.[17]

The game sailed along without incident through seven innings. The Reds led by a score of 4–1. In the bottom of the eighth inning, Durocher—who came into the game hitting a puny .191 on the season—

managed to poke a single into the outfield, his second hit of the day. Perhaps emboldened by his multi-hit performance, Durocher tried to steal second base and crashed into Bartell, as the Phillies shortstop smacked a hard tag on the sliding baserunner. Durocher jumped to his feet and punched Bartell. A scuffle ensued. When it ended, Durocher was ejected from the game. A more dramatic encounter was just three weeks away.

On Memorial Day, the Indians hosted the White Sox for a double-header at League Park II, in Cleveland. The Indians were in fifth place but trailed the league-leading Yankees by only 6 games. The White Sox were next to last, 11 games under .500 with a record of 14-25.

The umpires assigned to the series were Bill Dinneen and George Moriarty, both former players and veteran umpires. Dinneen, a pitcher, won 3 games for the Boston Americans in the first modern World Series, in 1903. In Game Two of the series he pitched the first shut-out in series history.[18] He was known as a sturdy, though overused, right-hander, completing 306 of his 351 starts in the Majors. In 1904 he completed all 37 games he started. Not surprisingly, arm trouble eventually forced him to retire as an active player.

Moriarty had a colorful thirteen-year career as a player, mostly with the Detroit Tigers; he also served as manager of the Tigers for two seasons. A mediocre hitter with a lifetime batting average of .251, he was best known for his daring on the base paths, especially for his ability to steal home, a feat he accomplished more than a dozen times.[19]

Dinneen and Moriarty were big men, both over six feet tall and weighing more than two hundred pounds. They shared another trait: they had earned reputations as men who did not back down from a physical challenge, either as players or umpires. In June 1922 Dinneen had tossed Babe Ruth out of a game when Ruth charged from left field to join an argument about a call at second base and spewed vulgarities at the umpire. Dinneen reported the incident to the league office, and the next day, when Ruth was notified before that day's game that he'd been suspended, he again confronted the umpire, calling him

"Yellow," and challenging him to a fight under the stands. Dinneen stood his ground, ripped off his mask, and said he was ready to fight Ruth, but the umpire was held back by Tris Speaker and Steve O'Neill of the Indians.[20]

Moriarty had been involved in multiple altercations as a player, most famously when he and Ty Cobb almost tangled. Moriarty supposedly handed Cobb a bat, saying that it wouldn't be a fair fight unless Cobb had a weapon in his hands.[21] Cobb, for one of the few times in his life, decided to back down. Willie McGill, a late nineteenth century pitcher who had witnessed some of Moriarty's youthful scuffles, said that Moriarty was "the fightingest kid I ever saw."[22]

Off the field, Moriarty had another distinction. He was an accomplished poet and lyricist. He published his poems in a syndicated newspaper column, specializing in elegies of baseball luminaries. As a songwriter, he wrote tunes titled "Mississippi Moon" and "Bonehead Plays." He was quite proud of his literary achievements and suspicious that others might take credit for his work. He had a long-running quarrel with former teammate and White Sox manager Donnie Bush, claiming that Bush had stolen part of a song he had written. Moriarty also alleged that George Gershwin and Irving Berlin "were stealing their hits from him."[23]

Bush had been fired as manager of the White Sox at the end of the 1931 season, replaced by Lew Fonseca, but the grudge between the umpire and the team was not yet settled or forgotten. On Memorial Day 1932, the dispute would erupt into a legendary altercation.

In the first game of the doubleheader, with Moriarty behind the plate and Dinneen umpiring the bases, the Indians bashed the White Sox 12–6, as Cleveland's Ed Morgan and Earl Averill combined to drive in 8 runs. In the nightcap, Moriarty was again calling balls and strikes, with Dinneen on the base paths. The White Sox took a 9–5 lead in the fourth inning and appeared to be on their way to a doubleheader split. Neither of the starting pitchers—Paul Gregory of the White Sox, Oral Hildebrand of the Indians—lasted through the third inning of the slugfest. By the seventh inning, both teams were relying on relief pitchers. The White Sox added 2 runs in the top of the seventh; the Indians countered with 2 runs in the bottom of the inning and another in the eighth.

The score stood at 11–8 going to the bottom of the ninth. Tensions between the White Sox bench and home plate umpire Moriarty had been rising throughout the 2 games. Moriarty and White Sox manager Lew Fonseca exchanged verbal insults, Fonseca claiming that Moriarty was "sneering" at his players. In the second game Moriarty engaged in loud arguments with both the White Sox catcher, Charlie Berry, and third base coach Johnny Butler, eventually ejecting Butler for swearing at him. Berry complained all afternoon about Moriarty's ball and strike calls.

In the bottom of the ninth, the Indians staged a rally, scoring 4 runs to register a 12–11 come-from-behind win. As White Sox players and Moriarty exited the field through the same tunnel to the clubhouse, the argument about Moriarty's competence raged on.

In the tunnel beneath the stands, Moriarty stopped. He was surrounded by Fonseca, Berry, reserve catcher Frank Grube, and pitcher Milt Gaston. Indians owner Alva Bradley also happened to be in the tunnel and witnessed what happened next. Moriarty, who had taken his fair share of abuse during the afternoon, offered a challenge: if the White Sox didn't like his umpiring, he'd be happy to settle the matter with his fists. The umpire said he was willing to fight the whole team.

Gaston stepped forward and said, "You might as well start with me." Moriarty didn't hesitate. He threw the first two punches, breaking his hand but landing solid blows that knocked Gaston to the floor. The other White Sox quickly came to Gaston's defense, knocking Moriarty to the ground, punching and kicking him.

The fight was eventually broken up when Bill Dinneen and several Indians players appeared in the tunnel. At first Dinneen offered to join the fight in support of his fellow umpire; then he acted as peacemaker and helped to pull the combatants apart. Moriarty was taken to the Cleveland Clinic where he was treated for his broken hand, plus cuts, bruises, and spike wounds.

Fonseca spoke to the press shortly after the incident, blaming the entire episode on Moriarty. "Everyone in baseball knows many stories of Moriarty's brawling tendencies," Fonseca said, "and his eagerness to start a fight at the slightest provocation."[24]

Following protocol, Dinneen and Moriarty filed a report on the incident with the American League office in New York.

News of the Memorial Day brawl in Cleveland between the White Sox players and George Moriarty reached American League president William Harridge at his offices in New York City. He took an overnight train, arriving in Cleveland on Tuesday morning, and demanded that all of those involved meet with him at a hotel near Cleveland's Union Station. Moriarty claimed he couldn't attend the gathering because he was suffering from a headache. This was understandable, considering the beating he had received at the hands of the White Sox players. Harridge arranged to meet and interview Moriarty at League Park later that afternoon.[25]

The meeting commenced with White Sox players—Milt Gaston, Charley Berry, and Frank Grube—along with manager Lew Fonseca and coach Johnny Butler—presenting their case. Also in the room: Cleveland owner Alva Bradley; Cleveland's general manager, Billy Evans, the former umpire who had previously engaged Ty Cobb in a bloody fist fight; and Moriarty's fellow umpire, Bill Dinneen, who had offered to lend a hand to Moriarty in the scuffle.[26]

Prior to President Harridge's appearance, the White Sox players had discussed and agreed upon their version of the incident. They contended that it was Moriarty who had started the altercation, first by provoking the players verbally, and then by punching Gaston. Moriarty, they said, had wound up on the floor because he had slipped and fallen. They denied trying to harm the umpire, but claimed they were trying to help him to his feet.[27]

After listening to the stories told by the White Sox at the hotel, Harridge and a stenographer met with Moriarty at the ballpark. For seventy-five minutes, the umpire answered questions and provided his side of the story. A few hours later, Moriarty returned to the hospital to have the broken bones set in his injured right hand.[28]

At 10:00 p.m. Harridge issued a statement: "During my twenty-one years in baseball, I have no recollection of an incident such as occurred after the second game of the Memorial Day doubleheader between the Chicago White Sox and the Cleveland Indians in the city of Cleveland."[29] He then addressed the fines and suspensions for those involved.

Gaston was dealt with the most harshly: fined $500 and suspended for 10 games. Fonseca, Berry, and Grube were fined: $500, $250, and $100, respectively. White Sox coach Johnny Butler was also disciplined: suspended 5 games for his use of "profane language addressed to Moriarty."[30]

As for Moriarty: Harridge indicated that he had been given "a severe reprimand for his neglect of duty."[31] The matter was settled. Harridge returned to New York. He would not have to deal with another major altercation for five weeks.

The White Sox's chances for the American League pennant were not imperiled by the fines and suspensions. After the Memorial Day losses, the team had a record of 14-27. They were mired in seventh place, 15 games behind the league-leading New York Yankees. No one had expected them to be contenders before the season, and no one expected them to mount a challenge in the latter half of the season.

While Milt Gaston was one of the better pitchers on the White Sox in 1932—he was 2-3 with a 2.84 ERA on Memorial Day—after the brawl, he won just 5 more games, finishing the season with a record of 7-17 and an ERA of 4.00. For his career, Gaston would lose 67 more games than he won, posting a career record of 97-164. Based on these numbers, Gaston holds the record for the worst win-loss record in history.[32]

Despite Gaston's failures on the mound, he never lost his love for the game. On the occasion of his one hundredth birthday, friends and family threw a party for him on Cape Cod. During the celebration, he rose and sang his favorite song: "Take Me Out to the Ballgame." Three months later, Gaston died in a nursing home. Before his death, he was the second-oldest living former Major Leaguer.[33]

9

Hornsby and Cuyler

While it was apparent at the end of May that the White Sox were not going to be factors in the American League, their crosstown rivals were in first place in the National League.

The Cubs had a 2½ game lead over the second-place Boston Braves, but the eight teams in the league were tightly bunched. The last-place Phillies, 8½ games out of first, still had pennant hopes. Despite leading the league, Cubs manager Rogers Hornsby had plenty of things to worry about, in particular the injuries that had limited English, Stephenson, Grimes, and Cuyler. Hornsby hadn't been able to put his regular lineup on the field since spring training.

Hornsby's main concern continued to be his outfield. In a moment of unfiltered frustration, Hornsby complained to a New York reporter, "How the hell can I win a pennant with this lousy outfield?"[1]

The problems started in the off-season when Hornsby gave his okay to a trade that swapped Hack Wilson to the Cardinals for Burleigh Grimes. So far, Grimes had proven to be a good addition to the pitching staff; he had won 3 games in May. But in spring training, Hornsby had been unable to find a suitable replacement for Wilson in the outfield. Danny Taylor had been given a shot at winning a regular spot, but after playing in just 6 games for the Cubs and hitting a meager .227, he was sold to Brooklyn. As soon as Taylor got to the Dodgers, his bat came alive. In 1932 Taylor would hit .324 for Brooklyn, the only productive season he would produce in his Major League career.

There were three other contenders for a starting position in the outfield—all of them still on the roster: Lance Richbourg, Johnny

Moore, and Vince Barton. Richbourg, obtained on waivers from the Braves, was intended to be Wilson's replacement, but he had little power.[2] Moore was an untested thirty-year-old who had played fewer than 100 games in the Majors. Barton had power, and Hornsby had devoted a considerable amount of time on Catalina Island in trying to improve his swing so that he could hit more balls in play and strike out less. Barton would last another two months with the Cubs and then be released; that would be the end of his Major League career. Barton's totals as a Cub in 1932: 134 at bats, 22 strikeouts, 3 home runs, a batting average of .224.[3]

Hornsby needed a healthy Kiki Cuyler in the lineup. Cuyler had been sidelined since he broke his left foot on April 24, and it would be another two weeks before he could play. In eight full seasons in the Majors, first with the Pirates and then with the Cubs, Cuyler had hit .309 or better seven times. He was a complete player who could run, field, throw, hit, and hit with power.

Signed by the Pirates in 1921 at the age of twenty-three, Cuyler made the jump from the Minor Leagues to the Majors in three years. He was an outstanding defensive outfielder with a strong throwing arm. With the Pirates, he had led the league once in triples and two times in runs scored. Four times—twice with the Pirates, twice with the Cubs—he had led the league in stolen bases.

In 1925, Cuyler's best season with the Pirates, he batted .357, drove in 102 runs, scored 144 runs, and collected 86 extra base hits. In the 1925 World Series against the Washington Senators, Cuyler had the game-winning hit in both Game Two and Game Seven. As a hitter, Cuyler even drew comparisons to Hornsby.[4] Both were line drive hitters with level swings that drove the ball to all fields.

Off the field, Cuyler was a model citizen. He was good looking with an abundance of curly hair and dark eyes. He was an excellent dancer. He did not smoke or drink. He was soft-spoken, polite, and a mentor to younger players. His first manager with the Cubs, Joe McCarthy praised him: "There was never a more valuable team player."[5]

If Cuyler had a weakness, it was that he was prone to injury. With the Pirates in 1927, he tore ligaments in his ankle sliding into third base. A year later, he crashed into an outfield wall during an exhibition game and jammed his wrist. The wrist injury bothered him all season and affected him both at the plate and in the field. He was healthy for most of the Cubs' pennant-winning year of 1929, though he was restricted to pinch hitting duties for three weeks after suffering a leg injury. So the broken foot in the spring of 1932 was part of a pattern.

With Cuyler still hobbled, Hornsby had one other option to address the outfield situation: he could put himself in the lineup.

In late May, that's what Hornsby did. He started himself in right field. He knew that, at best, it was a short term solution. The bone spurs in his right heel severely limited his mobility. His feet swelled up after every game. He couldn't run like he used to, or field adequately, or even hit with much authority. At age thirty-six, after a decade as the most feared hitter in the National League, Hornsby's career as a player was about over.

It wasn't just baseball that was on Hornsby's mind. He was still embroiled in lawsuits and a tussle with the IRS about unreported income. Nothing had been settled. He owed back taxes on his farm. Away from the ballpark, he was dealing with lawyers and a nervous wife. Hornsby's one form of recreation and relaxation continued to be betting on horse races, but he was losing regularly, and in order to cover his tax payments and gambling debts, he had begun to borrow money from some of his players—Bush, Malone, and English—as well as from one of his coaches, Charley O'Leary.

In the tense and joyless locker room, Hornsby kept to himself. The players grumbled among themselves about Hornsby's rules: a strict curfew, and a ban on movies and reading, which he thought were bad for the eyes. He also discouraged drinking and card playing.

The longest road trip of the season was coming up in June—22 games played over 26 days—and Hornsby wanted his team healthy and focused.

On the first of June, the Cubs were scheduled to play a home game against the St. Louis Cardinals, the defending National League champions. The pitching match-up was a gem: the veteran Pat Malone hurling for the Cubs against the sensational rookie, Dizzy Dean of the Cardinals.

Malone had a well-established off-field reputation as a part-time brawler and full-time drinker. With the possible exception of Ty Cobb, it's likely no one got into more fights than Malone, who was a skilled amateur boxer. Before Malone's buddy, Hack Wilson, was traded, they were a two-man wrecking crew. Over the course of several years, they challenged umpires, got in fights with players, went into the stands after unruly fans, assaulted bar patrons, and once invaded a hotel room to confront two men who happened to make some unkind remarks to them.

Wilson's days as a Cub were over, and Malone was no better behaved as a solo act, but on the mound he was all business: competitive, focused, and purposeful. Hornsby tolerated Malone's nocturnal habits because the pitcher was in his prime as an athlete and one of the better right-handers in the league.

Dean was a country boy who loved being the center of attention. He was brash and brazen around reporters, with a habit of slipping into Southern slang and boasting about his own accomplishments. The Cubs knocked him around in a game in late April, winning 12–7. In that game, Dean pitched like a mortal and kept his mouth shut after the drubbing, but since then Dean had pitched with confidence and displayed a fastball that was as good as any in the league.

On June 1, the sky was overcast and the air was heavy—pitcher's weather. Malone and Dean dominated their opposing lineups. The Cardinals scratched out a run and made it hold up for seven innings. Then it started to drizzle. In the top of the eighth the Cardinals scored two additional runs to go up 3–0, but before the Cubs could bat in the bottom of the inning the rain came down harder, and the umpires decided to call the game on account of the weather. The final score reverted back to the previous inning, wiping the additional runs out of the record books. The final result: a seven-inning, 1–0 win for the Cardinals.

In the clubhouse, Hornsby seethed that the Cubs were cheated out of a chance to tie the game in their last at-bats. But there wasn't time to waste. The Cubs had to be in Pittsburgh in less than twenty-four hours to play a 3-game series with the Pirates. The players showered and dressed, and then the team headed to Union Station to meet their train.

Despite wounded feelings and a lack of sleep, the Cubs' bats came alive the next day at Forbes Field, and they beat the Pirates, 9–5. Charlie Root hurled a complete game and notched his fourth win of the season. Woody English banged out 4 hits, including two doubles. Stevenson, Grimm, Hemsley, and Jurges collected two hits a piece; Jurges's blows drove in 3 runs. Hornsby—playing right field, batting clean-up, and carrying a .174 batting average—went hitless.

On June 3 the Cubs lost, 6–5, when Tony Piet hit an inside-the-park home run off Jakie May in the bottom of the eleventh inning. Once again, Billy Jurges, the Cubs' rookie shortstop, was the hitting star with 3 hits in 5 at-bats. He also clubbed his first home run of the season.

For Hornsby it was an especially bad day, one of the worst single game performances of his career. He came to bat six times with runners on base and failed to drive in a run. He also let 2 balls skip past him in right field. Hornsby's experiment with himself as the team's right fielder was about to end.

Except for a few Cubs and Pirates fans—and Hornsby, of course—no one in the baseball world paid much attention to the game in Pittsburgh, because the day—June 3, 1932—was to be enshrined in baseball history for reasons other than Hornsby's truly miserable performance.

In New York, John McGraw, the feisty and often reviled manager of the New York Giants, announced his retirement. McGraw had been involved in professional baseball for over forty years—the last three decades as the manager of the Giants. He was one of baseball's last human links to the premodern era, a time when baseball customs, traditions, and rules were still evolving. Through the years, McGraw had tried harder than most men to bend those rules, or evade them, for the purpose of winning or achieving a competitive advantage.

During McGraw's entire career he had been at war with owners, league presidents, other managers, umpires, and opposing players. He stayed in the game because of his uncommon success—a manager with a career record of 2,840-1,984 and 9 trips to the World Series. He could have had a tenth trip, but in 1904 after McGraw's Giants went 106–47 in the regular season to win the National League title, McGraw, and Giants owner John Brush, refused to participate in the World Series due to disagreements about the business arrangements—and, in part, due to McGraw's personal disdain for the American League and its president, Ban Johnson. Instead of playing the series against the Boston Americans—a team McGraw deemed vastly inferior to his own—McGraw simply proclaimed that the Giants were the world champions and didn't need to prove themselves against a team from an inferior league.

McGraw's retirement would grab the headlines, but what transpired at Shibe Park in Philadelphia, was just as notable. In that day's game the New York Yankees and Philadelphia Athletics, the two most potent offenses in baseball, scored 33 runs. The final tally looked like the score of a football game: Yankees 20, Athletics 13. But the story of the game belonged to Lou Gehrig, the Yankees' first baseman. Gehrig homered in each of his first 4 at-bats: 2 homers to left field, 2 to right field. In the ninth inning, he came up with the bases loaded and connected again, sending the ball high and deep, this time to center field. The ball traveled more than 450 feet in the air, and Gehrig was halfway to second base before the A's center fielder, Al Simmons, caught the fly ball as he was running away from home plate. Observers at the park had no doubt that if the ball had sailed over the fielder's outstretched glove, Gehrig would have easily scored on an inside-the-park grand slam home run. All three base runners were able to tag up and advance after Simmons's catch.

After the game Gehrig lamented the fact that his last at-bat resulted in an out. "I think that last one was the hardest ball I hit all day," he said. "Gosh, it felt good."

Although the media elected to focus on McGraw's retirement—an event that, one suspects, was silently cheered by umpires, opposing managers, and most of the league's players—Gehrig's feat was historic. It was the first time in the modern era that a batter had hit 4 home runs in 1 game, one of the rarest individual accomplishments in baseball history. In the twentieth century it was more common for a pitcher to throw a perfect game than it was for a batter to hit 4 home runs in a single game.[6]

For the rubber game of the Cubs series in Pittsburgh, it would be a battle of veteran right-handers: thirty-eight-year-old Burleigh Grimes for the Cubs, thirty-six-year-old Heine Meine for the Pirates. Once again, it was Jurges who got the Cubs' offense started, hammering a 2-run homer in the third inning to give the Cubs a brief lead. But the Pirates battered Grimes and came away with a 12–4 win.

Then it was back to the train station for both teams—and another lurching ride on the rails to Chicago—to play a make-up game, scheduled on June 5.

On the day of the Cubs and Pirates make-up game, Cubs president William Veeck submitted an official protest to John Heydler, the president of the National League, complaining about what the Cubs considered the hasty decision made by the umpires on June 1 to call the Cubs-Cardinals game in the 8th inning. A few days later, Heydler would consider and deny the protest, letting the 1–0 Cardinals' win go into the record books. For Dizzy Dean, it was the fifth win of his young career.

Hornsby had Lon Warneke rested and ready to pitch in the make-up contest, but the day was wet and overcast. Hornsby watched the drizzle from the edge of the dugout while the players loosened up, in case the rain stopped.

More than six thousand fans turned out in the gloom to eat peanuts, watch batting practice, and keep an eye on the sky to see if the sun might break through. The fans cheered enthusiastically when Cuyler ambled up to the plate to take batting practice. "Kiki, Kiki," the fans chanted. For nearly thirty minutes Cuyler swung the bat, testing his foot and working on his timing. After the batting practice, Cuyler jogged back and forth in the wet outfield grass.

Cuyler's presence briefly lifted the spirits of the rain-soaked crowd. But the rain continued to pour down, and the umpires decided that the field was unplayable. The game was called off.

It was a somber clubhouse. The Cubs players showered and dressed and packed their gear. The team would spend the next twenty-three days on the road.

10

Brooklyn

After a day off and another long train ride, this time to Brooklyn, the Cubs were rested and confident as they approached a 4-game series with the Dodgers. Brooklyn had lost 4 out of their last 5 games and was mired in sixth place, 6½ games behind the league-leading Cubs.

For second-year shortstop Billy Jurges, the games would be a chance to play in front of his family and friends. Jurges, born in the Bronx and raised in Brooklyn, had learned the game on New York City's sandlots. After two seasons of Minor League ball, he had been signed in 1929 by Cubs scout Jack Doyle and assigned to a class AA team in Reading, Pennsylvania.[1] Known for hard-nosed play on the diamond and a fiery temperament, he was more skilled as a fielder than as a hitter. Jurges played 88 games with the Cubs in 1931, batting just .201. In games against Brooklyn, he had done even worse, collecting only 7 hits in 55 at-bats. The series with the Dodgers offered him a chance to redeem himself in the city where he'd grown up.

Off the field, Jurges had been dealing with a personal issue. About a year earlier, he had met an attractive woman named Violet Popovich at a party. She was tall and dark-haired with ambitions to break into show business. She liked ballplayers and had been romantically linked with several National League players, including Al Lopez, the Dodgers catcher, and Leo Durocher, now the shortstop for the Cincinnati Reds.[2] Soon after Jurges and Popovich met, they began dating. Jurges's teammate Kiki Cuyler became worried about the relationship, though the grounds for his concern are not clear. Cuyler counseled the younger player to be cautious. When Jurges told Popovich he wanted to end the relationship, she resisted. During the Cubs' road trip, and while staying at his parents' house in Brooklyn, Jurges received several emotional phone calls from the young woman.

The games in Brooklyn would draw good-sized crowds. Despite the fact that the Dodgers hadn't finished higher than fourth during the past seven seasons under popular manager Wilbert Robinson, Brooklyn fans were passionate and devoted. In 1932 the Dodgers would draw 681,827 fans to Ebbets Field, trailing only the Cubs and Yankees in home attendance figures.

Ebbets Field was a jewel of a ballpark. Opened in 1913 on the site of a garbage dump, where pigs and goats rummaged for food, the park was located in a Brooklyn neighborhood appropriately called Pigtown. Designed by architect Clarence Randall Van Buskirk, it was constructed of steel, brick, and concrete, a studier and more fireproof structure than wooden stadiums of the era. It was also something of a work of art. At the main entrance, fans entered the ballpark through a domed rotunda made of Italian marble and crossed a white marble floor designed to look like a baseball, with red tiles representing the stitches on the ball. Van Buskirk's design elements also included decorative chandeliers and gilded ticket booths. Most notably, the seating was up close to the field, so that even those in the upper deck had a good view of the players, and fans in the lower level seats along the first and third base lines could converse with—or shout at—the players on the field.[3]

For Brooklynites, who felt a kinship with the Dodgers' players and believed the team was an integral part of the neighborhood, it was an intimate setting, one that encouraged fans to feel part of the action.

One of those fans was a young boy named Bernard Malamud, who lived with his father and younger brother at 1111 Gravesend Avenue, in an apartment above his father's small grocery store.[4] In the spring of 1932, Malamud had turned eighteen years of age. He had graduated from Erasmus Hall High School, and that fall he would enter City College of New York. He was a slender, studious boy who loved baseball, especially the Dodgers.

He attended home games when he could and followed the team's progress in the newspapers. In an interview in 1981 he would recall, "Baseball was the sport I became aware of first. In my neighborhood, every night in the summer, there was a crowd waiting at the corner candy store for the late newspapers with the later baseball scores. This was before people had radios."[5]

Like thousands of young boys across America—call them the boys of summer, if you will—Malamud was both a student of the game and an admirer of the athletes who played, though in Malamud's case, the adoration had an intellectual side to it. Over the years, an idea would come to him that the appeal of baseball arose from the fact that the players represented concepts larger than themselves. "I lived somewhere near Ebbets Field," Malamud reflected. "The old Brooklyn Dodgers were our heroes, our stars, like out of myths. Since the stadium was near, it had to concern you. You were concerned with the accomplishments of various mythological heroes."[6]

In June 1932, though, Malamud was just a teenaged fan, absorbing the pleasures of the game via the sports pages and an occasional day at the ballpark. Two decades later, Malamud would establish himself as a literary figure and publish his first novel, set in the world of baseball, with one of the key scenes inspired by an incident involving Cubs shortstop Billy Jurges and the young woman he had spurned.

Hornsby had Lon Warneke on the mound for the opening game of the series, and the rookie—nicknamed "The Arkansas Hummingbird" for his fastball—was pitching with two extra days of rest. The Dodgers started Dazzy Vance, still a formidable Major League pitcher at the age of forty-one.

A two-man umpiring crew was assigned to the series: Bill Klem and John "Beans" Reardon. Klem was in his twenty-ninth year as a Major League umpire and so highly regarded that he had earned the popular moniker "the Old Arbitrator." Players had another nickname for Klem. Because of his prominent lips and sagging jowls, they called him "Catfish" behind his back.[7] Klem hated the name Catfish and threw players out of games if he heard anyone refer to him by the name he despised. Reardon, in his seventh year as a Major League umpire, was noted for his profanity and combativeness on the field, though he seldom ejected players who talked back to him.[8] He encouraged and enjoyed the rough back-and-forth of commentary between players and umpires. He often chatted with fans during the game.

Klem and Reardon were an odd pair. Like Nick Altrock and Al Schacht, the pitchers-turned-entertainers, Klem and Reardon had a personal distaste for each other and spoke only when absolutely necessarily. Klem didn't approve of Reardon's casual interactions with the fans during games and his abundant use of profanity on the field. Another irritant: Reardon also insisted on wearing his chest protector on the outside. Klem had pioneered the use of a more pliable protector worn inside the shirt and took Reardon's rejection of his invention as a personal rebuke.

From 1925 through 1929, the Dodgers—then affectionately called the "Robins" after their manager Wilbert Robinson—finished in fifth place every year, right at the top of the second division. In 1930 and 1931 they had finished fourth. The 1932 Dodgers had added two former Cubs— Hack Wilson, obtained in the off-season, and Danny Taylor, purchased on May 7—but the rest of their lineup remained much the same as in previous years. Lefty O'Doul, their best hitter, was thirty-five years old and near the end of his career. Watty Clark, Dazzy Vance, and Sloppy Thurston anchored the pitching staff. A rookie with the enchanting name of Van Lingle Mungo was projected as a fourth starter.

The key player and third baseman for the Dodgers in the upcoming Cubs series would be Mickey Finn, normally a utility infielder. He was to play a significant role in every game of the series.

Finn's full legal name was Cornelius Francis Finn, but everyone called him Mickey. Like Billy Jurges, his fellow infielder on the Cubs, Finn was a hometown boy, born in Brooklyn. A two-sport athlete, Finn had been an alternate for the USA Olympic bobsled team at the 1932 Winter Olympics. Dripping wet, he weighed no more than 165 pounds, and he hadn't hit a home run since the end of the 1930 season. Brooklyn fans loved his fighting spirit. He was known as a scrapper. Once, in the Pacific Coast League, he had taken offense at some brushback pitches and gotten into a fight with Duster Mails, a pitcher with his own history of brawling.[9] Finn made it to the Major Leagues on grit and determination and baseball intelligence. He had barely made the team in spring training, and now at the age of twenty-eight, he was getting a chance to play regularly because the Dodgers' regular third baseman, Jersey Joe Stripp, was recovering from an injury. Finn was a good bunter and hit the ball in the gaps. He made plays in the field and ran the bases hard and broke up double plays. He was adored by the Brooklyn fans.

Now in the early weeks of June, Finn, improbably, was batting .327, the second highest average on the team. Finn was in the midst of his best Major League season, but he was a doomed man. This would be his last full year in the Majors and in exactly thirteen months, on July 7, 1933, he would be dead.[10]

The Cubs had scored single runs in the fourth and fifth innings and held a 2–0 advantage going into the bottom of the seventh. Warneke appeared to be cruising toward his eighth victory, but then the Dodgers staged a rally: a double, an error by Charlie Grimm, a fielder's choice, an intentional walk, a single to center, and a run-scoring groundout. Suddenly, the Dodgers had claimed a 3–2 lead and had runners on second and third with just one out.

Mickey Finn came to the plate. First base was open, but Hornsby decided to pitch to Finn, who proceeded to lay down a perfect squeeze bunt to bring home an extra run. By the time the inning was over, the Dodgers had scored six times. The final score was 9–2. The loss dropped the Cubs out of first place and put Hornsby into a foul mood.

In the second game of the series, Finn again played a key role. He went 2 for 5 and got hit by a pitch. Hornsby expressed his displeasure with Finn by shouting insults at him from the bench. The Dodgers took a 5–2 lead into the eighth inning, but the Cubs managed to come back and win 7–5, in 14 innings.

The next day Pat Malone was matched up against Van Lingle Mungo, pitching on his twenty-first birthday, a pairing of two of the most colorful and worst-behaved pitchers of this era. Malone's off-the-field reputation as a drinker and brawler was already well-established, thanks to his partnership over the years with Hack Wilson.

Mungo was at the beginning of a long and successful Major League career.[11] He would also compile an impressive resume of bizarre off-field incidents, including a spring training episode in Cuba in the early 1940s, when he went to bed drunk and woke up naked in a Havana hotel room with two exotic dancers. Leo Durocher, the manager of the Dodgers at the time, tells the story in his memoir *Nice Guys Finish Last*. Durocher liked taking his team to Havana for a few spring training games, partly because Durocher liked the Cuban night life, the race tracks, and the casinos. The president of Cuba at the time was Fulgencio Batista, and his soldiers—in uniforms and with guns and bayonets—provided security at the ballpark for exhibition games.[12]

This particular year Mungo was trying to stay sober and win a spot on Durocher's roster. Unfortunately for Mungo, he fell off the wagon and spent the night with a singer named Lady Vine and a female dancer named Gonzales. Ms. Gonzales had an angry and jealous husband who confronted the Dodger pitcher in the morning, with a butcher's knife, and threatened to kill him. Durocher explains that Mungo got out of town alive and relatively unscathed by hiding in a vegetable bin in the hotel basement and then being smuggled out to the airport on a luggage cart.[13]

On this day of June in 1932, Mungo was making just his eighteenth appearance in a Major League game. His reputation at this point in his career was simply that he had a lively fastball and some problems with his control. In his previous start, four days earlier against the Phillies, Mungo had walked eleven batters in eight innings.

In the first inning, Malone gave up a grand slam home run to his old drinking buddy, Hack Wilson, and in reprisal from that inning on, Malone greeted most Brooklyn batters with at least 1 pitch aimed at their head. Mungo pitched a complete game, allowing only 4 hits and 2 earned runs, walking just two batters and striking out 6. The Cubs failed to mount a serious challenge, but things turned nasty in the seventh inning when Al Lopez, the Brooklyn catcher, spiked Jurges on a hard slide into second base. Jurges was not to forget the incident.

Jackie May took over for Malone in the eighth and got some revenge, hitting Mickey Finn with a pitch, probably on orders from Hornsby. It was the second time in two days that Finn had been hit by a pitch, hardly a coincidence. Half-an-inning later, Mungo retaliated by hitting Gabby Hartnett. Both benches emptied and the players spilled onto the field.

It was up to the silently feuding umpires, Klem and Reardon, to work together to quell the uprising. The umpires stepped in between the teams and coaxed the players back to their respective dugouts, to the displeasure of the fans who made it clear that they wanted to see a brawl. The game ended with the Dodgers winning, 5–2.

On Friday afternoon for the series finale, it was Elks Day at Ebbets Field, and a lively crowd of more than twelve thousand fans showed up. Both teams were frustrated and itching for a fight in the final game of the series. And if that's what the hometown fans wanted to see, they didn't have to wait long for tempers to flare.

The trouble started in the bottom of the first inning. Burleigh Grimes was on the mound for Chicago. Danny Taylor, the ex-Cub, led off and reached on an infield single. Mickey Finn followed, tapping a ball back to Burleigh Grimes, whose throw to second base was dropped by Billy Jurges.

Without hitting a ball out of the infield, the Dodgers had runners on first and second. Lefty O'Doul came to bat and bounced a slow ground ball to Billy Herman. Jurges grabbed Herman's throw just as Finn arrived at second base, sliding hard into the bag, dirt flying, spikes raised. Jurges stepped on the base, barely avoiding Finn's spikes, and then expressed his displeasure with a few choice words directed at Finn.

For Jurges, who had just been charged with an error on a potential double play ball, it had been a tough series in his return to Brooklyn. In addition to dealing with an unhappy girlfriend off the field, he had been in the middle of a lot of tough action at second base. In other words, Jurges was primed to explode. If Jurges wanted a confrontation, Finn was ready to oblige. The fight that had been brewing throughout the series was inevitable.

Finn threw the first punch, which grazed Jurges's chin, and then a second punch, which landed on Jurges's shoulder. Woody English rushed in from third base, grabbed Finn in a bear hug, and threw him to the ground. Jurges and English jumped on Finn, and the three players wrestled in the dirt, throwing wild punches. Players from both benches hurried toward second base, and, for the second game in a row, it was up to the umpires to restore order. The umpires flung themselves into the melee and tried to separate the players. The fight delighted the fans to such an extent that they wanted to get in on the action.

When Finn finally landed a proper punch, smacking English square in the jaw, three spectators climbed out of their box seats, jumped over the railing, and dashed onto the field, running toward the brawl. One of them, it turned out, was Finn's brother. Spectators chanted, "Let Mickey fight!" Reardon intercepted the three fans before they could reach the players and sent them back to their seats.

When Finn finally rose from the ground, he was covered in dirt. Klem and Reardon, forced to speak to each, conferred briefly, then ejected both Finn and Jurges. The two infielders left the field peacefully, walking just a few feet apart, and disappeared into the Brooklyn dugout, which led to their respective dressing rooms. There was no resumption of the fisticuffs; the altercation had run its course on the field.

The game continued. Stan Hack replaced Jurges in the lineup, playing third base, while English moved to shortstop. Joe Stripp entered the game as Finn's replacement. In the fifth inning Rollie Hemsley hit a 2-run homer off Sloppy Thurston to give the Cubs a short-lived 2–0 advantage, but the Dodgers scored 2 runs in the sixth and 2 more in the seventh to take the lead. Stripp was the hitting star, doubling and tripling off Grimes, driving in 2 runs and scoring. The Dodgers hung on for a 4–3 victory, taking the series 3 games to 1.

The loss dropped the Cubs out of first place, but the players in the locker room didn't have much time to dwell on the disappointment of the Brooklyn series. They had to catch a train to Boston, where the road trip would continue.

11

Road Trips

For the first half of the twentieth century, baseball teams principally traveled from one city to another by train. The train was, in a sense, a rolling locker room with amenities like sleeping berths and dining cars. The long hours on the train—especially on an extended road trip like the one the Cubs were on—allowed for rest and conversation between destinations. The close quarters also allowed for both intimacy and conflict. Elden Auker, a 1930s era pitcher with the Detroit Tigers, describes the social interaction on what he called "the Tiger Special": "We were the closest bunch of men you ever saw, and traveling together by train did nothing but draw us closer. We loved each other like brothers. We traveled together, we slept together, we ate together, we played together, and we fought together."[1]

Players interacted in various ways, relaxing with games or conversation. In his book on the 1949 baseball season, the writer David Halberstam notes that players often passed the time by playing games, but that significant amounts of waking hours were devoted to shop talk: "The train was not only an opportunity for game playing—it was the center of an ongoing seminar about hitting and pitching."[2] On the Cubs' train, those seminars on hitting and pitching likely didn't include their manager. Outside of baseball, Rogers Hornsby's favorite activities were sitting in hotel lobbies and betting on horse races, neither of which he could do during long train rides. Hornsby tended to keep to himself when away from a ballfield.

Halberstam also observed that "The train was where the peer groupings took place, and where the subgroupings—by class, education, age, and position of importance on the team—were revealed. . . ."[3] On the 1932 Cubs, there were the older married veterans—Grimm, Cuyler, Bush, Root—and the young unmarried regulars—Warneke, Herman, Jurges—who were just establishing themselves at the Major League level. There were the drinkers and hell raisers—specifically, Malone and Hemsley, now that Wilson was gone—though Malone and Hemsley were more likely to get into trouble when the team was off the rails and near drinking establishments. Woody English, the best card player on the team, anchored the bridge table.

For the most part, these Cubs were a happy and well-balanced team. If there was an irritant in the mix of personalities, an individual whose very presence unsettled the harmony of group dynamics, it was the manager, the often stern and aloof Rogers Hornsby.

Despite the camaraderie, and the relative comfort of the team trains, the extended road trips took a toll on the players. By the time the Cubs left Brooklyn, they had played 7 straight games on the road—and they were just one-third of the way through what would be their longest road trip of the season.

Only hours after the brawl at Ebbets Field and the disappointing losses to the Dodgers, the Cubs were back on a train, traveling up the East Coast for a 2-game series with the Boston Braves, who had just moved into first place, a half-game ahead of the weary Cubs.

The Braves had finished 26 games under .500 in 1931. Going into the 1932 season they were considered one of the weaker teams in the league—in 1932 they would finish second to last in most offensive categories, including runs scored—but they had managed to stay in contention, thanks to a strangely cobbled together pitching rotation. The pitching staff included Tom Zachary, Socks Seibold, Ben Cantwell, Ed Brandt, Bob Brown, and Huck Betts. Zachary, remembered as the pitcher who served up Babe Ruth's sixtieth homerun in the final game of the 1927 season, was thirty-six years old and near the end of a long career. Seibold was also thirty-six, but less renowned, and he would win just 3 games in 1932, his penultimate year in the

Majors. Cantwell was a journeyman who had never won more than 9 games in a season. If there was an ace on the staff, it was Ed Brandt, who had compiled an 18-11 record the previous season. The staff was rounded out by a rookie named Bob Brown, who would earn 14 of his 16 career wins in 1932, and Huck Betts, a thirty-five-year-old who had been signed by the Braves, even though he hadn't pitched in a Major League game since 1925.[4]

On June 11, in the opening game of the series, Lon Warneke was matched up against Huck Betts. Although Betts pitched credibly, Warneke was slightly better. In a briskly played game of one hour and twenty-four minutes, the Cubs edged the Braves 2–1, and slipped back into first place. Billy Jurges went 1–3 and drove in the second and deciding run of the game. The next day Guy Bush outpitched Ben Cantwell 5–3, and Jurges, showing no ill effects from the fisticuffs with Mickey Finn, again paced the offense, banging out two doubles and a single and driving in a run. The Cubs left town with the satisfaction of a 2-game sweep.

An off day and a rain out provided the traveling Cubs with a chance to regroup before taking on the John McGraw-less Giants at the Polo Grounds. Since McGraw had retired and turned the club over to Bill Terry on June 2, the Giants had won 7 of their 9 games, including the last 5 in a row, jumping from last place to fourth place in the tightly bunched National League. Now just 4½ games out of first place, the Giants were back to playing solid baseball and ready for the Cubs.

Pat Malone was named the Cubs' starter for the first game of the series. Freddie Fitzsimmons, who had won twice during the Giants post-McGraw surge, would be on the mound for the Giants.

Fitzsimmons was a durable, overweight right-hander with unusually short arms and a quirky delivery. Casey Stengel called Fitzsimmons "The Seal," suggesting his arms reminded Stengel of flippers; another nickname was "Fat Freddie." Despite his physical limitations, he was an excellent fielder and a good hitter, cracking 14 homers in his career.[5] He had a decent fastball and curve, but the pitch he relied on and threw most often was a knuckleball that broke down sharply, like a spitball—what players called a dry spitter. He threw as many as fifty knucklers in a game, mixing it in with the other pitches.[6]

But it wasn't only the odd assortment of pitches that baffled hitters and allowed Fitzsimmons to pitch for nineteen years in the Major Leagues. It was his peculiar and disconcerting physical delivery. Leo Durocher, who batted and competed against Fitzsimmons for much of his playing career, offered an evocative and colorful description of Fitzsimmons on the mound: "If you ever saw Freddie pitch, you could never forget him. He would turn his back completely to the batter, as he was winding up, wheel back around and let out the most god-awful grunt as he was letting the ball go—rrrrrhhhhhooooo—like a rhinoceros in heat."[7]

Over the first seven innings of the game, Malone outpitched Fitzsimmons, and the Cubs held a 3–1 lead going into the bottom of the eighth. The Giants rallied by loading the bases in their half of the inning on 2 singles and a walk, and then with 2 outs, Fred Lindstrom hit a routine ground ball to Billy Herman at second base. That should have ended the rally, but the ball slipped through Herman's legs, allowing the tying runs to score. Bill Terry and Mel Ott followed with singles, suddenly giving the Giants the lead, and eventually the game, by a score of 6–3.

The second game of the series featured a matchup of future Hall of Famers, Burleigh Grimes and Carl Hubbell. Grimes came through with his best performance of the season, pitching a complete game and allowing just 7 hits. The Cubs won 2–1. The lone run for the Giants came on a solo pinch-hit home run by Sam Leslie.

The teams played a doubleheader at the Polo Grounds on Saturday before 25,000 fans. In the opening game the Giants scored 2 runs in the first and 2 more in the sixth off Guy Bush. Johnnie Moore smacked a 2-run homer for the Cubs in the seventh, but that was all the offense the Cubs would muster against Hi Bell and Dolf Luque, who combined to scatter 8 Cubs hits. In the nightcap Freddie Fitzsimmons started on two days rest and pitched well, hurling a complete game and giving up just 5 hits. But 2 of the hits were home runs, 1 each by Kiki Cuyler and Rollie Hemsley. For the Cubs, the dependable, and increasingly indispensable, rookie, Lon Warneke, raised his record to 9-3 by shutting out the Giants on 6 hits, 3 of them by Fitzsimmons.

After splitting the series with the Giants, the Cubs left town with a two-game lead over the Boston Braves in the tightly bunched league standings. The scramble of the pennant race had teams sliding back and forth between the first and second division on a daily basis. All eight teams were within 8½ games of the lead. If any team could put together even a modest winning streak, it would jump two or three places in the standings.

On the morning of June 19, the National League standings looked like this:

Table 1. National League Standings, June 19, 1914

Team	Wins	Losses	Percentage	Games Behind
Chicago	33	24	.579	————
Boston	31	26	.544	2.0
Pittsburgh	26	25	.510	4.0
Brooklyn	29	30	.492	5.0
New York	26	27	.491	5.0
Philadelphia	30	32	.484	5.5
St. Louis	26	29	.473	6.0
Cincinnati	28	36	.438	8.5

The reigning National League champions and preseason favorites, the St. Louis Cardinals, were in seventh place. The season had been a struggle. No one had emerged to replace Chick Hafey's bat in the lineup. In fact, only one starter was hitting over .300. Manager Gabby Street had counted on Paul Derringer and Bill Hallahan—who had combined for 37 wins in 1931—to be the aces of the staff. But by mid-June, they had just 9 wins between them; 6 by Hallahan, 3 by Derringer. Since both Burleigh Grimes and Flint Rhem had been traded, the team was relying on the colorful rookie, Dizzy Dean, to win, and win consistently.

Dean had almost as much talent as a starting pitcher as he did as a raw personality. In early June the Cardinals won 6 games in a row—it would be their longest winning streak of the season—and Dean got credit for two of the wins, allowing just 2 runs in 16 innings of work. Notably, in these two starts, Dean had good control, walking only three batters.

But Dean was disgruntled. In the midst of a mid-June road trip to the east, he expressed his dissatisfaction to a reporter of the *St. Louis Dispatch*.[8] He complained that he was underpaid and underappreciated. He threatened to quit the team. On June 15, in Philadelphia, he bolted, buying a one-way ticket back to St. Louis.

The Cardinals took it in stride, recognizing that Dean could be volatile and unpredictable but was also a pitcher with great potential. Branch Rickey acknowledged that Dean had "an unusual personality," and Gabby Street noted that he was "a hard proposition to manage."[9]

Dean's early season funk lasted two days. Rickey agreed to give him a payment of $225, and Dean sent a telegram of apology to his manager, asking for permission to rejoin the starting rotation in the next series. If he was allowed to pitch against the Giants in the Polo Grounds, Dean said he would "show you how a ball game should be pitched."[10]

True to his word, a contrite Dean took the train back east, got his start against the Giants on Tuesday afternoon, June 21, before a modest crowd of 4,000 fans, and pitched a complete game victory, 5–1, striking out eight and giving up just 6 hits. The Cardinals jumped to fifth place in the standings, 5 games out of first.

After splitting the series with the Giants, the Cubs had 8 more games to play before getting off the road, all of them against teams in contention. From New York, the Cubs traveled to Philadelphia to play the Phillies at Baker Bowl. The Phillies had a formidable offense with five .300 hitters in the lineup, paced by Chuck Klein. The series promised to be a slugfest.

The Cubs' hitters did their part, scoring 29 runs in the 4 games, but Chicago managed to come away with only 1 victory, 12–3, on June 21, with Pat Malone getting the win. In the other 3 games, Charlie Root, Burleigh Grimes, and Guy Bush had no luck in subduing the bats of the Phillies, who banged the ball all over Baker Bowl, scoring 37 runs on a total of 52 hits, including 19 extra base hits. Flint Rhem, facing the Cubs for the first time as a member of the Phillies, stopped the Cubs in the third game of the series. Chuck Klein did the most damage at the plate, going 9 for 17 with 3 doubles and 3 home runs in the 4 games.

Somehow the Cubs still had a game and a half lead, in the National League, over the second place Boston Braves. By taking 3 out of 4 from the Cubs, the Phillies had jumped into fourth, just 3½ games out of first.

The Cubs pushed on. The final stop on the road trip was St. Louis. Like the Giants and Phillies, the Cardinals were struggling to play .500 ball but were still right in the middle of the pennant race. After a slow start, the Cards had begun to play up to everyone's expectations and seemed to be rounding into form for the second half of the season.

In the first game of the series on Saturday afternoon, June 25, the Cubs pitched Lon Warneke, going on a full week's rest, coming off the shutout win over the Giants on the previous weekend. But the Cardinals jumped on Warneke and managed to hold on for a 7–6 win. On Sunday, the Cubs and Cardinals played a doubleheader before 31,000 fans. The Cards won the opener, 4–3, scoring 2 runs in the bottom of the ninth off Pat Malone, on a pinch double by Jimmie Reese. The nightcap featured a duel between the Cubs' Charlie Root and the Cardinals' brash rookie, Dizzy Dean. Root surrendered 14 hits but gave up only 3 runs. The Cubs managed to beat Dean by scoring single runs in the seventh and eighth innings, though Dean struck out 8.

In the final game of the series, and the last of the long road trip, Burleigh Grimes faced Paul Derringer, in a battle of two pitchers who had been teammates the previous season. On this day, Derringer was better. The Cards won, 4–1, taking the series, 3 games to 1.

With the road trip finished, the Cubs could enjoy one final train ride back to Chicago. Over the course of nearly four weeks and 26 games, the Cubs had won just eight times. They had fallen out of first place, but were still within 2½ games of the lead. The pennant race, if anything, had tightened even more as the season was about to reach the halfway mark.

There were no bands or cheering crowds to greet the Cubs upon their arrival at Union Station. It wasn't that Chicago had forgotten the Cubs. It was just that the energy of the city was focused in another place: Chicago Stadium, where both political parties would convene to select their nominees for president.

This was mid-summer of 1932, a crucial and troubling year for America. The Depression had crushed the spirits of many Americans, and no one was certain what leader, or what party, could unite the country and put it on a path to renewed prosperity. As the homeless suffered in shelters and Bonus marchers confronted Congress, most of America watched to see what would happen in the conventions being held in Chicago.

12

Chicago Conventions

While the Cubs were out of town on their twenty-six-day road trip, the city of Chicago hummed with activity as it prepared to host the presidential nominating conventions of both major parties.

The conventions would bring a stream of people to the city: party officials, campaigners, delegates, and reporters, people with money in their pockets who would boost the city's economy. The conventions were especially important to the big downtown hotels. For several weeks in the summer of 1932, they would be filled close to capacity.

Of all the hotels in Chicago, the most spectacular was the Stevens. It had become the largest hotel in the world when it opened in May 1927 and was owned and operated by Ernest Stevens, whose family also owned the Illinois Life Insurance Company.[1] The massive twenty-five-story structure had three thousand rooms, a large childcare center, a movie theater, a library, a bowling alley, retail stores, and a chip-and-putt golf course on the roof of the building.[2]

The youngest of Ernest Stevens's four sons was employed part-time as a bellhop in the hotel. Johnny Stevens—he was later known as John Paul Stevens—was twelve years old. At the time of the summer conventions, he was out of school and able to enjoy the hustle and bustle of guests checking into the hotel. Thanks to his father's hotel business, he was used to meeting famous and important people. In 1927, at the hotel, he met the renowned aviators Charles Lindbergh and Amelia Earhart.[3] He had also met Babe Ruth. As a young boy and a baseball fan, meeting Ruth was one of the thrills of his lifetime.

Although Johnny Stevens had grown up on the south side of the city, much closer to Comiskey Park than Wrigley Field, his allegiance was to the Cubs, not the White Sox. The 1932 White Sox were a bad team. They had two future Hall of Famers on the team—the thirty-one-year-old pitcher, Ted Lyons, and a young shortstop, Luke Appling, who was in his first full season in the Majors—but the rest of the team was a collection of modestly talented career backups. In 1932 a utility infielder named Red Kress led the team in home runs, with 9. The two best pitchers on the staff were Lyons and the forty-year-old Sad Sam Jones, each of whom would post records of 10-15 that season.[4]

During the season, the White Sox lost at home, and they lost on the road. They had a losing record each month of the season and a losing record against each of the other seven teams in the league. They would finish in seventh place with a dismal record of 49-102, a whopping 56½ games out of first. Only the inept Boston Sox, who would finish with just 43 wins, were worse. Home attendance for the White Sox was 233,198, an average of about 3,000 paid customers per game.[5]

Years later Stevens explained how he developed his loyalty to the Cubs as a youth: "The Cubs were the winning team at the time. They were a really strong team. I listened to many, many games and knew the Cubs inside and out."[6]

Johnny Stevens was another of the boys of summer, like the slightly older Bernard Malamud of Brooklyn. While Malamud kept track of the Dodgers through newspaper accounts of the team's games, Stevens was able to follow his Cubs in real time by listening to radio broadcasts. It had been the belief of William Wrigley and William Veeck that radio would encourage and expand the fan base of the Cubs, so while none of the New York area teams allowed broadcasts of their games, Cubs fans like Johnny Stevens could listen to games in their own homes. Stevens had attended only 1 Cubs game in person: the first game of the 1929 World Series, when the veteran pitcher, Howard Ehmke of the Philadelphia Athletics, a surprise starter, pitched an 8-hitter, beating the Cubs, 3–1, and striking out thirteen Cubs batters. But thanks to radio broadcasts, he didn't have to be at the ballpark to follow the team.

He could listen to the radio and hear one of the Cubs' announcers—Hal Totten, Bob Elson, Quin Ryan, or Pat Flanagan—call the games whenever the Cubs played.[7]

When he wasn't listening to Cubs games, and the weather was warm, Stevens played baseball in his backyard with his older brothers and other boys from the neighborhood. As the youngest and smallest of the players, Stevens was usually picked last, though it hardly diminished his enthusiasm for the game. The boys established an elaborate set of rules to govern play. Games were five innings long. Pitches had to be thrown underhand. There was a high brick wall at the back of the yard, and if a ball was hit over the wall, it was an automatic out. If a batted ball struck the family dog, Monday, the at-bat was replayed.[8]

Teams were chosen in the spring, and then the games commenced. The season usually ended on June 10, the date at which the Stevens family left Chicago for their summer home in Lakeside, Michigan, but this year was different. With the political conventions coming to the city in June, the boys' season extended until early July.

More than a year earlier, in the spring of 1931, Chicago elected Anton Cermak as the city's forty-fourth mayor. Cermak had defeated the incumbent, Big Bill Thompson, whose administration had been known mostly for its corruption and incompetence. For many of Chicago's ethnic minorities, Cermak was an appealing and refreshing change. It had been a bitter campaign in which Thompson ridiculed Cermak for his surname and birth in Eastern Europe. Cermak's famous response to Thompson's taunting was: "He doesn't like my name . . . it's true I didn't come over on the Mayflower, but I came over as soon as I could."[9]

Soon after his inauguration, Cermak began to lobby both political parties to bring their conventions to Chicago in 1932. Chicago had a long history of hosting presidential nominating conventions, beginning with the first national Republican convention in 1860, which selected Abraham Lincoln. In all, ten Republican and four Democratic conventions had been held in the city. No city had hosted more national nominating conventions.[10]

Cermak's primary motivation in working so hard to bring the conventions to Chicago was to highlight the city and his new administration, which had made significant progress in cleaning up the corruption of his predecessor. Al Capone was in jail, thanks to the creative legal work of a lawyer named Mabel Walker Willebrandt.[11] The crime wars and the shootouts on city streets were largely a thing of the past. Chicago's speakeasies were under wraps but not exactly out of business. In the downtown Loop area alone, there were reputed to be at least six hundred establishments that served alcohol.[12] Delegates to the conventions could find and enjoy them, if they wished.

In pitching his city as the location for the political conventions, Mayor Cermak offered other good and practical reasons to choose Chicago. Cermak noted that the city was situated near the geographical center of the country and functioned as the rail hub of the nation. It was a convenient location for anyone traveling from east or west, and there was ample hotel space to accommodate the delegates, campaigners, and reporters. Cermak recognized that the conventions would be good for the local economy, and no city in the country had been more adversely impacted by the Great Depression than Chicago. Furthermore, Chicago had an excellent facility in which to hold the proceedings: the Chicago Stadium, located at 1800 West Madison Street, in the heart of downtown. The arena was just three years old and had been built for sporting events and large conventions. It was large enough to accommodate more than twenty thousand people. The stadium had already hosted circuses, large church services, and sporting events, like hockey and boxing matches.

In February 1932, four months before the Republicans would gather for their convention, the venue presented a four-round boxing match between the legendary Jack Dempsey and a local fighter named Kingfish Levinsky.[13] Known as the Manassa Mauler, Dempsey was thirty-six and no longer the champion in the heavyweight division, but he was considering a comeback and remained one of the most famous living athletes of the century.[14] Less than five years earlier, he had fought Gene Tunney at Soldier Field, in Chicago, in the famous long count fight.

Since his loss to Tunney, Dempsey had boxed in various exhibitions while considering whether or not to attempt a full-scale comeback.

Levinsky was just twenty-one, and boxing pundits predicted a bright future for the youngster who had earned his nickname from working in the Maxwell Street fish market. Levinsky's sister, a flamboyant and foul-mouthed young woman known as Leaping Lena, worked in his corner during his fights.

The four-round fight was held on February 18, drawing a paid crowd of 23,322, and delivering gross receipts of nearly $75,000 for twelve minutes of action. Dempsey received $33,000 for his participation in the bout. Levinsky earned $11,000. But the fight, as it turned out, was not much of a contest. Levinsky battered the former champion. Whatever hopes Dempsey might have had about continuing his career had been dashed. After this fight, Dempsey turned his attention to other pursuits, working as a boxing referee and opening what would become a famous restaurant in New York City.[15]

Delegates to the Republican Convention began to arrive the second week of June. The official business of the convention would be conducted between June 14 and June 16, while the Cubs were playing their series with the Giants in the Polo Grounds. If convention goers wanted to break away from Chicago Stadium to see a ball game, the White Sox were in town and playing a 4-game series with the last-place Red Sox and the first-place Yankees.

It promised to be a lackluster convention for the Republicans, despite the fact that they controlled the Senate and the White House. President Hoover's absence from the proceedings was not unusual—candidates didn't show up at conventions in 1932—but there were no pictures of Hoover in the convention hall.[16] The party was not excited about the nomination of President Hoover for a second term, thinking that he was a losing candidate because of his dour personality, his policies, and the state of the economy. A half-hearted attempt to draft Calvin Coolidge went nowhere. The only other candidate to emerge was a relatively obscure senator from Maryland named James France. The delegates were equally unexcited by the vice president, Charles Curtis of Kansas, known as Egg Curtis for his passionate support of the poultry industry. But no one emerged to challenge Curtis for second spot on the ticket.[17]

The issue that consumed the most time and discussion was how the Republicans would address the question of Prohibition and present their position in the party platform. It was a topic the delegates wanted to avoid. Sen. Lester Dickinson of Iowa, a strong supporter of Prohibition, gave the keynote address. With just a fraction of the delegates present to hear his speech, he choose to avoid the matter altogether, saying not a word in support or opposition to Prohibition.[18]

Following tradition, President Hoover did not attend the convention. He remained in Washington and continued his normal schedule of activities: exercise at dawn, a bath, breakfast, desk-work until noon, a quick visit outside to pose for pictures and meet constituents, and then back to his office.

Hoover's favorite room in the White House was the Lincoln Study, which he used both for socializing and working. Hoover greatly admired Lincoln. This was the room in which the sixteenth president had signed the Emancipation Proclamation. There was a sitting area and built-in bookcases. Hoover worked at a desk that had been used by Woodrow Wilson. From this desk, Hoover could see the Washington Monument.

He could also see the tents and shacks erected by the BEF, who had camped on Anacostia Flats. If there was a single issue that focused the attention of the president in mid-June, it was what to do about the encampments and the BEF. Congress was still in session, debating the Patman Bonus Bill, which Hoover opposed. But he was aware of the intense feeling in the country about the bill. That June the president would spend many hours in the Lincoln Study planning strategy to deal with the continued occupation of the nation's capital by the Bonus marchers.

In Chicago, the delegates got down to business and cast their ballots, once again nominating Hoover and Curtis. When the official tally had been added up, the news was sent to Washington.

On the night of June 16, Hoover was told that the delegates in Chicago had voted. He was to be, as he expected, the party's standard bearer in the 1932 election. It was reported that Hoover accepted the news without jubilation or surprise. He said without emotion, "Well, it was not wholly unexpected. Guess I will go back to the office now."[19]

In Chicago, the convention ended. H. L. Mencken, reporting the proceedings for *The Baltimore Sun*, pronounced it "the stupidest and most boresome" of all the political conventions he had covered.[20] As the delegates left the convention hall, cleanup crews went to work restoring the facility and getting it ready for the next major event: the Democratic National Convention, which would begin in exactly twelve days.

The gathering of Democrats, unlike the Republican convention held two weeks prior, exuded vitality and optimism, the kind of reaction generated by confidence and positive thinking and symbolized by what became the party's theme song, "Happy Days Are Here Again." Amelia Earhart flew in for the opening ceremonies. At night, the city of Chicago staged fireworks displays over Lake Michigan.

The Democrats believed they could win the White House, and they had an array of candidates to choose from: Al Smith, the former governor of New York and the nominee in 1928; John Nance Garner of Texas, the politically powerful speaker of the House of Representatives; former Virginia Governor Harry Floyd Baker; Maryland Governor Albert Richie; the former secretary of war, Newton Baker; and Franklin Delano Roosevelt, the governor of New York.

Not all of these men were declared candidates. Some were favorite sons or simply preferred by a small but influential contingent of Democratic Party leaders who hoped their candidate might be drafted.

During the run-up to the convention, and in the days right before the proceedings convened, other names were whispered as possibilities, including Sen. Huey Long of Louisiana.

Mayor Cermak expected to wield a significant amount of power during the nominating process. The galleries would be packed with his supporters. Cermak also controlled the Illinois delegation and its fifty-eight delegates. He favored Illinois senator James Hamilton Lewis for the presidential nomination, and Lewis had done well during the primaries, but right before the start of the convention, Lewis decided to drop out. Cermak was ready with an alternate candidate: Melvin Alvah Traylor, the president of the First Union Trust and Savings Bank, Chicago's largest bank. Cermak instructed the Illinois delegation to support Traylor as its favorite son candidate.

Cermak understood that Traylor had very little chance for the nomination. It was well known that Cermak was not a fan of Governor Roosevelt. He would be willing to support other candidates before he would allow his delegates to cast ballots for the New York governor.

Although a majority of the delegates were elected officials from different layers of government who had been handpicked by the party, Roosevelt had the most pledged delegates, thanks to his success in the primaries, especially in the South and West. Roosevelt's candidacy was also bolstered by an extremely talented group of advisors, including Lewis Howe, James Farley, and Joseph P. Kennedy.

Three thousand delegates crammed into the city's hotels. The New York delegation occupied rooms at the Drake Hotel. Six delegations stayed at the Palmer House. The Sherman House hosted the Texas and California delegations, two key states in determining the outcome of the convention. The Stevens Hotel was the headquarters for twelve state delegations. Undoubtedly, some of the delegates sampled the charms and diversion of late-night Chicago, but the task in front of the Democrats was serious and profound. The nominee of the convention was very likely to become the next president at a critical time in the nation's history.

On June 29—a Wednesday—the convention got underway with a keynote address and passage of a platform that included a so-called "dry plank," calling for the repeal of Prohibition. Nominations and speeches dominated most of Thursday. The first roll call vote wasn't held until 4:30 a.m. on Friday.

It took four roll calls and some backroom deals brokered by Roosevelt's advisors for the New York governor to win the nomination. James Farley negotiated with the Texans, and Joseph Kennedy made a key phone call to William Randolph Hearst to put that delegation in Roosevelt's column. Eventually Mayor Cermak came around and released his Illinois delegation to join the bandwagon.

Through radio news and phone calls to his advisors, Roosevelt carefully monitored the drama of the convention from the governor's mansion in Albany. When he knew he had been selected to head the ticket, he made a bold and unprecedented decision: he would fly to Chicago to accept the nomination in person. The plane flight itself would be historic. The accepted mode of transportation for political candidates for almost a hundred years had been the train. It was the first time a president or candidate for president had flown to a political event. The next time a presidential candidate or sitting president would travel by air was in January of 1943, when Roosevelt—by then in his third term as president—flew in a Boeing 314 across the Atlantic Ocean to meet and discuss war strategy with Winston Churchill, at Casablanca.

The flight through a thunderstorm and strong winds, at an altitude of fifteen hundred feet, was a challenging adventure. The plane was uninsulated, so the interior was noisy and cold. One historian noted that the passengers endured "bone shaking vibration and thundering noise."[21] The plane landed at Buffalo, then Cleveland, to refuel. At Cleveland, five thousand people cheered the arrival of the Democratic nominee.

As the journey proceeded, Roosevelt worked on his acceptance speech at a small desk in the rear of the plane, composing the draft in pencil on legal pads. When the plane landed at Chicago's Municipal Airport—now known as Midway—a crowd of ten thousand had assembled to greet the governor. In the commotion at the airport Roosevelt's hat and glasses were knocked off. As the historian Steve Neal wrote, "It was unheard of for a political figure to attract such cheering throngs. Ordinary people were attracted to him in the same way that they thrilled to Babe Ruth and Charles Lindbergh."[22]

The comparison to Ruth and Lindbergh was apt. Roosevelt was about to become an American hero. The 1920s had more than its share of larger-than-life figures: the fictional Jay Gatsby; the aviators Lindbergh and Earhart; Al Capone; Jack Dempsey; Jim Thorpe; the two Babes, Ruth and Didrikson. But the national leaders—Harding, Coolidge, Hoover—had been distinctly bland individuals, lacking the ability to inspire.

Roosevelt combined the qualities of Lindbergh and Ruth. All three men were bold, proud, and self-confident. Like the aviator, Roosevelt was handsome and sophisticated. Lindbergh's main personal flaw was that he didn't like being in the public eye. In that regard Roosevelt was more like Ruth, a man who thrived on crowds and public actions.

The candidate was driven from the airport to the Congress Hotel, where he revised his speech in pencil and dressed in a blue suit. Someone tucked a rose in the lapel of his suit jacket.[23] He proceeded to Chicago Stadium to give his acceptance speech, taking the stage with the pencil protruding from his pocket. When Roosevelt appeared, an organist played "Happy Days Are Here Again."

He told the assembled delegates about his flight through stormy weather to arrive in Chicago to accept the nomination. Then he promised: "I pledge you—I pledge myself to a new deal for the American people."[24]

The campaign to change the lives of millions of Americans was underway.

As Johnny Stevens would have known, on the afternoon of the day that Roosevelt accepted the Democratic nomination for president the Cubs were playing a home game at Wrigley Field, trying to make it 3 in row over the Cincinnati Reds. But the Reds banged out a dozen hits, including a 3-run homer by Wally Roettger, and scored 6 runs to beat the Cubs, 6–3. Charlie Root took the loss. Despite the loss, the Cubs maintained their slim half-game lead in the National League, because the Pirates also lost, 5–4, to the Cardinals.

One bright spot for the Cubs was the continued good hitting by Billy Jurges. The shortstop hit in his fifth straight game since his injury, contributing a pair of singles and driving in two of the Cubs' runs. Jurges was becoming a significant contributor to the offense. More remarkable, but unknown to his manager or the fans, Jurges was performing well at the ballpark despite dealing with a tenuous off-field situation.

In a matter of days, an incident between Jurges and the woman he had been dating would change the course of the pennant race. The incident would take place in a Chicago hotel room, not at the Stevens Hotel, but at a small hotel on Chicago's North Side, near Wrigley Field.

13

Independence Day

Two days after Roosevelt's acceptance speech at the convention, the nation celebrated Independence Day. Americans turned out to commemorate Independence Day with parades, flags, picnics, fireworks, political oratory, and sporting events, including a full schedule of doubleheaders in the Major Leagues. The day began, however, with a tragedy, far removed from Major League ballparks.

Early that Monday morning in Butte, Montana, six teenage boys stole blasting caps and a case of dynamite from a storage shed and dragged the crate to the Meaderville Baseball Park. Shortly after daybreak, the boys started setting off small explosions to commemorate the holiday. Butte was a mining town, so residents were used to the ruckus of noise. But the steady round of percussive reverberations culminated in a sudden and unexpected blast that shook the ground for miles, as if an earthquake had hit. Window panes rattled and dogs cowered under tables. Adults and children rushed outside and observed a plume of smoke and dirt rising from the baseball field. Somehow the boys had managed to accidentally detonate the entire case of dynamite at once, blowing all six of them—quite literally—to pieces.[1]

From coast to coast, Americans played baseball: at fairgrounds, in city parks, on sandlots, in farm fields—anywhere ballplayers could find open space and a team to compete against. Town teams played rival town teams. Youth teams competed against each other. Rivalries were renewed. People came to watch, bringing young children and picnic baskets. In every possible way, and in multiple and unexpected venues, Americans gathered to celebrate the Fourth of July with baseball games.

In Anamosa, Iowa, the undefeated Anamosa Men's Reformatory prison baseball team, named the Snappers and coached by a fifty-six-year-old convicted murderer named Harry Hortman, prepared to play 2 games. The first game, oddly enough, was a road game. For obvious reasons, the Snappers played most of their games at home, on a field located within the friendly confines of the prison's walls. But the new warden, a cheerful and baseball-loving man named Charlie Ireland, had arranged for the first game to be played against a town team in Alburnett, sixty miles west of Anamosa. That game would be played in the morning and give the inmates on the Anamosa team a half-day of relative freedom outside the prison as they traveled to and from the site of the game.

The second game would be back at home, on the institution's field, against the Dubuque Meteors. The Snappers, who had 1 reliable pitcher, generally played just 1 game a week. With the prospect of playing 2 games on the same day—and having played just two days before, on Saturday, July 2, against a team from Martelle, Iowa—the Snappers needed to find an extra starting pitcher. To solve the problem, they recruited a ringer, a nineteen-year-old former Anamosa high school star named Darrell Meredith, to pitch the game against Alburnett. Meredith had once outpitched fellow Iowan Bob Feller in an American Legion game.[2] Dressed in the uniform of the Snappers, Meredith hurled a shutout, and the Snappers won 2–0. Back home that afternoon, with residents from the town of Anamosa admitted inside the walls of the prison to view the contest, the Snappers won again, this time by a score of 9–6 over the Meteors, keeping their undefeated season intact.

In Washington DC, members of the Bonus Expeditionary Forces, who had remained in the city after Congress had voted down the Bonus Bill, came together at the Anacostia Flats camp. The men most likely broke the monotony and tension of their long occupation with a game of baseball, playing on a field less than two miles from Griffith Stadium, where the hometown Senators took on the first place Yankees in a doubleheader.[3]

President Hoover did not participate in any public events over the holiday weekend. He left the city and spent the Fourth of July at Camp Rapidan, where he relaxed next to the calming waters of a mountain trout stream.

Another notable American with a more obvious connection to the world of baseball also took a personal vacation over the long Fourth of July weekend, and like the president, he went fishing. Passing through Minneapolis-St. Paul on his way to an undisclosed location in northern Minnesota, baseball commissioner Kenesaw Mountain Landis offered this comment to a reporter: "I'm sick of baseball. I'm going fishing and I don't care whether Babe Ruth decides to play polo instead of baseball."[4]

A few miles away from the encampment of the BEF, Hoover's home team Washington Senators were disappointed in their current record of 38-34. The first half of the season was coming to an end, and the Senators had dropped to fifth place in the standings. The league-leading New York Yankees would be at Griffith Stadium for the Independence Day doubleheader.

Over the previous three weeks, Manager Walter Johnson's team had slipped from 4 games behind the Yankees to 12½ games out of first place. The Senators had lost 11 of the 17 games during that stretch. Only Heinie Manush and Carl Reynolds were hitting above .300: Manush at .315 and Reynolds at .301. None of the other regulars—Joe Judge, Ossie Bluege, Sam Rice, Joe Cronin—were hitting above the .280s. Al Crowder, the ace of the staff, had a decent 3.60 ERA, but his record was only 9-9. The quixotic rookie, Monte Weaver, was a solid 9–5, and Lloyd Brown was 11–3. The rest of the staff was a disappointing 9–17.

Johnson retained some hope that the team would get back on track. If the pitching held up; if Manush and Reynolds continued to produce; if the rest of the lineup picked up the slack; then the team might climb back into the pennant race. But those were a lot of ifs. Before the slide started with a doubleheader loss to the lowly St. Louis Browns, on June 12, the Senators had been in contention, running ahead of the A's and just behind the Yankees.

Still the Senators went into the Fourth of July matchup with the Yankees with some degree of optimism. The first half of the season was nearly over. Their rookie sensation was carrying the pitching load. A couple of wins against the Yankees would be a great boost to the Senators' hopes for the second half.

A crowd of seventeen thousand turned out to see the games in Griffith Stadium. Monte Weaver was matched against the Yankees' ace, Lefty Gomez, in the first game. Gomez came into the game with a record of 14-1 and an 11 game winning streak. The Yankees got off to an early lead. In the top of the first, Weaver surrendered consecutive singles to Earle Combs, Joe Sewell, and Babe Ruth. Ruth's single drove in Combs. Then Lou Gehrig doubled Sewell home and sent Ruth to third. After Weaver retired Tony Lazzeri, Bill Dickey singled-in Ruth.

The Yankees were glad to have Dickey back in the lineup. Dickey had missed several games with a minor injury. He had returned just the day before, in Boston, and was greeted rudely in a play at home plate. In the third inning center fielder Roy Johnson had doubled off George Pipgras. Sparky Olson followed with a single to right field, and when Babe Ruth charged the ball, Johnson rounded third and tried to score. Ruth's throw to the plate was nearly perfect, but the ball and Johnson arrived at the same instant. Johnson charged into Dickey, knocking the ball out of Dickey's glove. The ball rolled to the stands, while Dickey lay in the dirt momentarily stunned. One of Dickey's teeth had been knocked loose. To add insult to injury—quite literally, in this case—the official scorer gave Dickey an error for not holding onto the ball.

But Dickey was back behind the plate for the opening game in Washington. Lefty Gomez was in command and protected the 3-run lead through three innings, but in the fourth, Senators shortstop Joe Cronin hammered a pitch into the left field bleachers with Heinie Manush on base to make it a 1-run game. Weaver pitched solidly through the seventh inning, scattering 8 hits with mathematical precision and shutting down the Yankees' lineup. Neither team scored again until the bottom of the seventh.

Carl Reynolds singled off Gomez to start the rally. Wes Kingdom, playing on the occasion of his thirty-second birthday, also singled—one of the 11 hits he would collect in his short Major League career. Reynolds, the potential tying run, advanced to third base on Kingdom's hit. After Roy Spencer flied out, Walter Johnson sent a utility infielder named John Kerr up to the plate to bat for Monte Weaver.

Reynolds took a generous lead off third base, trying to distract Gomez. Dickey tried to pick him off, but the catcher's throw hit Reynolds, and the ball scooted toward the stands. Yankees third baseman Joe Sewell chased after the ball and retrieved it in time to make a throw to the plate.

It was a moment of déjà vu for Dickey. Sewell's throw—just like Ruth's throw the day before in Boston—arrived at the same time the runner did. Reynolds, a former football player, slammed into Dickey with a fierce body block. Reynolds was called safe. Reynolds rose from the dirt and turned to go back to his dugout. But Dickey took exception to the way Reynolds had run into him at home plate, climbed to his feet and followed him. When Reynolds turned around, Dickey threw a well-aimed right-handed punch that landed on Reynolds's jaw, breaking it in two places. As the two ballplayers scuffled on the ground and home plate umpire George Hildebrand tried to break it up, Wes Kingdom advanced to third base. When the dust settled, Hildebrand ejected Dickey. Reynolds was taken to the hospital.

When Kerr finally got a chance to complete his at-bat, he hit a sacrifice fly that scored Kingdom and gave the Senators the lead. Washington ended up winning the game, 5–3, putting an end to Gomez's winning streak.

In the second game, the Senators' bats came alive—perhaps fueled by their anger over the injury to Carl Reynolds. Washington jumped out to a 6–0 lead with Lloyd Brown on the mound. By the end of the sixth inning, the Senators had stretched the lead to 10–2. The final count was 12–6.

Despite allowing 6 runs, Brown pitched a complete game. Ruth homered—his twenty-third of the season—and drove in 2 more runs. At this point in the season, Ruth was on pace for 160 RBIs. But the hitting stars of the day were in the other dugout. Sam Rice had replaced Reynolds in the lineup and collected 4 hits. Manush added 3 hits, including a homer, and the Senators scored their 23 runs on 16 hits. The Senators were pleased with two solid wins, but they still had a lot of ground to make up.

The consolation for the Yankees was that they still had a comfortable 7½ games over the second-place Tigers and Athletics—and they were headed back to New York for a twenty-one game home stand.

The incident at home plate in the first game would prove costly to both the Yankees and the Senators. Immediately after the game, Washington Senators owner Clark Griffith fired off an angry telegram to American League president William Harridge. The telegram read:

"Witnessed today most atrocious act one ball player ever perpetrated on another when Catcher Dickey swung mighty blow on Reynolds when he was not looking and broke Reynolds's jaw. Am asking you impose maximum fine on Dickey and that he be suspended until Reynolds is able to return; also Dickey or New York Club shall pay Reynolds's hospital and doctor bills."[5]

For the second time in six weeks, Harridge was being asked to adjudicate a violent incident involving players and determine an appropriate punishment. It didn't take him long to make a decision. Harridge suspended Dickey for thirty days and fined him a thousand dollars. For the Senators, it appeared that Reynolds would be lost for the remainder of the season.

In the National League, the Boston Braves won 2 games from the Philadelphia Phillies, and the Cincinnati Reds beat the St. Louis Cardinals in the first game of a scheduled doubleheader. The second game was called on account of darkness, after 13 innings with the score tied at 3–3.

The Cubs were in Pittsburgh. The Pirates and Cubs had switched places, once again, at the top of the National League standings. Going into the twin bill, the Cubs trailed by half-a-game.

In the first game of the doubleheader, the Cubs produced 4 runs in the top of the first inning to stake Burleigh Grimes to the lead. The

Pirates came back with a run in the bottom of the inning and another in the second, but then, in the third inning, Grimes couldn't get anybody out. Charlie Root relieved. The Pirates put more men on base. By the end of the inning, six Pirates had crossed the plate, and the Pirates had an 8–4 lead. The Pirates were powered by Pie Traynor with 4 hits, Arky Vaughan with 3 singles, and Paul Waner, who had a single, a double, and a triple.

In the nightcap, Guy Bush got the starting assignment for the Cubs against Glenn Spencer. The Cubs took the early lead in the fourth on a 2-run homer by Kiki Cuyler, his second of the season, adding a third run in the sixth. The Pirates tied the score in the bottom of the sixth, but the Cubs came back to take the lead again with single runs in the seventh and eighth.

But Bush, who would give up 13 hits to the Pirates, couldn't hold this lead either. He gave up runs in the bottom of the eighth and ninth, forcing extra innings. Hornsby decided to stick with Bush, but in the bottom of the eleventh, the Pirates scored the winning run with 2 outs.

The Cubs' clubhouse was dejected. The Cubs had dropped, in a matter of just over twenty-four hours, from first place to third place. Improbably, the Boston Braves, thanks to their doubleheader sweep over the Phillies, now claimed second place.

Things got worse for the Cubs after the games. Reserve catcher Rollie Hemsley got into the spirit of the Fourth of July holiday and started lighting firecrackers. The celebration ended when one of the firecrackers blew up in Hemsley's face, scorching his eyebrows and damaging one of his eyes.

For Hornsby, that meant one less Cubs player who would be available for duty for the foreseeable future. It would be a somber train ride back to Chicago.

Although Major League Baseball action was complete, the nation continued to celebrate the Fourth of July holiday west of the Mississippi River.

In Reno, Nevada, 8,000 boxing fans watched Max Baer, a promising California heavyweight, win a twenty-round decision over King

Levinsky, the former fish peddler from Chicago who had defeated Jack Dempsey in Chicago Stadium in February. Less than two years later, Baer would capture the heavyweight title by knocking out the Italian giant, Primo Carnera, in the 11th round of a bout at Madison Square Garden Bowl, in Long Island City. Levinsky, who retired in 1939, fought all of the top contenders in the heavyweight division but never earned a title fight for himself. Still, in the fifteen months prior to the Baer fight, the gate receipts at his fights totaled a quarter of a million dollars.[6] It is probable, based on what percentage of the gate he earned, that he was the highest-paid athlete in Chicago.[7]

The last flickers of America's Fourth of July celebrations in 1932 occurred on the West Coast. Appropriately enough, the day was celebrated at baseball parks. Just as the day had started with the tragedy at a baseball field in Montana, the day ended with a different kind of disaster after the conclusion of a baseball game.

In Seattle, Washington, just a few hours after the Seattle Indians of the Pacific Coast League lost a doubleheader to the San Francisco Mission Reds, the baseball park burned to the ground. Dugdale Park, named for D. E. Dugdale, the father of Seattle baseball, was an old-style park with a wooden grandstand and high board fences. The grandstand caught fire first, and then the fire roared through the bleachers and torched the outfield fences. The fire was first reported just after midnight, but firefighters arrived too late to save the park. The cause of the blaze was unclear, though it was eventually designated an accident by the authorities. Some local residents speculated that the fire started in an oil drum or that maybe a faulty hot water heater spit out the first spark. Fans had noticed boys in the grandstand throwing firecrackers at each other at the end of the game as the crowd cleared out, suggesting that perhaps a smoldering ash from the firecrackers had ignited the stands.[8]

The cause of the fire hardly mattered. By morning, the old park was a pile of rubble, nothing but gray smoke, twisted metal piping, and scorched lumber.

14

Double X

In some years the first half of the baseball season resembles a meandering prelude to the spectacle of a hot summer pennant race. But not so in 1932. The first half had been as exciting and dramatic as any half-season in baseball history: McGraw's retirement; Gehrig's four-homer game; the Moriarty-White Sox fracas; the Dickey-Reynolds fight; the debut season of talented and colorful rookie pitchers; the return to dominance of the New York Yankees; the seven-team pileup of teams battling for the National League pennant; and, of course, Babe Ruth.

Although some fans clung to the fanciful notion that teams holding first place on the Fourth of July were bound to meet in the World Series—that would mean a Yankees-versus-Pirates fall classic—John Kiernan, writing in the *New York Times*, disputed the myth: "The theory that the ball clubs leading the major leagues on the Fourth of July are due to meet in the world's series has been badly dented from time to time. The classic clout at the ancient theory, of course, was the victory of the Braves in 1914. That team was in last place on the Fourth of July and swept to four straight over the great Athletics in the world's series in October."[1]

Kiernan's reasoning didn't stop fans from speculating. In actuality, due to scheduling and rainouts, only two teams—the Philadelphia Phillies and the Cincinnati Reds—had completed half of their games. But on the morning of July 5—a rest day for most teams, with only 2 single games to be played—baseball fans throughout the nation took a long look at the standings in their morning newspapers and assessed their team's chances of making it to the World Series.

The pennant race in the National League was a tossup. Seven teams—all but the struggling Cincinnati Reds—were still solid contenders. While the Pirates clung to a game-and-a-half lead over the Cubs, the seventh place Brooklyn Dodgers were only 5½ games out of first. Even the last-place Reds were close enough to be contenders if they had a good second half.

The second half of the season would see any number of changes in the standings. But on the morning of July 5, the National League standings looked like this:

Table 2. National League Standings, July 5, 1914

Team	Wins	Losses	Percentage	Games Behind
Pittsburgh	37	29	.561	———
Boston	39	34	.534	1.5
Chicago	37	34	.521	2.5
Philadelphia	39	38	.506	3.5
St. Louis	35	35	.500	4.0
New York	32	34	.485	5.0
Brooklyn	35	38	.479	5.5
Cincinnati	34	46	.425	10.0

The American League standings had a very different look. One team—the New York Yankees—clearly stood out. The two teams tied for second—the Detroit Tigers and the preseason favorite Philadelphia Athletics were 7½ games behind the first-place Yankees. By comparison, in the National League, the seventh-place Dodgers trailed the first–place Pirates by only 5½ games.

On July 5, each of the top five teams in the American League had more wins than the league-leading Pirates of the National League.

Table 3. American League Standings, July 5, 1914

Team	Wins	Losses	Percentage	Games Behind
New York	50	23	.685	——
Detroit	41	29	.586	7.5
Philadelphia	43	31	.581	7.5
Washington	40	34	.541	10.5
Cleveland	39	34	.534	11.0
St. Louis	35	36	.493	14.0
Chicago	26	44	.371	22.5
Boston	14	57	.197	35.0

Joe McCarthy, now forty-five years old and in his second season as manager of the Yankees, had to be pleased with his team's performance in the first half of the season. He also must have been intrigued that his former employer, the Chicago Cubs, was in the mix of National League teams with a chance to make it to the fall classic.

A World Series between Hornsby's Cubs and McCarthy's Yankees would have been an appealing matchup, for both franchises and both managers. For Hornsby, it would be a chance to win a second World Series as manager over a team led by Babe Ruth. For McCarthy, it would be an opportunity to win his first world championship by beating the Cubs.

But McCarthy had his concerns. The loss of Bill Dickey was a significant blow. Dickey had been one of the most productive Yankees during the first half of the season, batting .323 with 11 doubles and 55 RBIs. There were other potential issues: an aging Babe Ruth, who might need to be rested in late summer in order to preserve his energies for the postseason; two young starting pitchers—Gomez and Allen—

who would be under more scrutiny and stress, if the race tightened in August and September; and the lack of production from the shortstop position, a persistent problem for the club over the past few years.[2]

The bigger worry, however, was what kind of a move the Philadelphia Athletics might make in the second half of the season, with their lineup of power hitters and a pitching staff led by Lefty Grove. They were too strong a team to discount.

Grove was 12–3 with a 1.89 earned run average through the first half of the season, and he'd beaten the Yankees head-to-head three times in May and June. Fortunately, the Yankees only had to face the A's five more times. The rest of the A's pitching staff had been mediocre, performing far below what was expected of them. Rube Walberg and Roy Mahaffey were a combined 11–16, giving up an average of 5 earned runs per nine innings. George Earnshaw's record was a solid 13-6, but he'd been allowing almost 5 runs a game, too.

No matter what the pitching staff was doing, the team was scoring runs. Al Simmons was productive with 16 homers and 67 runs batted in, and although Mickey Cochrane, Mule Haas, and Jimmie Dykes were having subpar years—batting in the .260s and .270s—the slack was picked up by Jimmie Foxx who, at age twenty-four, had emerged as the best power hitter in the Major Leagues.

Without question, the hitting star of the first half of the 1932 season was Jimmie Foxx, nicknamed "Double X," or simply, "The Beast."

Thorough all of April and May, and into early June, Foxx's batting average was above .400. On June 25, he was on pace for 68 home runs. As late as July 1, Foxx was still hitting .388. On July 5, Foxx was still batting a hefty .380 with an OBP of .476 and a slugging average of .785. He had knocked in 89 runs with 12 doubles, 7 triples, and 29 home runs. Although Foxx had not homered in the last eleven days, he was still on pace to hit 60 home runs for the season.

McCarthy was well aware of how a power hitter could carry a club. McCarthy, after all, had a front row seat on the Cubs' bench the year that Hack Wilson slammed 56 home runs and propelled the 1929 Cubs into the World Series. McCarthy had a couple of pretty fair hitters in his own lineup, but neither Ruth nor Gehrig was going to keep pace with the A's slugger in 1932.

From the beginning, Foxx—born James Emory Foxx on a tenant farm in rural Maryland, in October 1907—was a natural athlete. Working alongside his father on the farm, he developed stamina and a muscular build. By his teens, he was playing sports. He was strong, and he was fast. His father, Dell, a talented town team baseball player, encouraged Foxx to take up baseball, but Foxx also competed in basketball, soccer, and track.[3]

At the age of sixteen, after three seasons of high school baseball, Foxx showed up at a Minor League tryout; he came straight from the farm dressed in overalls. The manager of the Easton team—a club in the Eastern Shore League—happened to be John Franklin "Home Run" Baker, just two years removed from the Majors, where he had acquired his nickname by leading the American League in home runs four consecutive years.[4]

Home Run Baker knew something about power hitting, and he spotted the potential in the high school prospect. Foxx was offered a contract to play for Easton during the summer. In July the Philadelphia A's purchased the rights to his contract. He played credibly for Easton—his position at the time was catcher—and in the fall, he returned to Sudlersville to begin his senior year of high school, but he dropped out in February to join the A's for spring training.

Foxx showed up in training camp as a raw seventeen-year-old with unlimited potential. He got only 9 at-bats with the A's that season—collecting 6 hits, but no homers—and spent most of the season in the Minor Leagues, honing his skills and preparing himself for the Majors. In 1926 and 1927 Foxx managed to earn a place on the Major League roster, but he saw little playing time on a team that had established Mickey Cochrane—four years older than Foxx—as its regular catcher. But Foxx was gifted athletically and learned to play first base, third base, and the outfield.

146

In 1928 Foxx—at the age of twenty—got to the plate for 400 at-bats. He played 20 games at catcher, 30 games at first base, and 61 games at third base. Like Babe Ruth a decade earlier, he was too valuable as a hitter not to be in the lineup almost every day, so Connie Mack had to find a place for him to play regularly.

A year later, Jimmie Foxx became the A's regular first baseman on the first of the three consecutive World Series championship teams. In those three seasons Foxx hit exactly 100 home runs, drove in 393 runs, and batted .327. He finished in the top five of the American League in each of those seasons in home runs and slugging average, behind Ruth, Gehrig, and his own teammate, Al Simmons.

His exploits attracted attention—and so did he. He was handsome and strong and well spoken. He had bright blue eyes, dark hair, dimples, and an engaging smile. His fingernails were carefully trimmed and manicured. He cut off the sleeves of his uniform to display his impressive biceps.[5]

When the coiled power of his swing was unleashed and he made full contact, his home runs had both impressive arc and astounding distance. But what most captivated observers around the league was not just the frequency of his home runs, or the distance they traveled, but the actual sound of the ball coming off his bat. Like Ruth, players noted that the collision of Foxx's bat with a pitched ball generated a different kind of sound—a vibration, a crack—that was unlike what other players could produce.

At the beginning of the 1932 season, Foxx made a modest change in his approach. He switched to a lighter bat with a thinner handle, hoping that he could generate more bat speed and power.[6] He got off to a rousing start, homering in 4 of his first 5 games—2 homers against the Yankees; 2 more against the Senators. His home run off Lefty Gomez at Yankee Stadium on opening day flew past the flagpole in center field, landing an estimated 468 feet from home plate. By the end of May, he had 17 homers and was batting .417. Though his team struggled to keep pace with the league-leading Yankees, Foxx provided the punch in the batting order that kept the A's in the pennant race.

In late June, the A's had played a 2-game weekend series at Yankee Stadium. At the time, the A's were tied for second place with the surprising Detroit Tigers, 7½ games out of first. The first game of the series was played on a Saturday afternoon before a sparse crowd. Roy Mahaffey started for the A's against Lefty Gomez of the Yankees, the ace of the Yankees' pitching staff. Gomez came into the game with a record of 13-1 and an ERA of 3.14.

The Yankees scored early in the first inning on a 2-run homer by Lou Gehrig and added 2 more runs to build a 4–0 lead going into the top of the fourth inning. Gomez had not yet allowed a hit. After walks to little-used backup catchers Johnnie Heving and Al Simmons, Gomez again faced Jimmie Foxx.

Gomez respected Foxx's bat—he had given up Foxx's mammoth home run on opening day—but with runners on base, he couldn't afford to pitch around him. Once again, Foxx connected and sent a ball soaring skyward. The ball landed in an empty seat in the upper deck in left center field. If it had traveled a slightly different trajectory, more toward center, observers felt it might have gone out of the stadium. Gomez later remarked that Foxx's home run that day "broke seats in the third deck at Yankee Stadium. You can't walk that far in an hour and a half."[7] To mark the spot, a double X was painted on the seat where Foxx's shot came to rest. The double X was retained through the years, until Yankee Stadium was renovated in the 1970s.[8]

Joe McCarthy had seen Foxx's exploits. If the Yankees manager was going to worry about something outside of his clubhouse—outside his control—it would likely be Jimmie Foxx. What Foxx might be able to do in the second half of the season—and how he might inspire or carry his team on his back—was anybody's guess.

1. Before his prowess as a hitter was recognized, Babe Ruth was the best left-handed pitcher in baseball, posting a career record of 94-46 and an ERA of 2.28.
He completed 107 of his 148 starts in the Major Leagues. Credit: Francis P. Burke Collection, Wikimedia Commons.

2. (*above*) Woody English was a solid contributor to the Cubs for most of a decade and became team captain in 1932 when Charlie Grimm replaced Rogers Hornsby as manager. Though not a power hitter, English had a knack for getting on base via both hits and walks. National Baseball Hall of Fame and Museum, Cooperstown NY.

3. (*left*) Jimmie Foxx emerged in 1932 as baseball's most dangerous hitter, challenging Babe Ruth's single-season home run record. He captivated fans with both his on-field performance and his good looks. National Baseball Hall of Fame and Museum, Cooperstown NY.

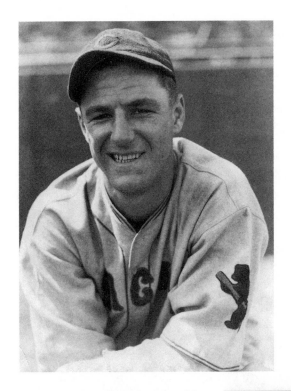

4. (*above*) Billy Jurges had an eventful 1932 season—barely making the team in spring training, getting shot by his jilted girlfriend in July, and coming back to play a key role in the Cubs' pennant drive. National Baseball Hall of Fame and Museum, Cooperstown NY.

5. (*right*) A much-traveled infielder, Mark Koenig played for five Major League teams and enjoyed important roles on the 1927–1928 Yankees and the 1932 Cubs. He was at the center of the dispute that precipitated Babe Ruth's called shot in the 1932 World Series. National Baseball Hall of Fame and Museum, Cooperstown NY.

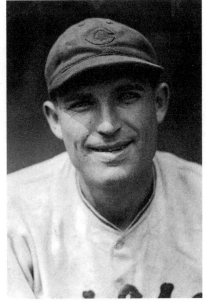

6. Described by Ruth biographer Leigh Montville as "an odd, foul-mouthed little man, an ego-driven, tobacco-chewing puritan with electric white hair shooting out of his head, a hanging judge with the wrath of God carved across his face," Judge Kenesaw Mountain Landis was a fierce but fair arbiter of the rules of baseball during his twenty-four years as the game's commissioner and ultimate authority. National Baseball Hall of Fame and Museum, Cooperstown NY.

7. Manager Joe McCarthy (*center*) won his first world championship in 1932, thanks to the power hitting of Babe Ruth and Lou Gehrig, who combined for 75 home runs and 288 runs batted in. National Baseball Hall of Fame and Museum, Cooperstown NY.

8. (*left*) George Moriarty was a man of multiple talents. As a player he was known for his ability to steal home and a willingness to get into fights. After his playing days ended, he managed and umpired in the American League for a total of twenty three seasons. Outside of baseball, Moriarty was an accomplished poet and lyricist. National Baseball Hall of Fame and Museum, Cooperstown NY.

9. (*below*) Charlie Root was the sturdy backbone of the Cubs' pitching rotation for sixteen years, posting a record of 201-160 and pitching more than 3,000 innings. His legacy is defined more by his career accomplishments than by his famous confrontation with Babe Ruth in the 1932 World Series. National Baseball Hall of Fame and Museum, Cooperstown NY.

10. If not for a coal mining accident that required amputation of four toes, Red Ruffing might have made it to the Major Leagues as an outfielder. He was an excellent hitter and often used as a pinch hitter, but he is best remembered as a pitcher who won 274 regular-season games and appeared in seven World Series. National Baseball Hall of Fame and Museum, Cooperstown NY.

11. (*top*) Lon Warneke emerged in 1932 as the best pitcher on a talented Cubs pitching staff. His 22 wins and 2.37 ERA were the best in the National League. After a fifteen-year Major League career, Warneke umpired for seven years in the Major Leagues then returned to his native state of Arkansas, where he ran for and was elected county judge. National Baseball Hall of Fame and Museum, Cooperstown NY.

12. (*bottom*) One of the smartest men to ever play Major League Baseball, Monte Weaver had graduated from the University of Virginia with a master's degree in mathematics before deciding on professional baseball as a career. In his rookie season of 1932, he had a record of 22-10. National Baseball Hall of Fame and Museum, Cooperstown NY.

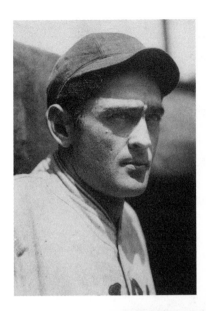

13. A shy country boy from the Deep South, Guy Bush was nicknamed "The Mississippi Mudcat." In 1932 he was the principal antagonist during Babe Ruth's called shot at bat in Game Three of the World Series. Bush is also linked to Ruth by the fact that he surrendered Ruth's last home run in 1935. National Baseball Hall of Fame and Museum, Cooperstown NY.

14. (*below*) Kiki Cuyler was one of the outstanding outfielders of his generation, with a lifetime batting average of .321. He played on World Series teams with both the Pittsburgh Pirates and the Chicago Cubs. National Baseball Hall of Fame and Museum, Cooperstown NY.

15. The loquacious and boastful Dizzy Dean created headaches for his owners and managers, but no one denied his skill on the mound. From 1932 through 1936, he won 120 games, lost only 65, and led the National League in complete games four years in a row. He was a fan favorite from his first day in the Majors to his last. National Baseball Hall of Fame and Museum, Cooperstown NY.

16. Bill Dickey was acknowledged as one of the game's best catchers, both for his offensive and defensive skills. Bob Feller called him "the best all-around catcher of them all." Although he was suspended for a month in 1932, he was a key contributor to the Yankees' success in that season. National Baseball Hall of Fame and Museum, Cooperstown NY.

17. Charles Ireland was the eighth warden of the Iowa Men's Reformatory
in Anamosa, Iowa, serving in that capacity from January 1, 1932, until his
death on June 27, 1933. A compassionate and outgoing man—and a loyal
Cubs fan—Ireland was harshly criticized in the media for taking two prison
inmates to World Series games in Chicago, in October 1932. Credit: Steve
Wendl and the Anamosa State Penitentiary Prison History Website.

18. The Iowa Men's Reformatory baseball team was virtually unbeatable during the 1932 season. Pictured here in front of the assistant warden's house, the team poses with fellow inmate and longtime manager, Harry "Snap" Hortman. Credit: Steve Wendl and the Anamosa State Penitentiary Prison History Website.

19. Violet Popovich was a sensation in Chicago during the summer of 1932. She wore this stunning outfit—white crepe dress with red trim, white hat, red shoes—to her July 15 court appearance before Judge John Sbarbaro. Credit: Bill Hageman. From the private collection of Jack Bales.

20. Known for a powerful, level swing, Rogers Hornsby was able to drive the ball to all fields. He hit over .400 three times and finished his career with a .358 batting average. For a decade he was the most feared hitter in the National League. He was less successful as a manager. Wikimedia Commons.

21. Throughout his long career, Babe Ruth sustained major and minor injuries, but demonstrated a remarkable capacity for recovery. On July 5, 1924, Ruth was knocked out after running into a concrete wall in Griffith Stadium. Trainers revived him, and he stayed in the game. National Photo Company Collection (Library of Congress).

22. In the spring of 1948, Babe Ruth donated the original manuscript of his autobiography, *The Babe Ruth Story*, to Yale University. In a ceremony at Yale Field, Ruth handed the manuscript to the captain and first baseman of the Yale Bulldogs baseball team—George H. W. Bush. Ruth died ten weeks later. Credit: National Archives.

15

Wicked Chicago

On the afternoon that Billy Jurges was shot in the Hotel Carlos, the Cubs were scheduled to play a single game against the Philadelphia Phillies. That the shooting took place in Chicago was not a surprise. That the scene of the crime was the Hotel Carlos was also not a surprise.

Over the years, Cubs players regularly rented rooms in the Hotel Carlos, located within easy walking distance of the ballpark and various night spots. In addition to Jurges, Kiki Cuyler and reserve outfielder Marv Gudat had rooms at the hotel for the 1932 season. Cuyler had been a resident for several years. In the past, Riggs Stevenson and Hack Wilson had lived in the building. Hack was well-known at the various watering holes in the neighborhood, though his preferred place to drink was an establishment in Cicero called the Hole in the Wall, which was also a favorite hangout for Al Capone and his crowd.

The hotel had been the scene of an earlier tragedy involving a Cubs player. In the early morning hours of May 28, 1930, Hal Carlson, the Cubs' pitcher who was due to start that day's game, suffered a stomach hemorrhage and died.[1] Carlson had been in poor health for years. As a machine gunner in World War I, he had been gassed in combat and suffered recurring health problems throughout his Major League career. When Carlson fell ill, shortly after midnight, he thought he was suffering from stomach ulcers. He called Ed Froelich, the Cubs' clubhouse attendant who lived in the hotel. Froelich summoned three Cubs players who also lived in the building: Kiki Cuyler, Riggs Stevenson, and Cliff Heathcote. When Carlson's condition worsened, Froelich

149

called the Cubs' team physician, John Davis, but he arrived too late to do anything to save Carlson.[2]

In contrast to Carlson's death in the middle of the night, the shooting of Billy Jurges occurred in broad daylight, just hours before the scheduled game with the Phillies. For Chicagoans—and Cubs fans in the Midwest—it was a startling development in the midst of a pennant race.

From its beginning, Chicago had been a rough and charming town, a city of big ambitions where disputes were sometimes settled in episodes of violence. In its early days it was populated mostly by fur traders, hard drinkers, adventurers, speculators, and various risk takers. The city took pride in its authenticity and resilience. Long hard winters required men and women who could withstand adversity. After the Great Chicago Fire of 1871 destroyed much of the city, including more than seventeen thousand buildings, the city rebuilt and perservered. Over the years, a distinctive skyline evolved and the city sprawled west and south away from the southern end of Lake Michigan.

In the first three decades of the twentieth century, Chicago earned a reputation for its durability and tolerance of illicit behavior. Before the city became known for its speakeasies and the murderous reign of Al Capone, it was famous for the Everleigh Club, the classiest and most successful brothel in Chicago's rich history.

The club was owned and operated by two sisters, Minna and Ada Everleigh, who grew up in a wealthy Virginia family, journeyed west as aspiring actresses, and later invested their inheritance in a brothel in Omaha. A few years later, they moved their business to Chicago, bought a three-story double townhouse at 2131–2133 South Dearborn Street, and created a "men's club" that featured crystal chandeliers, gold spittoons, a gold piano, elaborately decorated sitting rooms, a library, a fancy dining room with a gourmet menu, and thirty boudoirs with mirrored ceilings and brass beds. The sisters opened the Everleigh Club to clients on February 1, 1900.[3]

When the Everleighs retired and left town in 1911—to travel in Europe—Chicago was said to have more than a thousand brothels and at least five thousand full-time prostitutes. No one knows how many other young women were working part time as independent contractors.

Mayor Carter Harrison and other reformers had tried their best to clean up the town and restore at least a semblance of order and morality, but the city quickly returned to its old ways. Shortly after World War I ended, Prohibition had become the defining reality of the city. For more than a decade Chicago endured political corruption, hustlers, gangsters, resistance to the rule of law, and the exuberance of the Roaring Twenties. Once again, Chicago became known for—and to a degree, pleased by—its reputation as a city devoted to pleasure and instant gratification.

Saul Bellow, a Chicago writer of a later era, wryly noted that "The people of Chicago are very proud of their wickedness.[4]

By 1932 the Depression had sapped some of the city's strength and energy. That year an estimated 660,000 Chicagoans were jobless and seeking work.[5] Families without an income were evicted from apartments and lived on the street. Because neither the federal government nor the state government contributed resources to the relief effort, the city of Chicago dipped into its coffers and allocated $2.5 million for emergency relief aid.[6] But people who tried to survive on public assistance received barely enough to live on.

One positive for the city: criminal activity had declined. The corrupt ex-mayor, Bill Thompson, had been voted out of office and replaced by Anton Cermak. Al Capone was in jail, though he was not exactly out of business yet. Since his conviction on tax evasion charges in October 1931 and while his case went through the federal courts on appeal, Capone had the luxury of living in an over-sized cell on the fifth floor of the hospital ward of the Cook County jail. He shared his cell with his personal bodyguard. Capone's jailers, especially Warden David Moneypenny, made every effort to make sure he was comfortable. Capone was allowed a comfortable mattress, a radio, unrestricted visitation rights, and access to a phone so that he could be in touch with family, friends, and business associates. He used the phone to call his bookies and make bets on horse races. The radio allowed him to listen to broadcasts of the Cubs' games. His wife delivered hot meals to the jail. Capone's mother sent him a Thanksgiving dinner. On one occasion, Capone ordered cake and ice cream to be delivered from a local restaurant for himself and his fellow inmates.[7]

For more than six months, Capone was allowed to use his cell as an executive office.[8] Capone's visitors included other mobsters, including his mentor, Johnny Torrio. New York gangsters Lucky Luciano and Dutch Schultz also paid social calls. Capone settled a dispute between Luciano and Schultz, holding the meeting in the jail's death chamber. Capone presided over the meeting while sitting in the electric chair.[9]

But Capone's pleasure in following the early season exploits of the 1932 Cubs, as well as his enjoyment of the other amenities provided by his friends in high places, came to an end in early May. When his legal appeal reached the United States Supreme Court and was turned down without comment, Capone was ordered to report to the federal penitentiary in Atlanta, Georgia.[10] On May 3, a team of federal agents, including Eliot Ness, arrived at Cook County Jail to transfer Capone to Atlanta. Capone dressed for the occasion: silk underwear, tailored suit, fedora; he carried a rosary and $231 in cash.[11] The security detail took every precaution to ensure that there would be no incidents. They escorted Capone out of town and transported him by train to Atlanta.

Capone still had hopes that his lawyers might secure his release or get his sentence reduced, but he had no choice but to adjust to prison life. He cobbled shoes as his work assignment. A few weeks after arriving at the federal penitentiary, he organized a prison baseball team and installed himself as first baseman.[12] Unfortunately, Capone could neither hit nor field. Playing the game frustrated him. So he switched to tennis as his recreational sport of choice.[13]

Capone's departure from Chicago didn't mean that the city had been tamed or that illicit socializing had significantly diminished. There were an ample number of speakeasies in operation—though still illegal—as well as legal jazz clubs and other places for social gathering.

On the north side of Chicago, near Wrigley Field and in the neighborhoods where many of the Cubs' players lived, a vibrant nightlife thrived. Since Major League baseball games were played during the day, ball players had many free nighttime hours. That included both the eligible bachelors, as well as the married players, especially those who had come to Chicago for the season and left their families behind.

The Green Mill at 4800 North Broadway, which had been one of Al Capone's favorite hangouts, was just a twenty minute walk from Wrigley Field. Machine Gun Jack McGurn, one of Capone's cronies, served as manager of the Green Mill.[14] When Capone visited, he preferred to sit at a table near the back where he could watch the two doors and be the first to see whoever happened to enter the establishment.

One of Capone's rivals, Bugs Moran, co-owned the Sheridan Wave Club on Waveland Avenue with his partner, Potatoes Kaufman. The club was reputed to operate the best casino in town and admission was by invitation only. Even closer was Marigold Gardens, a former beer garden that was located just two blocks from the Hotel Carlos. It was a legitimate business that served food and featured various kinds of entertainment. Popular jazz singer Ruth Ettig—married to a hoodlum named Moe Snyder—performed regularly on the outdoor stage, and sports fans frequented the club to watch prize fights.

In addition to organized crime, there was an abundance of unorganized crime in Chicago. It was a great era for young hustlers who wanted to mingle with famous athletes and make a quick buck, here or there, with a scheme. One of those young hustlers was a stocky young man with a receding hairline. His name was Sparky Rubenstein.

Rubenstein was twenty-one years old in the summer of 1932. He had grown up on the west side of the city, in the Maxwell Street neighborhood, near where King Levinsky and his sister, Leaping Lena, had been raised. As a youth, Rubenstein got in various scraps: juvenile delinquency, truancy, fist fights. He dropped out of school around the age of sixteen. By his late teens, he was making a living on the streets, selling racing tip sheets and scalping tickets to athletic events.

He had an interest in sports and liked being around athletes. He was hired by the Cubs to sell scorecards outside Wrigley Field.[15] At a downtown gym, he met an aspiring boxer named Dov-Ber Rosofsky, who later changed his name to Barney Ross. Ross's early career as a prizefighter was bankrolled by Al Capone, who claimed to have made a great deal of money betting on Ross's fights.[16]

Eventually the career paths of Rubenstein and Ross diverged. The fighter went on to become one of the leading lightweight fighters in his sport. Rubenstein moved to Dallas, Texas, where he opened a nightclub and changed his name to Jack Ruby.

At night, Cubs players who lived near Wrigley Field could find diversion and entertainment at any number of clubs or speakeasies within walking distance of the ballpark. As professional athletes, they had money in their pockets. It was inevitable that their social lives would become entwined with the lives of the Chicagoans who rooted for them.

And it was hardly surprising that these ballplayers—easily recognized, idolized by fans—would sometimes find themselves entangled in relationships with adoring female fans.[17]

One of these fans was Violet Popovich, the young woman who had fallen in love with Billy Jurges.

Born and raised in Chicago, Popovich was an aspiring showgirl who had survived a difficult childhood and was trying to make a name for herself as an entertainer.[18] She was the oldest of her four siblings; her brothers, Michael, Milos, and Marco, had been born at two-year intervals after Violet. The Popovich children grew up in what can only be described as an extremely dysfunctional family. Less than four weeks after Violet was born, Violet's father beat her mother so severely that she required medical attention for numerous bruises and two black eyes. Mirko Popovich—known as Mike—had a good job as the night electrician at the Insurance Exchange Building on Jackson Boulevard, but he had a nasty temper and a gambling habit that put a strain on the family finances. For recreation he liked to play poker and shoot craps. Sometimes he won big, but usually he lost more than he won. Violet's mother, Margaret, endured Mirko's moods and beatings, but left him several times, only to return and suffer more abuse. In May of 1919 Margaret filed for divorce, charging "extreme and repeated cruelty." Violet, at the age of eight, was forced to testify in the divorce proceedings, and the divorce was granted in March 1920.

Since Margaret was unable to provide a home or support, the Circuit Court of Cook County ordered the Popovich children to be placed in the Uhlich Orphan's Asylum, at 2014 Burling Street. Mirko was required to pay alimony to Margaret and child support to the Uhlich facility. For nearly a decade, the children bounced in and out of the Uhlich home, sometimes living with their father, who took them to work with him and at night put them to bed on cots in the basement of the Insurance Exchange Building. Despite steady work, Mirko was frequently delinquent on his support payments, necessitating repeated court appearances. When Violet was older, she moved back in with her mother, and for a while they lived together under her mother's maiden name as Margaret and Violet Heindl.

In 1922 Mirko remarried, wooing and winning a female janitor named Anna Sopcak, who worked in the Insurance Exchange Building with him. Anna, a German immigrant and recent widow, could not read or write in English, but she had inherited nearly six thousand dollars from her dead husband, which made her an especially appealing marriage candidate. She turned the money over to Mirko, who promptly used the funds to purchase a six-flat duplex apartment building at 538–540 Belden. Surprisingly, this turned out to be a successful investment, though he continued to be delinquent on alimony and support payments.

One of Anna's daughters, known professionally as Betty Subject, befriended Violet when she was a teenager and got her involved in show business. Betty was nearly a decade older than Violet and had been in several successful productions, playing the lead in a Broadway show titled *September Morn*, but Betty's main talent seemed to be the capacity to fall in love. By the age of twenty-seven, she had been engaged to at least five men and wed four times, including a brief marriage to Harold Powell, the musical arranger of *September Morn*.

Likely with Betty's help, Popovich landed a small role in a traveling revue called *Vanities* that was produced on Broadway by Earl Carroll. Popovich took a stage name and began calling herself Violet Valli. She was introduced to the whirl of big city social life, which included parties with famous people, including baseball players. One of the other young actresses playing in *Vanities* happened to be Violet Arnold, who was engaged to Bill Dickey, the catcher for the New York Yankees.

Popovich reportedly started dating baseball players, mostly National Leaguers, and at a party in 1931, she met Billy Jurges, a native of Brooklyn who had played Minor League ball in Reading, Pennsylvania and was just beginning his Major League career with the Chicago Cubs. A spark was lit. The following year, Popovich was back in Chicago, living with her mother on North LaSalle Street and working as a cashier in a cigar store.

After all she had gone through in her life—the poverty and violence of her early childhood, the instability and breakup of her family, and her limited success as a showgirl—Violet thought she had found something solid and lasting in her relationship with Billy. He was young and attractive and fun to be around. He had a good future, and not so incidentally, he was in the public eye, a baseball player whose name appeared in the sports pages of the daily newspapers. Thousands of loyal fans read the box scores or listened to the games on the radio. Being with Billy satisfied Violet's desire for stability and respectability.

But the relationship soured. Violet learned that friends and teammates of Billy had warned him to stay away from her, and Billy had told her that he wanted to break up. When the Cubs were in New York—during the series with the Dodgers, when Jurges got in a fight with

Mickey Finn—Violet had called Billy at his parents' house in Brooklyn, and they had argued on the phone.

The day before the Cubs were to return to town and Billy would be back in room 509 at the Hotel Carlos, Violet rented her own room at the hotel. Her plan was to meet Billy on the morning of July 6 and plead with him to continue the relationship.

That morning Violet sat at a desk in her room on the second floor of the Hotel Carlos, drinking gin and thinking about murder. She took out a piece of paper and addressed a letter to her brother Mike, who worked at a local YMCA. The note read:

Dear Mike,

I have just a few minutes of waiting before I see Billy so I'll write and try to explain everything. I know you'll understand.

To me, life without Billy isn't worth living, but why should I leave this earth alone. I'm going to take Billy with me. We are getting along famously, just as everything should go, but a few people like Ki-Ki Cuyler and Lew Steadman forgot there might be anything fine and beautiful in our love and dragged it in the mud. I know what I'm doing is best for me and I hate to do it. . . . but ? ? ?

My last wish is that you, mother, and the boys go to California and enjoy life to the greatest extent, and remember father once in a while. I can't write any more. I'm so nervous. I love all of you.

Violet[19]

Violet placed the letter on her desk. She pushed a .25 caliber handgun into her purse and walked out of the room. The door clicked shut behind her.

She called Jurges from a phone in the lobby and said she wanted to talk to him. Jurges was nonchalant. He said, "C'mon up."

Before Violet got to Jurges's room, she stopped at Cuyler's room and knocked. Cuyler didn't answer the door. He had probably already walked to the ballpark for that afternoon's game. But she had a key to the room. She opened the door and entered the room. She wrote out a note and taped it to Cuyler's mirror. It said, "I'm going to kill you."[20]

By the time Violet got to room 509, she was agitated, but the gin had steadied her nerves. She wanted to give Jurges one more chance, hoping he would reconsider. She took a deep breath and knocked. Jurges opened the door and let her in.

They had a brief conversation. She told Jurges that she didn't want to break up. Years later, Jurges recalled how he had responded to Violet. "I'm not going to go out on any more dates," he said. "We've got a chance to win the pennant. I've got to get my rest."

Violet asked for a glass of water. Jurges went to the bathroom, filled a glass, and brought it back to her.

At that point, Violet pulled the gun from her purse and pointed it at her head. Jurges responded immediately, lunging for the gun, and trying to wrestle it out of her hands. They struggled for control of the weapon. Jurges recalled three shots: the first ripped into his right side, colliding with a rib as it passed through his body. Another shot hit him in the hip—he must have turned sideways once the shooting started—and the third shot went through the palm of his left hand as he finally grabbed the gun away from Violet.

Violet ran out of the room. Jurges stumbled backwards, collapsed on his bed, bleeding and trying to assess his wounds. There was a lot of blood. A terrifying thought rushed through Jurges's mind: *I'm going to die.*

Marv Gudat was in the lobby of the Hotel Carlos when he heard three sharp explosions coming from the vicinity of Jurges's room. Gudat was reminded of the Fourth of July. His first thought: Jurges is setting off firecrackers. Gudat rushed up the stairs. The door to 509 was ajar. Jurges was in the hallway, holding his side. He said, "Get a doctor!"

Someone called for help. Soon an ambulance screeched to a halt outside. A doctor arrived and took the elevator to the fifth floor and proceeded to Jurges's room. He took a quick look at the blood and the wound and came to the same bleak conclusion that Billy had: the man was probably dying. The doctor thought Jurges might die within half an hour. He told the wounded man, "You've got it bad."

Police officers arrived on the scene and located Violet, who had returned to her room. She had suffered only a slight wound to her hand. The half-empty bottle of gin and suicide note rested on the table in her room. When police searched the room, they also found a black and white photo of Popovich: a photograph showing her with lush black hair and a broad smile.

Moments later, Dr. John Davis, the Cubs' trainer, appeared and went to Jurges's room. Davis had a different impression of the severity of Jurges's wounds. "You'll live," Davis said. After treating Jurges, Davis also looked at Violet's wounds. Then the police and ambulance crew escorted the wounded lovers into the back of the vehicle. Sirens screamed. The ambulance raced to Illinois Masonic Hospital.

A few hours later, Popovich was transferred to Bridewell Hospital, where she received medical treatment for her wounds. Then she was moved to the Cook County jail.

The news of the shooting spread by word of mouth. A man on the street told Woody English about it as English walked to the ballpark from his hotel a few blocks from the Hotel Carlos. When John Davis got to the ballpark, he assured Hornsby and Jurges's teammates that the shortstop would recover from his wounds.

It was a warm mid-summer afternoon in Chicago, a perfect day for baseball. A few indifferent clouds drifted over Wrigley Field. The stands were partially filled with about ten thousand paying customers scattered throughout the park.

Hornsby's thoughts turned to his lineup. If there had been one unexpected bright spot to the season, it was the superb and reliable defensive play of Jurges and Herman at short and second. Since the first of June, Jurges had been hitting .296, with some power, too. He had 7 doubles and 2 homers in that five-week stretch, and he'd gotten clutch hits in several games. He also had an 8-game hitting streak.

The Cubs' manager had struggled with the lineup all season: Stevenson, still limping on his bad leg; English missing all of April with a broken finger; Cuyler out from April 24 until June 8 with a broken foot. In Pittsburgh, after the Fourth of July doubleheader debacle, the reserve catcher, Rollie Hemsley, had been lighting firecrackers when one blew up in his face, burning his left eye. Hemsley had never been much of a hitter—he would hit a mere .238 for the season, only .262 for his career. If he went blind, his Major League career would be over, and the Cubs would be looking for a new catcher to back up Gabby Hartnett. And now it was Jurges who was out of action.

Hornsby moved Woody English from third base to shortstop. On the last road trip, the rookie, Stan Hack, had finally started to hit, raising his average to .235. Hack was a good fielder, and Hornsby didn't have any other option. Hack would have to play third base until Jurges got back in the lineup. He had Warneke scheduled to pitch.

Warneke was shaky from the start but managed to pitch out of a bases loaded situation in the seventh inning. The Cubs pushed across a run in the second, another in the fourth, 2 in the fifth, and single runs in the sixth and seventh. Warneke completed the game, scattering 8 hits. The Phillies left 12 runners on base. The Cubs won 6–1, but they dropped another half-game behind in the pennant race. Throughout the game, Hornsby had kept one eye on the scoreboard to see how Pittsburgh was faring. The Pirates won 2 games from the Giants—back-to-back doubleheader sweeps for the Pirates. The Pirates were the hottest team in the league and had won 13 out of their last 15 games.

But the good news: the Cubs had broken their 4-game losing streak. They were ready to start the second half of the season.

Jurges spent the afternoon in the hospital. If the nurses let him, he probably listened to the Cubs' game on a radio. Although his injuries weren't serious or life threatening, he was in pain and kept asking for medication. He phoned his father in Brooklyn and told him not to worry. He said he was recovering and would be okay.[21]

That evening a group of Chicago's reporters and photographers were admitted to Billy's room to ask what had happened. Billy was photographed reclining in the bed with a slight smile on his face.

Flashbulbs exploded around him like fireworks as Jurges patiently answered questions.

Jurges recounted his version of the incident. Violet had called him on the phone, he said, and asked if she could come to his room. When she arrived, she asked for a drink of water. When he returned from the bathroom with the water, she had pulled out a pistol and pointed the gun at her own head. Jurges tried to grab the gun away from her, but she squeezed the trigger three times—pop, pop, pop. Fortunately, Jurges told the reporters, Dr. Davis was at the hotel and able to reassure him that the wounds would not be fatal. His life was spared because the bullet struck a rib on its passage through the lower abdomen.

From his hospital bed, Jurges tried to downplay the incident, acknowledging that he was lucky to survive but stating that Violet had come to his room to commit suicide, not to harm him.

Photos of Jurges in his white hospital gown appeared in Chicago papers the next day. Newspapers around the country picked up the story and ran their own version of the events based on the wire reports coming out of Chicago.

The shooting was reported on the sports page of the *New York Times* under a headline that read "Bill Jurges Wounded by Girl He Rejected." Violet Popovich was described as "a pretty brunette" and "a woman scorned."[22]

The eighteen-year-old Bernard Malamud probably read this newspaper account in his father's store. Two decades later, he would recall the event as he sat in front of a typewriter trying to write his first book. The story of Jurges and Popovich would inspire a key scene in that novel, a work that Malamud titled *The Natural*.

16

Harry Hortman and Charlie Ireland

The shooting of Billy Jurges was widely reported in big league cities.[1] For Cubs fans in particular, it was especially disturbing news. Jurges had been a pleasant surprise at the plate and over the past few weeks had been getting key hits in crucial games.

For one Cubs fan—fifty-four-year-old Harry Hortman—the Jurges story summoned painful memories, mirroring circumstances from his own life. Hortman was a permanent resident of the Iowa State Men's Reformatory in Anamosa, Iowa. He had been in prison for the past thirty years serving a life sentence.[2]

Hortman's crime had been committed in Cherokee, Iowa, on November 30, 1901, when he was a young man who drank too much and lacked ambition. He worked part time as a hack driver. But in the late spring of 1901, he had fallen in love with a pretty young woman named Florence Porter, who worked as a waitress at the C. E. White Hotel in Cherokee.

But like the romance between Billy Jurges and Violet Popovich, the relationship between Hortman and Porter seemed to be coming to an end. Porter told Hortman that she wanted to break up. Hortman refused to accept her decision and made one last attempt to reconcile. On the morning of November 30, he took a few drinks to calm his nerves, borrowed a pistol from a friend, and went to confront Porter in her room on the second floor of the White Hotel.

They argued briefly, then Porter tried to flee, running out of the room and descending the wooden staircase on the outside of the building.

Hortman followed, raised the pistol, and shot twice, hitting Porter in the back.

The young woman crumbled at the foot of the stairs. Hortman threw down the gun and turned himself in to authorities. Porter, gravely wounded, was transported to her family home, where she died eight days later. On her deathbed, she forgave Hortman, saying that she knew Hortman meant no real harm and only committed the act because he had been drinking and lost control.

A month later, expressing remorse and admitting to the crime, Hortman stood before a judge to be sentenced. Hortman's attorney pleaded for leniency, citing the circumstances, his client's drinking problem, and his otherwise clean record, but the judge sentenced Hortman to be hanged at the state prison in Anamosa.

For two years, Hortman worked in the print shop at the Anamosa State Penitentiary uncertain about his ultimate fate, while his attorney continued to pursue the legal case, filing motions, and appealing for a new sentencing hearing. In March of 1904 Hortman's case was heard before a judge in Cherokee who revoked the death sentence and resentenced Hortman, to life in prison.

Harry Hortman had escaped the hangman's noose and faced the prospect of a life behind bars. His family—both parents and his brother, Roy—moved from Cherokee to Anamosa to be close by. His father ran a hardware store.

By the summer of 1932, Hortman had spent three decades in prison and was the institution's longest serving inmate. He had acquired the nickname Snap.[3] His parents had died. He had been allowed to travel with an escort back to Cherokee for their funerals and burials. He was fifty-four years old and in declining health. He had served his sentence under the administrations of four wardens. He was a model inmate with a spotless record. He worked as a nurse in the prison hospital. He served as a mentor to new inmates. He played clarinet in the Men's Reformatory band.

But his passion was baseball. He was a proud fan of the Chicago Cubs and the coach of the highly successful reformatory team.[4] To honor him, the team called themselves the Snappers. One of his duties at the prison was to control the cellblock radios, and when the Chicago Cubs began broadcasting their games in the 1920s, the warden gave Snap permission to tune the prison radios to those broadcasts. From April to September, inmates and reformatory personnel followed the fortunes of the Cubs.

There are only a few existing photographs of Snap Hortman. One photo, taken in the late 1920s or early 1930s, shows Hortman with his team of inmate ballplayers. The thirteen Caucasian men are posed in front of the assistant warden's house, standing in ascending order, left to right, from shortest to tallest. The men are looking in the direction of the photographer, hands cocked on their hips, attired in white, baggy uniforms. At the far right in the picture, Snap Hortman faces the camera, dressed in dark pants and wearing what looks like a black peacoat. He is unsmiling and has his arms crossed. A baseball cap shades his face.

Other than Hortman, there were few inmates with long sentences. The players on the reformatory team came and went, then returned to life outside the prison walls. The one constant at the Men's Reformatory over the years was Snap Hortman. In a sense Hortman was to the Men's Reformatory Snappers what John McGraw was to the New York Giants.

In July of 1932, the warden of the Men's Reformatory in Anamosa, Iowa, was a man named Charlie Ireland. He was responsible for managing the correctional facility that now housed more than a thousand inmates.

Ireland was a native Iowan who had been raised on a farm near Clinton. He was a sturdy, cheerful, outgoing man who had enlisted in the army at the age of twenty-one and served in the Philippines during the Spanish American War. After his army discharge, he took a job at the prison—known at that time as the Anamosa State Penitentiary—and worked for two years as a guard and storekeeper.[5]

Later he worked at the Anamosa National Bank and opened a restaurant called The Grill Café. He married Jennie Northrup soon after he returned from the Philippines, and they began raising a family in

Anamosa. Ireland's natural affinity for people, and his gregarious ways, prompted him to engage in a variety of civic enterprises. He was active in the community, joining various social groups and fraternal organizations. In particular, he was known for organizing and promoting auto races at the Jones County fair.

Inevitably, Ireland got involved in politics. He joined the Republican Party and worked for the election of his fellow Iowan, Dan Turner, who had also served in the army in the Philippines. When Turner was elected governor of Iowa in 1930, he offered Ireland the job of warden at the Men's Reformatory. Ireland was installed as the new warden on July 1, 1932.

Like Hortman, Charlie Ireland was a devoted Cubs fan. A friendship quickly developed between the warden and his best-known inmate. Ireland encouraged Hortman's interaction with other inmates and provided new uniforms for the baseball team, with the word *Snappers* boldly displayed on the uniforms.

Over the summer, the 1932 Major League baseball season would bring the two men closer together.

When Charlie Ireland took over as warden, the Men's Reformatory already had a variety of recreational programs for the inmates. In addition to the baseball program, there was a football team, track and field competitions, boxing and wrestling tournaments, theatrical performances, and a band that played concerts for Anamosa town residents on Sunday afternoons in the park across the street from the institution. For a few years, Snap Hortman served as the director of the band.

These programs were not unique to the Men's Reformatory.[6] The prison reform movement of the late nineteenth and early twentieth centuries had emphasized rehabilitation and programs that would facilitate the return of inmates to society. Correctional facilities had begun to offer educational and recreational programs.

Baseball was the most popular of the recreational activities. When allowed to do so, inmates cleared space for fields and maintained the grounds for intramural games. Bleachers were erected for spectators. Teams were organized by work assignments—the print shop, the kitchen workers, the boiler room—and all-star teams were chosen to compete against outside competition. Local town teams and semi-pro teams would visit prisons for exhibitions.

Baseball was particularly popular in youth reformatories.[7] The most prominent of these facilities was located in Baltimore, Maryland, the site of St. Mary's Industrial School for Boys, which is famous as the place where Babe Ruth learned to play baseball.

For more than a dozen years, Ruth lived at the institution, going to school, learning a trade, and developing his baseball skills. He left for good in 1914—a raw but talented nineteen-year-old, signed to a professional contract by Jack Dunn.

Ruth's story encouraged an Indiana governor to think that the next Babe Ruth—or if not that, at least a Major League talent— might be playing ball in one of their institutions. In the late 1920s Gov. Harry Leslie of Indiana, happened to see a game between the Indiana Reformatory team and a semi-pro team. The inmate team featured a good-fielding and hard-hitting shortstop who "could hit the ball savagely."[8] The young man—another loyal Chicago Cubs fan—had played for several town teams in Indiana before being arrested and convicted of a robbery. The shortstop's name was John Dillinger.

Governor Leslie, who had been an athlete at Purdue University, saw potential and took a personal interest in Dillinger's case. "The kid ought to be playing major league ball," the governor said, and added, "It might be an occupation for him later."[9] Leslie might have been right about Dillinger's potential but was wrong about his career path. Released from prison in May 1933, Dillinger embarked on a crime spree, allegedly robbing a dozen banks over the next thirteen months. He remained passionate about the Cubs, and in the summers of 1933 and 1934, he attended games at Wrigley Field, sitting in the right-field bleachers, disguised as a mailman and using the alias Jimmy Lawrence.[10] The last game he saw was on July 8, 1934. The Cubs blasted the Pirates that day,

12–3. Two weeks later, Dillinger was shot dead in Chicago outside the Biograph Theater.

Although Dillinger didn't become a professional ballplayer, two other former convicts, both incarcerated at Sing Sing in Ossining, New York in the 1930s, followed Ruth's footsteps from institutional life to professional careers.

The team at Sing Sing was known as the Black Sheep, and for several years, they were led by Piggy Sands and Alabama Pitts. Sands completed a twelve-year sentence at the prison. He reportedly hit .440 and often hit homers that carried more than four hundred feet on the fly.[11] After his release, Sands, an infielder and catcher, played for the Indianapolis Clowns, a barnstorming team that played in the Negro American League.[12]

Certainly the most famous prison ballplayer of the era was Alabama Pitts. Convicted of a theft of seventy-six dollars, Pitts was given a sentence of eight to sixteen years in 1930. An outstanding athlete, excelling at both baseball and football, Pitts's exploits were reported in newspapers across the nation. The *Los Angeles Times* called Pitts "the most prominent jailbird athlete in America."[13] Warden Lewis Lawes arranged an early discharge for Pitts, which cut three years off his sentence.

Pitts was signed immediately by the Albany Senators of the International League, but the signing was opposed by league president Charles H. Knapp, who said that Pitts's participation would be "against the best interests of the game."[14] Fans disagreed and wanted to see him play.[15] Eventually the issue landed on the desk of Judge Landis who ruled that organized professional baseball would allow Pitts to play.[16]

Unfortunately, Pitts wasn't as talented as everybody thought, though he continued to be popular with the fans. Huge Minor League crowds turned out to see him play, but he slowly sank in the Minors, playing for six years and ending up in a Class D league. His life ended tragically when he was stabbed to death in a bar fight at the age of thirty-one.

Nobody as notorious as John Dillinger, or as talented as Sands or Pitts, played on the Snappers. The stars of the 1932 team were Sam Yorty, a bank robber, and Casey Coburn, a car thief.[17] Although Anamosa had a town team that played in a regional semi-pro league, large numbers of Anamosans turned out to watch the Snappers play their games.[18] As of July 9, the Snappers remained undefeated with a record of 9-0 with 12 games left to play, most on Saturday afternoons on the field inside the prison.

The team's biggest fan was Charles Ireland, the fifteen-year-old son of the warden. In early January the Ireland family had moved into the warden's quarters on the second and third floors of the facility's main administration building.[19] Inmates had repainted the interior. The state of Iowa had helped to refurbish the residence, and the Irelands moved some of their own furniture—a round oak table, a red horsehair sofa—into the common areas. The residence contained parlor areas, a dining room, five bedrooms, and three bathrooms. Above the residence, a ballroom was used for parties and receptions; the reformatory orchestra–under guard–would sometimes be invited to play for social events. The family was served by four inmates—a man who cleaned and did chores, a chef, a table waiter, and a chauffeur who drove the family car.[20]

For Charles, that first year living inside the Men's Reformatory was an adjustment and a period of excitement. On Saturdays his father brought home bags of candy, purchased at the reformatory commissary. Charles was free to visit the warden's office and look at the intake register as new prisoners arrived. He could go to the guards' barbershop on the first floor. And when there was a baseball game, a guard would escort him past the locked entry doors to the bleachers next to the ball field. His mother kept a scrapbook with reports on the season's games and a group photograph of each of the teams that came to play against the Snappers.[21]

The Snappers' games were reported in the local papers, and Charles, a future journalist, began to do some sports reporting about the games, contributing his stories to the *Des Moines Register*, Iowa's largest newspaper.[22]

Like other boys of summer, especially those who were Cubs fans, it was an exciting time, and while Charles could see the Snappers play in person, he had to rely on the newspapers and the radio to follow the National League pennant race.

And like other Cubs fans, he hoped that the loss of Billy Jurges would not be a too damaging blow to the pennant hopes of the Cubs.

17

Sbarbaro's Courtroom

While Jurges was still in the hospital and his assailant remained in jail, the Popovich case entered the legal system on July 8, landing on the desk of John Sbarbaro, a forty-two-year-old municipal court judge.

Sbarbaro was an unremarkable physical presence, a man with soft pale features, a high forehead, and slicked-back, black hair. He wore wire-rim glasses that gave him a scholarly appearance. To the casual courtroom observer, Sbarbaro appeared to be an introverted and unassuming man. The judge was persistent and cautious, and there was nothing flamboyant about him on the bench.

But Sbarbaro was no stranger to crime or the drama of violent outbursts in Chicago. The judge had lived on the periphery of law and lawlessness for more than a decade, first earning a reputation as a businessman and mortician involved with Chicago's gangster elite and later becoming a member of the legal establishment. His political career was advanced, thanks to the support and endorsement of the corrupt mayor, Big Bill Thompson.

He lived a strange but interesting double life, common among politicians in Chicago during the era. He stored liquor for Al Capone in his garage. He ran a reputable business. He had served in city government and was a visible candidate for public office. In 1926 placards bearing the words "John Sbarbaro for Municipal Judge" were attached to cars in the funeral procession for Hymie Weiss, a gangster murdered in broad daylight on orders from Al Capone. In one notable incident, two years later, Sbarbaro himself was the target of assassination. During the primary campaign for city elections in February 1928, the homes of a number of Chicago politicians were bombed. In mid-February Sbarbaro's home was hit. The blast destroyed Sbarbaro's garage, severely damaged his house, and blew the judge and his wife out of bed.[1]

Sbarbaro had longstanding business connections to Chicago's gangsters, mostly through his professional services as a mortician. His funeral parlor was located just north of the Loop, at 708 North Wells Street. Sbarbaro and his family lived in the rooms above the mortuary. As Chicago's gang wars heated up during the 1920s Prohibition era, there was plenty of business, and Sbarbaro earned the reputation of being the gangs' favorite undertaker.

Funerals for gangsters were gala affairs, attended by the family and friends of the deceased, as well as law enforcement, politicians, and rival gangsters. In the 1920s the funerals were frequent enough to provide irregular and unscheduled social events for the prominent members of the community.

The most spectacular funeral of the era was a celebration of the short life of Dean O'Banion. For several years he had an alliance with Johnny Torrio and Al Capone that allowed him to control the illegal liquor business on the North Side of Chicago.[2] O'Banion, a former altar boy at the Holy Name Cathedral in Chicago, co-owned a flower shop at 738 North State Street, across the street from the church.[3] He was the florist of choice for Chicago's gangsters, just as Sbarbaro was the undertaker of choice. He lived in a twelve room apartment within walking distance to Wrigley Field and earned an estimated one million dollars a year from bootlegging, supplying liquor to individuals and speakeasies on Chicago's North Side. But in the fall of 1924, he made the mistake of double crossing Torrio and Capone. On the morning of November 10, O'Banion was gunned down in his flower shop.[4]

O'Banion's body went to the Sbarbaro Mortuary. He "lay in state" for three days in a casket that cost $10,000.[5] Lavish floral displays surrounded the casket. O'Banion's widow sat in a chair near the casket, weeping, and moaning, "Why, oh why?" Capone, who had been involved in ordering O'Banion's execution, sent a large bouquet of roses with a card that read "From Al." Members of the Chicago Symphony played at his service. A cortege a mile long—including three marching bands and a police escort—followed the hearse from the funeral home to the cemetery, where between fifteen and twenty thousand mourners—or voyeurs—attended the burial. Father Patrick Malloy, who had known O'Bannon as an altar boy, conducted the graveside services.[6]

This was one of the worlds in which Sbarbaro lived and did business.

At the same time Sbarbaro was embalming slain gangsters, he was moving ahead in his legal career. In the early 1920s he secured a position as an assistant state's attorney under Robert Crowe, the ambitious state's attorney for Cook County.[7] One of Sbarbaro's first cases involved an investigation into the disappearance and death of Leighton Mount, a Northwestern University student whose decomposed body was discovered in May 1923, near the Lake Street pier in Evanston, twenty months after his disappearance.[8] Mount appeared to have been bound with ropes. Crowe assigned Sbarbaro and several other assistant attorneys to the case. A grand jury was convened. The key legal issue was whether or not the death was accidental—possibly as the result of a fraternity hazing incident–or a murder. Several witnesses suggested, somewhat improbably, that Mount could have committed suicide. Testimony by key witnesses was wandering and elusive; others recanted their testimony or offered contradictory statements; one witness refused to tell all he claimed to know because he thought "the men at the top" might find out. Crowe could not get a murder indictment. The case remained unsolved.

A year later, on May 21, 1924, a fourteen-year-old boy named Bobby Franks was abducted and murdered in Chicago. Franks had been walking home from school after staying late to participate in a baseball game. His body was dumped in a drainage culvert on Chicago's North Side, near Wolf Lake, and discovered the next day. The crime produced a torrent of sensational newspaper headlines and stirred public interest.

Crowe recognized that this was the kind of high-profile murder case that would attract national attention and generate extensive coverage in the Chicago daily papers. The victim was young and from a prominent and wealthy Chicago family. Furthermore, the attack was especially brutal: the boy's body was naked with copper-colored stains on his face and genitals; there were bruises and deep gashes on his face.[9] Unlike the Mount case, there was no question, this was to be a murder investigation.

There were certain similarities between the two cases. Mount and Franks were both young and members of well-known families. Their deaths had been violent and, in Crowe's mind, premeditated. In each case, the killer—or killers—had stuffed the bodies into hiding spaces where they would not be easily discovered. Crowe had been frustrated by the Mount case, unable to find key physical evidence or obtain eye-witness testimony to reveal the motive and circumstances of the death. Nothing had turned up to point to the killer.

But eight days after Bobby Franks's death, investigators traced a pair of horn-rimmed glasses, found near the body, to a young man named Nathan Leopold. Crowe sent two detectives to Leopold's house to bring him in for questioning. Leopold's family was wealthy and well-known in Chicago, and at first Crowe did not think of him as a suspect. Crowe questioned Leopold in room 1618 at the Hotel LaSalle, a location chosen so that reporters would not learn the identity of the young man or suspect anything about the nature of the investigation. Not satisfied with Leopold's responses and curious about the man's relationship with a friend named Richard Loeb, Crowe ordered Leopold held for more questioning and, on May 30, asked detectives to locate Loeb and bring him in for an interview. Crowe did not immediately suspect Loeb of being involved in the crime—no evidence connected him to the crime scene—but Crowe thought that Loeb might be induced to reveal information about Leopold.

Although Crowe participated directly in the questioning of Leopold and Loeb during these first interviews, he quickly assigned three assistant attorneys to the case. One of them was John Sbarbaro. Most likely, Crowe picked Sbarbaro because he had been impressed with Sbarbaro's work on the Mount case. The other two assistant attorneys were Joseph Savage and Milton Smith.

Loeb and Leopold were questioned in separate rooms. The sessions were lengthy and lasted all day. Leopold acknowledged that the glasses at the crime scene belonged to him, but he claimed to have lost them when he'd been bird watching in the area. At first, the boys' stories seemed to hold up. Crowe set a midnight deadline. If there wasn't a break in the case by that time, or meaningful revelations by the boys, he would have them released.

Just before midnight, however, the prosecutor received new information. Both boys had insisted that on the day of the crime, they had been riding around in Nathan's red Willys-Knight sports car. The auto was easily recognizable since it featured "red disk wheels, nickel-plated bumpers, and a tan top."[10] The boys claimed they had picked up two girls and gotten drunk, and then they had driven around, hoping the girls would eventually have sex with them.

The key to the story was the car. Sven Englund, the Leopold family chauffeur, told investigators that the car had been in the family garage that day while he worked on it. Nathan had left the house in a green car—a vehicle driven by Richard Loeb.

Now Crowe believed the boys were lying about the car and their whereabouts on the day of the murder. In an interrogation room, Crowe questioned Loeb more assertively with an angry quaver in his voice, shouting his questions faster and louder.

Sbarbaro was present in the room, too, sitting near Loeb as the exchange took place. Loeb stuck to his story, claiming the chauffer was mistaken or lying.

Shortly after 1:00 a.m. Crowe decided to take a break. The prosecutor was as fatigued as the suspect and ready to let the boys go. He left the room and walked down the hall to his office, leaving Sbarbaro alone with Loeb.

In stark contrast to Crowe, Sbarbaro's demeanor was dispassionate and soft-spoken. Patiently, Sbarbaro went back through the details of Loeb's concocted story: the car, the party with the girls, the drinking and driving around. It was a good alibi if it all held together, because the boys claimed only to know the first names of the girls, so they would be impossible to trace.

But Sbarbaro didn't believe Loeb's story and sensed that the boy was nervous. He offered the young man a glass of water, which Loeb drank quickly. Loeb trembled and his face lost color. He slumped in his chair.

Again, Sbarbaro explained calmly that he knew the alibi was a lie because of what Englund had told them.

Loeb suddenly blurted out, "For good Christ's sake! Is he sure?"

Sbarbaro waited patiently. Loeb said nothing, avoided Sbarbaro's eyes, stared at the window and shivered. Finally, he asked Sbarbaro to bring State's Attorney Crowe back into the room so he could make a statement. Minutes later, Loeb confessed.[11]

The confession that John Sbarbaro coaxed out of Richard Loeb was the turning point in the investigation of the murder of Bobby Franks. Within the hour, Leopold also confessed. The boys pled guilty, and in September, they were sentenced to life imprisonment. Only the impassioned pleas and oral argument of their attorney, Clarence Darrow, saved the two young men from the death penalty.

Compared to the Leopold and Loeb case, the nonfatal shooting of the Cubs' shortstop by a love-stricken young woman should have seemed like small potatoes. But Judge Sbarbaro knew that the daily newspapers in Chicago would play up the story as much as possible. He had seen it happen before.

In the spring of 1924, just before the murder of Bobby Franks, two other murders captured the attention of the city. In March, a woman named Belva Gaertner shot and killed her lover; three weeks later Beulah Annan shot and killed her lover. None of the parties involved knew each other—though alcohol and handguns played a role in each tragedy—but Gaertner and Annan were soon to be linked as their crimes enchanted the public. Both women were soon exonerated, thanks to acquittals by all-male juries. The cases were extensively covered by a *Chicago Tribune* reporter named Maurine Watkins, who later turned this raw material into a play. If Judge Sbarbaro was a theater-goer, he would have known that *Chicago*, the play, ran for more than 170 performances on Broadway in 1927. He might even have seen Cecil B. DeMille's silent movie version of Watkins's play that came out that same year.[12]

By 1932 Watkins had retired from journalism to write for the theater and movies, but Sbarbaro knew there were plenty of Chicago reporters who would be eager to focus on the story of a young ballplayer shot by his jilted girlfriend. Born and raised on the north side of Chicago, Sbarbaro was a lifelong Cubs fan. He would do everything he could to prevent this case from distracting the Cubs and their pursuit of a pennant.[13]

What Sbarbaro didn't know yet was that the case would become more complicated than it seemed at first. There were letters—love letters from Jurges to Popovich—that had fallen into the wrong hands. Sbarbaro would stay busy during the summer trying to keep the situation under control.

On July 9, a character named Lucius Barnett appeared and came to Violet's rescue. Barnett was something of a hustler, thrice-married and with a criminal past. He lived at 2434 Burling Street, not far from Wrigley Field and the Hotel Carlos.[14] He claimed that he and Violet were acquainted because they attended the same church. The exact nature of his relationship to Violet was never clear, but he saw an opportunity in the young woman's misfortune. Barnett posted a $7,500 bond to secure Violet's release. Barnett escorted Violet out of the county jail and faced a small crowd of curious reporters. He spoke a few words to the reporters, assuring them that Violet was a young woman with fine moral character who attended church regularly. And then Barnett whisked Violet away from the reporters.

Meanwhile, back at the ballpark, the Cubs went on a brief winning streak. Hemsley recovered from his eye injury and was available for duty. Malone followed Warneke in the rotation and beat the Phillies

7–0, pitching a 5-hit shutout. Eight players collected base hits, including the new third baseman Stan Hack, who contributed a pair of singles. The Cubs completed a sweep of the 3-game series with the Phillies on Friday, winning 6–4 behind little-used Bob Smith.

It seemed as though the shooting of Billy Jurges had suddenly awakened the Cubs and inspired the team to focus and compete harder, something Hornsby seemed incapable of achieving from his position as manager. The Boston Braves came to town, and the Cubs won 3 games out of 4 in the series. Guy Bush outpitched Socks Seibold in the series opener, winning 5–2. The following day Lon Warneke hurled a 6-hit shutout, the fifth straight complete game win for the Cubs' pitching staff. On Monday, the winning streak was halted. Pat Malone started and failed to retire a batter, departing after the first five Braves reached base. Hornsby sent Malone back out to the mound on Tuesday to try his luck again. A large weekday crowd of 28,000 fans showed up for the game, and this time, Malone came through, pitching a complete game and holding the Braves scoreless until the sixth inning. With the score tied at 3 in the bottom of the ninth, Malone got a two-out single, advanced to second on Billy Herman's single, and scored the winning run on a bloop double by Woody English.

A week had passed since Billy Jurges had been shot, and the Cubs had won 6 out of 7 games at Wrigley Field. Fan support continued to be strong and enthusiastic. Sunday crowds in July averaged close to 40,000, and weekday attendance was good, too; 28,000 fans had come out on a Tuesday afternoon to see the final game of the Braves' series.

Unfortunately, the Cubs had failed to gain any ground on the league-leading Pirates since the doubleheader loss in Pittsburgh on July 4. Over that same stretch, the Pirates had won 7 of 9 games. The race remained close, with the Braves and Cardinals trailing the Cubs by 2 games and 4 games, respectively. For the Cubs, the rest of the month would be lackluster. They would win 10 games and lose 10 games, losing ground to the Pirates, who continued to build their lead.

The frustration was felt throughout the organization. William Veeck, never a big supporter of Hornsby, was getting impatient and weighing his options.

Jurges and Popovich saw each other in court on July 15. Jurges arrived first, dressed in a conservative business suit and accompanied by Dr. John Davis and Pat Malone. Sbarbaro's courtroom was packed with spectators and newspapermen.

A few minutes later Popovich entered the courtroom. She had dressed for the occasion. She wore a white crepe dress trimmed in red, a white hat, and red shoes. She carried a white purse. Her left forearm was covered in white bandages. All heads turned in her direction. As a local celebrity, she appreciated the audience and the attention. Appropriately, the young woman offered a shy smile to the assorted onlookers in the gallery. She looked stunning.

Judge Sbarbaro ordered Jurges and Popovich to stand before the bench. A photographer captured the scene: a debonair Jurges looking directly at Popovich, both of them smiling. They appeared mischievous and slightly embarrassed, like young lovers who had been caught playing a prank. They were flanked by their lawyers in conservative business suits.

Sbarbaro asked Jurges several questions about the shooting, which the shortstop answered with reluctance. Then Jurges said, "I have no desire to testify."

"Do you think you'll have no more trouble?" Sbarbaro asked.

"No," said Jurges. "I wish to drop the case."

Then the judge turned to Popovich and asked her about her plans.

"After what's happened," Violet said, "I feel I owe it to my self-respect to consider the matter a thing of the past."[15]

The judge had mingled with the most respectable and most illicit characters in society over the course of a dozen years in public life as an entrepreneur, attorney, politician, and judge. He had stored booze for Al Capone, embalmed the bullet-riddled corpses of slain gangsters, coaxed a confession from one of the century's most infamous murderers, and been blown out of bed when his residence was bombed in the middle of the night. He was a survivor and had come far enough in his life to earn a modicum of power and influence.

Sbarbaro looked around the courtroom and sized up the situation. He took his time, giving the appearance of sober deliberation. He was confident his heart was in the right place. He would do what was best for the city of Chicago.

"Then the case is dismissed for want of prosecution," Sbarbaro said, "and let's hope that no more ballplayers are shot."

Moments later, outside the courtroom, Popovich summed up her feelings: "If I happen to see Bill again, it will just be impersonal."[16]

At Wrigley Field that afternoon, it was Ladies Day. Nearly 20,000 women were admitted to the park free of charge to watch the Cubs play the Brooklyn Dodgers. The Cubs banged out 12 hits and outscored the Dodgers, 8–3. Hornsby inserted himself into the starting lineup, played third base, singled twice, and drove in 2 runs—just his fourth and fifth RBIs of the season. Charlie Grimm homered and drove in 4 runs. Lon Warneke pitched a complete game, scattering 8 hits.

After a loss to Brooklyn the next day, the Cubs closed out the home stand by winning 3 out of 5 games against the New York Giants. On July 19, Warneke got his fourteenth win—his fourth at Wrigley since July 6—to keep pace with the Pirates, now leading the Cubs by 2 games. The Cubs were now just 2 games out of first place.

On July 21, the Cubs took the train to Pittsburgh to play a 2-game series. But with a chance to pull into a virtual tie for the National League lead, the Cubs faltered. With Billy Jurges back in the lineup—the Cubs had gone 11–4 in his absence—the Cubs lost back-to-back games, 3–1 and 11–8. Jurges went 3–8 in the 2-game series, with a double. Jurges was, once again, the starting shortstop. Woody English returned to third base. Stan Hack went back to the bench.

With her legal problems temporarily resolved, Violet Popovich continued to attend games at Wrigley Field as a fan. She liked to sit in the box seats behind first base, a location that allowed her to look across the diamond, directly into the Cubs' dugout.

As it turned out, the shooting of Billy Jurges briefly revived Violet's career as an entertainer. A few weeks after the shooting, she returned to the world of entertainment with a new act that she performed in Chicago theaters and nightclubs. She used her stage name, Violet Valli, and billed herself as "The Girl Who Shot for Love." An advertisement in the Chicago Tribune under the title "Amusements," described the show as "A Screamingly Funny Burlesque Production" entitled "Bare Cub Follies."[17]

Violet's fifteen minutes of fame was going to last all summer.

18

Legs of Glass

The shooting of Billy Jurges was not the only story of domestic violence that attracted national attention in early July 1932. On the same day that Jurges was shot, Smith Reynolds, the twenty-year-old heir to the Reynolds tobacco fortune, suffered a gunshot wound to the head and died a few hours later in a hospital in Winston-Salem, North Carolina. He had spent the evening at a party with his wife, Libby Holman, a torch singer and musical theater star in New York. Friends reported that Reynolds and Holman had quarreled before going upstairs. Holman told the police that her husband shot himself on an upstairs sleeping porch after the dinner party. She claimed that she was in the next room when she heard the gunshot. The authorities investigated the incident as a suicide but later brought murder charges against Holman and a man at the party, who was alleged to have been Holman's lover and possibly her accomplice.[1]

There was less grim, and less dramatic news, elsewhere in the newspapers. The cost of mailing a first class letter had risen from two cents to three cents. Customers who still had a supply of two cent stamps lined up at post offices around the country to buy one-cent stamps.[2] Two American aviators were attempting to set an around-the-world speed record. James Mattern and Bennett Griffin had reached Berlin. They had beaten Amelia Earhart's time for the Atlantic crossing and were nearly eleven hours ahead of the record pace set by Wiley Post and Harold Gatty. After posing for pictures and drinking glasses of lemonade, Mattern and Griffin were back in the air and headed to Moscow in their Lockheed Vega airplane on the next leg of their trip.[3]

In political news, Al Smith, the defeated and still bitter rival of Franklin Roosevelt, announced that he would support the Democratic Party and its ticket, spurning the solicitation of his supporters to run on a third-party ticket for the presidency. In Washington DC, President Hoover battled with Congress over legislation supported by John Nance Garner, speaker of the House of Representatives and Democratic nominee for vice president. The bill would have provided benefits and loans from the Reconstruction Finance Corporation to individuals as well as banks and ailing businesses. Attempts to revise the bill to satisfy both sides had failed.

In a separate legislative matter, Congress appropriated $100,000 to be used to purchase train tickets for members of the BEF so they could leave the city and return to their homes. The government set a deadline of July 15 for the offer to be accepted and for the BEF to leave Washington.[4] The cost of the tickets would be considered loans to the demonstrators and later subtracted from their bonus checks. Walter Waters rejected the proposal and continued to raise funds independently to help feed and supply the veterans.[5]

Three weeks had passed since the Senate had resoundingly rejected Patman's Bonus Bill. Washington DC Police Chief Pelham Glassford continued his efforts to urge the BEF to leave the city. He conferred regularly with Waters and personally toured the Marks and Anacostia camps—riding his motorcycle into the camps—to show his concern and respect for the marchers. On two occasions—in late June and again on July 1—he paid for hundreds of dollars of food that was delivered to the camps.[6] On the evening of July 10, Glassford showed a movie on the baseball diamond at Camp Marks—a brief newsreel that touted the opportunities of mining for gold in the west.[7] The film was intended to show the marchers that there were better prospects for the unemployed in the western states.

Five thousand men attended Glassford's film, but his pleas went unheeded. The stalemate between the Bonus marchers and the government continued.

Despite the loss of Bill Dickey, the Yankees kept winning. After the Fourth of July debacle in Washington, the Yankees sported a record of 50-22 and maintained a solid lead in the American League pennant race, with the second-place Tigers and Athletics trailing by 7½ games. A month later, when Dickey returned, the lead would be 7 games, as the Yankees would win 18 games and lose 12 during his absence.

Dickey was replaced in the lineup by Arndt Jorgens, a twenty-seven-year-old catcher who had been Dickey's backup since 1929. Jorgens was born in Norway but raised in America, where he came to love the game of baseball. One doesn't associate Norway with Major League Baseball, but Jorgens, in fact, wasn't the first Major Leaguer to have been born in Norway. John Anderson, who had a fourteen-year career, and Jimmy Wiggs, a three-year Major Leaguer, were also native Norwegians.[8]

With only 186 at-bats prior to 1932, Jorgens had been used sparingly by the Yankees. He would manage to play eleven seasons in the Majors, finishing his career with a meager .238 lifetime batting average and a total of just 4 home runs, 2 of which he would hit during the 1932 season.

But in July of 1932, with Dickey suspended and half the season looming ahead of the Yankees, Jorgens was called upon to fill in and produce. Just a week after taking over as the starting catcher, Jorgens clubbed his second Major League home run in a 15–4 romp over the St. Louis Browns. During his stint as Dickey's replacement, he would hit just .176 and collect only 3 extra base hits. But he was adequate, and the Yankees maintained their lead.

With the exception of Tony Lazzeri, the rest of the Yankees' lineup continued to batter opposing pitching staff. Lazzeri, who hit just .237 in July, still managed to produce runs, scoring 22 and knocking in 21. Frank Crosetti, the rookie shortstop whose main contribution was his defense, hit .256—a few points above his season average—and drove in 20 runs. Every other Yankee in the starting lineup—Sewell, Combs, Chapman, Gehrig, and Ruth—hit .308 or higher in July. Sewell homered 6 times—his best previous full year homer total was 7—and recorded 22 RBIs. Combs and Chapman combined for 19 doubles, 6 homers, and 38 RBIS. But the team was paced by its two biggest stars. Gehrig hit a robust .349 with 5 homers and 30 runs batted in. Ruth was even better, with 8 homers in the month, 34 RBIS, and a batting average of .418, despite missing four days due to a serious leg injury.

As vital as Dickey was to the pitching staff and to the offensive production of the lineup, for the month he was suspended, the Yankees performed as well as if he had been in the lineup every day.

While the Yankees surged, the Washington Senators struggled to stay in the race. In July the Senators almost kept pace with the Yankees, compiling a record of 19-14 for the month. The player who stood out was the rookie pitching sensation and math wizard: Monte Weaver. Weaver won all 8 games he started. He beat every team in the league at least once—except for the Red Sox—and he managed to beat the White Sox and the Browns, twice each. For the month of July in 1932 Weaver was the best pitcher in baseball.

The Senators dealt with the loss of Carl Reynolds by installing forty-two-year-old Sam Rice in right field. Rice hit .350 in July—and .323 for the season—though he was primarily a singles hitter and finished the year with just 1 home run and 34 RBIS. As consequential as the loss of Reynolds seemed at the time, the Dickey haymaker that sidelined Reynolds would have little, if any, lasting impact on the pennant race.

Every baseball season is a collection of linked stories, and the drama of the second half of the 1932 American League season belonged to Jimmie Foxx, the principal actor of consequence. Although there were teams in the pennant race with a chance to overtake the Yankees, fans and reporters focused on Foxx's challenge to Babe Ruth's single-season home run record.

On July 8, in the first game of a doubleheader with the Chicago White Sox, Foxx had hammered a 2-run homer. It was his thirtieth of the season, and it came in his team's seventy-seventh game. The A's had played half their games, and Foxx was now exactly halfway to tying Babe Ruth for the single-season home run record.

Two days later, the A's outslugged the Indians in Cleveland in a contest that lasted 18 innings and took four hours and five minutes to complete. Fans who liked offensive fireworks got their money's worth. The final score was 18–17. In the seventh inning alone the teams combined to score 13 runs, 7 by Cleveland, 6 by the A's. The game seemed likely to end in the seventeenth when Jimmie Foxx hit a 2-run homer to give the A's a 17–15 lead, but the Indians came back in the bottom of the inning to tie the game, thanks to a double followed by 3 singles.

Foxx came to the plate 10 times and recorded the following statistics: 1 walk, 2 singles, 3 home runs, 4 runs scored, 8 runs batted in. It was Foxx's single most productive day of the season.

He continued the slugging over the next 11 games, clubbing 6 more homers. That gave him 39 home runs in 92 games, a pace that would extrapolate out to a new single-season record of 65 home runs.

Despite the slugging of Foxx—and outstanding hitting by his teammate Al Simmons, plus Lefty Grove's pitching—the A's still badly trailed the New York Yankees. Unless the Yankees went into a slump, the season would end with the A's a long way behind the Yankees in the standings, but it looked more and more likely that by the end of the season, baseball would have a new home run king: the muscular and youthful, Jimmie Foxx.

On Monday, July 18, the day before Foxx hit number 39, the Yankees were playing the White Sox at home in Yankee Stadium before a small weekday crowd of 5,000 fans. Milt Gaston, two months after being knocked out by the umpire George Moriarty, was the pitcher for the White Sox. George Pipgras was the starter for the Yankees.

The White Sox took a 2–0 lead in the top of the second, but in the bottom of the inning, Gaston surrendered a lead-off home run to his former roommate, Lou Gehrig. Tony Lazzeri followed with another solo homer. By the end of the inning, the Yankees had taken a 4–2 lead. Gaston pitched six innings and left with the Yankees leading, 5–2.

In the top of the seventh, Carey Selph, a utility infielder, pinch hit for Gaston. Selph lifted a soft fly ball to right field in the direction of Babe Ruth. As Ruth ran for the ball, his right leg buckled and he crumpled to the outfield turf. The ball fell safely and Selph made it to second with a double before the ball was retrieved.

Ruth lay on the ground in obvious pain. Later, he would say that the pain was so intense that it felt like a knife stabbing him. Players and coaches surrounded Ruth, helped him to his feet, and assisted in getting him to the dressing room. An examination by Yankees trainer Doc Painter confirmed that Ruth had a serious injury. It was reported that Ruth had suffered "a rupture of the sheath of the extensor muscles in the rear of his right leg."[9] Painter estimated that Ruth would be out of action for at least three weeks.

On Tuesday, Ruth recuperated at home with an electric heating pad on his leg. He and Claire lived in his eleven-room apartment at 345 West 88th Street.[10] Claire did her best to nurse the Babe back to good health. Ruth was visited by Artie McGovern, his personal trainer, and McGovern sounded slightly more optimistic after the visit, suggesting that Ruth might be able to resume playing in a week or so.[11] Ruth called the injury a "charley-horse."[12]

The next day Ruth made an appearance at Yankee Stadium, sitting with a delegation of Australian cricketers. While Ruth explained the nuances of American baseball to the visiting athletes, the Yankees put on a good show for their guests, beating the White Sox 7–2, and sweeping the 5-game series. The Yankees' attack was paced by Frank Crosetti who homered and drove in 4 runs. Sammy Byrd, Ruth's capable replacement in right field, went 3–5 as the Yankees' lead-off hitter.

Ruth had a long history of injuries, illnesses, and misadventures that compromised his health and playing time. Fortunately for his employers, he was both lucky and a quick healer.

In 1915, while a pitcher with the Boston Red Sox, Ruth broke a toe kicking a bench in a fit of frustration and missed two weeks of action.[13] A few years later, Ruth damaged his knee on a slide into third base. He lay on the ground in pain until he was finally carried to the dugout by his Red Sox teammates.[14]

There was more drama to come when Ruth joined the Yankees in 1920. That season Ruth pulled a rib muscle in April, strained muscles in his leg in May, was knocked unconscious while running the bases when a throw from White Sox shortstop Buck Weaver struck him in the forehead in June, jammed a wrist in July, injured a knee in August, and missed games due to an infected insect bite in September. Ruth also wrecked his car in July, rolling it upside down, though he walked away from that accident with only a bruised knee. Despite the injuries and mishaps, it was still an outstanding season for Ruth. He led the league in home runs (54), runs scored (158), runs batted in (137), and slugging average (.847).[15]

Ruth had another stellar season in 1921 and stayed healthy until the World Series, when he suffered an abrasion on his arm in the World Series matchup with John McGraw's Giants.[16] The injury didn't heal properly, even after being lanced, and amputation was briefly discussed. Ruth missed 3 games.[17] The Giants won the best-of-nine series, 5 games to 3.

In 1925 Ruth suffered from his most famous affliction, what came to be known as "The Bellyache Heard Round the World." In the off-season Ruth's weight had ballooned up to 260 pounds. When he reported for spring training in St. Petersburg, he had a fifty-inch waist—larger than his chest measurement—and he was grossly out of shape. In Florida he fished and golfed and fornicated. He ate too much. He drank too much. On the trip back to New York, as the Yankees stopped in several towns to play exhibitions, he began to feel sick. He had stomach cramps and a fever. On April 7, in Asheville, North Carolina, he collapsed on a train platform. Later, as the train was approaching New York, he fell in the train's washroom and banged his head. He was knocked out. In New York he was carried off the train on a stretcher and taken by ambulance to St. Vincent's Hospital. Again, there were rumors that he had died. Some speculated that his distress was caused by a variety of venereal diseases. On April 17, he had an abdominal operation to deal with what his physician called an intestinal abscess. He recovered but played in only 98 games that season and posted, for him, mediocre numbers. At age thirty-one, some observers thought that Ruth's career was pretty much over, that the years of neglect and abuse had permanently maimed his body.[18] He bounced back in 1926, and over the next six seasons, he batted .354 and averaged 50 home runs, 147 runs scored, and 155 runs batted in.[19]

Ruth continued to dismay his teammates and fans with various wounds, afflictions, theatrics, and off-field shenanigans, but as his biographer Robert Creamer wrote, "He dramatized his injuries; no player in big league history was carried off the field on his shield as often as the massive Bambino. But he could ignore both illness and injury and play superlatively well despite them."[20]

Ruth was a remarkable physical specimen. He was not just larger and stronger than most of the players of his era, he also had innate physical gifts that contributed to his success on the field. In September of 1921, near the end of his stellar season, he was examined by two psychologists at Columbia University. The scientists conducted a series of tests, measuring his strength, response time, his vision, his hearing, and the steadiness of his nerves. They even tested his attention span.

The Babe aced the tests. On every assessment, Ruth was superior—and in some cases, far superior—to average human beings. Not surprisingly, the psychologists determined that Ruth generated great power and force when swinging a bat, though they concluded that he could improve in this area if he kept breathing when he swung the bat, rather than holding his breath. But Ruth also had extraordinary eyesight—clearly a necessity for a hitter—extremely good hearing, and perhaps most significantly, scored at the very top of the scale in terms of how steady his nerves were and how focused he was when confronted with a single task.

In other words, as a social animal on a weekend night of drinking and womanizing, Ruth might be wild and impulsive and unpredictable and self-destructive, but as a batter facing a pitcher with a ninety-mile-per-hour fastball, he was steady, focused, and absolutely locked in. He was a creature of moments. At the plate, he was an athlete with superior mental and physical skills.

The results of the tests were reported in the *New York Times* the next day.[21] A longer article, titled "Why Babe Ruth Is Greatest Home-Run Hitter," was written by Hugh Fullerton and published in *Popular Science Monthly*.[22]

There's no evidence that Ruth read either of the stories. But then, he already knew what he could do.

As it turned out, Ruth's injury—once again—healed more quickly than anyone expected. On Thursday, July 21, just three days after collapsing in the outfield, Ruth was back in uniform for a game between the Yankees and the Red Sox. With 1 out and the Red Sox leading, 2–1, in the bottom of the eighth inning, Lazzeri walked and Crosetti singled him to third. Ruth was called upon to pinch hit for Arndt Jorgens. Ruth limped to the plate. He didn't look capable of running the bases, but he stood in the batter's box, looking for a pitch to hit. He walked. The rally died as Red Ruffing, also pinch hitting, grounded into a force play and Sammy Byrd struck out.

Two days later, in the first game of a doubleheader, Ruth again appeared as a pinch hitter, and again he walked, though this time it was not an intentional base on balls. Ruth continued to suit up for games, but McCarthy was reluctant to put him back in the lineup where he'd have to perform in the outfield.

Ruth had two more pinch hitting appearances—singling and driving in 2 runs in a game against the A's and drawing another walk in a game against the Indians—before McCarthy reinserted him in the starting lineup in a game in Cleveland on July 28, ten days after his injury. Against the Indians, Ruth looked completely recovered. He went 3–4 at the plate with 2 home runs and 7 RBIS. After his fourth at-bat, Sammy Byrd entered the game as his defensive replacement.

In the 9 games when the Yankees were without either Ruth or Dickey in the starting lineup, they had won five times and lost four times. No question, the team was deep and talented, even with two regulars sidelined. When Ruth returned to the lineup, the Indians and A's were tied for second, 8½ games behind.

The Yankees still had 56 games to play, but they were in control, and Dickey was eligible to come back in eleven days.

Yankees fans breathed a temporary sigh of relief. Even though they'd seen this drama played out before over the course of Ruth's career— illness or injury, followed by a full recovery—the Babe was no longer a babe. He was thirty-seven, the second-oldest player on the team. Only Herb Pennock, at age thirty-eight, was older.

Yankees fans—not to mention his manager, Joe McCarthy—had to wonder, and worry, whether or not Ruth could make it through the rest of the season without another serious injury or health scare.

19

The End of the Hornsby Era

Herbert Hoover and William Veeck had little in common other than their Midwestern birthplaces, but in July 1932, the men faced critical decisions that would define their tenures and reputations.

After the defeat of Patman's Bonus Bill by the Senate on June 17, President Hoover and government officials hoped that the World War I veterans would peacefully disperse and leave Washington. But only a few thousand of the demonstrators left the city, and others arrived to take their place. In early July the police estimated that more than twenty thousand were still encamped in the city, most at Camp Marks on the Anacostia Flats.[1] The men—including some with their families—were living in makeshift wooden shelters and tents at Camp Marks or elsewhere in the city. Others occupied vacant government buildings in downtown Washington. Some slept on the Capitol lawn.

The Bonus Army had taken up permanent residence. Hoover was increasingly concerned that the standoff between the government and the protestors would result in more direct conflict.[2] Police Chief Glassford agreed. Confrontation was not Hoover's strong point or preferred method of handling a crisis, but logic, coddling, and negotiation had failed. By the end of July, Hoover had come to the conclusion that the protestors had to be removed, forcefully if necessary.

On July 28, Hoover made the decision to have Army Chief of Staff Gen. Douglas MacArthur evacuate the camps and disperse the protestors. Following MacArthur's orders, Maj. George Patton led a cavalry assault on Camp Marks. His troops rode through the camp with sabers drawn. Tear gas scattered the occupants. MacArthur's infantry followed, brandishing bayonets. The troops set fire to the shelters. Flames and smoke soared skyward. For several hours, chaos ensued.

This is what had become of the Hoover presidency in its fourth year: American troops attacking homeless and impoverished World War I veterans in the streets of the nation's capital.

Hoover watched the torching of Camp Marks from the windows of the Lincoln Study, frustrated by his inability to settle the conflict in a less bellicose way. He may have realized that he was watching the future of his presidency in the smoke and flames that rose above the city.

In Albany, hearing the news of the dispersal of the Bonus Army, Franklin Roosevelt surmised what the events in Washington meant for his candidacy. Speaking to his friend and advisor, Felix Frankfurter—whom Roosevelt would appoint to the Supreme Court in 1939—Roosevelt said, "Well, Felix, this elects me."[3]

In spite of the drama in Washington DC, the world of baseball moved inexorably forward. On the day the Bonus Army was routed just a few miles from Griffith Stadium, the Senators were on a fifteen-day road trip, losing a game in St. Louis to the lowly Browns. The Senators, at that point, were 12 games out of first place, clinging to fourth place in the standings. Their only reliable pitcher was the splendid rookie, Monte Weaver, who ended the month with a record of 16-5.

The Yankees, still without the services of Bill Dickey, finished the month of July with an 8-game lead over the Philadelphia Athletics. Babe Ruth had recovered—once again, miraculously—and returned to the starting lineup in Cleveland ten days after collapsing in Yankee Stadium. The Babe celebrated his return by going 3–4 and knocking in seven runs.

In the National League, the Pittsburgh Pirates were in first place, with a 5-game lead over the second-place Chicago Cubs. The Boston Braves and Philadelphia Phillies were tied for third, 10 games behind the Pirates. The Pirates had built their lead despite a brutal schedule in July, playing 38 games, including 10 doubleheaders, over the course of 31 days. Their record for July was a strong 25-13, winning 11 of those games by 1 run.

With eight weeks left in the regular season, fans in Pittsburgh and New York had reason to begin dreaming that the Pirates and Yankees might meet in the World Series in a rematch of the 1927 series—a series won by the Yankees, 4 games to none.

In late July, the Chicago Cubs were struggling. Between July 18 and July 28, they won only four times, 3 of the wins posted by Lon Warneke, their only consistent starter. After the Cubs lost 3 games out of 4 to the Dodgers, William Veeck had reason to be frustrated and angry.

Veeck was about to make two decisions that would have an impact on the pennant race and the World Series—and, in a grander sense, on the history of the game itself.

Since the death of William Wrigley in January, Veeck had been making all of the baseball decisions for the franchise. Philip Wrigley admitted that he had little interest in the day-to-day operations of the ball club. And what Veeck wanted to do now was to change managers. It is unlikely that the elder Wrigley, if alive, would have approved, but Veeck was in charge now.

The Cubs lost to Brooklyn, 4–2, on Tuesday afternoon, August 2, with Danny Taylor and Hack Wilson—both ex-Cubs—getting key hits in the 3-run eighth-inning rally that erased a 1-run Cubs lead. After the game, the Cubs traveled to Philadelphia for another 4-game series. During the train ride, Veeck talked to Hornsby in his private compartment. That evening, Veeck met with Hornsby again, this time in Veeck's hotel room at the Ben Franklin Hotel. When Veeck and Hornsby emerged from the meeting, Veeck announced that Hornsby had been fired as manager. Charlie Grimm would take over the managerial duties. Hornsby was given his unconditional release.[4]

Veeck and Hornsby held an informal but cordial press conference and insisted that the dismissal of Hornsby had to do solely with "big differences of opinion about the ball club and how it should be handled."[5] But Veeck had several other unstated reasons for getting rid of

Hornsby. It was increasingly obvious that most of the players didn't like Hornsby or trust his judgement as manager. As a player, Hornsby had declined to the point where he was a liability, both at bat and in the field. And finally, Veeck was well aware of Hornsby's off-field problems and the fact that he had borrowed money from his players to finance his gambling addiction.

Hornsby's precarious financial situation was likely the final strike.[6] In particular, Veeck had reason to be concerned by Hornsby's debts to gamblers, covered for the time being by loans the manager had solicited from his players. The disaster of the Black Sox Scandal, and what it had meant for Chicago baseball, was little more than a decade in the past. Now that baseball had a powerful commissioner strongly opposed to the association of players and gamblers, it was incumbent upon Veeck to act decisively to clear up the matter of Hornsby's loans and, in so doing, protect the franchise.

Veeck wrote out an agreement by which Hornsby's debts to the players would be paid off out of the salary still owed to Hornsby. Both men signed it. Veeck kept the original of the agreement. Hornsby took a copy.

It was the fourth time in six years that Hornsby had been fired or traded. The next day Hornsby was on a train back to Missouri where he would wait out the rest of the season on his farm. He would find another job in baseball. He had no doubts about that.

Grimm was well liked by his teammates. He was a fun-loving man who liked to play the banjo and drink beer. He promised to be a leader with a much gentler touch than Hornsby. Grimm was also a respected ballplayer in his prime: an excellent fielder and a productive hitter. At the time Grimm became playing manager, he was hitting .290, third best in the club behind his roommate, Riggs Stevenson, and the rookie, Billy Herman.

He immediately relaxed a few of the clubhouse rules established by Hornsby. Players could now smoke in the clubhouse before games. In tone and attitude Grimm was as different from Rogers Hornsby as a man could be. To express their enthusiasm over Grimm's selection, the Cubs players chipped in to purchase a large floral horseshoe, which was presented to Grimm on the field prior to his first game as manager.[7] It was ironic, but not necessarily deliberate, that the shape of the arrangement conjured the image of racehorses.

As if to confirm the rightness of Veeck's decision, the Cubs won their first game under Grimm's guidance by a whooping score of 12–1, over the Phillies, in the hitter-friendly confines of the rickety and poorly designed structure known as the Baker Bowl.[8] The Cubs scored 8 runs in the second inning and banged out 14 hits. Every player in the lineup contributed. Cuyler homered and five players had multi-hit games. Pat Malone went the distance to pick up his eleventh win of the season. That same afternoon, the Pirates lost a doubleheader to the Dodgers by scores of 7–4 and 6–5. In one day the Cubs had moved to within 3½ games of first place.

Veeck had another decision to make. The removal of player/manager Hornsby opened a roster spot. Jurges was back in the lineup, seemingly fully recovered from being shot, but the Cubs needed to add a utility infielder. How Veeck decided to replace Hornsby would impact the pennant race, and more.

Two thousand miles to the west of Chicago, the ex-Major Leaguer Mark Koenig was playing shortstop for the San Francisco Mission Reds of the Pacific Coast League.

After Koenig had been released by the Tigers in spring training, unable to make the club as a pitcher, he accepted an assignment to the Mission Reds. A couple of the 1932 New York Yankees had gotten their professional starts in San Francisco—Lefty Gomez and Frank Crosetti—so Koenig, though a veteran and not a rookie prospect—had some hopes that a Major League scout would spot him, especially if he played well for the Mission Reds.[9]

The Mission Reds shared a ballpark with the San Francisco Seals. In the late summer of 1932 the Seals added a youngster named Vince DiMaggio to their squad. Vince had a couple of younger brothers who would come to games and hang around the park—Joe, who would later play for the Yankees, and Dom, who would later play for the Red Sox.

Joe—the middle brother, a raw seventeen-year-old—had been offered a tryout with the Mission Reds, but he wouldn't start his professional career with the Seals until the fall of 1932.[10]

At that time, Joe's position was shortstop, so the future Yankee must have watched the former Yankee play the position.[11] Joe would have noticed Koenig's strong arm, but likely was more impressed with the way Koenig handled a bat. For much of that season Koenig led the Pacific Coast League in hitting. A year later, it would be the eighteen-year-old Joe DiMaggio—after switching positions from shortstop to outfielder—who would lead the Pacific Coast League in hitting, compiling a record 61-game hitting streak in June and July of 1933.[12]

As for Koenig, he had played baseball from the beginning. Born and raised in San Francisco, he broke into professional baseball as a sixteen-year-old, playing for the Moose Jaw Millers of the Western Canada League. At first, he didn't show much promise, batting .202 with the Millers and committing 54 errors in 84 games during his first season with the club, but he made it to the Majors in 1925 and played on the powerhouse New York Yankees' teams from 1925 to 1930, the teams that featured Babe Ruth and Lou Gehrig. The switch-hitting Koenig was a key part of the Yankees in these years and played in 3 World Series. He forged a bond with Babe Ruth. Batting second in the order, Koenig was often on base when Ruth came to the plate. On the next-to-last day of the season in 1927, Koenig had faced Tom Zachary of the Senators and tripled in the eighth inning, bringing Ruth to the plate. Ruth homered—his record sixtieth. Koenig was at home plate; he became the first Yankees player to congratulate Ruth on setting the record.[13]

In the spring of 1930, Koenig was replaced as the Yankees' shortstop by Lyn Lary.[14] On May 30 of that season, Koenig and starting pitcher Waite Hoyt were traded to the Detroit Tigers for a trio of players: Ownie Carroll, Harry Rice, and Yats Wuestling. In retrospect, one wonders what the Yankees were thinking. The trade was clearly one-sided, in favor of the Tigers. Ownie Carroll did not win a game for the Yankees so he was dealt in midseason to the Cincinnati Reds. Harry Rice appeared in exactly 100 games for the Yankees in 1930, then was waived in the off-season. Yats Wuestling had 41 hits in his Major League career, but just 11 with the Yankees.

The Tigers clearly got the better deal. Koenig played in 182 games over two seasons, mostly at shortstop, and hit .247. Waite Hoyt was in the middle of a Hall of Fame career. At the time of the trade, he was just thirty years old and had 169 Major League victories. After the trade, he won another 70 games in the Majors—a dozen with the Tigers in 1930 and 1931. He was sold to the Philadelphia A's thirteen months to the day after he had been traded to Detroit; by the summer of 1932, he was pitching for the New York Giants. He pitched in the National League for the final seven years of his career. In 1969 Hoyt was inducted into the Baseball Hall of Fame.

In early August of 1932, Koenig was knocking the cover off the ball in the Pacific Coast League. He was doing a decent job at shortstop—fielding was never his strong suit—and he was batting .370, second in the league. Koenig was making the case that he belonged in the Majors.

William Veeck noticed.[15] On August 5, the Cubs paid $10,000 to buy Koenig's contract. When he arrived in Chicago, he would have a Cubs uniform waiting for him. He would wear number nine—Hornsby's old number.

20

The Boys of Summer

Three years earlier, on September 6, 1929, Mark Koenig and his Yankees teammates had traveled to Ossining, New York to play an exhibition game at Lawes Field, twenty-six miles north of Yankee Stadium. The Yankees were going to compete against a team of prisoners housed at Sing Sing prison.

The caravan of cars left in the late morning, driving north along the Hudson River. Most of the Yankees' regulars made the trip, including Babe Ruth, Lou Gehrig, Earle Combs, Benny Bengough, and Lyn Lary.[1] In addition to the ballplayers, a number of reporters accompanied the team to record the event.[2] The *Sporting News* reported that Ruth drove "his big motor car, wearing spotless white flannels and arriving in a blaze of glory."[3]

The Major League schedule called for the Yankees to play 26 more games, but for them, the season was as good as over. After the three consecutive pennants from 1926 through 1928, and the back-to-back World Series sweeps of 1927 and 1928, the 1929 season had been a grave disappointment. Four days before the trip to Ossining, the Yankees played a Labor Day doubleheader against the league-leading Philadelphia Athletics, losing by scores of 10–3 and 6–5. Following the doubleheader victories, the A's closed out the series with a 10–2 crushing of the Yankees, on Tuesday afternoon. When the series ended, the Yankees were 14½ games out of first place.

Yankees manager Miller Huggins had already begun to think about restructuring the roster for the 1930 season. It was likely that the thirty-two-year-old outfielder Bob Meusel, a valuable bat in the middle of the lineup during the pennant-winning years, would be traded over the winter. Other key members of the team—Bengough, Lary, Koenig—were rumored to be expendable. No one expected the Yankees to trade Lou Gehrig—he was just twenty-six years old—but even he had failed to live up to expectations. "It is known," the *Sporting News* reported, "that Huggins has been greatly disappointed by the all-around work of Lou Gehrig who seems to have fallen for an inferiority complex and whose tremendous drop in batting has had a lot to do with the failure of the team."[4]

But Huggins had to be pleased with the season that Babe Ruth was having. At age thirty-four, the oldest of the Yankees' regulars, Ruth was well past the midpoint of his career, but in 1929 he managed to bat .345 and lead the league in homers with 46 and a slugging average of .697. He would place second to Al Simmons in runs batted in with 154. Ruth's numbers were remarkable considering he missed 19 games, mostly in the early part of the season. In May, he jammed his wrist; soon after that injury, he came down with a bad chest cold; and then on June 7, he was sent to St. Vincent's Hospital in New York for a physical exam where he was diagnosed with heart murmurs, forcing him out of the lineup for over two weeks.

Ruth was not the only Yankee with health problems in 1929. What was not yet fully known by the Yankees or the baseball world was that Miller Huggins himself was gravely ill. Throughout the season, the manager had been bothered by a persistent carbuncle on his face. He had missed 3 games due to flare-ups of the boil, which was, in fact, a symptom of a more serious condition known as erysipelas, a blood infection. It is probable that he could have been cured by a regimen of penicillin, but the drug hadn't been developed yet. On September 20, two weeks after the exhibition game in Ossining, Huggins would enter St. Vincent's Hospital. Five days later, at the age of fifty, Huggins would be dead.[5]

The Yankees arrived in Ossining at noon, parked their cars near the entrance to the prison, and were escorted through the iron gates by prison guards to the residence of Warden Lewis Lawes, where the team ate lunch. After the meal, the Yankees were given a tour of the facility. Not surprisingly, Ruth was the center of attention and prisoners called out greetings as Ruth passed the cells. Warden Lawes's tour included a visit to the death house to see Sing Sing's famous electric chair. In its forty years of service, hundreds of inmates had been put to death in the chair, including Leon Czolgosz, the assassin of Pres. William McKinley, and Father Hans B. Schmidt, the only Roman Catholic priest to be executed in the United States.[6] More recently, on January 12, 1928, Ruth Snyder and Judd Gray, the "Sash Weight" killers, were put to death in the chair after a well-publicized trial.[7] Many years later, Julius and Ethel Rosenberg would be executed in this room at the Sing Sing prison.

Babe Ruth sat down in the electric chair and had a moment of sober reflection. Then the Yankees dressed in their uniforms and took the field to play the one of the Sing Sing teams that participated in what was called the Mutual Welfare League. Prisoners filled the bleachers. Townspeople sat in separate bleachers behind a wall. As the two teams warmed up, Ruth joked with the crowd and signed autographs for the prisoners.[8]

The visit to the execution chamber had failed to dampen the spirits of the Yankees. Although they no longer had a realistic chance at repeating their American League championship, the players had come to Ossining to play baseball. For one afternoon, the Yankees were just boys playing a summer game in front of a small contingent of local fans. There was no big stadium, no pressure, and nothing riding on the outcome of the contest. For a few hours, there was just sunlight, green grass, a dirt infield, an outfield fence, and the crack of a bat hitting a ball.

When the game began, Ruth was the focal point and hitting star, bashing a double and 3 home runs. The first of the home runs was a long blast that cleared the forty foot high center field fence and landed near the prison administration building. Original estimates put the length of the homer at over 600 feet. More recent, and more accurate, measuring indicates a blast of about 550 feet.[9]

After the game, the prisoners returned to their cells and work duties. Their afternoon of being baseball players and fans was over. The Yankees motored back to the city.

In the summer of 1932 the Men's Reformatory Snappers in Anamosa, Iowa, had no exhibitions scheduled with Major League teams over the summer, but they continued in their winning ways. By the end of July, their record had improved to 11-1, the lone defeat being a 3–2 loss to the Cedar Rapids Iowa City Railway and Light Company team.

For fifteen-year-old Charles Ireland, it was his first summer living at the Reformatory. On the weekends, the community gathered to hear the prison band give concerts in the park. A colony of painters and artists, led by Grant Wood, traveled to Anamosa from Stone City to display and sell their art. Charles worked at the local newspaper office, learning the journalism trade and writing a few sports stories that he submitted to the papers in Des Moines.

The Cubs were not in first place, but they continued to play good baseball. Charles read the box scores in the paper and listened to games on the radio.

It was the radio that allowed Charles and most fans across the country to follow baseball games in real time. In 1932 there were about 125 million citizens. Only 15 percent of those—18 million or so—lived in cities with Major League teams. America was still a rural nation, and radio was transforming the way the game could be enjoyed. The writer Willie Morris recalled summer days when he was a youth in rural Mississippi, watching sandlot baseball and listening to Gordon McLendon call a Major League game on the radio:

> On Sunday afternoons we sometimes drove out of town and along hot, dusty roads to baseball fields that were little more than parched red clearings, the outfield sloping out of the woods and ending in some tortuous gully full of yellow paper, old socks, and vintage cow shit. . . . It was a wonderfully lazy way to spend those Sunday afternoons—my father and my friends and I sitting

in the grass behind the chicken-wire backstop with eight or ten dozen farmers, watching the wrong-handed catcher go through his contorted gyrations, and listening at the same time to our portable radio, which brought us the rising inflection of a baseball announcer called the Old Scotchman. The sounds of the two games, our own and the one being broadcast from Brooklyn or Chicago, merged and rolled across the bumpy outfield and the gully into the woods; it was a combination that seemed perfectly natural to everyone there.[10]

This was how the summer of 1932 passed for Charles Ireland: watching the Snappers play on Saturday afternoons and following Cubs games on the radio. He must have harbored thoughts, as his Cubs climbed in the standings, that his team might win the National League pennant.

His father had thoughts about that, too. On an afternoon late in the summer, he sat beside Snap Hortman, and they talked baseball. Hortman, in failing health, told the warden that if he could see the Cubs play one time, he'd be ready to die. The warden made him a promise: if the Cubs made it to the World Series, he'd buy tickets to the game and take Hortman as his guest.[11]

21

Judge Landis Intervenes

For Cubs fans in the Midwest, the managerial transition and the surge of the Cubs gave rise to talk of a World Series—a meeting with the mighty Yankees of New York. Now it was Chicago fans, not Pittsburgh fans, who harbored hopes of a World Series meeting with the Yankees.

When Charlie Grimm took over on August 3, the Cubs trailed the league-leading Pirates by 5 full games. Over the next nine days, the Cubs won 6 of 8 games to overtake the Pirates, who lost 7 of 8 games during that same span. At the end of the day on August 12, the Cubs had the lead in the National League pennant race by half a game.

Under their new manager, the Cubs had found various ways to win. Some days their bats came alive and they scored a lot of runs. In the hitter-friendly confines of the dilapidated structure known as the Baker Bowl, the Cubs scored 12 against the Phillies on August 4, then 10 runs in each game of a doubleheader against the Phillies on August 6. But the Cubs didn't just win the blowouts; they also managed to win the close, low-scoring games. Three of their 6 wins in this stretch were by 1 run, including a come-from-behind 4–3 thriller over Carl Hubbell and the Giants, and then, two days later, a 10 inning, 3–2 win over the Pirates, in Pittsburgh.

Quite simply, the Cubs were on a hot streak, and the Pirates were folding.

As a team, the 1932 Pirates were a bit of a mystery. They were over-achievers. Granted, their roster included four outstanding players, all of whom were destined for the Hall of Fame in Cooperstown: Pie Traynor, Arky Vaughn, and the Waner brothers, Paul and Lloyd, aka Big Poison and Little Poison, respectively. But the Pirates had mediocre pitching, with a rotation of Larry French, Bill Swift, Heine Meine, Steve Swetonic, and Bill Harris. As a team they were very poor defensively, especially in the infield. They committed the third-most errors in the league and turned the fewest double plays.[1]

In fact, the 1932 Pirates were not outstanding at anything. The only offensive category in which they would lead the league was triples; they collected 90 three-baggers during the season. They would hit a grand total of 47 home runs, tied for last in the National League with the impotent Cincinnati Reds. The Pirates were a team of singles hitters, a team capable of making enough good baseball plays in a game to grind out wins. By the end of the season they would be 18 games over .500, but they would be outscored by their opponents 711–701.

Here it was August, and the Pirates, despite a miserable start to the month—offsetting their brilliant July—were still in the pennant race. They continued to be the main challenger to the Cubs.

Shortly after Charlie Grimm replaced Rogers Hornsby as the manager of the Chicago Cubs, Commissioner Kenesaw Mountain Landis began hearing allegations about his most dreaded subject: baseball and gambling. Landis was well aware that Hornsby, recently banished back to life as a gentleman farmer in Missouri, had little restraint when it came to betting on the horses. But Landis wondered now, amid new reports and insinuations about players on the Cubs' team, whether or not Hornsby might be just the tip of an iceberg.[2]

Landis took it upon himself to investigate the reports. On August 11, he traveled to Pittsburgh, ostensibly to watch the top two teams in the National League battle it out in a single game—the game won by the Cubs in the tenth inning to snatch the league lead away from the floundering Pirates—but Landis's real reason for being in Pittsburgh was to meet face to face with Charlie Grimm and ask about the firing of Hornsby.

Grimm and Landis met behind closed doors. Reporters stood outside in the hallway. When they emerged to speak to the media, Grimm insisted that gambling was not a topic. He and Landis had just talked about the Cubs and the pennant race and how Grimm liked his new position. Grimm implied that neither Hornsby, nor the circumstances of Hornsby's removal as manager, was a topic. The writers pressed Grimm on the subject.

Then Grimm said, "You can say that Guy Bush is not guilty of gambling."[3]

Bush? What was Grimm talking about?

The reporters had a field day with this information, or Grimm's slip of the tongue, whatever it happened to be. The next day Chicago's afternoon papers printed speculative stories, under bold headlines, suggesting that gambling, indeed, was going on between members of the Cubs organization and bookies. Cubs players were making bets at illegal betting parlors near Wrigley Field, specifically the handbook located at Broadway and Belmont. The article alleged that two Cubs—unnamed—were using women described only as "blondes" to place bets for them.

The bettors were losing more often than they won.[4] Some Cubs were putting up money for other Cubs. Debts were being incurred, and creditors wanted their money. At least one individual, an article alleged, owed $38,000. The print articles didn't name names, but the papers ran photos of Bush, Veeck, and Hornsby, linking them and implying some kind of conspiracy or cover-up.

The gambling rumors, as well as the suggestion that Judge Landis might be getting ready to investigate, infuriated William Veeck, who put out an angry statement that evening, calling the *Chicago Daily News* reports cheap and cowardly attacks in the midst of a pennant race. Veeck defended his players' honesty and argued that the managerial change he had negotiated was strictly to increase Chicago's chances of winning a pennant.

Finally, Veeck asserted, "Hornsby's dismissal was due entirely to a difference of opinion on the way the club should be handled. If he gambled on horses, I know nothing about it."[5]

But Veeck wasn't in a position to put an end to the rumors. The unstated question before the public seemed to be: what did Judge Landis know about the allegations and what was he going to do about it?

Landis was a humorless man with great power. He was not easily intimidated or dismissed. One of Ruth's biographers described the judge in these words: "He was an odd, foul-mouthed little man, an ego-driven, tobacco-chewing puritan with electric white hair shooting out of his head, a hanging judge with the wrath of God carved across his face."[6]

Judge Landis was not a man to mess with or provoke.

As a federal judge, Landis had investigated gambling rings in Chicago.[7] He knew the landscape. Maybe Landis believed Grimm and Veeck about the circumstances of Hornsby's firing, maybe not. Landis and Hornsby had some prior history on this subject.

Just a few years after the Black Sox Scandal, when Hornsby was still a member of the St. Louis Cardinals' organization, Landis had requested that Hornsby meet him in the Commissioner's Office in Chicago. In Hornsby's book, *My War with Baseball*, Hornsby recalled that Landis's office "looked like a federal courtroom," and "some guy was taking a transcript." Soon after Hornsby arrived, Landis began an interrogation:

"Mr. Hornsby," Landis started out, "I've received varied reports and strong rumors that you bet on race horses.

"Well, Judge Landis, they aren't just rumors. I bet on horses. That's my only recreation."

"Then I'm ordering you to stop. It's gambling."

"I know it's gambling, and baseball and gambling don't mix. That's why I never play cards in the clubhouse with the other players. They're playing for money. I wait till later and maybe pick out a horse."

"That's some excuse. And you're going to stop."

"Look at it this way. I don't drink, smoke or go to movies. Don't even read anything but the baseball box scores. Don't even go to the races over once or twice a year. I can relax by betting a horse now and then."

"It's gambling," responded Landis, "It's gambling."[8]

Whether Hornsby considered betting on horse races to be gambling or not, he certainly hadn't paid any attention to Landis's admonition or command—"you're going to stop." Landis was unable to persuade Hornsby to curb his betting habits and was unwilling to punish him if he didn't.

It was no secret that Hornsby bet on the horses. Nobody expected him to stop—not even Landis. And it was no secret that Hornsby's losses were greater than his gains. He had to pay back his creditors somehow, and Hornsby already had a mountain of debt and other financial obligations, considering his ongoing legal cases and his failing farm. It should have come as no surprise, to Landis or anyone who knew Hornsby, that he was going to have to borrow money to support his habit.

After the discussion with Grimm in Pittsburgh, Landis followed the Cubs to St. Louis. He set up another meeting for August 13. It was a Saturday; the Cubs were scheduled to play the Cardinals that afternoon.

The inquiry in St. Louis, in the heat of the 1932 pennant race, took place in Landis's hotel suite at the Park Plaza Hotel. Once again, reporters were in hot pursuit, stationed outside the room while Landis conducted the meeting.

Landis arrived with his executive secretary, Leslie O'Connor, and a stenographer.[9] Four members of the Cubs organization were at the meeting: Cubs players Guy Bush, Pat Malone, and Woody English, as well as Cubs coach Charley O'Leary. The eighth man in the room was the ousted Cubs manager, Rogers Hornsby, who had been summoned from his farm, just north of the city.

Judge Landis started by questioning Bush. What financial transactions had Bush had with Hornsby over the years? Bush said that Hornsby had borrowed $5,000 from him in 1929 and that loan had been repaid.

But Hornsby had borrowed another $2,000 from him, just a few weeks ago, right before the Cubs left on their current road trip.

Why did Hornsby need the money? Bush said Hornsby told him it was to pay back taxes.

Landis asked O'Leary and English the same question. Hornsby owed O'Leary $2,000 and English $1,200. It seems that Hornsby had made the rounds with his hat in his hand to collect whatever he could from his players and coaches. He had also borrowed $250 from Malone about three weeks ago, but that debt had been repaid.

When Landis finally got around to questioning Hornsby, the topic was why he had needed to borrow the money. Hornsby was the highest paid player in the National League. Hornsby muttered something about paying taxes and interest on the mortgage he had on the farm. Also, Hornsby admitted, he had other financial obligations.

Then Landis steered the conversation toward Hornsby's gambling. Did Hornsby make bets on horse races with other players, specifically Guy Bush? Hornsby denied it. Bush was especially upset and kept breaking into the dialogue between Landis and Hornsby to assert his own innocence. Did Hornsby use the money he'd borrowed to bet on the horses or pay off gambling debts? Hornsby denied both.

Then Landis asked when Hornsby had most recently placed a bet on a horse race. At first, Hornsby claimed not to remember, saying maybe two or three years ago. Nobody in the room would have believed that. When Landis pressed Hornsby on whether or not he'd placed a bet in the past year, Hornsby became impatient and made it clear he wasn't going to reveal any more about his gambling habits. "Put in my position," Hornsby said, "I am not going to say. I refuse to answer that question."[10]

Landis returned to the question as to whether Hornsby had been placing bets with any of his players. Hornsby and the players in the room were in agreement that whatever betting Hornsby did, he did it on his own. That was good. Now the question for Landis was how Hornsby, the deposed manager of the Cubs, was going to repay the players he had borrowed from.

At this point, Hornsby presented Landis with a piece of paper—his copy of the agreement he'd reached with Veeck in Philadelphia. It took Landis a moment to realize what he was reading. Referring to Veeck, Hornsby said, "He will show you the same one, the original, if you want it. These gentlemen were all present when it was drawn up."[11]

For whatever reason, none of the Cubs in the meeting had thought to bring the Veeck-Hornsby agreement to Landis's attention until now. For that matter, no one else associated with the Cubs—neither Veeck nor Grimm—had seen fit to enlighten the commissioner about the arrangement.

It wasn't often that Landis was kept in the dark, but he pressed on with a few more inquiries, primarily about the $38,000 that some Cubs allegedly owed to some unidentified person. No one in the room could offer much insight about that particular rumor, though Bush was especially irritated that he'd been connected to a gambling scheme of some kind. Or maybe, as a married man, what irked Bush the most was the linkage of his name with two or more mysterious women known as "blondes."

Eventually the meeting ended. Hornsby went back to his farm. The Cubs went out to Sportsman Park to get ready to play the Cardinals.

Landis took the train back to Chicago. But not before releasing a transcript of the meeting to the press.

So why did Landis release the transcripts? It was a sensitive time in the pennant race to bring up such a provocative issue, as Veeck had pointed out. Did Landis want to put an end to the speculation about the Cubs being engaged in excessive gambling or betting? The meeting didn't clear the names of English, O'Leary, Malone, or Bush, and they were small fish compared to Hornsby; only Hornsby had a long and well-known history of gambling.

Most likely, in releasing the transcript Landis was warning Hornsby—or, more specifically, warning any owner or general manager who might consider hiring Hornsby in the future—that the commissioner was keeping a close eye on Hornsby's off-field activities.

It was also possible that Landis just wanted to assert his authority. Maybe the release of the transcripts was strictly a matter between the two Chicagoans, a specific rebuke from Landis to Veeck that the commissioner was not to be trifled with. Landis would not have been happy that Veeck had negotiated the payback of Hornsby's loans without consulting him.

22

Stretch Run

Neither the meeting with the commissioner nor the subsequent disclosures from the transcript managed to rattle the Cubs. Woody English was in the lineup for the Cubs that afternoon, and he didn't seem distracted by the probing questions in Landis's hotel room. He contributed 3 singles in 4 at-bats, stole a base, and scored a run. Charlie Root pitched a complete game 7-hitter and allowed only 1 run. The Cubs won, 3–1.

On Sunday, however, the Cubs lost a doubleheader to the Cardinals, who were now creeping back up in the standings. In the first game Tex Carleton shut out the Cubs on 7 hits and won a pitcher's duel with Pat Malone, 2–0. The game marked the first appearance in a Cubs uniform of newly acquired Mark Koenig, who collected a pinch hit single in the eighth inning, batting for Malone.

In the nightcap, there was another pitching duel, with Dizzy Dean going 10 innings to beat Guy Bush, 2–1. It was Dean's fifth appearance and fourth start of the season against the Cubs. The winning run was scored, with 2 out in the bottom of the tenth on a single, by Cardinal center fielder, Ernie Orsatti.

The good news for the Cardinals was that they had won 7 of their last 8 games and now trailed the Cubs by only 6 games, but the Cards were still in sixth place. The main effect of the Cardinals double win over the Cubs was that the whole National League pennant race had tightened.

After the loss to Dizzy Dean and the Cardinals, the Cubs returned home with a half-game lead over the second-place Pirates. The team was met by hundreds of cheering fans at the Illinois Central Station.[1] It's hard to overstate how excited Cubs fans were by the turn of events: Hornsby out as manager, the popular Grimm installed as the new skipper; the team no longer sinking in the standings but actually in first place.

The team had a day of rest before resuming play on August 16, designated "Charlie Grimm Day" at Wrigley Field. An enthusiastic crowd of more than 32,000, many wearing white straw hats, turned out for the Tuesday afternoon game between the Cubs and the Boston Braves, the first of a 4-game series. Jack Bramhall's band, featuring a booming tuba, noisily serenaded the crowd with pop favorites, including the Democratic Party theme song, "Happy Days Are Here Again."[2]

Before the game could start, ceremonies were held at home plate to honor the grinning Grimm. Huge floral displays in the shape of horseshoes—a subtle, though probably unintentional visual reminder that Hornsby's gambling addiction had contributed to Grimm's hiring—were brought forward to surround the new manager. Then Grimm was presented with gifts, including silverware and a platinum watch. At last, the game got underway with a healthy Billy Jurges at shortstop—his first appearance on the field at Wrigley since he was shot by Violet Popovich in the Hotel Carlos on July 6. Lon Warneke took the mound for the Cubs, trying for his eighteenth win.

The game was scoreless until the top of the eighth when the Braves staged a rally, scoring 3 runs and forcing Grimm to make an uncharacteristic pitching change in mid-inning. The Cubs had scratched out just 2 hits by that time—one by Jurges—and hadn't threatened to score.

The straw-hatted crowd had quieted and was ready to head for the exits when the Cubs suddenly came to life in the bottom of the ninth. After 1 out, Billy Herman doubled to left, and Woody English followed with a double to center to knock in the first Cubs run of the game. When Kiki Cuyler contributed a third straight double—his first hit of any kind in a week—the Cubs had a legitimate rally going. Riggs Stevenson quickly followed with a single that scored Cuyler and tied the score. The crowd cheered wildly. The tuba in Jack Bramhall's band boomed even louder. Dozens of straw hats sailed out of the stands in celebration. The game was delayed for a few minutes while the ushers cleaned up the field.[3]

The rally wasn't over. Frank Demaree singled to put the winning run on second base. The day's honored guest, Charlie Grimm, stepped to the plate with a chance to be the hero. But Grimm popped up for the second out. Hartnett reached base, thanks to an error on his ground ball, loading the bases for Billy Jurges.

Jurges ended the day's drama, and the game, by ripping a line drive over the head of Wally Berger in center field. Stephenson jogged home with the winning run.

Another deluge of straw hats floated onto the field. Improbably, but appropriately, on Charlie Grimm Day the Cubs had managed to secure a victory, 4–3.

If a single game can be said to turn a season around for a team, then the Cubs' comeback win on Charlie Grimm Day might have been that key game. It was the first game of a 20-game home stand, several of the games ending in dramatic fashion, delighting the Wrigley Field crowds.

The day after the Grimm game, the rejuvenated Cubs played a nineteen-inning game against the Braves, earning a 3–2 triumph, thanks to 12⅔ innings of excellent relief pitching by Bud Tinning. Guy Bush relieved Tinning in the nineteenth and pitched one inning to earn the win. The third game of the series also went to the Cubs, 4–3, this time in 15 innings. On Friday, August 19, Koenig replaced English in the lineup, and Koenig responded with a pair of singles.[4] The series ended with the Braves getting a win, 6–5—all 4 games of the series being 1-run affairs. The two teams had played 52 innings of baseball in seventy-four hours.

If the Cubs were tired, it didn't show. Winning begat winning and invigorated the team, just as it was energizing their fans in the city. The Phillies were coming to Wrigley Field for another 4-game series, and while the Cubs had only a slim 2-game lead over Brooklyn, 2½ games over Pittsburgh, and 5 games over the visiting Phillies, optimism was building.

If there was still cause for concern, it was that the Cubs' best hitter and most potent offensive weapon, Kiki Cuyler, remained in a slump, hitting in the .260s—70 points below his lifetime average—with just 4 homers in the year. Cuyler had averaged 14 homers and 103 RBIs per season in his four years with the Cubs, but in his injury-plagued 1932 season, Cuyler's bat had suddenly lost its pop, and despite the key double he contributed in the ninth inning rally on Grimm's day, he was not hitting consistently or with much authority.

It's possible that Cuyler was distracted. Although Billy Jurges had recovered from the gunshot wounds he suffered at the Hotel Carlos on July 6, and the shortstop was back on the field for the Cubs, the drama involving Violet Popovich had become stranger and more ominous for both Jurges and Cuyler over the past five weeks.

Soon after the shooting and her release from jail, Violet Popovich had entrusted a cache of love letters—approximately two dozen—to Lucius Barnett, the man who had provided bail for her. The letters were from Jurges to Popovich—or at least most of them were; Barnett later claimed that some of the letters he possessed had been written by Cuyler.[5] Barnett devised a plan for the letters. At first, he told Popovich that he planned to bring a suit against Jurges and Cuyler for $50,000. The grounds for the suit were not clear to Popovich or anyone else.

With the letters in his possession, Barnett proposed a new plan: publishing the letters in a booklet and selling them at Major League ballparks. The title of the booklet was to be "The Love Letters of a Shortstop." The contents, one presumes, would be embarrassing to both Jurges and Cuyler. Popovich was to get a $2,500 advance. If the books sold enough copies, she'd get at least another $2,500—perhaps as much as $20,000. But Popovich wanted no part of the deal. "I think too much of Bill," she explained. She wanted the letters back.[6]

Popovich took her concerns directly to Judge John Sbarbaro. On August 12, she appeared in the judge's courtroom. A few minutes later, the judge took her into his chambers for a private conversation. Exactly what Popovich told Sbarbaro was never revealed, but the next day, several Chicago policemen attempted to arrest Barnett on a charge of blackmail. Barnett kicked one officer in the groin and tried to flee. Popovich happened to be on the scene and witnessed the police struggling with Barnett, who was taken into custody and charged with "extortion, larceny, disorderly conduct, resisting a policeman, and assault."[7]

Two days later, on August 15, Barnett was brought before Judge Sbarbaro to face these charges. Again Popovich was present, sitting in the back row of the courtroom. Sbarbaro fixed bail at $10,000. A week later, Barnett was back in front of the judge. Popovich's attorney acknowledged that some of the letters had been returned to his client but that others, perhaps the more salacious items, were still in Barnett's possession. He set a September court date for Barnett to answer to the multiple felony charges. The judge made it clear that all of the letters in question were to be returned—and were not to be seen by or leaked to the public.

The judge left no doubt as to his personal loyalties and motivation: "I want to keep this case under my jurisdiction to prevent embarrassment to the Cubs so that their chances of winning the pennant will not be harmed," he stated. "I don't want this thing to worry Jurges."[8]

Jurges was hitting .246 since his return from the shooting. Sbarbaro might have been more concerned about Cuyler. But both Cubs could now feel some measure of relief that the judge would protect their privacy—if not for their sake, then for the good of the team.

The Phillies came to town on Saturday, August 20. To give a boost to the offense Grimm moved Koenig into the starting lineup for the Phillies' series. In the first game, with the Cubs trailing 5–3 in the bottom of the ninth, Koenig stepped to the plate with two runners on base and slammed a game-winning 3-run homer. Grimm suddenly looked like a genius. The Cubs won the next 3 games by scores of 2–0, 8–4, and 5–1.

Then the Dodgers came to town. Wrigley Field was packed with more cheering crowds; 82,000 fans paid to see the 3 games. The Cubs swept Brooklyn, three straight. In the final game of the series the Cubs scored 9 runs in the third inning to take an early and insurmountable lead.

Thanks to the sweep, the Cubs stretched their lead over the second-place Dodgers to 6½; the Pirates were third, 7 games back. The Cubs had won 7 in a row.

The home stand continued with the New York Giants arriving for a 5-game series, starting with a Saturday doubleheader before a crowd of 41,000. In the first game Freddie Fitzsimmons was matched against Burleigh Grimes. Kiki Cuyler blasted a 3-run homer in the first inning to give the Cubs an early lead, and Grimes pitched his best game of the season, a complete game 6-hitter; the Cubs won, 6–1. The Cubs won the nightcap too, 5–0 behind the pitching of Bob Smith.

On a rainy Sunday, Cuyler was again the hero, driving in 4 runs with a pair of singles, his sixth homer of the season, and a game-winning sacrifice fly in the bottom of the ninth. The Cubs triumphed, 5–4. Cuyler was starting to make a little noise with his bat. The winning streak had reached 10 games.

After a Monday rainout, the Giants pitched their ace, Carl Hubbell, on Tuesday against Charlie Root. Hubbell took a 2–0 lead to the bottom of the seventh before the Cubs staged a rally, capped by Cuyler's 2-run homer to take the lead. Four in a row over the Giants, and the best was yet to come.

The finale of the Giants series had a little bit of everything: a partial eclipse of the sun, blue skies, a rainstorm, and another afternoon of heroics by Kiki Cuyler. Judge Landis was on hand to witness the game, sitting in his customary box along the third base line where he was joined by Cubs president William Veeck.[9] If Landis and Veeck were still feuding over the Hornsby matter, it wasn't obvious.

The solar eclipse began at 2:07 p.m. in the afternoon, about an hour before the scheduled game time, and by 3:18 p.m., four-fifths of the sun was obscured by the moon. Fans and players—not so safely—stared at the event through dark glasses. As soon as it was light enough to play ball, Lon Warneke took the mound for the Cubs. He failed to record a single out and was replaced by Bud Tinning, with the Giants leading, 3–0.

Freddie Fitzsimmons pitched for the Giants, who added a run in the second before the Cubs began to chip away at the lead. Cuyler tripled off the center field scoreboard in the third to knock in 1 run. Then the rains came, forcing a twenty-seven minute delay. When the skies cleared, Stephenson rapped a double to score Cuyler. Then the clouds rolled back in. The teams played on through the drizzle. Grimm knocked in a run later in the inning to cut the Giants lead to 1 run.

The score was 5–4 with a light rain falling as the game moved to the bottom of the ninth. It was slowly darkening, the field was wet, and the base paths were muddy. Fitzsimmons was still pitching for the Giants. Some of the day's fans had already departed, heading for home and dry clothes, when the Cubs mounted a small rally. With 2 outs and Frank Demaree on first, Woody English singled to right field, and Demaree trudged through the mud to reach third base. Bill Terry came to the mound to talk to Fitzsimmons, taking as much time as the umpires would allow, hoping that the game might be stopped on account of the weather before Cuyler got to bat. Terry decided to change pitchers. Hi Bell was the new hurler. Bell took some warm-up pitches. Cuyler waited.

Finally, Cuyler, already with 3 hits in the game, stepped to the plate. Once more, as he had done throughout the series with the Giants, he delivered, singling to right to drive in the tying run.

The umpires decided there was enough daylight for one more inning. Guy Bush took over the pitching duties for the Cubs in the top of the tenth. Bush had no more success than Warneke had had nine innings earlier. Bush walked a batter, hit a batter, hit another batter, gave up a run-scoring single and then uncorked a wild pitch. Leroy Herrmann replaced Bush on the mound. The half-inning ended with the Giants ahead, 9–5.

In the bottom of the tenth, Jurges and Gudat made quick outs. It looked like Cuyler's ninth inning heroics were going to be wasted. But Mark Koenig stepped to the plate and blasted a homer to right field. Zach Taylor, the seldom-used reserve catcher, delivered a pinch hit single, and Billy Herman followed with another single.[10] The tying run came to the plate in the person of Woody English—with Cuyler on deck.

Unfortunately, no one in the stands had a movie camera. This would have been an inning to capture on film. English singled and Taylor scored. Now the tying run was on first base. Cuyler stepped into the batter's box.

On the fifth pitch, Cuyler swung and drove the ball through the rain into the right-field stands for a game-winning home run.

Cuyler sloshed gleefully around the bases as his teammates poured out of the dugout to greet him at home plate. Fans rushed onto the field. A sodden William Veeck vaulted over the third base railing in his excitement and fought his way through the mob to congratulate Cuyler.[11]

It had been an extraordinary game, another miracle finish, a game forever to be known to Cubs fans as the Cuyler game, a victory every bit as sweet and memorable and important as the Grimm game.[12] The winning streak was now 12 games.

In historical hindsight, though, maybe the most notable fact was simply this: despite the rain, 35 hits, 19 runs crossing the plate, multiple pitching changes, stalling by the Giants—not to mention the eclipse—the game was reportedly played in a time of just two hours and fifteen minutes.

The 5-game sweep of the Giants virtually ended the pennant race. The Cubs now had a 7 game lead with less than a month to play. Cuyler had broken out of his slump. Koenig had hit .408 since being rescued from the Minor Leagues. Under Grimm's leadership in August, the Cubs had gone 22–5.

The Cardinals came to town on the first of September, and the Cubs stretched the winning streak to 14 games before losing 3–0 in the second game of a doubleheader on September 3.

The pitcher who finally stopped the Cubs' streak was the Cubs' nemesis, Dizzy Dean. Dean would go on to lead the league in strikeouts, tie for the league lead in shutouts, and win 15 games. It wasn't good enough to carry his team to the pennant, but it foretold a bright future for the opinionated and loquacious rookie.

After the series with the Cardinals, the Cubs went back on the road: Cincinnati, Boston, Brooklyn, New York, Philadelphia, and once more to Cincinnati, for a makeup game. They won 9 and lost 8 on the road trip.

On September 20, needing just one more win to clinch the national league pennant, the Cubs returned to the friendly confines of Wrigley Field to host the Pirates in a doubleheader. It was Riggs Stevenson Day at the ballpark. Guy Bush pitched the first game for the Cubs, going for his nineteenth win.

It was another damp day in Chicago as an early afternoon mist turned into a light rain. The game was tied, 2–2, in the bottom of the seventh when the Cubs came to bat. Billy Jurges singled, then Bush was safe on an error. Billy Herman sacrificed the runners to second and third and Woody English was intentionally walked to load the bases.

The next batter—who else could it be?—was Kiki Cuyler. The inexorable late-season pennant drive by the Cubs had come, once again, to this: Cuyler at bat with runners on base in a crucial situation. And Cuyler delivered, smashing a triple into the left field corner. Three runs scored, and the Cubs held on for a 5–2 win. The last Pirate batter was retired on a ground ball. Bush rushed off the mound, snatched the ball from Grimm's glove at first base, then climbed into the stands to embrace his wife and present her with the ball.

A season of adversity had turned into a pennant and a trip to the World Series.

The next day the Cubs met to make decisions on who would get World Series shares. For some players, a full share would be equal to half or more of the player's annual salary. With sellout crowds at Yankee Stadium and Wrigley Field, the winning shares might be worth as much as nine thousand dollars.[13]

Nineteen members of the Cubs took part in the voting.[14] As team captain, Woody English ran the meeting. It was agreed that decisions had to be unanimous. The nineteen players voted full shares for themselves, plus full shares for Charlie Grimm, and the two coaches, Charley O'Leary and Red Corriden. Half-shares were voted for traveling secretary Robert Lewis, trainer Andy Lotshaw, and the three players who had joined the team in July and August: Leroy Herrmann, Frank Demaree, and Mark Koenig.

Most of the players wanted to give Koenig, a key player in the final weeks of the pennant race, a full share, but there were two holdouts: Koenig's fellow middle infielders, Billy Jurges and Billy Herman. The decision would have repercussions.

The name of Rogers Hornsby was barely mentioned. He had been the Cubs' manager for 99 games, but the team did not grant him even a partial share. When news reached Hornsby at his farm in Missouri, he grumbled that he deserved a full share and said that he would appeal the decision to Commissioner Landis. Hornsby needed the money. During the summer, the IRS had filed suit against Hornsby claiming that he owed the government $8,412 in back taxes.[15]

With the pennant race settled, Chicago began preparations for hosting World Series games. The city allocated $40,000 to construct additional seating at Wrigley Field.[16] Ticket sales soared.[17] Carpenters began hammering away. Temporary bleachers in right field and left field would boost capacity from 38,000 to nearly 50,000 seats.

Less than forty-eight hours after the pennant-clinching game, the city of Chicago honored the Cubs with a parade. Fans gathered at Wrigley Field to send the team off on a six-mile route that wound through Lincoln Park and ended at the Loop. Violet Popovich was spotted in the cheering crowd at Wrigley Field, a few blocks away from the Hotel Carlos, where just seventy-eight days earlier she had waved a gun in Billy Jurges's face and tried to kill him.

More than a hundred thousand—maybe a hundred and fifty thousand—Chicagoans lined the streets, a turnout that was bigger than the parade for Charles Lindbergh in 1927. An American Legion fife and drum corps marched at the head of the parade. Confetti and ticker tape and loose paper cascaded down on the twelve cars carrying the team. Twenty motorcycle police rode along as escorts. Fans yelled encouragement and congratulations. Auto sirens blared. Factory whistles blew.

At the stage on the west side of City Hall, a beaming Mayor Anton Cermak spoke first. He welcomed the team and paid tribute to the efforts of the late William Wrigley to bring a championship to Chicago. Cermak touted the World Series as a financial bonanza for the city—perhaps adding more than $700,000 of revenue to Chicago in terms of ticket sales, restaurant receipts, hotel bookings, and assorted services. Addressing manager Grimm, Cermak said, "Charlie, this is a rare occasion and a most gratifying one for me, for you, and for the whole of Chicago." The World Series, Cermak went on, would "attract the attention of the whole country to this city."[18]

Cermak, in his first term, had pulled off a trifecta: hosting both national presidential nominating conventions and the World Series in the same year.

William Veeck said a few words. Then the players took turns being introduced and speaking briefly. Finally, the police escorted the team back to Wrigley Field, where they played and lost a meaningless game to the Pirates by a score of 7–0. Now a matchup with the Yankees loomed. The Cubs had six days to prepare.

23

Yankees Coast

At the end of August, the Yankees were firmly in control of the American League pennant race with a record of 91-38. The team won 9 of the last 10 games it played in August, part of a 24 game home stand, stretching their lead over the second-place Philadelphia Athletics to 11½ games. The Washington Senators were a distant third in the league standings, 17 games out of first place.

The recently injured Ruth had returned from his leg injury. He was batting a robust .351 with 39 home runs. The rest of the lineup was also producing: Gehrig had a .342 average with 31 home runs; Combs was hitting .325; Ben Chapman was at .306; Bill Dickey at .303; Tony Lazzeri at .298.

Ruth and Gehrig each already had over 100 RBIS. Tony Lazzeri was next with 96, and Ben Chapman had 86 RBIS. All four players would drive in over 100 runs in 1932—combining for a whooping total of 508 RBIS on the season. Even Joe Sewell, dismissed as "an old man discarded by the Indians," was quietly having one of the best seasons of his career, hitting in the .280s and smashing a career-best 11 home runs.[1] The only weak spot in the Yankees' lineup was at shortstop. Lyn Lary and the rookie Frank Crosetti were splitting time at the position, both struggling to reach the .240 mark.[2] As Westbrook Pegler would note in his column later in the month, "The fact is the Yankees have not been very stable at shortstop since the best days of Mark Koenig."[3]

Koenig, of course, was now employed by the Cubs in the National League. He was batting .408 for the month of August and had hit safely in 12 of 13 games since being inserted in the regular lineup. Koenig's clutch hitting had been one of the main reasons that the Cubs had taken control of the National League pennant race.

The Yankees' pitching staff continued its fine work, too. The rookie, Johnny Allen, was 14-2. Lefty Gomez had a record of 22-6. George Pipgras was 14-7. Red Ruffing was 16–6, with the team's best ERA of 2.74, not to mention a batting average of .314, 75 points higher than the team's shortstop combination. Ruffing also had a couple of home runs and 17 RBIS.

With the pennant race virtually decided, Manager Joe McCarthy had some decisions to make, namely what players might need a rest before the World Series, which was scheduled to start in four weeks. In particular, he worried about Ruth, recovering from his leg injury and occasionally needing a few days off to be fully rested and ready for the postseason.

McCarthy had a capable replacement for Ruth, a reserve outfielder named Sammy Byrd. Byrd already had acquired the nickname of "Babe Ruth's Legs," since he often replaced Ruth in the late innings. Byrd was a young man, born more than a decade after Ruth. He would turn twenty-five on October 15. In his four seasons with the Yankees, Byrd had played in about half of the Yankees' games, mostly as a defensive replacement, sometimes as a pinch hitter. He hit in the .280 range and had some power. He could play any of the outfield positions. On opening day in 1932 he had started in center field in place of Earle Combs and smacked 2 home runs in the 12–6 shellacking of the A's, a decisive win for the Yankees in what was harbinger of things to come.

Byrd had southern roots, born in Georgia and raised in Alabama, and although he was a skilled baseball player, his best sport was golf. After eight years in the Majors—six with the Yankees, two with the Cincinnati Reds—he would play his last Major League game at the age of twenty-eight and then switch sports to pursue a career as a professional golfer. He won six times on the Professional Golfers Association tour, notching wins at the Greater Greensboro Open and the Texas Open, and played twenty times in the sport's major championships.[4] He finished third in the 1941 Masters Tournament, fourth in the 1942

Masters, and lost 4–3 in the match play finals of the 1945 PGA championship to Byron Nelson. Byrd holds the unique distinction of being the only Major Leaguer to play in a World Series game and also compete at the Masters Tournament.

Ruth should have taken golf lessons from Byrd. Ruth was a devoted and accomplished amateur golfer, often competing in tournaments against professional golfers, but he was no match for Byrd on a golf course.

On the first of September, the Washington Senators came to Yankee Stadium for a 3-game series. Herb Pennock pitched the opener for the Yankees, opposed by General Crowder of the Senators.

After Crowder's opening day ten-inning shutout of the Red Sox in April, he had struggled. At the end of July, he was a disappointing 11-13 and was giving up close to 4 runs a game. In August, however, Crowder put up a record of 7-0—two of the wins came in relief roles—and he also notched a save. He was a workhorse. For the season, he would appear in 50 of the team's 154 games.

Against the Yankees, Crowder pitched masterfully, allowing just 6 singles—one of them a pinch single by Red Ruffing, who McCarthy often used as a pinch hitter. The Senators won, 6–2. Crowder blanked Ruth in 4 at-bats. The next day, the Senators won again, this time behind Firpo Mayberry; again, Ruth went hitless in 3 at-bats. In the final game of the series, Washington's rookie ace, Monte Weaver, was relieved in the seventh inning by Lloyd Brown, with the Senators holding a 5–4 lead. But in the bottom of the ninth, Brown surrendered a 2-run, two-out, game-winning homer to Tony Lazzeri, allowing the Yankees to salvage 1 game of the series. Ruth went 2–5, with a triple and a single. Red Ruffing pitched a complete game for this seventeenth win.

The Senators left town, and the next day the Yankees played a makeup contest with Boston, the league's worst team with a record of 37-95. McCarthy gave Ruth the day off. A crowd of only ten thousand fans showed up for the Sunday contest. The Yankees banged out 12 hits and won, 8–2. Byrd went 0-3 as Ruth's replacement in the outfield.

On September 5, the Yankees ended their home stand with a Labor Day doubleheader against Philadelphia. If the A's had any hope of mounting a September stretch run to overtake the Yankees, it was time for Connie Mack's team to make a statement. The A's trailed the Yankees by 10½ games. A doubleheader sweep, plus some September heroics from Jimmie Foxx—now with 51 homers—would be needed in order to pull off the comeback.

Yankee Stadium was packed with 70,772 loudly cheering fans. It was the largest crowd that would see the Yankees play all season, and it didn't take long for the Yankees to give their supporters something to cheer about. A's starter George Earnshaw retired only 1 batter in the Yankees' half of the first and gave up 6 runs. The Yankees coasted to an 8–6 win. Lefty Gomez was hardly dominant, but he pitched all nine innings to improve his record to 23-6. The nightcap followed the blueprint of the first game. With the rookie, Johnny Allen, on the mound, the Yankees jumped out to a 5–0 lead after 3 innings and breezed to a 6–3 triumph. Allen's record improved to 16-2. The Yankees' lead was now 12½ games, with 18 games to play. The pennant race was essentially over.

For the A's in the doubleheader, Foxx managed a double in 8 at-bats and wasn't a factor in either game. Ruth started both games, hitting his 40th home run in the opener and collecting a single in the nightcap. Byrd replaced him in the late innings in both games.

McCarthy felt relieved and confident, but he didn't yet know that something was wrong with Babe Ruth. Although he had been productive in the doubleheader, he wasn't healthy. A day after the A's doubleheader, Ruth began to experience sharp pains on his right side, and this time, it didn't seem to be a baseball-related injury. The Babe's wife, Claire, accompanied him on the first leg of a short road trip, but in Detroit the pains got worse. He left the team without playing a game. Babe and Claire took a train back to New York.

In Detroit, Sammy Byrd replaced Ruth in the starting lineup for the 6-game series. Batting in the leadoff spot, Byrd went 13-28 in the series, with 5 extra base hits, including 3 home runs and 8 RBIs. It was more evidence that, as great as Ruth was, he was just one cog in a very powerful and efficient offensive machine. Still, McCarthy had reason to be concerned.

While the Yankees were exhausting themselves in Detroit—two of the games went 14 innings; another went 10 innings—Ruth went to see his doctor, Edward King, in New York.[5] Ruth trusted King, who had treated Ruth's famous bellyache in 1926 and was also the doctor who examined and treated Miller Huggins when the Yankees' manager was dying.

This time, Ruth, the noted hypochondriac, had something real to worry about. The illness was not diagnosed, or at least it was never publicly reported, but Ruth had a fever and was losing weight.[6] Whatever Ruth's ailment was, it was a setback and knocked him out of action for more than two weeks. Ruth later claimed it was an attack of appendicitis. If so, for whatever reason, Dr. King decided not to operate. He prescribed cold packs and bed rest. Ruth rested for ten days. He appeared at the stadium for an hour-long workout on September 17, but was unable to hit a single ball into the stands during his batting practice. "I don't feel as though I could break through a pane of glass," he said, noting that, "You know, they had me packed so deep in ice I don't feel thawed out yet."[7]

A few days later, Ruth returned to the lineup, trying to play himself back into shape in the final 5 games of the season. But the results weren't promising. He still looked weak and depleted, managing just 3 hits in 16 at-bats, though 1 of the hits was his forty-first homer, in Boston on the final weekend of the season.

It was now questionable if Ruth would play in the World Series, or if he did play, if he would be able to contribute or make an impact.

While the Yankees coasted to their first pennant in four years and Ruth took half the month off to recuperate from his peculiar and undefined illness, the baseball world focused on the exploits of Jimmie Foxx.

Foxx had entered September with 48 home runs and 23 games to play, then homered three times in the first four days of the month. He was having one of the greatest offensive seasons in baseball history. Only

Hack Wilson and Babe Ruth had ever hit more than 50 home runs in a season; Foxx was now the third member of that exclusive club. And because he had been on the A's roster since he was seventeen, people tended to forget that he was just twenty-four years old.

Fans recognized that Foxx had a shot at Ruth's single-season home run record. Ruth had hit 17 in September 1927. Foxx needed just 12 in his final month to reach the magic mark of 60. He had already hit 12 or more homers in three months, consecutively in May, June, and July; after the Labor Day doubleheader with the Yankees, Foxx needed 9 homers in 16 games.

He didn't homer in a 2-game series with the Indians, but he collected number 52 at Tiger Stadium on September 11, a 2-run blast in the seventh inning off Buck Marrow. A week passed before he homered again, this time at Comiskey Park. After the series with the White Sox, the A's returned to Shibe Park to close the season with a 2-game series against the Yankees and 3 games with the Senators.

The Yankees had already clinched the pennant, and only seven thousand fans attended the Wednesday afternoon game. Red Ruffing pitched for the Yankees, going for his nineteenth win in his final regular-season appearance of the year, and little-used Sugar Cain, a twenty-five-year-old rookie, took the mound for the A's. The A's won, 8–4, scoring half their runs in the bottom of the eighth inning. Foxx contributed a solo homer in the seventh inning.

On Thursday, this time with a crowd of 9,000 in the stands, the A's concluded their season series with the Yankees, and Foxx provided some fireworks to enliven the day. In the third inning, facing Lefty Gomez with the bases loaded, Foxx connected for a grand slam, pushing his RBI total for the year to 161. Only five players in Major League history—Hack Wilson, Lou Gehrig, Chuck Klein, Al Simmons, and Babe Ruth—had ever knocked in more runs in a season. Foxx added to his home run and RBI totals with a solo homer in the seventh off Wilcy Moore.

Foxx's home run total now stood at fifty-six, tied with Hack Wilson for the second most homers in a season. Three games were left on the schedule. The task of tying or breaking Ruth's single-season record was formidable but possible. The Washington Senators, still in contention for second place in the league, came to Philadelphia. The Senators were 2 games behind the A's, needing 3 straight wins to claim second place.

Monte Weaver, the best rookie pitcher in the American League and sporting a record of 22-9, was relieved in the fourth inning after giving up 5 runs, including home runs by Mule Haas and Al Simmons. The A's won, 8–4, and clinched second place. Foxx had 2 hits but no home runs.

The next day, Jimmie Foxx faced Bill McAfee in the first inning with the bases loaded and crashed a home run into the left field stands. It was home run number 57, not to mention his second grand slam in three days. The A's eventually squandered their lead, losing to the Senators, 8–7. Foxx came to bat four more times, but failed to homer. After the game, both teams boarded trains and traveled to Washington, where they would play the last game of the regular season.[8]

The final game of Foxx's 1932 season was played on Sunday, September 25. In Washington, Sugar Cain was the starter for the A's, matched up against General Crowder, who would pitch the season finale, just as he had hurled the season opener. It was Crowder's league-leading thirty-ninth start of the season. President Hoover, who had watched Crowder perform on opening day, was not in the stands. Hoover was six weeks away from the election that would determine his—and the country's—future course.

Like the opening day game that the Senators had played against the Red Sox, it was a pitcher's duel. Washington got a run in the first, and the score stayed at 1–0 until the bottom of the eighth when the Senators got an insurance run. It looked like Crowder would pitch shutouts in both the opening and closing games of the season if he could hold the A's scoreless in the ninth.

In his first three plate appearances, Jimmie Foxx had walked and reached base on a pair of singles. After Al Simmons made an out leading off the ninth, Foxx came to the plate for his final at-bat of the season. Fittingly, Foxx homered, number 58, and Crowder lost his bid for his fourth shutout of the season.

After retiring the next two batters, Crowder walked off the mound with a record of 26-13. He had won his last fifteen decisions. He led the league in wins, starts, innings pitched—and in hits allowed. He finished with an ERA of 3.33, the fourth best mark in the American League and the lowest ERA he would post in his eleven-year career. Along with the rookie, Monte Weaver, Crowder had kept the Senators in the pennant race but the team would finish a disappointing third.

Of historical interest: the Senators' 2–1 win over the A's was played in one hour and seventeen minutes. The 3 games in the series between these two teams were completed in five hours and seven minutes, or an average of one hour and forty-two minutes per game. Compare that to the length of a typical Major League game today: in 2018, the average length of a game was three hours and four minutes.[9]

The dominance of the Yankees, especially considering the strength of their two closest competitors, the Athletics and the Senators, is evident in the final standings.

Table 4. Final Standings, [1932]

Team	Wins	Losses	Games Behind
New York	107	47	———
Philadelphia	94	60	13
Washington	93	61	14
Cleveland	87	65	19
Detroit	76	75	29.5
St. Louis	63	91	44
Chicago	49	102	56.5
Boston	43	111	64

Jimmie Foxx had achieved one of the greatest offensive seasons in baseball history. His individual efforts may have been overshadowed

Table 5. Four-Season Stats Comparison

		AB	Runs	Hits	2B	3B	HR	RBI	BB	Average	OBP	SLG
Ruth	1921 season	521	177	204	44	16	59	171	144	.377	.511	.845
Ruth	1927 season	540	158	192	29	8	60	164	137	.356	.486	.772
Wilson	1929 season	585	146	208	35	6	56	191	105	.356	.454	.723
Foxx	1932 season	585	151	213	33	9	58	169	117	.364	.470	.749

by the Yankees' march to the pennant, the various dramas involving Babe Ruth, the antics of Dizzy Dean, the Memorial Day brawl in Cleveland, the shooting of Billy Jurges, and the firing of Rogers Hornsby, but Foxx was just twenty-four years old. No one, not even the Babe, had demonstrated such power at that age.

Inevitably, Foxx's season would be immediately compared to two recent record-breaking years: Ruth's 1927 season and Hack Wilson's 1929 season. Although in historical terms, the greatest individual offensive output of them all—at least to this date in history—was Ruth's 1921 season, when he personally out-homered eight different Major League teams.

A comparison of these four seasons tells the story (see table 5).

Before the World Series began, however, the Yankees had to handle a few housekeeping tasks. On September 23 the team had met to decide on how to distribute their World Series money. It was expected to be the richest postseason in baseball history.[10]

A World Series share, especially for players with an average salary, could be as much as 25 to 50 percent of his salary. With few guaranteed contracts or opportunities for additional income, average roster players benefitted greatly from the World Series money. This was true not just for the pennant winners in each league, but also for players on teams that finished in the top four of their respective leagues.

In the off-season, most players needed a second source of income. Some returned to farms. Others parlayed their baseball fame into entertainment gigs. Joe McCarthy had a vaudeville act, as did other ballplayers, like the Waner brothers. Lefty Gomez also briefly appeared on stage, earning more money for a five-week engagement than he'd earned in salary during the 1932 season.[11] Big stars like Babe Ruth and Lou Gehrig organized barnstorming teams that traveled across the country playing local teams and giving fans far away from major cities an opportunity to see big leaguers in action. The teams organized by Ruth and Gehrig were known as the "Bustin' Babes" and the "Larrupin' Lou's."

The Yankees were far more generous than their World Series opponent from Chicago, spreading the wealth amongst players and various club personnel. In all, the Yankees voted shares or awarded cash to thirty-nine members of the organization. Full shares were granted to McCarthy, his three coaches, and twenty two players, including two members of the team—pitchers Danny MacFayden and Wilcy Moore—who had joined the team midway through the season.[12] Partial shares were approved for several players who were traded or injured during the season, and cash grants, ranging from $350 to $1,000, were designated for the trainer, the road secretary, the groundskeeper, the clubhouse attendant, the clubhouse messenger, and the mascot.[13]

Perhaps as the Yankees divided up the shares, they took note of the half-share voted by the Cubs to their ex-teammate, Mark Koenig. That issue would emerge in dramatic fashion a week later when the two teams met in the World Series.

24

The World Series Begins

Four years had passed since the Yankees had last played in a World Series game and fan interest in New York was intense, though one of the team's most notable supporters—Franklin Roosevelt, the state's governor—would miss the first 2 games of the series. As the Yankees prepared for Game One at Yankee Stadium, Roosevelt was campaigning for the presidency in the Southwest. On the eve of the series opener, he was giving a speech in Lamy, New Mexico. But the governor's itinerary would bring him to Chicago for Game Three, where he was expected to see the Yankees perform in Wrigley Field.

The Yankees' number one fan was a resident of the city, a man named Bill Robinson, known more popularly by his nickname, Bojangles. The entertainer—a dancer and vaudeville performer—was renowned for his devotion to the Yankees and made it a point to attend every Yankees World Series game.[1]

In 1932 Robinson was fifty-four years old and a nationally recognized celebrity, earning more in a few weeks than most Major League ballplayers earned in a season. He was famous and wealthy and recognized informally as "the mayor of Harlem." Soon he would embark on a movie career that would make him even more famous and wealthy.[2]

At a time when African Americans were banned from the white Major Leagues, and when African Americans were restricted by law and custom to the indignities of segregation in housing, public transportation, and accommodations—including segregated seating in many Major League ballparks—Robinson often traveled with the Yankees and was welcome in their clubhouse.

A skilled athlete, Robinson was not a sedentary fan. He had an unusual talent: he could run backward almost as fast as he could run forward.[3] From 1930 until 1977, he was listed in the *Guinness Book of World Records* as holder of the record for the fastest time in the one hundred yard backward dash.[4]

Robinson was also a man who liked to gamble—on virtually everything, from boxing matches to horse races; from card games to pool matches to dice games—and, of course, on baseball games. Before the 1932 World Series, he made a bet on the Yankees to win the series in a 4-game sweep. He got 6–1 odds and put up $2,000.[5] He would be in the crowd at Yankee Stadium for the opening games of the series.

Bill Robinson wasn't the only Yankees supporter eagerly anticipating the series. A fan from Kansas City, Kansas, named Bill Cunningham, had arrived in New York ten days early in order to be first in line when bleacher seats went on sale the day of the game. Others lined up behind him. Despite occasional rain showers and inclement weather, Cunningham stayed in place. He wasn't alone. Fifteen New York City police were assigned to keep order as the line grew in length.[6]

Inside the stadium, workmen were busy decorating with bunting and banners. Yankees players took batting practice on Tuesday afternoon and invited Cunningham to enter the stadium and watch from a seat behind the Yankees' dugout. He was assured that he could return to his spot at the head of the line when the practice was over. Babe Ruth recognized Cunningham's presence by coming over to where he sat and autographing a ball for him.[7]

The managers of the Yankees and Cubs had already gone on the record with their own predictions. Charlie Grimm boldly declared, "We're going to win." He expressed confidence that his pitching staff could handle the potent Yankees' lineup, even Babe Ruth. Joe McCarthy, noting his concern about Ruth's physical status, was somewhat more reserved, telling the press, "We are confident of victory, but, I hope not overconfident."[8] McCarthy's mother, Susan, interviewed in Buffalo, New York, had no doubt that the key to the series was the

Table 6. Yankees Player Stats, 1927 vs. 1932

Playing Position	1927 Yankees	Batting Average	HRS	RBIS	1932 Yankees	Batting Average	HRS	RBIS
First base:	Lou Gehrig	.373	47	175	Lou Gehrig	.349	34	151
Second base:	Tony Lazzeri	.309	18	102	Tony Lazzeri	.300	15	113
Shortstop:	Mark Koenig	.285	3	62	Frank Crosetti	.241	5	57
Third base:	Joe Dugan	.269	2	43	Joe Sewell	.272	11	68
Outfield:	Babe Ruth	.356	60	164	Babe Ruth	.341	41	137
Outfield:	Earle Combs	.356	6	64	Earle Comb	.321	9	65
Outfield:	Bob Meusel	.337	8	103	Ben Chapman	.299	10	107
Catcher:	Pat Collins	.275	7	36	Bill Dickey	.310	15	84
		-	ERA			-	ERA	
Pitcher:	Waite Hoyt	22-7	2.63		Lefty Gomez	24-7	4.21	
Pitcher:	Wilcy Moore	19-7	2.28		Red Ruffing	18-7	3.09	
Pitcher:	Herb Pennock	19-8	3.00		Herb Pennock	9-5	4.60	
Pitcher:	Urban Shocker	18-6	2.84		Johnnie Allen	17-4	3.70	
Pitcher:	George Pipgras	10-3	4.11		George Pipgras	16-9	4.19	

Yankees' right fielder: "Babe Ruth will be back in there, and you can bet he'll hit them hard and long."[9]

With the Yankees as heavy favorites due to having the more powerful offense and a manager with World Series experience, speculation among sportswriters centered on whether this Yankees team or the 1927 Murderers Row team was the more outstanding club.[10] A side-by-side statistical comparison shows the 1927 team to be, by the numbers, the more dominant team. The 1932 Yankees were significantly better at only one position: catcher.

As Bill Cunningham waited in line, as workmen prepped the stadium for the games, and as sportswriters debated the relative merits of the two teams, more than a thousand cheering Chicagoans showed up at Chicago's Union Station on Monday, September 26, to shout encouragement as the Cubs team boarded a train bound for New York. The train was dubbed "The Cub Special," and the Cubs' entourage totaled seventy-four individuals, counting players, coaches, trainers, and wives. Charlie Grimm's wife, Lillian, passed out sewing kits to the women.[11]

The players passed the time with games and baseball talk. Woody English, the best bridge player on the team, dominated the card games. Burleigh Grimes played ping pong with Charlie Root. Guy Bush, named by manager Grimm as the Game One starter, nervously smoked cigars.[12]

After twenty-one hours on the train, the Cubs debarked at Pennsylvania Station. Given that the weather was cold and damp, Grimm canceled practice and held a short afternoon team meeting. After listening to Grimm, the players scattered, many of them intending to enjoy a night at the city's theaters. One player stayed in his hotel room: Guy Bush. "Maybe the show would get my mind off the game," he mused, "but on the other hand I always found theatres were not so good for my eyes."[13]

The first game of the series was played on a cold, wet Wednesday, the twenty-eighth of September. A heavy morning downpour drenched the field. Then the rain subsided. Tarps protected the infield, but the outfield was soaked.[14] When the gates opened, Bill Cunningham was first to enter the stadium, hurrying to the bleachers to secure his unreserved seat.

Finally, the sun broke through. Acting New York City mayor, Joseph McKee—known as "Holy Joe"—threw out the first ball.[15] The game began at 1:48 p.m., eighteen minutes late, and the stadium was only a little more than half-filled. The total paid attendance would be recorded as 41,459, a far cry from the more than seventy thousand who attended the Labor Day doubleheader with the Athletics, just three weeks earlier. The inclement conditions had kept many at home, and the empty seats meant smaller checks for owners and players.

For Guy Bush, this was the biggest game the thirty-one-year-old right-hander had ever been asked to pitch. He was in his ninth full season with the Cubs and had recorded double-digit wins in each of the past seven years. Born and raised in Mississippi, where he worked on the family cotton farm, Bush was a country boy, just twenty-one years old when signed by Cubs scout Jack Doyle, for the sum of $1,200.[16]

Doyle had been impressed by Bush's stamina and durability after seeing him pitch both ends of a doubleheader, shutting out a Minor League team from Vicksburg, Mississippi. Doyle had been right in his assessment. In 1927 Bush pitched a complete eighteen-inning game against the Boston Braves, facing seventy one batters in a contest that lasted nearly four hours. Over the previous seven seasons, he had averaged 12 complete games and over 200 innings a year. He had pitched in the 1929 World Series, allowing just 1 earned run in 11 innings of work.

Bush was thin and handsome, with slicked-back black hair, a swarthy complexion, and notably large ears. On the mound, he had a good fastball and a curve that he delivered with a high leg kick and a long stride toward the plate. If he had a flaw, it was that he tended to be nervous, sometimes with lapses in his control.

Red Ruffing, the Yankees' starting pitcher for Game One, had a background similar to Bush's: poor and rural. At the age of thirteen, Ruffing had dropped out of school to work in an Illinois coal mine, where the labor was demanding and dangerous. He showed promise as a young outfielder on the company team, managed by his father. Two years later, however, his right foot was crushed between two coal cars, requiring the amputation of four toes.[17] Still, he pursued a baseball career, though as a pitcher, not as an outfielder. He signed with the Boston Red Sox organization, making it to the Majors at the age of twenty. He spent five dismal seasons with the Red Sox, losing more games than he won for the perennial cellar dwellers.[18] After his trade to the Yankees in the fall of 1929, he became one of the top pitchers in the league and still holds the Yankees' team record for most wins by a right-handed pitcher, with 234.

Ruffing was also a good hitter. He retired with a .269 lifetime batting average and 36 career home runs; his managers often used him as a pinch hitter.[19] In fact, based on career statistics, Ruffing was a more dangerous home run hitter than four members of the 1932 Yankees' starting lineup: Frank Crosetti, Joe Sewell, Ben Chapman, and Earle Combs.[20]

Because Ruffing didn't join the Yankees until the 1930 season, he had never pitched in a World Series. In that regard Bush was more prepared for the Game One experience than Ruffing.

The four men picked by Commissioner Landis to umpire the World Series were Bill Klem and George Magerkurth of the National League; Bill Dinneen and Roy Van Graflan of the American League. For this first game, Dinneen would call balls and strikes, Klem would be at first base, Magerkurth at second base, and Van Graflan at third base. The umpires would rotate clockwise, game by game, during the series.

The Cubs scored first, getting 2 runs in the top half of the first inning. Billy Herman led off with a single to center, and Woody English followed with a single to right that skipped past a stumbling Babe Ruth. As Ruth lurched after the ball—resembling "a fat man trying to catch a rabbit," as one writer put it—Herman scored and English made it to third.[21] English came home on a single by Riggs Stevenson.

The score remained 2–0 going to the bottom of the fourth. Bush easily retired the first nine Yankees batters in order, but in the fourth, he walked the lead-off man, Earle Combs, retired Sewell on a bouncer to Grimm at first, and then surrendered an RBI single by Ruth. The next batter, Gehrig, homered, and the Yankees had their first lead of the game.

Ruffing was far from perfect. He would walk 6 in the game and give up 10 hits, but he held the Cubs scoreless from the second inning through the sixth. In the bottom of the sixth with the score still 3–2, the Yankees drove Bush out of the game. He loaded the bases, walking the first three batters—Sewell, Ruth, and Gehrig. Lazzeri popped out, but Dickey singled to center driving in 2 runs. Chapman reached first on a fielder's choice when Herman tried to throw Gehrig out at the plate. Then Bush walked the weak-hitting Crosetti to reload the bases. Burleigh Grimes replaced Bush and retired one batter before Combs singled in 2 more. Thanks to 4 walks and some shaky play in the field, the Yankees had scored 5 runs on just 2 singles, leaving 2 runners on base.

At the end of the inning, the score stood 8–2. Each team scored four more times, making the final a decisive 12–6 win for New York. Throughout the game there was constant chatter back and forth between the teams. Ruth, the vocal leader of the Yankees, reminded the Cubs—and his former teammate, Mark Koenig—how unfair it was that the Cubs had failed to vote Koenig a full share of World Series money. From game to game, the bench jockeying would only get worse, more profane, and more personal. As for Koenig, he jammed his wrist in Game One and was unable to play in the rest of the series, except for one brief pinch hitting appearance in Game Three. Billy Jurges replaced Koenig in the lineup.

In the locker room, a reporter asked Ruth how his appendix felt. "Fine," Ruth answered. He had received 2 walks but hit only 1 ball out of the infield. "I'm not strong, you know," he added, "not quite full of the old power."[22]

Game Two was played under better weather conditions and with a slightly larger crowd in attendance. Paid admissions totaled 50,709. The pitching matchup was between the respective team's young starters, Lefty Gomez, winner of 24 games during the regular season, and Lon Warneke, who had finished his first full year in the Majors with 22 wins. Only two Major League pitchers had won more games during the season: General Crowder of the Senators with 26 wins and Lefty Grove of the Athletics with 25 wins. The game would be the best pitching matchup—and lowest-scoring—game of the series.

Once again, the Cubs scored in the top of the first. Billy Herman lashed a lead-off double past Sewell at third and advanced to third when Kiki Cuyler reached on Crosetti's error. With runners at first and third, Riggs Stevenson hit a sacrifice fly to Combs in center. But the Yankees quickly countered in their half of the inning. Like Bush the day before, Warneke's control got him in trouble. He walked Combs and Sewell to put two runners on, with Ruth coming to plate. Ruth struck out, but Gehrig followed with a 2-strike single to right, scoring Combs. Then Dickey singled in Sewell to give the Yankees a 2–1 advantage.

The Cubs tied the game in the third, thanks to another misplayed ball in right field by Ruth, who allowed Stevenson's base hit to scoot past him. Frank Demaree, in his first-ever World Series at-bat, also singled to right to score Stevenson. If the powerful Yankees had a weakness, it seemed to be the defensive play of their right fielder. His miscues in both games resulted in runs for the Cubs.

At the plate, Ruth did most of his damage by waiting out Cubs pitchers for walks. With 1 out in the bottom of the third, and after fouling off several pitches, Ruth drew a walk. Gehrig followed with an infield single, and both runners advanced when Billy Jurges charged Lazzeri's slowly hit ground ball and threw the batter out at first. Warneke walked Bill Dickey to load the bases, and Ben Chapman hit a line drive single to center to drive in 2 runs and give the Yankees the lead at 4–2. Gehrig led off the fifth with a hard hit single to right and later scored on an RBI single by Dickey, which ended the scoring as both starting pitchers completed their starts.

Grimm was philosophical and upbeat in his analysis of the first 2 games. He praised Gomez, calling him, "One of the greatest pitchers I ever saw." He told his team to be patient. They would do better once they got back to Chicago. "I promise you a different story out there," he said.[23]

With a 2–0 lead in the series, the Yankees' clubhouse was in excellent spirits. Gehrig with 5 hits, including a home run and 3 RBIs, had paced the offense in the first 2 games. McCarthy cautioned his team against overconfidence, reminding them that they were headed to Wrigley Field for the next games, where the Cubs might be tougher to beat.

Al Schacht, the former Washington Senators' pitcher and coach, who now entertained spectators with pantomimes and gags in pregame festivities, visited the Yankees' clubhouse. Schacht was unimpressed with the Cubs' lineup, asking, "Where is their power?"[24] It was a question the Cubs hoped to answer at Wrigley Field.

Less than two hours after the end of the second game, both teams were aboard trains, headed for Chicago.

For Babe Ruth, he was reliving the experience of 1918. Here was the Babe, on a westbound train, traveling to the Midwest to play a World Series game against the Chicago Cubs. Much had changed over the course of fourteen years. Ruth was still the focus and main concern of the Cubs, but now he was a New York Yankee, and now he was feared less as a dominating pitcher and more as the most powerful hitter in the history of the game, though his performance in New York suggested that he might not be healthy enough to be a significant factor in the series.

For Joe McCarthy, it would be a bittersweet homecoming, returning to Wrigley Field to lead the Yankees against a Cubs team he had helped to build and manage—before being relieved of his responsibilities and replaced by Rogers Hornsby. Most of the core players on the Cubs—Cuyler, Bush, Malone, Grimm, Root, Hartnett, English—had played for McCarthy on the 1929 World Series team.

In cities and small towns along the route, fans came out to greet the trains carrying the two teams. When the Yankees' train stopped in Elkhart, Indiana, to change engines, fifty youngsters charged onto the train and searched for ballplayers. They found Babe Ruth and mobbed him. Ruth and other players signed autographs for their young fans, and then the youths were shooed off the train.[25]

The trains of both teams arrived at LaSalle Street Station to be greeted by large and cheering crowds of Chicagoans. The Cubs' train pulled in first. Despite the two losses in New York, there was a tide of optimism in the air, an excitement that the World Series had come back to Chicago for the first time since the disaster of 1929. The Cubs' fans pinned their hopes on Charlie Root, the steadiest of the Cubs' pitchers in their long history. One observer noted, "all Chicago has now turned its eyes on Charlie Root, upon whose stout right arm has fallen the responsibility of halting the onrushing Yankees."[26]

Chicagoans gave an equally mighty welcome to the Yankees when their train reached the station, recognizing Joe McCarthy, the former Cubs manager, and the large figures of Ruth and Gehrig. Traffic was blocked outside the station, and motorcycle police had to clear a path for cabs to escort the Yankees from LaSalle Street to the Edgewater Beach Hotel. An uglier scene presented itself at the hotel. That crowd taunted the Yankees, and someone spit in the direction of Babe Ruth and his then-wife, Claire. McCarthy had a brief meeting and calmly told his team, "Don't get excited. Just imagine you're down on the South Side getting ready for a series with the White Sox."[27] He set a midnight curfew and let the players go on their way. The Ruths spent a quiet night in the hotel. Gehrig and some of his teammates went to a party.[28]

The excitement at the LaSalle Street Station for the arrival of the Yankees' and Cubs' trains was just the warm-up. Chicago had geared up for the largest celebration the city had ever seen: a torch-lit parade with banners and music to welcome Franklin Roosevelt.

Roosevelt had completed a three-week campaign swing in the West—speaking at rallies in Topeka, Salt Lake City, Denver, Seattle, Portland, San Francisco, Los Angeles—and then back through the Southwest and the Midwest. The San Francisco speech on the subject of wealth was later hailed as one of the great political speeches of the twentieth century. Along the way, Roosevelt's train would stop in small towns, and he would stand on the platform at the rear of the train and give a short speech.

By the time he arrived in Chicago, the campaign had reached millions of people, and the tone of the campaign had become nastier. Hoover accused Roosevelt of being a Capitalist. Roosevelt's vice-presidential candidate, John Nance Garner, attacked Hoover as a Socialist. Roosevelt focused on making speeches about what he intended to do if elected to the presidency.

The Chicago crowd along the parade route from the train station to the Congress Hotel was boisterous and rowdy. People waved kerosene torches in the air. Others held red stick flares. Music blared as bands marched behind Roosevelt's white convertible. Roosevelt rode through the cauldron of sound, waving energetically to his supporters. Observers estimated the crowd as large as 200,000 people. The city of Chicago was excited.

25

The Crowd Gathers

On the morning of October 1, Ruth and Claire left the Edgewater Beach hotel and went to visit a young Chicagoan who had been injured in a bombing.

A few weeks earlier, Leo Wilbur Koeppen, a sixteen-year-old, had been walking home with three friends. Around 10:00 p.m., as the four young people were passing by the home of Supreme Court Judge John P. McGoorty, Koeppen noticed the lit fuse of a bomb in their path. When he tried to kick it out of the way, the bomb exploded. The blast shattered windows and rattled the doors in the judge's house. Koeppen and his companions were tossed in the air. One of Koeppen's friends was burned on her arms and legs. Koeppen was the most seriously injured, suffering wounds to his face and eyes.

It was the seventy-eighth recorded bombing in Chicago since the start of the year—most of which were related to organized crime.[1]

Ruth had heard of the boy's situation and had been told that Koeppen loved baseball. The boy was a Cubs fan, but nevertheless a baseball fan. As he had many times in the past, and would do again in the future, Ruth was moved to do something to perk up the boy's spirits.

When Ruth and his wife arrived at Koeppen's room at the Chicago Hospital, the boy's head was tightly wrapped in bandages. Doctors had determined that he was permanently blinded, but Koeppen had not yet been given this diagnosis. No record exists of how long Ruth stayed in the boy's room, but they talked for a while about baseball. Koeppen affirmed that he was a Cubs fan and hoped that they might get a win in that day's game. Before leaving the hospital, Ruth presented the boy with an autographed baseball.

Ruth also promised to hit a home run in that afternoon's game.[2]

Leo Wilbur Koeppen wasn't the only young boy looking forward to Game Three of the World Series. In Anamosa, Iowa, fourteen-year-old Charles Arthur Ireland was awakened before dawn by his father and told to get ready for a trip to Chicago.

True to his promise to Snap Hortman, Warden Ireland had purchased tickets for the 3 World Series games scheduled for Wrigley Field. In order to attend the games, however, he had to cancel plans he'd made to visit his daughter, Maisie, in Grinnell, and to listen to a speech by his friend and political ally, Dan Turner.

The visit could wait, and the warden could miss Dan Turner's speech. The opportunity to see the Cubs play in the World Series took priority.

An inmate named Shorty Wakefield drove the car. Warden Ireland sat beside him in the front seat. Charles Ireland and Snap Hortman were in the backseat. The car was a new 1932 Ford V-8, the first vehicle of its kind in the county, a source of great pride for the warden. Wakefield served as Charlie Ireland's driver on long trips. He had been convicted of stealing copper tubing from a hardware store and sentenced to three years in the reformatory. Although Wakefield had become eligible for parole and early release eight months earlier, he had refused the parole and asked to stay on at the reformatory until he completed his original sentence. Wakefield knew there was little chance he could find employment outside the prison, and he liked driving the warden's car.

The day was overcast but dry. The Ford stirred up clouds of brown dust as Wakefield steered the car past farms and through a procession of small towns. Although Iowa farmers had suffered badly for over a decade, the summer of 1932 brought even more widespread and severe consequences of the Great Depression. Foreclosures had forced some families off their land. Other farms had simply been abandoned, and even those farms that had managed to survive were in bad shape. In the towns, buildings were boarded up and failed banks had shuttered their doors. Through the gray morning light, the hollow shells of vacant buildings and empty houses gave the appearance of ruin and desolation.

They stopped for lunch at a small diner and then got back in the car. At Clinton, the car clattered over the Lyons-Fulton Bridge—a steel-trussed structure with a wooden deck—and the Ford carried them from Iowa to Illinois. A hundred feet below the car, the Mississippi River coursed dark and foreboding, the great river more than a mile wide at this point.

That afternoon they reached Chicago. The car rolled through the city streets. Charles and Snap peered out at the tall buildings and pedestrians and passing vehicles. Streetcars screeched past them on iron rails. Homeless men sat slumped on curbs, holding their heads in their hands. Newspapers swirled in the street. Charles looked up in awe at the skyscrapers. Except for the courthouse and the three-story towers on the prison, no building in Anamosa was more than two stories in height.

Wakefield parked the car near Wrigley Field, and they walked to their gate. Fans had been in line outside the park for bleacher and general admission seating since before 6:00 a.m., and once-seated, these same fans had waited six more hours before the first ballplayers appeared on the field for warm-ups. The mood outside the ballpark was still one of keen anticipation. Men in overcoats and derby hats jostled shoulder-to-shoulder as they milled about the entrances. Some smoked cigarettes, flipping the butts into the street when they were finished. All of the excited talk was about the game.

Inside the park, Charles settled into his seat, again sitting next to Snap Hortman. The uniqueness of the experience made an indelible impression. Fifty-eight years later—by then a retired newspaper man living in California—Charles Ireland would recall that afternoon with exquisite pleasure: "Sometimes I feel," he said, "that I am the only person who sat beside a prison lifer at a World Series game."

Charles Ireland was joined in that crowd by thousands of boys close to his age—other boys of summer, dedicated young baseball fans, some of them seeing their first Major League game. Many of the boys lived in the Chicago area, but others came from out of state.

Early that morning, Lincoln and Charlie Landis, formally dressed in white shirts and dark sports jackets, boarded a train in Logansport, Indiana, and headed for Chicago, where they were to meet their uncle—they called him "Uncle Squire"—who also happened to be the commissioner of Major League Baseball. For Lincoln and Charlie, it would be their first time in attendance at a Major League game. They would have excellent reserved seats, front row on the third base side, near the Cubs' dugout.[3]

Johnny Stevens, the son of hotelier Ernest Stevens, was also in the crowd. Like the Landis boys, Stevens would be in the reserved seats along the third base line behind the Cubs' bench. He clutched a scorecard in his hands.

Two boys from the Chicago suburbs, twelve-year-old Lowell Blaisdell and eleven-year-old Irving Boim, attended the game with their fathers. Decades later, both boys would recall in vivid detail their memories of that day.

Lowell Blaisdell and his father did not have reserved seats. They lived in Elmhurst on the west side of Chicago and left for Wrigley Field at 6:30 a.m. in order to line up for general admission bleacher tickets. They parked near Wrigley Field, and Lowell's father paid a young boy a dollar to watch his car. Then they walked to the ticket office behind the scoreboard and stood in a long line. Lowell later recalled that when the gates opened, they rushed "with a horde of others" to grab a non-reserved seat in the right-field bleachers, "six tiers up from the right-field fence." The fence, Lowell remembered, was made of wire and about five feet high. They sat in their seats from 8:30 a.m. until game time—four-and-a-half hours.

Irving Boim—later a Minor League pitcher, mostly in the Pirates organization—also attended with his father. Years later, he recalled his father waking him between 3:00 a.m. and 4:00 a.m., in order to get ready. They rode the elevated train to Belmont Street, near Wrigley, then walked to the ballpark and stood in the long line for the unreserved bleacher tickets. They finally found seats in the temporary wooden bleachers over Sheffield Avenue.[4]

The Ireland party watched the park fill with spectators. The fans, especially those who arrived early to get the bleacher seats, waited a long time before any of the players appeared. The teams finally came out to warm up around noon.[5] They went through their workouts, the Yankees attired in their gray pinstriped road uniforms, the Cubs in white jerseys and pants with red and blue accent stripes. They tossed the ball back and forth, like teenagers warming up for a sandlot game; a few players ran sprints or stretched in the outfield.

There was no mistaking Babe Ruth: he was the largest of the Yankees' players, pot-bellied with thin legs and a powerful torso. He wore the distinctive number three on his broad back. This was Ruth's nineteenth season as a Major Leaguer, and he had played before Chicago crowds at Comiskey Park, but this was his first appearance at Wrigley Field. Fans taunted him and threw lemons in his direction. Good naturedly, Ruth tossed them back to the fans.

When Ruth took batting practice, everyone's attention focused on his swings. Cubs fans near home plate yelled insults and hurled more lemons at the Yankees' slugger. As if to answer the crowd's taunts, Ruth lifted one fly ball after another into the right-field stands; nine balls in all sailed over the wall. Ruth shouted at his hecklers: "I'd play for half my salary if I could hit in this dump all the time."

Fifteen minutes before game time, Franklin Delano Roosevelt, the governor of New York and now the Democratic candidate for president, arrived with his contingent. Chicagoans cheered Roosevelt's arrival, though most of them knew that he was a Yankees fan. The governor was accompanied by his wife, Eleanor, and their son, James. Eleanor wore a black felt hat with a silver donkey pinned to it. It was reported that this was the first Major League baseball game she had ever attended.

The entourage included Chicago mayor Anton Cermak, and the party was seated along the first base line, near the Yankees' dugout.

Roosevelt had been a baseball fan since he was a boy. At Groton, he lacked the skill to play on the school team, so he was put on a team called the Bum Base Ball Boys.[6] But his enthusiasm for the game never waned. He was manager of the baseball team at Harvard. As a young man, he went to the Polo Grounds to watch the Giants and Yankees play.[7] In 1917 he was called on to substitute for Woodrow Wilson at the opening game ceremonies in Washington DC and threw out the first ball.

He was a fan of high-scoring games, remarking in a letter to the Baseball Writers Association in January of 1937, "I am the kind of fan who wants to see plenty of action for his money. My idea of the best [baseball] game is one that guarantees the fans a combined score of not less than fifteen runs, divided about eight to seven." He was a devotee of the lively ball style of play, not a fan of old school John McGraw style baseball.

It was well known that Roosevelt was a proud Yankees supporter, and a fan of Babe Ruth because for the fan who liked action and lots of scoring, no one epitomized that kind of play better than Ruth.

For all of their differences in terms of education and sophistication, Roosevelt and Ruth shared some traits. Both men were gregarious, supremely self-confident, fearless in their professional pursuits, and bold actors in public. They loved crowds and being the center of attention. Neither man was shy about making bold predictions, and both men knew how to charm an audience—in Roosevelt's case, with words; in Ruth's case, with action.

It is fair to say that on this date—October 1, 1932—they were the two most famous men in America, creatures of their particular time and place in history. But if one man attracted more attention on this day, it had to be Ruth. This was the World Series, the stage where Babe Ruth excelled, and the crowd was here to see what he could do against their hometown Cubs. It would also be the last time that Franklin Roosevelt played second fiddle to another person in a public setting. As for Roosevelt, the future president could have not picked a better game to attend.

Moments before the game started, the two managers, Joe McCarthy and Charlie Grimm, made their way to the governor's box for introductions and a brief chat. When speaking to McCarthy, Roosevelt made a gesture with his right arm, swinging it toward the right-field bleachers, as if to indicate he'd like to see the boys in pinstripes hit a few balls in that direction.

Soon all eyes focused on Governor Roosevelt. He had been given the honor of throwing out the ceremonial first pitch. James Roosevelt helped the governor rise to his feet. Franklin Roosevelt cocked his right arm back and tossed the ball to Gabby Hartnett.

It was time to play ball.

26

The Called Shot

Wrigley Field was filled to capacity. The games in New York had failed to sell out, but nearly fifty thousand fans—the official count was 49,986—now crammed into Wrigley's seats, including the bleacher seating atop scaffolding on Waveland and Sheffield Avenues, just beyond the outfield walls, and the temporary bleachers in front of the right-field wall.

In the front-row box seats along the third base line, the commissioner of baseball, Kenesaw Mountain Landis, sat with his eleven-year-old nephews, Lincoln and Charlie. Landis leaned forward to watch the action, his chin resting on the railing. He peered intently at the players going through their final warmups. Also on the third base side of the diamond, young Johnny Stevens waited anxiously for the game to begin. In this same section of the stands, two fans—Matt Miller Kandle and Harold Warp—came prepared to film some of the action on their 16 mm cameras. Kandle was accompanied by his daughter, Gladys.

Yankees fans were clustered on the first base side. Bill Robinson, the Yankees' most loyal fan, had accompanied the team to Chicago and had a seat near the Yankees' dugout with a good view of the on-deck circle and home plate. Willie Veal Sewell, the wife of the Yankees' second baseman, was nearby with the wives of other Yankees' players. They were close enough to hear the players talking to each other. If Violet Popovich had a ticket to the game—there's no evidence that she did—this was her preferred seating area, too, so that she could gaze into the Cubs' dugout during the game.

The Roosevelts were settled into their seats on the first base side of the diamond, also near the Yankees' dugout, sitting with Chicago Mayor Anton Cermak.

Out in the right-field bleachers, Lowell Blaisdell sat with his father, six rows up from the playing field. Irving Boim and his father were a little further back, in the bleachers over Sheffield Avenue. Somewhere in the vast crowd, Jimmie Foxx and Mickey Cochrane, of the second-place Philadelphia Athletics, were seated with their wives. Cincinnati Reds outfielder Babe Herman, who would be traded to the Cubs in the off-season, sat behind home plate.

Warden Ireland, his son, and the two inmates of the Anamosa Men's Reformatory, Snap Hortman and Shorty Wakefield, were in the reserved seats.

In the press box more than a hundred newspapermen from around the country hunched over their typewriters: Irving Vaughn and Edward Burns of the *Chicago Daily Tribune*; Warren Brown of the *Chicago American*; the New York reporters, Richards Vidmer of the *New York Herald Tribune*, John Drebinger of the *New York Times*, Joe Williams of the *New York World Telegram*. There were many others: notably, the syndicated columnists, Westbrook Pegler and Grantland Rice. In future years, their observations and reports on the Yankees' half of the fifth inning would be painstakingly parsed and analyzed.

Radio announcers perched in front of their microphones, ready to bring the game live to more than a million radios across the nation: located in farm houses and city apartments and offices; speakeasies, and the backrooms of bookie joints. Snap Hortman's fellow inmates at the Men's Reformatory in Anamosa, Iowa, would be among those tuned in.[1] In Brooklyn, eighteen-year-old Bernard Malamud probably listened to the game on the radio in his father's store. One baseball notable who had declared that he would not be listening and had no interest in the outcome of the game remained at home on his farm north of St. Louis; that would be Rogers Hornsby.

Calling the game for the Mutual Broadcasting System, the Cubs' regular-season announcers, Quin Ryan and Bob Elson; for CBS, Ted Husing and Pat Flanagan; for NBC, Graham McNamee and Tom Manning.

It was a crisp fall day in Chicago, nearly perfect weather for baseball. The temperature at game time hovered in the low seventies, the skies were slightly overcast, and a breeze was blowing out, whipping the American flag on top of the pole in center field. The Chicago Board of Trade band played "The Star Spangled Banner," and then the Cubs ran out onto the field.

The veteran Chicago right-hander, Charlie Root, took the mound for the Cubs. He was tough-minded and durable, averaging 255 innings and 18 wins a year for the Cubs over seven seasons, and he was respected as a no-holds-barred competitor. Nicknamed "Chinski" for his willingness to throw his fastball inside and high to hitters, Root was noted as a pitcher who commanded respect when he was on the mound. For the seventh-straight season he finished with 14 or more wins. He had thrown 216 innings and completed 11 of 23 starts. He pitched 16 times in relief. He had posted a record of 15 wins and 10 losses.

With Koenig injured, Billy Jurges remained in the lineup at short-stop. Moore replaced Demaree in center field. Hartnett remained behind the plate. Stevenson and Cuyler flanked Moore in the outfield; English, Herman, and Grimm filled out the infield.

The lead-off hitter for the Yankees in the first inning was Earle Combs. With the count at 2–2, Combs hit a hard ground ball to the normally reliable Jurges at short. Jurges fielded the ball cleanly but threw it wildly over Grimm's head and into the Yankees' dugout, allowing Combs to reach second base. The next batter, Joe Sewell, walked on 5 pitches. Ten pitches, two baserunners, no one out, and Babe Ruth coming to the plate. Root and Hartnett conferred, meeting halfway between the mound and home plate.

Over the years, Ruth had played many games in Chicago as a member of the Boston Red Sox and the New York Yankees, but this was his first at-bat at Wrigley Field in a regular season or World Series game.[2] A roar came up from the crowd as Ruth approached the plate; hoots and jeers rang out. A few lemons were tossed in the direction of the home plate. The bench jockeys in the Chicago dugout chimed in with insults and derisive commentary.

If Ruth was fazed at all, he didn't show it. He relished being the center of attention. As Richards Vidmer, writing the next day in *New York Herald Tribune*, would report: "The very first time [Ruth] came to bat in the opening inning, there was confidence in his manner. He paused to jest with the Cubs, pointed to the right-field bleachers and grinned."[3]

Root threw 2 balls to Ruth, both low. Eight of his first 12 pitches had been called balls. On the thirteenth pitch of the first inning, Root delivered a hittable pitch and Ruth took his first official swing at Wrigley Field, connecting and driving the ball in a steep, soaring arc over the right field fence, over the heads of the fans in the bleacher, who stared in amazement at the flight of the ball. As the ball neared the bleachers, Irving Boim held his cap aloft, in the hope that he might catch the ball, but it cleared the temporary bleachers and returned to earth on the far side of Sheffield Avenue. Root watched Ruth trot gleefully around the bases. The Yankees had a quick 3–0 lead.

The Cubs countered with 1 run in the bottom of the first against Yankees starter, George Pipgras, when Kiki Cuyler doubled to drive in Billy Herman, who had walked.

Root appeared to settle down a bit in the second inning, striking out Pipgras and getting Combs to fly out to Johnny Moore in center. Then Sewell once again walked on 5 pitches, as Root struggled with his control. With the crowd buzzing, Ruth stepped to the plate for another battle with Root. This time the count went to 3–2. Sewell took off with the pitch; Ruth swung and drove a long fly ball toward right field. Fans in the temporary bleachers in right rose up in anticipation of a second homer by Ruth, but Cuyler sprinted back and made the catch a few feet in front of the fence for the final out of the inning.

The Cubs failed to score in their half of the second, then Gehrig led off the third with a solo home run to increase the Yankees' lead to 4–1, but the Cubs managed a rally against Pipgras in the bottom of the third. With 1 out, Cuyler matched Gehrig's blast with a line drive homer into the right-field bleachers. Stevenson followed with a bloop single into short right. Moore forced Stevenson at second, but then Grimm lined a single to right that bounced away from Chapman, permitting Moore to score.

With the score at 4–3 in favor of the Yankees going to the top of the fourth, the game was turning into exactly the kind of contest that Governor Roosevelt favored: a high-scoring affair with plenty of action and the two teams closely matched. The Cubs tied the score in the bottom of the fourth, thanks to some sloppy fielding on the part of the Yankees. Jurges reached on a single to left and advanced to second base when Ruth misplayed the ball. The crowd gave Ruth a thorough razzing for bungling the play. Ruth doffed his cap sarcastically in response. With 2 outs, Woody English hit a hard grounder to the right side of the infield that Lazzeri booted. English reached first base safely and Jurges scored from second base. On the third pitch to Cuyler, English tried to steal second base and was thrown out to end the inning.

With the score now tied at 4–4, the game moved to the top of the fifth inning, the occasion of the most famous and meticulously analyzed at-bat in the history of baseball.

Joe Sewell led off the inning for the Yankees. He slashed a ground ball to the left side of the infield, out of the reach of Woody English, but snared by Jurges at deep short. Jurges made the long throw across the diamond in time to retire Sewell at first. Sewell jogged back to the dugout.

The scene was set. History was about to be created. Ruth walked to the plate. The hoots and jeers and catcalls rang out. Up in the stands along the third base line, Matt Kandle and Harold Warp switched on their movie cameras to capture the moment.

Consider the setting: Ruth was in the batter's box with fifty thousand people watching him and fixated on what was going to happen next. Gehrig was in the on-deck circle. Claire Ruth was watching from her seat just behind the Yankees' dugout. At the plate, Ruth stood one hundred feet away from Judge Landis on the third base side, and one hundred feet away from Franklin Roosevelt on the first base side. Charlie Root stood directly in front of Ruth, sixty feet away.

Ruth's task was to concentrate on the moment. A Major League pitch takes about one second to go from the pitcher's hand to the catcher's mitt. We know from Hugh Fullerton's experiment at Columbia University in 1921 that Ruth had unusual powers of concentration.

Consider also that the Cubs in their dugout were doing everything possible to disturb Ruth's frame of mind; they were screaming insults at Ruth. The next day the *New York Times* would publish an article on the game in which the writer would benignly comment that the Cubs "directed some uncomplimentary remarks at [Ruth]."[4]

The leading bench jockeys on the Cubs were Burleigh Grimes and Guy Bush. They were on the top steps of the dugout. Bush cupped his hands around his mouth so that his words would travel unambiguously to Ruth's ears. The remarks—to contradict the *Times* reporter—were much harsher than "uncomplimentary." Ruth's physique and manhood and racial heritage were called into question.

One specific insult was certain to reach Ruth's ears—a racial obscenity. Since his boyhood at St. Mary's, Ruth had been sensitive to and enraged by one particular word—the word suggesting that he might have African-American ancestors or parentage.[5] Variations on that word and its connotation had been directed toward Ruth off and on during his career. He had almost fought Johnny Rawlings in the Giants' locker room when Rawlings dared to use the word. Guy Bush, now perched at the edge of the dugout as if he were about to charge toward Ruth at home plate, taunted Ruth with the slur. The words burned the ears of Judge Landis, sitting just a few feet away from the Cubs' dugout with his nephews.

Ruth did not ignore the words tossed at him. He engaged with the Cubs' bench, shouting back at them. He might also have heard his wife call out. From the first base side, Claire Ruth shouted to her husband, "Remember the little boy."[6]

At some point, Charlie Root threw a pitch for a called strike. Ruth raised a finger in the direction of the Cubs' bench. One strike. The next two pitches were balls. One of the balls was in the dirt and got away from Gabby Hartnett, who turned and retrieved it. Ruth grinned and gestured. He pointed somewhat ambiguously with his bat and raised his arm, pointing toward the Cubs in the field, or toward Root, or at some unspecified distant location. The record is not clear about what Ruth intended to communicate.

The fourth pitch from Root was also a called strike. The count stood at 2 balls, 2 strikes.

Root's next delivery was a slow curve, breaking down and out of the strike zone. Ruth swung, upper cutting the ball, his first swing of the at-bat. Bat and ball connected. The ball arched into the sky, over Root's head, over Johnnie Moore's head in center field, and over the patrons in the seats, flying past the flagpole in the deepest part of the park. Home run.

From his seat along the first base line, Franklin Roosevelt turned to his son, James, and said, "Unbelievable." Then as Ruth circled the bases, Governor Roosevelt loudly exclaimed, "You lucky bum. You lucky, lucky bum."[7]

Ruth trotted around the bases, continuing the dialogue with the Cubs' bench and gesturing with his hands that the Cubs should get back in the dugout and sit down. He trotted all the way around the bases and shook hands with Gehrig, then disappeared into the Yankees' dugout.

Gehrig stepped to the plate and hit Root's first pitch into the right-field stands. The Yankees had taken the lead, 6–4. The crowd quieted.

Each team added a run. The final score was 7–5.

The Cubs' locker room was dejected. With their supporters cheering them as they left the field, the team acknowledged they had disappointed their fans. Manager Grimm summed it up this way: "Don't it make you sick you can't win even one game for a bunch of folks like that." Grimm promised a better outcome in Game Four. He would send Guy Bush to the mound. But everyone knew that no team had ever come back from a 3–0 deficit in the World Series.

By contrast, the visiting Yankees were jubilant and exuded confidence. The Yankees had now won 11 straight World Series games—4 straight in 1927, 4 straight in 1928—and were on the verge of another series sweep.

Reaching the locker room, Babe Ruth—suddenly healthy again after a sluggish September—was still celebrating his 2 home runs. "Did Mr. Ruth chase those guys back to the dugout?" he shouted. Then he answered his own rhetorical question: "I'll say Mr. Ruth did."[8]

Bill Robinson entered the room and joined the celebration, shaking hands with the Yankees players, then jumping onto a trunk and dancing. Players gathered in a circle around Robinson, cheering and clapping as he performed.[9]

Before dressing in street clothes and preparing to go back to the Edgewater Beach Hotel, Joe McCarthy had a few words of advice for his team, "Get your bags tomorrow morning, fellows. I think we'll be leaving right after the game."[10]

27

The World Series Ends

After the game, the Roosevelt party returned to the Congress Hotel, where the governor and his wife shared an ice cream soda.[1] That evening Roosevelt attended a formal dinner at the Stevens Hotel, hosted by the Illinois Democratic Party. Johnny Stevens, after an exciting afternoon at the ballpark, was likely in the room for the event.

Following an introduction from gubernatorial candidate Judge Henry Horner, Roosevelt delivered a speech to an enthusiastic crowd of more than three thousand fellow Democrats. Roosevelt praised Mayor Cermak's leadership, the pioneer spirit of the city, and Chicago's ethnic diversity. Then he stressed his position on the repeal of the Volstead Act, stating that "When Prohibition is out of the way—and I am confident it will be soon—we will be able to give our attention to other problems."[2]

After more cheering and congratulations, the governor was whisked away to his waiting campaign train for an overnight trip to Detroit. There he would enjoy a reception, another parade, and a speaking engagement on Sunday night to six thousand people at the naval armory, where he would proclaim, "Americans everywhere must and shall choose the path of social justice."[3]

The game on Saturday had ended a bit after 5:00 p.m., a little before dusk. Warden Ireland had reserved two rooms at a hotel near Wrigley Field, and after dinner, Ireland's party returned to their rooms for the evening. For Charles Ireland and the two inmates from the Men's Reformatory it had been a day of intense excitement. It's unlikely that even the Cubs' loss dampened their spirits. From the windows of their hotel rooms, the vast sprawl of the city of Chicago must have seemed like a magical place—a city of three million people, where citizens roamed the streets freely and the traffic never stopped moving, and the lights burned all night long.

Shorty Wakefield and young Charles Ireland shared one room. The other two men—the warden who had traveled the world, and his prisoner, who had spent all of his adult life in the Men's Reformatory—settled down in an adjacent room. Before going to sleep, Warden Ireland locked the door.

The next day the Ireland party left their hotel and returned to Wrigley Field for Game Four. The Ireland contingent hoped that the Cubs might claim a victory so they could stay in Chicago an additional night and attend Game Five. Cubs fans who looked at the headlines of Chicago's morning papers must have winced:

The *Chicago American*: "Ruth and Gehrig Rout Cubs with Homers."

The *Chicago Tribune*: "Root Sees Ruth, Gehrig Ruin Perfect Pitches."

Looking ahead, though, optimistic Cubs fans figured: If the Cubs could scratch out a win on Sunday, they'd be able to pitch their ace, Lon Warneke, on Monday and perhaps force a Game Six back in New York.

It was another warm and sunny day for a ball game and not as windy as it had been on Saturday. By game time, the temperatures had reached into the high seventies. Once again, a sell-out crowd packed into the stands—though swarms of gnats whirred around the heads of fans in lower level seats. The official paid attendance was reported as 49,844.[4]

Governor Roosevelt was not among the spectators. He was in Detroit, the final stop on his month-long campaign trip before returning to Albany.[5]

Prior to the game, Joe McCarthy held a meeting with the Yankees in their locker room. McCarthy reported that he'd received a strongly worded message from Judge Landis that the two teams were ordered to clean up their language. If not, players on both teams faced heavy fines. Landis—sitting with his young nephews—had clearly heard the profanity, insults, and racial invective. McCarthy read the Landis note to the players and cautioned them to refrain from using inappropriate language.[6]

The instruction from the commissioner carried a lot of weight. The Yankees' dugout was quiet during the game. Joe Sewell later said, "We sat there like mummies. One thing you didn't do in those days was monkey around with Judge Landis. He was the *law* in baseball."[7]

The Yankees' starter for Game Four was Johnny Allen, the rookie who had posted a 17-4 record during the regular season. The Cubs countered with Guy Bush, loser in Game One and the chief antagonist of Babe Ruth in Saturday's game.

Bush's first pitch to Earl Combs, the Yankees' leadoff hitter, resulted in a line drive that nearly beheaded the pitcher. Bush got his glove up in time to deflect the ball, but it skidded past second base and into short center field. Sewell followed with a swing at Bush's next offering and grounded a single to right field.

Two pitches, two runners on base, and Babe Ruth coming to bat. The sequence was eerily similar to the previous day's game. After all the hollering at Ruth during Game Three's fifth inning, Bush was now in a position to let his pitching do the talking. The crowd buzzed in anticipation.

The first pitch was a called strike. The next pitch was a fastball thrown right at Ruth, hitting him squarely on the right forearm. Ruth flicked at his jersey, as if the pitch meant nothing to him. In truth, Ruth was in pain, but the Babe laughed audibly enough that fans could hear him. On his way to first base, Ruth called out to Bush, "Hey, Lop Ears, was that your fastball you hit me with? I couldn't feel it. I thought it was one of those gnats flying around here."[8]

Whether Bush intended to hit Ruth—which was entirely possible—or whether he just had a momentary loss of poise and control is a question that can't be answered. Over his career, Bush had reasonably good control, walking fewer than three batters per nine innings. But Bush had struggled with his control in Game One, and like Root the day before, Bush seemed to come undone when facing the top of the Yankees' batting order.

Things didn't get much better for Bush. With the bases loaded and nobody out, Lou Gehrig stepped to the plate. Gehrig smashed a long fly ball to left-center that looked like it might result in a grand slam, but Cubs center fielder, Frank Demaree, caught the ball as he crashed into the wall.[9] All three baserunners advanced. The Yankees led 1–0. After Lazzeri walked on a 3–2 count to refill the bases, Charlie Grimm decided to change pitchers. Lon Warneke came in and retired the next two batters.

Guy Bush's day was over. He had faced five hitters and retired only Gehrig on a 400-foot fly ball.

Bush would get one more chance to pitch to Ruth before their careers ended. It would be a few years later, in Pittsburgh, in a regular-season game with little impact on the pennant race. That final encounter between Bush and Ruth, however, would have lasting historical significance.

The Cubs came back to score 4 runs in the bottom of the first, knocking Allen out of the game. Wilcy Moore replaced Allen. It was the third time in 4 games that the Cubs had taken a lead in the early innings. The big blow was a 3-run homer by Frank Demaree. Relief pitchers finished the game for both clubs.

Warneke yielded a 2-run homer to Lazzeri in the third, cutting the margin to 4–3. Jackie May replaced Warneke in the fourth when the Cubs' pitcher developed a sore elbow. But it was not a lead that May and the Cubs could maintain. By the top of the seventh, it was a tie game, 5–5.

If the Cubs and their fans had any hopes of preventing a 4-game sweep by the Yankees, that notion dissolved in the seventh. Dickey opened the inning with a single, and after Chapman's flyout, Crosetti slammed a double off the right-field fence. Red Ruffing, the winning pitcher in Game One, pinch hit for Wilcy Moore and was intentionally walked to load the bases. Three straight singles—a bloop by Combs, a liner to right by Sewell, and a ground ball single by Ruth—brought home 4 runs. Gehrig was hit by a pitch and Bud Tinning replaced May. Eventually the inning ended with the strikeout of Dickey, who had started the rally.

Herb Pennock hurled three scoreless innings, and to complete the rout, the Yankees scored 4 more runs in the top of the ninth, including a second 2-run homer by Lazzeri. The lopsided final score of 13–6 was indicative of the Yankees' domination in the series. The total number of runs scored in the contest set a single-game World Series record.

The Cubs' clubhouse was subdued after the game. Charlie Grimm lit a cigarette and addressed his team. "We won together and we lost together," Grimm said. "It's no disgrace to lose to a ball club like that."[10]

After the game, the Yankees celebrated. "I'm the happiest man in the world," declared Yankees manager Joe McCarthy.[11] It was sweet vindication for McCarthy to capture the world championship at Wrigley Field, just two years after having been dismissed from his managerial position with the Cubs.

Judge Landis and American League president William Harridge entered the Yankees' locker room and offered their congratulations. Players gathered around McCarthy and burst into song, singing a raucous and off-key version of "The Sidewalks of New York."[12]

Ruth, who had contributed little to the Yankees' offense in what would be his final World Series game, wrapped his aching right forearm in hot towels. But he was gleeful, too, congratulating McCarthy with a handshake and shouting, "Boy, what a victory."[13]

The celebration continued on the train back to New York. There was more singing and shouting and boasting. The champagne flowed.

No one on the Yankees' train was happier than Bill Robinson. He had just won $12,000 in a bet that the Yankees would sweep the Cubs in four straight. As the train sped through the night on iron rails, Robinson tap-danced up and down the aisles.

28

Postgame

A splendid season filled with drama, on and off the field, had come to an end. Attendance at Major League games had dropped to the lowest figure in thirteen years. Fewer than seven million fans paid admissions to see big league baseball. The total attendance number for all Major League teams was 6,974,566, a 30 percent drop since 1930. The Cubs and Yankees topped the attendance standings; the Cubs drew 974,688 fans to Wrigley Field, edging out the Yankees who drew 962,320 to Yankee Stadium. The St. Louis Browns were last in attendance. Only 112,558 fans showed up to watch the Browns, averaging less than 1,500 spectators per game. The hapless Browns would post the worst attendance figures in the Majors for a decade, every year from 1930 through 1939.

Despite the low attendance figures, increasing numbers of Americans listened to the games on their radios. Two networks—NBC and CBS—carried the World Series games nationwide, reaching more than twenty million fans who listened at home or in public places, like gas stations or cigar stores.[1] Snap Hortman's fellow inmates at the Men's Reformatory weren't even the only incarcerated fans to hear the World Series. The warden at San Quentin prison in California allowed inmates to listen to Game Four of the series. For many of those inmates, it was the first time they had ever heard a baseball game on the radio.

With the conclusion of the 1932 season, teams were quick to make plans and adjust their rosters for the 1933 season.

For the Philadelphia Athletics, the season had ended without a fourth consecutive trip to the World Series, and Connie Mack acted swiftly.

He sold off a trio of his star players, completing the deal on the same day that the Yankees and Cubs played Game One of the World Series. Mack sold Mule Haas, Jimmy Dykes, and Al Simmons to the White Sox for the sum of $100,000.

Mack explained the sale was due to financial considerations. "We went into the red heavily," Mack said. "We had one of the highest salaried clubs in the league, including the Yankees with Babe Ruth's $75,000, and our attendance figures were far below those of last year."[2]

Mack praised all three of the players, calling Simmons "the greatest outfielder I ever managed," noting that Dykes had "his greatest season at third base," and praising Haas as "a valuable man."[3] Over the next three seasons, the acquisition did little for the White Sox franchise, which finished sixth, eighth, and fifth with the three former Athletics on their roster.

A year later, Mack trimmed his payroll some more, sending Mickey Cochrane to the Tigers and Lefty Grove to the Red Sox.[4] Mack held onto his most valuable asset, Jimmie Foxx, for three more seasons. Foxx averaged 43 homers and 135 RBIs a season during those years, but Mack's depleted roster finished third, fifth, and eighth. In December of 1935, Mack sold Foxx to the Red Sox for $150,000.[5]

Mack had responded to the demands of the times. The Depression years had been agonizingly difficult on Major League Baseball. Players, owners, and fans suffered. Mack believed he had saved his franchise from insolvency by breaking up one of the most powerful and balanced rosters in the history of the game. Cochrane had several more productive seasons. Simmons, Grove, and Foxx played into the 1940s before retiring. As for the Athletics, they went from being one of the greatest teams of all time to one of the worst. From 1935 through 1946—twelve seasons—the A's finished in last place nine times.[6]

Connie Mack wasn't the only owner to make dramatic changes after the 1932 season. On October 4, Clark Griffith announced simply that "he had decided to make a change" and fired popular manager Walter

Johnson, the most iconic figure in the history of the Washington Senators. The "Big Train," as he was known to fans, was forty-four years old and had achieved modest success as the team's manager, leading the club to a sixth-place finish in 1929, a second-place finish in 1930, and third-place finishes in 1931 and 1932. Johnson's teams had held their own against the Yankees and Athletics, the two most powerful clubs in baseball during those years, but the Senators' owner wasn't satisfied.[7] Johnson was replaced by a younger man, Joe Cronin, who turned twenty-six years old a week after he was named manager. Cronin would be the team's playing manager for the next two seasons before Griffith made another change, trading Cronin to the Red Sox for Lyn Lary and $225,000.[8]

There was also some unfinished business for Commissioner Landis. The series had generated good crowds and a considerable amount of revenue to be split among the two World Series teams and the first division teams in each league. The players share was $363,822.27, slightly less than the payouts to the Yankees and Cardinals in 1928 or to the Cubs and Philadelphia Athletics in 1929. On a team by team basis, the split broke down like this:

Yankees: $152,805.35
Cubs: $101,870.24
Second place Athletics and Pirates: $29,786.67
Third place Senators and Dodgers: $18,174.44
Fourth place Indians and Phillies: $6,612.23

A full share for the Yankees' players and coaches was $5,231.77. It was a significant allocation, considering the regular-season salaries of the players. Excluding the contracts of Ruth and Gehrig, the average Yankee earned about $10,000 a year.[9] Bill Dickey and Earle Combs had salaries of $12,000. Tony Lazzeri had a contract for $12,000. Herb Pennock earned $10,000. Joe Sewell and Red Ruffing were both paid $8,000. Lefty Gomez, the ace of the pitching staff, but just in his second full season, earned $7,500. And Sammy Byrd, who played an important role in being "Babe Ruth's Legs," was paid just $6,500 in salary in 1932; Byrd's World Series earnings nearly doubled his annual income.

The Cubs had voted fewer total shares. Each full share for a Cubs player or coach was worth $4,245.60; Mark Koenig's share, of course, was half that. Except for Rogers Hornsby, who had a $40,000 contract in 1932, other Cubs salaries for that year are hard to verify, but salary information for 1930 is available. Cubs players in 1930 earned the following: Guy Bush $11,000; Kiki Cuyler $17,000; Woody English $12,000; Charlie Grimm $15,000; Gabby Hartnett $18,000; Pat Malone $14,000; Charlie Root $16,000; Riggs Stevenson $16,000. Despite the Depression and salary cuts on other ball clubs, William Wrigley was noted for his fairness and open pocketbook, so it's likely that these key players on the 1932 Cubs were earning roughly the same salaries in 1932 that they did in 1930. The World Series full share money of just more than $4,200 would have added 25 percent to 30 percent to their income for the year—no small potatoes in this particular year.[10]

For first and second year players, in particular—like Billy Herman and Billy Jurges, the two holdouts on the vote regarding Koenig's share—the World Series money was a significant augmentation to their earnings for the year.

Of course, one person questioned whether the distribution of World Series money had been fair. That person was Rogers Hornsby, still fuming after the vote by the Cubs to deny him any share of the World Series money, even though he had managed the club for the first 99 games of the season. In addition, Hornsby argued—and sincerely believed— that he had been the architect of the Cubs' pennant-winning season, nurturing and teaching the young stars of the team: Herman, Jurges, and Warneke.[11]

Hornsby took his complaint directly to Commissioner Landis. In late September, shortly after the Cubs had cast their vote on World Series shares, Hornsby wrote a letter to Landis. For Hornsby, facing possible foreclosure on his farm and having his paycheck garnisheed by Veeck to pay back the loans to his players, a share of the World Series money would provide temporary relief for his troubled finances.

Landis responded on October 14, citing an obscure league rule that only players on a team's roster after September 1 were automatically qualified for a World Series share. If a player was not on a roster at that date, the team's vote had to be unanimous for him to receive a share. Hornsby was not happy and blamed Veeck for putting pressure on the players to deny him a share.[12] But he had no further recourse.

With Hornsby's complaint out of the way, Landis turned to an issue that personally bothered him: the half-share voted to Mark Koenig. Unlike Hornsby, it wasn't Koenig who raised the issue—one might say that, in fact, it was Babe Ruth who raised the issue or at least made a very public and dramatic case for Koenig.[13] Landis wanted to know exactly why the Cubs had not given a full share to Koenig, considering all he had done to help them win the pennant. He called Charlie Grimm to his office in Chicago and told him, "You can tell your boys that everybody feels bad about them voting Koenig only a one-half share and they won't get their checks until next January."[14]

The players saw it differently, at least Jurges and Herman did. As Jurges explained, "He did win the pennant for us, but he didn't play that many ball games, and he wasn't entitled to it," though Jurges later conceded, "If we had to do it all over again, we'd probably give him a full share."[15]

Woody English, the Cubs' captain, had returned to his home in Newark, Ohio, where he spent the off-season, when Landis's secretary, Elinor Donohue, phoned and said the judge wanted to meet with English in person. English hurried to Chicago.

English arrived at Landis's home, where the judge was recovering from the flu. The white-haired Landis was in bed on the second floor. English climbed the stairs. The judge asked English to get him a glass of water. Then the two men talked.[16]

Landis asked English a series of questions about how the team had arrived at its decision. English explained that, as captain, he ran the meeting. Grimm and the coaches did not participate. It was strictly a vote of the players who had been on the roster all season. There were two holdouts—Jurges and Herman, though English refused to name them in the judge's presence—and the argument was that Koenig, who had participated in just 33 games, had not been on the roster long enough, or played in enough games, to justify a full share.

In the end, Landis set aside his own feelings and agreed that the decision had been reached fairly and logically and within the rules set forth by baseball.[17]

29

Fans Return Home

After Game Four of the 1932 World Series, the Irelands and their guests retraced their route and returned to Anamosa on Sunday evening. When Hortman arrived back in the prison, he was greeted and enthusiastically cheered by his fellow inmates, then locked in his cell.

The warden and his son returned quietly to the comfort of the family quarters and went to bed.

The games were over and the baseball season had ended, but the news that Warden Ireland had gone to the World Series games in Chicago with two prisoners—one of them a convicted murderer serving a life sentence—soon became public knowledge. On October 7, the headline in the *Des Moines Register* boldly proclaimed: "Herring Charges Iowa Warden Took Convicts to World Series."

Clyde LaVerne Herring, a fifty-three-year-old Democrat, was running against Warden Ireland's friend and political ally, Dan Turner, for the governorship of Iowa. Turner, a Republican who had rewarded Ireland by appointing him to the position of prison warden at Anamosa, was the incumbent, hoping to win a second term as governor.

Herring was an energetic and ambitious man who had grown up on a farm in Michigan. As a young man he left the farm to move to Detroit and take a job as a jewelry clerk. He served in the military during the Spanish-American War, returned to farming, and then held a job as the representative of the Ford Motor Company in Iowa. He was a shrewd and successful businessman who became wealthy by acquiring valuable real estate in Des Moines. In time he became involved in Democratic politics, running for governor in 1920 and senator in 1922, though he lost both races.

But in 1932, with Franklin Roosevelt at the head of the ticket, and with the country in despair as the Great Depression deepened, the Democratic Party once again turned to Herring and made him their nominee for the governorship.

The most compelling issue in the governor's race—as it was in the presidential contest—was the state of the economy, especially the agricultural economy in the Midwest. Land values had declined during the 1920s, and farm foreclosures had forced many Iowa farmers to give up their land. Prices had plummeted. By the fall, corn was ten cents a bushel, oats seven cents a bushel. It cost farmers more to plant a crop than they could expect to receive once it was harvested. It wasn't any better with livestock. Pork was three cents a pound, beef five cents a pound.[1]

But the economy was not the only topic in the latter stages of the governor's race. Herring seized on Ireland's World Series trip and turned it into a political issue. Speaking at a fundraising dinner, Herring proclaimed: "Here is a situation and spectacle unsurpassed in the history of American criminology." Later in his speech, Herring described the trip as "an out of state pleasure jaunt, which thousands of law-abiding citizens would have liked to take themselves, but could not because they did not have the money."[2]

It was, according to Herring, "the last word in pampering criminals." Herring demanded that Governor Turner immediately remove Ireland from office, and promised that, once elected, he would make "a full and complete investigation of the trip."[3]

Reporters came to Anamosa to get a reaction from Warden Ireland. Ireland responded calmly to questions and explained that the trip had been planned for several weeks: there was no element of secrecy involved; he had used his own car; no state money had been used to transport the inmates to or from Chicago. Ireland had personally paid for the hotel rooms and all the meals on the trip. Ireland described the impulse for the trip as a "humanitarian gesture," noting that Snap Hortman was a model prisoner and a good influence on the inmate population, especially new and young inmates. He described Hortman as "very feeble" and "not a dangerous character."[4]

A month later, the nation voted. On November 8, 1932, Franklin Delano Roosevelt was swept into office, winning over 60 percent of the popular vote and 42 of the 48 states in an historic presidential election. Regional affiliation of the candidates made little impact on voters. President Hoover—born in Iowa, raised and educated in Oregon and California—won only six states, all in the Northeast: Maine, Vermont, New Hampshire, Delaware, Connecticut, and Pennsylvania. Governor Roosevelt—born and raised in New York, educated at the Groton School and Harvard—won all the states in the South, the Midwest, the Southwest, and the Far West. Roosevelt won Hoover's Iowa with 58 percent of the vote. Farmers throughout the Midwest—the region most severely impacted by the Great Depression—celebrated Roosevelt's victory.

Clyde Herring rode Roosevelt's coattails into office to become Iowa's twenty-sixth governor, the rare Democrat to hold the Iowa governor's seat in the early part of the twentieth century. He was inaugurated on January 12, 1933.[5]

Herring never followed up on his campaign promise to investigate the warden's journey to Chicago with his son and the two inmates. There were more important matters for the new governor to tackle. The farm rebellion continued with increasingly violent and confrontational actions. On April 27, 250 angry farmers stormed into the Plymouth County courthouse and abducted District Judge Charles C. Bradley as he was about to conduct a foreclosure hearing.[6] Bradley was taken to a rural crossroads and threatened with lynching before he was released. Fearing more outbursts and violence against authorities, Governor Herring proclaimed martial law in the county and ordered out the Iowa National Guard to protect public officials.[7]

Just months after Herring's inauguration, the scandal involving Warden Ireland's trip to the World Series was largely forgotten.

At the Anamosa Men's Reformatory, things returned to normal. As winter turned to spring and the snow melted, the inmates began to think again about baseball. Soon the Snappers were back on the field, under Hortman's leadership. And Cubs games were heard on the prison radio.

In the off-season William Veeck made one significant trade in order to bolster the Cubs' offense. He swapped reserve catcher Rollie Hemsley, pitcher Bob Smith, and outfielders Johnny Moore and Lance Richbourg, plus cash, to the Cincinnati Reds for outfielder Babe Herman.[8] Over the previous four seasons with Brooklyn and Cincinnati, Herman had averaged 23 home runs and 107 RBIs per year, batting over .300 in each of those seasons.

The Cubs opened defense of their National League pennant on April 12 with a home game against the St. Louis Cardinals, a contest that featured Lon Warneke and Dizzy Dean, the two young pitchers who had played such prominent roles in their rookie seasons. Warneke was the winning pitcher on this day, hurling a 6-hit shutout for a 3–0 win.

Despite the opening-day win, the Cubs got off to a sluggish start and by the end of June were just 1 game over .500 with a record of 36-35, good for fourth place in the standings, 7 games behind the league-leading, and eventual pennant-winning, New York Giants.

On July 6—one year to the day after Violet Popovich shot Billy Jurges in the Hotel Carlos—baseball held its first All-Star Game at Comiskey Park, in Chicago. The game was the brainchild of Arch Ward, the *Chicago Tribune* sports editor. It was intended to be a one-time affair, designed to publicize the Chicago World's Fair, but it turned out to be so popular that the game became an annual event. In the inaugural game of 1933, the American League defeated the National League, 4–2. The star of the game was Babe Ruth, who hammered the first home run in All-Star Game history and also made a fine running catch in the outfield on his aging and spindly legs.

Warden Ireland did not live to see if the Cubs would be repeat National League champions and return to the World Series. On June 27, Charlie Ireland experienced a shortness of breath. In the warden's living quarters, he lay down on the red horsehair sofa and his family gathered around him. Shortly thereafter, at 3:10 p.m. in the afternoon, he died, the victim of a heart attack.

For the men in the prison, it was shocking news. The prison newspaper ran an obituary and a tribute to the man who had defied convention, just nine months earlier, by taking Shorty Wakefield and Snap Hortman to the World Series. In the lead story, the *Men's Reformatory Press* reported: "The sudden death of our Warden has been a great shock to us all and his passing leaves a void in our hearts that cannot be filled." The obituary concluded: "You played it on the level, Warden Ireland, and we shall miss you."[9]

Harry Hortman lived for fourteen months after the death of Warden Ireland and died in the Men's Reformatory hospital on August 6, 1934. The cause of death was reported as a blood clot in his heart, though he had been in declining health for several years. At the time of his death, he had spent almost all of his adult life—more than twelve thousand days and nights—as a prisoner. His death was reported in the local papers, which noted that he had compiled "an enviable record as a model prisoner."[10]

Although many of the Men's Reformatory inmates who died while incarcerated were interred in the prison cemetery, Hortman had saved money specifically for the cost of transporting his body by train back to his hometown in western Iowa. In Cherokee he was given a funeral and then buried next to his mother and father, in the Oak Hill Cemetery.[11] The Hortman graves are unmarked.

30

Ruth's Legacy with the Cubs

In 1918—a year after the end of World War I, a year before the Black Sox scandal—Babe Ruth and his Boston Red Sox teammates had beaten the Chicago Cubs with outstanding pitching. In that series, the Red Sox and Cubs combined to score just 19 runs in 6 games. Fourteen years later, Ruth's 1932 Yankees overpowered the Cubs with hitting. In 1932 the Yankees and Cubs produced 19 runs in a single game—Game Four—and a total of 56 runs in the 4 games of the series.

The comparison of runs scored from these two Ruth-dominated series, in 1918 and 1932, illustrates, first, that the eras were strikingly different in terms of how the game was played; and second, that Babe Ruth dominated in both eras, first as the best left-handed pitcher in baseball, then as the game's most dangerous and powerful hitter.

Although Ruth would play two more full seasons after 1932, he had played in his last World Series. He had established his place in baseball history and his uniqueness as an athlete. No other player so successfully bridged a transition in equipment, rules, and game strategy over the course of a career.

It was Ruth himself—his capacity for sensationalizing the home run, his personal popularity, his ability to draw fans to the ballpark simply through his presence in a lineup—who dictated the changes the game went through over time and helped to enlarge its audience. Those who have argued that Ruth saved baseball after the Black Sox Scandal make a valid point, but whether or not that is true, Ruth's particular and peculiar skill at hitting a baseball rewrote not just the record books but the way the game was perceived in the minds of fans and played on the field.

In all the years of Ruth's career, he played in only 12 games against the Cubs. Ruth's reputation and, in part, the legacy of his accomplishments are permanently linked to his performance in the 7 World Series games he played against Chicago.[1]

First, Ruth's dominance as a pitcher—illustrated in these statistics from his two outings against the Cubs in the 1918 series:

Games started: 2
Games completed: 1 (a shutout)
Games won and lost: 2–0
Innings pitched: 17
Hits allowed: 13
Earned run average: 1.06

Second, Ruth's batting record in the 1918 and 1932 World Series:[2]

At bats: 20
Hits: 6
Walks: 4
Batting average: .300
Runs scored: 6
Triples: 1
Home runs: 3
Runs batted in: 6

Ruth's timeless connection to the Cubs is assured because of one single moment of baseball history: Ruth's at bat against Charlie Root in the fifth inning of Game Three of the 1932 World Series.

The tantalizing but unanswerable question is : What was Ruth's intention when he pointed or gestured during his at bat in the fifth inning of Game Three of the 1932 World Series? Did the Babe— who throughout his career proved himself capable of extraordinary feats on and off the field—predict the monstrous home run he hit off Charlie Root?

One of Ruth's most recent biographers, Leigh Montville, notes multiple occasions on which Ruth delivered on his prediction to hit a home run.[3] Montville maintains it was Ruth's nature to dramatize the moment:

"He called shots all the time. He loved to create situations. It was for other people to determine what they meant. Did he call a shot here? That will probably never be answered to every nitpicker's satisfaction. He definitely created a situation. He challenged his entire environment, whipped up all parties, then made them shut up. The specifics might be hazy, but the general story was not wrong."[4]

Robert Creamer, one of the Babe's earlier biographers, articulated a similar position:

"It is an argument over nothing, and the fact that Ruth did not point to center field before his home run does not diminish in the least what he did. He did challenge the Cubs before 50,000 people, did indicate he was going to hit a home run and did hit a home run. What more could you ask?"[5]

Some facts are not in dispute. Ruth came to bat with the score tied, the Cubs' bench tried to provoke Ruth, he made some gestures, and there was provocative taunting back-and-forth between Ruth and Cubs, primarily Guy Bush and Burleigh Grimes. It wasn't all about Koenig and his half-share; the derisive comments from the Cubs were directed right at Ruth.

Then after 2 balls and 2 called strikes, after more finger-pointing, hand-waving, arm-cocking, and bat-pointing by Ruth, he did swing at a pitch and hit the longest home run ever blasted at Wrigley Field.[6]

The homemade videos by Kandle and Warp are clear about one thing: Ruth had quieted Guy Bush and his tormentors on the Cubs' bench, and without question, Ruth enjoyed the moment and that particular home run as much as any he'd hit in his career. But the two videos are inconclusive on the question of where exactly Ruth was pointing. It's impossible to tell—even by studying the videos frame by frame—the angle and direction of Ruth's gesture, let alone what was going on in Ruth's mind at the time.

The at bat can also be seen as a piece of the larger narrative. A perfect storm of circumstances created the opportunity for Ruth to enact this drama: the firing of Rogers Hornsby, the Cubs' signing of Mark Koenig, and the team's decision to vote Koenig only a half-share of the World Series money.

Many things are remarkable about this story: the World Series setting; the Wrigley Field crowd; the presence of Governor Roosevelt in the crowd; the jawing back-and-forth between Ruth and Guy Bush; Ruth's concentration at the plate in the midst of all these distractions; Ruth's pointing; the prediction, whatever it was; the length of the home run; Ruth's home run trot; the way that event has transported itself into our collective mind and memory. Whether or not it actually happened, it has become a cornerstone of Ruth's legend.

Most baseball fans wish they could have been there to witness it firsthand, to make their own judgment about the meaning of what happened.

In an interview for Ken Burns's documentary on the history of baseball, Negro League legend Buck O'Neil, a veteran of sixty years of professional baseball, was asked, "Is there one moment in all of baseball you wish you could have seen?"

And O'Neil answered: "I wish I could have been there when Babe Ruth pointed and hit the ball out of the ballpark in the 1932 World Series. I wish I could have seen that."[7]

There were eyewitnesses, of course, more than fifty thousand of them: fans, players, radio announcers, dozens of sportswriters, four umpires, two amateur videographers, Chicago's mayor, a future justice of the United States Supreme Court, and a future president of the United States.

Ruth was coy, giving ambiguous responses in the years that followed. He never clearly claimed or disclaimed the key part of the story: whether he had actually pointed to the spot where the ball eventually landed. Over time, the legend matured and became more alluring for just this reason.

One person who fiercely denied the premise of the story was Charlie Root, the Cubs' pitcher who delivered the pitch that Ruth knocked past the flag pole. Three decades after the game, Root responded to a fan who wrote and asked him about it: "Babe Ruth did not call his shot," Root wrote. "If he had pointed as they say, he would have been knocked on his fanny."[8]

On the last day of Root's life, he told his daughter, Della, "You know, Della, I gave my life to baseball, and I'll only be remembered for something that never happened."[9]

For Game Three, Della, and Root's wife, Dorothy, were seated behind the Cubs' dugout—in the same vicinity as Judge Landis, his nephews, and the videographers Kandle and Warp. Dorothy later summed up what Charlie would have done if Ruth had pointed. Dorothy Root said that her husband would have "thrown right at his head."[10]

But Ruth did point. It was after the third pitch. The Kandle and Warp films aren't clear as to the direction of the pointing, but Ruth's right arm is extended and slightly elevated. The fourth pitch was high and inside, evening the count at 2–2. The home plate umpire, Roy Van Graflan, recalled that Ruth then said, "Let him put this one over, and I'll knock it over the wall out there."[11]

Consider for a moment, as Root and others have said, that if Ruth was predicting a home run, verbally or by gesturing, what Root's reaction would have been. Would he have thrown a pitch directly at Ruth? It was a tie game. Root was an intense competitor. The Cubs were desperate to get a win at home and give themselves a chance to even the series on Sunday. Ruth was an easy target, the largest man on the field, and not particularly mobile. If Root had wanted to silence Ruth by hitting him—as Bush tried to do the next day—it would have been easy. But it would have given the Yankees the lead-off man and go-ahead run at first base, with no one out and Lou Gehrig coming to the plate. Decades later, with the fact of the Yankees' 4-game sweep of the Cubs recorded in the books, it might have seemed like an appealing idea to hit Ruth with a pitch, but it wouldn't have made sense in those circumstances to put Ruth on base.

What Root did was deliver a slow curve on the outside of the plate—by most accounts, it would have been called a ball, low and outside—in an effort to fool Ruth and strike him out. But Ruth was guessing along with Root.[12] For most left-handed batters, it would have been a perfect pitch to slice into left field for a single. But that's not what Ruth did: he golfed it, driving the ball over the fence in center field.

Skeptics have pointed to the fact that few of the sportswriters in attendance referred to Ruth's home run as a "called shot" in their stories that appeared the next day. But an exhaustive analysis by John Evangelist Walsh in "Babe Ruth and the Legend of the Called Shot" suggests that of thirty-seven bylined reports that appeared a day or two after the game, seventeen writers either "clearly stated" or "clearly implied" that, in some way, Ruth predicted his home run before the fifth pitch of the at bat.[13] Joe Williams of the *New York World-Telegram* was the first, filing his story on the evening of October 1, and writing that Ruth "on the occasion of his second round-tripper even went so far as to call his shot." Over the next two days, more writers weighed in. John Drebinger of the *New York Times* noted that Ruth "carried on a pantomime act while standing at the plate" and "in no mistaken motions" signaled that he would hit the next pitch for a home run. Paul Gallico, writing for the *New York Daily News*, was even more direct: "He pointed like a duelist to the spot where he expected to send his rapier home and then sent it there." Gallico also refers to Ruth's actions before the hit as being in "the universal language that everyone understands—pantomime."[14] In fact, just a few years later, the baseball clown and mime Al Schacht would perfect a pantomime routine that recreated that particular moment.

Less attention has been paid to the reaction of the announcers in Wrigley Field who described Ruth's at bat. The original recordings of those broadcasts are no longer in existence, but remnants of them—supposedly recorded in real time, rather than recreated—have been released on compact disc.[15] Quin Ryan's call of Ruth's at bat goes like this:

"Here's the one and one pitch. (inaudible) Strike two. Babe let that one go past him also. He never took the bat off his shoulder. One and two on Ruth. Now Babe raises that finger again and looks out at Charlie, who gets the sign from Gabby. Into the windup. Here's the one and two pitch. Swing. A long drive. It's toward that center field corner. (Inaudible) . . . almost the exact spot that Babe had been pointing to. Here's Ruth around second on his way toward third. (Chuckling) As he comes into third (laughter), he thumbs his nose in the direction of the Cubs' dugout. Here he is around third base, heading for home."[16]

Note that if this is an authentic recording, Ryan missed one pitch in the count. Ruth swung on the fifth pitch of the at bat, not the fourth.

A longer description features the voice of Tom Manning, who was in front of the microphone for NBC radio. A print version appears in Curt Smith's book *Voices of the Game*. Here is the key excerpt:

Babe Ruth steps into the batter's box. Now Charlie Root gets the sign from his catcher, Gabby Hartnett. Here's the first pitch. And it's a strike—right down the middle! And the fans are certainly giving it to Babe Ruth now. Looking over at the Cubs' bench, the Cubs are all up on the top step. And they're yelling "flatfoot" and throwing liniment and everything else at Babe Ruth! But he steps out of the batter's box. He takes a hitch in his trousers, knocks the dust off his shoes. And now he's back in there again. And Root winds up again and here it comes! And it's outside—and it's evened up on Babe Ruth! Boy, what a powerful figure he is at that plate! And once again, Root gets the signal, winds up, here it comes. . . . and it's called strike two! And the fans are giving it to him from all corners of this Wrigley Field. The Cubs are up on the bench—they're all hoping that Babe Ruth will strike out. Again, Charlie Root winds up. And here's that pitch—and it's high inside, and it drove Babe Ruth out of the batter's box! And the count is ball two and strike two. And, boy, the Cubs are giving it to the Babe now! Oh, oh, Babe Ruth has stepped out of the batter's box. And he steps about two feet away from home plate. Now he steps toward the Cubs' dugout! We thought for a moment that he was going over and toss his bat at them or something! No, he's smiling at them! He takes off his hat, he holds up his two fingers with his right hand. Now he drops his bat and he's indicating that the count is ball two and strike two. He gets back into the batter's box. The umpire again warns the Cubs! Charlie Root gets his signal. And Babe Ruth steps out of the batter's box again! He's holding up his two and two. Oh, oh, and now Babe Ruth is pointing out to center field and he's yelling at the Cubs that the next pitch over is going into center field! . . . Someone just tossed a lemon down there. Babe Ruth has picked up the lemon and now he tosses it over to the Cubs' bench. He didn't throw anything, he sort of kicked it over there. After he turns, he points again to center field! And here's the pitch . . . It's going! Babe Ruth connects and here it goes! The ball is going, going, going—high into the center field stands, into the scoreboard! And it's a home run! It's gone. Whoopee! Listen to that crowd![17]

Not surprisingly, in the years that followed, most Cubs players—Hartnett, Grimm, Herman, English, Jurges, Grimes—and Ruth's former teammate, Mark Koenig—backed Root's description of events, saying that Ruth did not point and call his shot. Most Yankees—Gehrig (watching from the on-deck circle), Gomez, Pipgras, and Sewell—went along with the version of the story that Ruth predicted the home run.

Ironically, one of the Cubs who supported the Yankees' version was Guy Bush, the pitcher who had screamed obscenities at Ruth from the Cubs' dugout. No one was closer to the action, or more involved in the sequence of events leading up to the climactic moment, than Bush, who played a key role in the drama. In 1964 Bush wrote, "Ruth was talking to me at the time when he raised his right hand. It is my belief he pointed to center field. The only thing I am sure of he hit the next pitch in [the] center field stands."[18]

As the decades passed and the legend grew from a story about one at bat in a game to an iconic moment, those who witnessed the event recalled it in various ways. Two of the more prominent witnesses were Lincoln Landis, nephew of the commissioner, and Johnny Stevens, the future Supreme Court justice.

The memories of both of them, perhaps reformed by the passage of time and the appeal of the story, supported the version that said Ruth pointed:

Landis said, "I remember this moment very clearly. It really frustrated me to read that there were those who questioned whether he called his shot. I thought, That's horrible. To me, there was absolutely no question." And Landis added: "And I remember how the fans behaved. To my mind, they couldn't believe what they had seen. He could not do this. He could not predict his shot and then deliver. But he did."[19]

In September 2008 Stevens told an interviewer, "He definitely pointed toward center field."[20]

When Ruth retired in 1935 the *Chicago Daily Tribune* reported that "one incident epitomized his whole career." Then, in recounting the Ruth home run in Game Three, the article concluded "Ruth held up two fingers and then pointed to deep right center field. In any one else, it would have been braggadocio, but not in Ruth. Root pitched again and Ruth planted the ball just where he had pointed."[21]

True or not, the legend was born in Chicago, and Chicago was determined to own it.

Epilogue

The Babe Calls His Last Shot

After the triumph of the 1932 World Series, Babe Ruth played two more seasons, but 1932 turned out to be Ruth's last great season and his last World Series. He hit .301 with 34 homers in 1933 and .288 with 22 homers in 1934; despite a talented roster, neither the 1933 nor 1934 Yankees advanced to the World Series, much to Ruth's frustration.[1]

Ruth realized that he was no longer able to perform at the highest levels as an everyday player, and he had no desire to stay in the game as a part-time player or an occasional pinch hitter. At thirty-nine, he was, for baseball purposes, an old man. He could not ignore the reality of age and the inevitable physical deterioration. Ruth's body was a wreck. He was overweight, and his legs were gone. If he had been a thoroughbred racehorse, his owner would have shown him mercy and shot him.

To the Yankees' organization—namely, Jacob Ruppert—Ruth was now more trouble than he was worth. Ruth was still popular and still the highest paid player in the game, but Ruppert slashed Ruth's salary from $75,000 in 1932, to $52,000 in 1933, and then to $35,000 in 1934. Ruth was costly as a fading superstar.

Ruth's clearly stated ambition was to be a manager, ideally with the New York Yankees. But the Yankees had a manager: Joe McCarthy. Although Ruth was convinced that he was ready and able to manage, and had earned the right, thanks to his stellar career—he also realized that the Yankees had no intention of replacing McCarthy.

Ruth was open to considering other options. Managerial positions opened up every year, and now Ruth's name was tossed about as a potential manager—in Cleveland, in Chicago, in Detroit. But nothing came of these rumors. All of those managerial jobs were offered to other candidates.[2]

One possibility arose while Ruth and Claire and their daughter, Julia, were on a worldwide tour after the 1934 season. On the first leg of the trip—Hawaii, Japan, China, and the Philippines—Ruth played baseball with a team of American All-Stars, managed by Connie Mack. When the baseball games ended, Ruth and his family continued on an around-the-world cruise traveling to Java, Bali, the Suez Canal, Paris, and London, before returning to New York.

As Ruth traveled through Europe, Boston Braves owner Judge Emil Fuchs contacted Jacob Ruppert about acquiring Ruth in some kind of transaction. Fuchs's motives were similar to his motives in bringing Rogers Hornsby to Boston in 1929: to prop up his financially stressed franchise. Ruppert and Fuchs saw ways they could mutually benefit from an arrangement in which Ruth was released by the Yankees and signed by the Braves.

The two owners struck a deal. In the winter of 1935, Babe Ruth returned to Boston.

Fuchs signed Ruth to an artfully obscure contract that convinced Ruth he could become manager of the Boston Braves in 1936, after serving for a year as an assistant manager, a position that had never existed previously in Major League Baseball.[3] For Fuchs, the deal brought Ruth to Boston in order to save the franchise, if indeed Ruth could draw fans to the ballpark to support what would be a losing team. The contract was worded so that Fuchs was not bound to promote Ruth to manager.

So Ruth, out of shape but as hopeful as a rookie, arrived in St. Petersburg, which coincidentally was also home to the Yankees' spring training camp. Claire, a stabilizing influence, accompanied her husband to Florida. Local fans used to seeing the Babe in Yankees pinstripes now saw him, fat and lumbering, in the uniform of the Boston Braves. The Braves had only one established star—the twenty-nine-year-old outfielder, Wally Berger—and few even moderately talented players with Major League experience: pitchers Huck Betts and Ben Cantwell; infielder Pinky Whitney.[4] In the Braves' training camp, Ruth was reunited with Rabbit Maranville, an old buddy from his years in Boston. When Ruth had played for the Red Sox, he'd enjoyed the company of Maranville. Rabbit had spent the first nine years of his career in Boston with the Braves and had returned to the club in 1929. He was now forty-three years old and in his twenty-third Major League season. Ruth's wildest days were behind him, but Maranville was an old friend, and one of the few players of Ruth's generation who had been able to match him, drink for drink, antic for antic.

Ruth did his best to get his aging body in shape. He stretched and ran and worked out. He played first base in some exhibition games. He took batting practice. The local fans loved seeing the Babe, back in St. Petersburg for spring training, even though he was wearing a different uniform. A huge crowd showed up on March 16 to see the Braves play the Yankees in an exhibition game.[5]

The season opened in Boston against the New York Giants. One of the best left-handed pitchers in baseball—Carl Hubbell, who had struck out Ruth and four others in succession at the 1934 All-Star Game—was on the mound for the Giants. No reasonable fan would have bet money that the Braves would win that game, but Ruth singled in a run in the bottom of the first and, later, scored. In the fifth inning, he homered—once again on opening day. The Braves won; Ruth participated in all of the scoring. The great Carl Hubbell took the loss.

The next day, Ruth was once again the hitting star. Perhaps Jacob Ruppert, sitting in his office at the brewery, wondered if he'd made a smart decision to cut ties with the greatest player in the history of the game.

Then Ruth began to strike out and fly out. He was ineffective, at bat and in the field. Fans, especially on the road, still came to see him, but the pop was gone from his bat. His legs were shot. He couldn't run the bases or field his position. Ruth knew it was time to quit before he embarrassed himself further. He also now realized that Fuchs had no intention of honoring the deal to make him manager. Although he wanted to quit, he felt a kinship and loyalty to the fans and with the teams who had made plans to honor him with Babe Ruth Appreciation Days; so the disconsolate Ruth agreed to stay on through one last road trip—a long, sad farewell that required him to play games in five National League cities.

The road trip started in St. Louis, where the Braves lost 2 out of 3 games. In the final game Ruth went 0-4 against Dizzy Dean, striking out once. Then the Braves played 2 games in Chicago at Wrigley Field, the site of Ruth's heroics in the 1932 World Series. The Braves lost the first game, but won the second, 4-1. In the sixth inning, in Ruth's penultimate at bat in Wrigley Field, he lofted a home run into the right-field stands, his third of the season. On his last at bat in Chicago, he flied out to deep center field.

After Chicago, the Braves took the train to Pittsburgh for 3 games with the Pirates at Forbes Field. Ruth was batting .157 for the season. On Thursday, May 23, the Pirates won, 7–1. Ruth went 0-4. But he had one good at bat, hitting a ball deep to right field that Paul Waner jumped to catch at the wall, robbing Ruth of an extra base hit. In the bottom of the sixth, as Ruth plodded out to right field, he passed Waner and said, "Say, you're a mighty little fellow to be such a big thief."[6]

That night in the ballroom of the Schenley Hotel, Ruth attended a testimonial dinner honoring his friend, Rabbit Maranville, who had played four seasons in Pittsburgh.[7] There was food and drink, an orchestra, and speeches. Ruth rose from his chair and gave a short, emotional tribute, toasting his fellow ballplayer and calling Maranville his brother. The occasion and Ruth's own words brought tears to his eyes. After the celebration ended, Ruth and Maranville spent the night partying, but Ruth played the next day, hitting a single and 2 long fly balls, both caught by Waner near the right-field fence. Again the Pirates prevailed, this time by a score of 7–6.

On the final day of the series, Babe walked to Forbes Field from the Schenley Hotel. It was May 25, a chilly Saturday, and he was in an uncharacteristically gloomy mood. As always, a group of boys—boys of summer who loved baseball—waited outside the players' entrance. On the two previous days, Ruth was accompanied by Claire and he had stopped to chat with the youngsters and sign scorecards, but on this day he was alone and just passed out printed business cards with his name stamped on them.[8]

One of those boys was twelve-year-old Paul Warhola. He lived a few blocks away from Forbes Field with his parents and two younger brothers, John and Andy. Sometimes Paul and his brother John would attend the games together. His youngest brother, Andy, who would later become a renowned artist, was not interested in baseball.[9] Paul Warhola sold newspapers and peanuts at Forbes Field, so he was able to see the Pirates play on a regular basis. When the game started, Warhola went inside the ballpark to sell his newspapers.

During batting practice, Ruth broke his bat, so he was using a new bat when he faced Red Lucas in the first inning and hit a high fly ball toward the right-field stands. Once again, Paul Waner raced back and tried to make the catch, but the ball cleared the right-field fence and landed in the lower stands, just beyond his outstretched glove. When Ruth came to bat again in the third, Lucas had been removed and replaced by Ruth's old nemesis, Guy Bush, who had goaded him throughout the 1932 World Series and hit him with a pitch the last time they'd faced each other. Ruth got a measure of revenge, hitting his second home run of the day, a Ruthian blast that landed in the upper deck.

In the fifth inning, Ruth faced Bush again and singled. By Ruth's fourth at bat—his third time to face Bush—in the top of the seventh, he was relaxed and joking with a cluster of fans sitting alongside the first base line. Paul Warhola, now sitting behind home plate, heard someone call out to Ruth, "Hey, Babe, hit one over the roof." Ruth turned and pointed his bat at the eighty-six-foot-high roof in right field.

No one in the ten-year history of Forbes Field had ever hit a ball over the roof. To the delight of the crowd, he pointed. Nine hundred and sixty-five days had passed since Ruth's called shot in Chicago. Could he do it again?

On the second pitch from Bush, a thigh-high fastball that creased the center of the plate, Ruth connected and the ball ascended. Fans stared in awe. In right field, Paul Waner simply turned and watched the flight of the ball. The ball kept rising and soared over the roof, landing on top of a house at 334 Joncaire Street, and then bouncing down Bouquet Street, where it was retrieved by a boy named Wiggy DeOrio.[10]

Ruth trotted around the bases, celebrating regular-season home run number 714. After he touched third base, he looked over at Guy Bush on the mound. Ruth's old nemesis tipped his cap in a gesture of respect and admiration. Bush later said, "It was the longest cockeyed ball I ever saw hit in my life."[11]

Gus Miller, the head usher at Forbes Field, estimated the distance between home plate and the house where the ball landed at six hundred feet.[12] The measurement was imprecise, as Ruth's biographer, Robert Creamer, notes, but it was one of the longest of Ruth's many long home runs, in the same category as on exhibition home run off Huck Betts in North Carolina, or the home run at Sing Sing, or his most famous homer at Wrigley field.

No matter how far it traveled, it was historic: the final home run of his career.

The score of the game hardly mattered, but for the record, the Pirates won, 11–7. Ruth had driven in 6 of the Braves 7 runs. Ruth left the game after his seventh inning homer, pausing briefly in the Pirates' dugout on his way to the Braves' locker room. Ruth sat down next to Pirates rookie pitcher, Mace Brown, and said, "Boy, that last one felt good."[13]

Ruth dressed and left the ballpark, heading down Sennott Street toward the Schenley Hotel. He wore a cap and his trademark light camel-hair coat, pulled up tight under his chin. Boys ran up to him, seeking autographs or a word or two, but he stared straight ahead and walked silently in the direction of the hotel.

Thirteen-year-old Sam Sciulla accompanied him all the way to the trolley tracks on Forbes Avenue. Despite Ruth's heroics inside Forbes Field, he seemed unhappy. More than seventy years later, Sciulla recalled, "He was not a well man that day. He was depressed and glad to get out of Pittsburgh."[14]

The game in Pittsburgh was the last time that Ruth dominated a game and mesmerized a crowd as a player. The rest of Ruth's season—3 games in Cincinnati, 3 games in Philadelphia—were uneventful. In Cincinnati he went 0–6 in the series, though he drew a pair of walks. At Philadelphia, he played in 3 more games, going 0–3, drawing 2 more walks, and earning an assist in his final game. His last at bat was a weak ground ball to the first baseman.

He was finished. He never stepped on a Major League baseball field as a player again.

The numbers for the 1935 season were ugly. Final stats: Ruth played in 28 games for Boston, batting .181. In 72 official at bats, Ruth managed only 13 hits. Six of the hits were home runs, including the 3 he hit in Pittsburgh. He struck out 24 times. Somewhat remarkably, considering how poorly he hit during the season, he was walked 20 times in 92 plate appearances. He still retained the aura of the hitter he once had been. In the eyes of National League pitchers, he was still the "Sultan of Swat" with the potential to homer each and every time he came to the plate.

It is almost impossible to express how bad the 1935 Boston Braves happened to be. They won only 38 games. They finished last—26 games out of seventh place; 61½ games behind the pennant-winning Chicago Cubs. Ben Cantwell, one of the team's starting pitchers, compiled a record of 4 wins and 25 losses. Although Ruth had only 72 at bats, he finished second on the team in home runs with 6.[15]

In the field, Ruth could no longer turn left or right to chase fly balls. Wally Berger had to cover not only his position in center field but half of Ruth's position in right. "He'd go in pretty good to field a ball, but he couldn't turn on those damn knees and ankles," Berger said. "So that made my job no easier. Every time there was a ball hit out toward Babe, I'd be there to back him up."[16]

Ruth's career as a player had come to an end.

In the post-Ruth years, the New York Yankees continued to dominate the American League. From 1935 through 1943, Joe McCarthy managed the Yankees to seven American League pennants and five World Series triumphs, including another 4–0 sweep of the Cubs in 1938. Gehrig had four more productive years before he was diagnosed with the deadly disease that carries his name. Replacing Ruth, and then Gehrig, as the premier ballplayer on the club, was a new star, the California-born Joe DiMaggio, former shortstop of the San Francisco Seals and now the Yankees' center fielder.

In retirement, Ruth was restless. He passed the time with a variety of hobbies: golf, bowling, fishing, and hunting. He refereed wrestling matches. He made public appearances. He lived the sad and often disconcerting life of a former star and celebrity—always recognized, still loved—but was no longer a significant part of the game he once dominated. On July 4, 1939, he joined with other members of the powerhouse 1927 Yankees team at Yankee Stadium for a ceremony to honor Lou Gehrig, stricken with ALS and now dying. Gehrig gave his famous "Luckiest Man" speech.[17] Ruth came up to Gehrig, put his arm around him, and whispered something in his ear. Gehrig smiled. It was the first time in five years that the two men had spoken.[18] The ceremony foreshadowed Ruth's own farewell at Yankee Stadium only eight years later.

Ruth played himself in *The Pride of the Yankees*, a successful Hollywood film of Gehrig's life, released in 1942, shortly after Gehrig died. Ruth lost forty-seven pounds for the role.[19] In 1941 he was invited to play a series of three golf matches against his old baseball rival Ty Cobb, to raise money for several charities, including the United Service Organization.[20] It was becoming more apparent that America would be drawn into the conflict in Europe, and after Pearl Harbor, Ruth participated in various fund raising events in the summers of 1942 and 1943. The historian Robert Elias wrote "Probably no ballplayer crusaded more than Babe Ruth. Retired and in his late forties, Ruth was a patriotic symbol, ranking just below the flag and the bald eagle."[21]

An occasion featuring Babe Ruth was sure to draw a crowd. On August 23, 1942, the Yankees and Indians played a doubleheader before 69,136 fans at Yankee Stadium, and between games, fifty-five-year-old Walter Johnson pitched to the forty-eight-year-old Babe in an exhibition of pitching and hitting. To the delight of fans, Ruth hit Johnson's fifth pitch into the lower right-field stands. It was the last time he would appear in the stadium and knock a ball over the fence in fair territory.

Early in the 1943 season Ruth appeared at Griffith Stadium in Washington DC, for a charity game between the Senators and a team of U.S. Navy All-Stars, based in Norfolk, Virginia. Shirley Povich, baseball writer for the *Washington Post*, organized the event. Kate Smith and Bing Crosby performed. Comic Al Schacht was also on hand. Prior to the game between the Senators and the All-Stars, Schacht performed a routine. Schacht's finale was a pantomime of Ruth's "called shot," with all the pointing and gesturing that fans recalled. After Schacht replicated Ruth's home run swing, Babe Ruth—the real Babe Ruth—jogged onto the field and "trotted around the bases with his famous mincing, home run gait." Then the Babe gave a two-minute speech urging spectators to contribute to the war effort. The crowd of 29,221 responded by purchasing nearly $2,000,000 worth of war bonds.[22]

In July, Ruth took part in two exhibitions, one staged at Fenway Park in Boston in front of twelve thousand fans and another held at Yankee Stadium. Both events also featured Ted Williams. In Boston, Ruth and Williams had a home run hitting contest. Williams hit 3; Ruth, limping on a bad knee, failed to drive a ball over the fence. A few weeks later, Williams and Ruth entertained fans with a charity game in New York played to benefit the Red Cross. This time when the two met, Williams asked Ruth to sign a baseball for him—the only time Williams approached another player about an autograph. Ruth wrote: "To my pal Ted Williams from Babe Ruth."[23]

Ruth became ill in late 1946. His symptoms: terrible headaches and difficulty in swallowing. He spent eighty-eight days in the hospital for observation and treatment as his health declined.[24] On April 27, 1947, a few months after his release from the hospital, Ruth was the guest of honor at Babe Ruth Day at Yankee Stadium. The Yankees hosted the Indians, and a crowd of 58,339 attended the game. Ruth used Bob Feller's bat as a steadying cane when he walked slowly to home plate to give a short speech. Later that summer, he served as honorary chairperson of the Hearst Sandlot Classic, an All-Star Game played at the Polo Grounds, featuring the best high school ballplayers of America.[25]

In the last year of his life, he collaborated with two ghostwriters— Bob Considine and Fred Lieb—on *The Babe Ruth Story*, an autobiography of sorts. He donated a copy of the manuscript to Yale University, handing over the pages to the Yale University baseball team's captain and first baseman, a youngster named George Herbert Walker Bush.

Ruth entered Memorial Hospital in New York City in the summer of 1948. During the last weeks of his illness, crowds gathered outside the hospital, hoping to catch a glimpse of him so they could wish him well. Pres. Harry S. Truman and Cardinal Francis Spellman made phone calls to the hospital to check on his condition. He died on August 16, 1948, a Monday, succumbing to cancer at the age of fifty-three.

Ruth lay in state in Yankee Stadium. More than seventy-seven thousand people passed by the open coffin in silence, heads bowed in respect. Men and women cried. Some held their young children aloft so they could peer into the casket and glimpse the body of the greatest ballplayer America had ever produced. Ruth was honored in death as if he were a pope or a president.

His funeral was held in St. Patrick's Cathedral in New York City on August 19. The Yankees were in Washington that day, winning 8–1 behind the 5-hit pitching of Allie Reynolds. The right fielder for the Yankees on that afternoon was a future Hall of Famer, a twenty-three-year-old rookie and rising star named Yogi Berra.

A huge crowd stood in the street outside the cathedral to watch the funeral procession escort Ruth's body to the Gate of Heaven Cemetery in Hawthorne, New York.

A week after Ruth's death, the 1948 Hearst Sandlot Classic was played at the Polo Grounds. Joe DiMaggio served as honorary chairperson of the event, taking the role that Ruth had played a year earlier. Fittingly, the 1948 game was dedicated to Ruth, who had grown up on the fields of St. Mary's Industrial School for Boys and was known for his devotion to young athletes and the game of baseball in general. Ruth's will specified that 10 percent of his estate was to go "to the interests of the kids of America."[26]

The Polo Grounds was an appropriate site for the tribute to Ruth. In 1920, Ruth's first season with the Yankees, the team had played its home games on that field, where Ruth hit his very first home run as a Yankee, on May 1, 1920, a warm Saturday afternoon. A crowd of twelve thousand was on hand to witness the occasion. The pitcher who gave up that historic home run was Herb Pennock, a future teammate of the Babe's.

Before the Hearst Sandlot game in 1948, Ruth's memory was honored with a series of tributes. Various celebrities and individuals who had a connection to Ruth's life took part in the event. Johnny Sylvester, for whom Ruth had dedicated the 3 home runs he hit in the 1926 World Series, was in attendance. The Broadway star Robert Merrill sang "My Buddy."

As part of the pregame ceremonies, Ruth's contemporary Al Schacht, the baseball comic and mime, was on hand to honor Ruth by performing one of Schacht's most famous routines, a pantomime of Ruth's called shot in Wrigley Field during the 1932 World Series.

No film crew or amateur videographer was at the Polo Grounds in 1948 to record the moment, so we have to imagine Schacht's reenactment.

Schacht would have strolled to the plate with a bat on his shoulder and taken Schacht's place in the batter's box, facing the third base dugout and the imaginary hecklers who yelled at him as the imaginary pitcher delivered the first 4 pitches. As Ruth had done, Schacht would have gestured back at the bench jockeys, signaling with his fingers how many strikes he had left, and then, finally, pointing—famously, mystifyingly—his right arm extended at the pitcher, or perhaps at the Cubs in the field, or most improbably, at some spot in deepest right-center field. Then, on the fifth pitch, Schacht would have swung, the bat slicing upward through the air, his torso and hips swiveling, the bat held high for just a second or two. Schacht's audience could have imagined the reaction: fans rising to their feet, cheering wildly.

And in the thick of the echoing cheers, Schacht would have trotted around the bases—just as Ruth had done so many times in his career, exulting in the triumph of the moment.

Extra Innings

The rosters of the 1932 Yankees and Cubs were stacked with baseball talent. In all, a record number of players—thirteen, to be exact—participated in the 1932 World Series and later were voted into the Hall of Fame.[1]

Ten Yankees—Ruth, Gehrig, Lazzeri, Sewell, Dickey, Combs, Gomez, Ruffing, Pennock, and manager Joe McCarthy—earned plaques in Cooperstown. In addition, general manager Ed Barrow, who played a key role in putting the team together, is enshrined in the Hall of Fame.

Although the 1932 Cubs lacked a single big star—like power hitter Hack Wilson, who led the 1929 team—they were a strong team with a quality pitching staff and solid performers at every position. Five Cubs players—Cuyler, Hartnett, Herman, Grimes, and player/manager Rogers Hornsby—are members of the Hall of Fame, although Grimes and Hornsby were honored primarily for their careers with other ball clubs.

The Cubs made it back to the World Series before the Yankees. In 1935 the Cubs would win 100 games, paced by a core group from the 1932 team—Hartnett, Hack, Herman, Jurges, Root, Warneke—plus new additions Phil Cavarretta and Chuck Klein. In the decade from 1929 to 1938, only the Cardinals—who won four World Series in this span—were a consistently better team in the National League. Much of the Cubs' success through the 1930s was due to the players selected and groomed by Joe McCarthy during his stint in Chicago.

Starting in 1936, the Yankees would begin their run of 4 straight World Championships, from 1936 through 1939, featuring the new face of the franchise: a young outfielder from the West Coast named Joe DiMaggio.[2]

One last reflection on the 1932 Cubs and Yankees: seven players on the 1932 Cubs became Major League managers. In addition to Hornsby and Grimm, the list includes Stan Hack, Gabby Hartnett, Billy Herman, Burleigh Grimes, and Billy Jurges. As managers, those seven former Cubs won 2,766 Major League games. Only two Yankees players ever managed: Ben Chapman for a couple of seasons with the Philadelphia Phillies, and Bill Dickey for part of the 1946 season with the Yankees.

THE 1932 CHICAGO CUBS:

Kiki Cuyler Cuyler hit over .300 ten times in his Major League career and finished with a career batting average of .321. Four times he led the National League in stolen bases. Elected to the Hall of Fame in 1968.

Gabby Hartnett Hartnett was the greatest catcher in Cubs history, hit .297 for his career, earned an MVP award in 1935, and managed the Cubs from the middle of the 1938 season through 1940. Elected to the Hall of Fame in 1955.

Billy Herman Herman played on four World Series teams—three with the Cubs, one with the Dodgers—over a stellar fifteen-year playing career. He achieved a .304 lifetime batting average. He managed both the Pittsburgh Pirates and the Boston Red Sox. Elected to the Hall of Fame in 1975.

Burleigh Grimes As a member of the Cubs, Grimes posted only 9 of his 270 Major League wins. He earned the majority of his victories pitching for the St. Louis Cardinals and was the last of the legal spitballers. Elected to the Hall of Fame in 1964.

Rogers Hornsby One of the greatest hitters of all-time with a career batting average of .358. He led the National League at least twice in every offensive category: hits, runs scored, doubles, triples, home runs, runs batted in, walks, batting average, and slugging percentage. Elected to the Hall of Fame in 1942.

Woody English English retired in 1938 with a career batting average of .286 and moved back to his hometown of Newark, Ohio. He came out of retirement to coach the Grand Rapids Chicks of the All-American Girls Professional Baseball League from 1952 to 1954.[3]

Charlie Grimm The man they called "Jolly Cholly" had a long association with the Cubs as a player, manager, coach, front office executive, and broadcaster. Grimm was a superb fielder and batted .290 for his career. As a manager, he led the Cubs to pennants in 1932, 1935, and 1945, though the Cubs lost each of those World Series matchups. When Grimm died in 1983, his widow received permission to scatter his ashes on the playing field at Wrigley Field. A legend has developed that Grimm's ghost haunts the ballpark.[4]

Riggs Stevenson Due to injuries, Stevenson played in just 1,310 games over fourteen seasons but hit .336 during his career. With the exceptions of Shoeless Joe Jackson and Lefty O'Doul, Stevenson retired with the highest career batting average of any modern era player who is not in the Hall of Fame.[5]

Stan Hack A fan favorite who was known as "Smiling Stan" for his cheerful disposition, Hack posted a career batting average of .301. He was an excellent fielder, a perennial league leader in stolen bases, and 1 of 7 members of the 1932 Cubs who went on to be a big league manager.

Billy Jurges The volatile shortstop played twelve years in the Majors, appeared in 3 World Series, was named to three National League All-Star teams, and briefly managed the Boston Red Sox. He battled teammates, opposing players, and umpires throughout his career. His most memorable confrontation was in 1939 with 250 pound umpire George Magerkurth over the arbitrator's call on a foul ball. The argument escalated to the point where the two men spit at each other and then exchanged blows. Both were fined and suspended. Later in life, Jurges reflected on his passion for the game by saying, "All I wanted to do was play baseball."[6]

The Pitching Staff The core of the Cubs' 1932 pitching staff—Guy Bush, Charlie Root, Pat Malone, and Lon Warneke—compiled exceptional career statistics. Together that four-man rotation won 704 Major League games over the course of fifty nine combined seasons. All four pitchers were 20-game winners in one or more seasons. Year after year they were among the league leaders in wins, games pitched, complete games, ERAs, shutouts, and winning percentages. Root is the all-time leader in games won as a Cub, with 203 wins. Warneke posted eleven consecutive years of double-digit wins and twice led the league in shutouts. After his playing days ended, Warneke became a Major League umpire; later in his life, he entered politics, serving ten years as a judge in Garland County, Arkansas.

THE 1932 NEW YORK YANKEES:

Babe Ruth Ruth was inducted into the National Baseball Hall of Fame in 1936, joining Ty Cobb, Honus Wagner, Christy Mathewson, and Walter Johnson, as the first class of inductees.[7]

Lou Gehrig The "Iron Horse" was struck with a mysterious illness and took himself out of the lineup in the spring of 1939, when he felt he could no longer contribute. He had played in 2,130 consecutive games. He was soon diagnosed with amyotrophic lateral sclerosis (ALS)—now called Lou Gehrig's Disease—and died at the age of thirty-six on June 2, 1941. Elected to the Hall of Fame in 1939, shortly after the end of his playing career.

Tony Lazzeri Overshadowed by the other power hitters in the Yankees' lineup, Lazzeri was a dominant and feared hitter throughout his career. Elected to the Hall of Fame in 1941.

Joe Sewell Sewell was the hardest man to strike out in the history of baseball. In nearly 8,000 plate appearances over a fourteen-year career, Sewell struck out only 114 times. He was a polite, soft-spoken man with a Southern drawl, reflecting his Alabama roots. In his later years, he attended baseball card shows, always dressed impeccably, offering anecdotes about his years with the Yankees. Elected to the Hall of Fame in 1977.

Bill Dickey One of the great catchers in baseball history, Dickey was known for both his superb defensive skills and his ability to hit. Elected to the Hall of Fame in 1954.

Earle Combs The speedy Combs was overshadowed by many of his Yankees teammates in the 1920s and 1930s, but he was a valued lead-off man whose contributions as a fielder and baserunner contributed to the great Yankees teams of the era. He led the league in triples 3 times. Elected to the Hall of Fame in 1970.

Lefty Gomez Gomez was a mainstay of the Yankees' pitching staff for nearly a decade, pitched on 5 world championship teams, and posted a perfect 6–0 record in World Series competition. Nicknamed "Goofy," Yankees fans loved him, and he was renowned for his sense of humor. Elected to the Hall of Fame in 1954.

Red Ruffing Ruffing remains the all-time Yankees leader in wins by a right-handed pitcher with 231 victories. Elected to the Hall of Fame in 1967.

Herb Pennock An outstanding left-hander who played eleven seasons with the Yankees, Pennock appeared in 5 World Series, posting a perfect 5-0 record. Elected to the Hall of Fame in 1948.

Joe McCarthy In his twenty-four-year career as a manager—five years with the Cubs, sixteen years with the Yankees, three years with the Red Sox—McCarthy took nine teams to the World Series and won 7 championships. He finished his career with the highest winning percentage of any manager in baseball history. Elected to the Hall of Fame in 1957.

Ed Barrow Barrow managed Detroit and Boston before becoming a front office executive with the Yankees in 1920. He deserves much of the credit in building the Yankees' dynasty over the next quarter of a century. Elected to the Hall of Fame in 1953.

THE OTHER MANAGERS AND BALLPLAYERS OF 1932:

Jimmie Foxx The successor to Babe Ruth as the premier power
hitter in baseball, Foxx ended his career with 534 home runs.
At the time, he was second only to the Babe in career home
runs. Elected to the Hall of Fame in 1957.

Dizzy Dean One of the game's most colorful and oft-quoted ballplayers, Dean backed up his bragging with five outstanding seasons, averaging 24 wins a year from 1932 through 1936. In 1934
he posted a regular-season record of 30-7, leading the Cardinals
to the World Series. He won 2 games in that series, including
a 6-hit shutout in Game Seven. He led the league in strikeouts
and complete games four years in a row. Elected to the Hall of
Fame in 1953.

Monte Weaver The reserved and erudite right-hander had only
one outstanding season—his rookie year in 1932, during which
he finished fifth in *The Sporting News* MVP voting. He compiled a 71-50 career mark. He was plagued with minor injuries,
switched to an all vegetarian diet, lost nearly thirty pounds,
and retired at the age of thirty-three. During World War II, he
served in the Air Force. After the war, he relocated to Florida,
where he bought and managed orange and grapefruit groves.

Milt Gaston Gaston might have had the worst win-loss record in
Major League history, but he never lost his enthusiasm for the
game. At a party to celebrate his one hundredth birthday, he
rose out of his chair, stood straight up, and heartily sang, "Take
Me Out to the Ballgame."

Walter "The Big Train" Johnson The Big Train was the dominant
pitcher of his era, winning 416 games and leading the league
in strikeouts 12 times. As a manager, he posted a 530-432
career record with the Senators and Indians, though he never
took a team to the World Series. Elected to the Hall of Fame
in 1936.

Connie Mack It is a good bet that Mack's remarkable longevity as a Major League manager will never be equaled. He managed for fifty-three years, starting in 1894, and won and lost more games than any other manager in history. His career win-loss record stands at 3,776 wins and 4,025 losses. He managed some of the best and worst teams ever to play the game. Elected to the Hall of Fame in 1937.

John McGraw One of the most colorful and successful managers of his era, the legendary McGraw retired with a record of 2,840-1,984, 10 National League pennants, and 3 world championships. Elected to the Hall of Fame in 1937.

THE BOYS OF SUMMER:

Lincoln Landis Of all the boys of summer who witnessed Babe Ruth's historic at bat in Wrigley Field on October 1, 1932, no one was more convinced than Lincoln Landis that Ruth had, indeed, pointed to centerfield before he homered off Charlie Root. A framed print of Robert Thom's famous painting *Called Shot* showing Ruth at the plate, pointing to the outfield—hung in Landis's home office.[8]

Charles Ireland After writing for local Iowa newspapers, Charles Ireland moved to California and continued his career as a journalist, first as a sports reporter for a daily paper in Santa Barbara, and later as that paper's editor-in-chief. One of his prized possessions from his days in Iowa was the scrapbook that his mother had made for him of the Snappers 1932 baseball season.[9]

Lowell Lawrence Blaisdell Blaisdell was a lifelong Cubs fan and later a college History professor. He retired as a professor emeritus from Texas Tech University. During his academic career, he published numerous articles on history and several on baseball. He was also the author of a biography of screwball pitcher Carl Hubbell.

Irving "Pro" Boim Boim was nicknamed "Pro" for his uncanny ability to do impressions of Major League stars, such as Lou

Gehrig and Babe Ruth. He pitched the University of Michigan to the 1942 Big Ten championship. While serving in the U.S. Navy, he struck out Ted Williams twice in a service league game at the Naval Air Station in Pensacola, Florida. After the war, Boim pitched for nine years in the Minor Leagues, in the Pirates, Reds, and White Sox organizations. Although he never made it to the Majors, he had a forty-year career as an elementary school gym teacher and baseball coach.

Bernard Malamud The young Brooklyn Dodger fan grew up to be one of America's most original and renowned fiction writers. In 1952 he published his first novel, *The Natural*, a story set in the world of baseball featuring a protagonist, Roy Hobbs, who makes a comeback after being shot by a female fan in a Chicago hotel room. This key dramatic episode in the book was inspired by two real-life incidents, both involving baseball players, and both occurring in Chicago hotel rooms: first, the shooting of Billy Jurges by Violet Popovich in 1932; second, the shooting of Eddie Waitkus, a former Cub, in 1949, by Ruth Ann Steinhagen, an obsessed fan.[10]

John Paul Stevens Stevens served in the U.S. Navy during World War II, attended the Northwestern University School of Law, clerked for Supreme Court Justice Wiley Blount Rutledge, and went on to a distinguished career as a lawyer. He worked as a staff lawyer on U.S. Representative Emmanuel Cellar's congressional subcommittee investigating the antitrust exemption of Major League Baseball.[11] In 1975 Pres. Gerald Ford nominated Stevens to the United States Supreme Court, where he served for more than thirty-four years. He remained a proud fan of the Chicago Cubs. One of the decorations on the wall of his office at the Supreme Court was a framed scorecard from Game Three of the 1932 World Series, a contest he had witnessed as a twelve-year-old fan. On September 14, 2005, at the age of eighty-five, Stevens wore a Cubs jersey to Wrigley Field and threw out the ceremonial first pitch before a game between the Cubs and Reds.[12]

FANS IN THE STANDS:

Violet Popovich We do not know for certain if Violet Popovich—devoted Cubs fan, distraction, local celebrity—was at Game Three of the 1932 World Series, though it is certainly possible. We do know that a few years later, she and her siblings moved—as she had proposed in her suicide note to her brother—to the sunny state of California, settling in Los Angeles. Her taste in men continued to gravitate toward professional athletes. She was briefly married to a former heavyweight boxer named Charley Retzlaff, whose career ended in January of 1936 when he was knocked out in the first round of a bout against Joe Louis. She and Retzlaff lived on a farm in North Dakota, but the rural life didn't appeal to Violet. Eventually she moved back to Los Angeles. Violet's career as a showgirl never blossomed, but she spent most of the last sixty years of her life in Los Angeles on the fringes of the entertainment industry. She lived in Studio City and worked at a film studio. She died in 2000 at the age of eighty-eight and was buried in a section of Forest Lawn Cemetery known as "Enduring Faith."

John Sbarbaro For the rest of his life, Judge Sbarbaro remained a loyal Cubs fan. In the November elections, two months after the end of the 1932 World Series, Sbarbaro lost his judgeship in the Democratic sweep and returned to private practice, forming a law firm with Benedict J. Short. Sbarbaro remained active in Republican Party politics and civic organizations. He was president of the Chicago Stags, a professional basketball team that played in the Basketball Association of America and later played in the National Basketball Association, from 1946 to 1950. The Stags were the forerunners of today's Chicago Bulls. On March 17, 1960, Sbarbaro was a passenger on Northwest Orient Airlines Flight 710 when the plane exploded and broke apart in the air over Tell City, Indiana. All sixty-three passengers on board died. Speculation arose that the plane was destroyed by a bomb, though an investigation by the Civil Aeronautics Board suggested the more likely cause was metal fatigue, causing the right wing to detach from the aircraft. More than six hundred people, many of them judges and lawyers, attended Sbarbaro's funeral.[13]

William Veeck Sr. The man who built a pennant-winning team through trades and acquisitions died of leukemia at the age of fifty-six in October 1933, just a year after his Cubs had competed in the 1932 World Series. On his deathbed, Veeck was treated to sips of French champagne, compliments of one of the Cubs' biggest fans: Ralph Capone.[14]

Bill "Bojangles" Robinson The celebrated entertainer known as "Bojangles" achieved fame and fortune as a vaudevillian, dancer, and movie star, appearing both as a solo act and in films with Shirley Temple and other stars. He was a passionate and lifelong fan of the Yankees, befriending ballplayers, other athletes, and celebrities. At his funeral, the Reverend Adam Clayton Powell gave the eulogy; Joe DiMaggio, Jackie Robinson, and Joe Louis served as pallbearers. During his lifetime, Bill Robinson earned considerably more money than any baseball player of his era. Unfortunately, he gambled away most of his wealth and died almost penniless.

Matt Kandle Kandle died in 1951 without realizing the full historical importance of the video he had taken at Wrigley Field in 1932. In 1975, Kandle's great-grandson, Kirk, took the two-minute film to a *Louisville Courier-Journal* reporter who had written a story about Ruth's legendary at bat, but images from the film were not published or available to the public until October 1980.[15]

Harold Warp Warp's video of the Ruth at bat was shown at family reunions many times over the years, along with other Warp family home movies, but no one recognized the significance of the film until 1999 when Warp's great-nephew, James Jacobs, authenticated the film.[16]

Al Capone The most notorious of all Cubs fans, Capone was transferred from the Atlanta Federal Penitentiary to Alcatraz Federal Penitentiary in August 1934. He was paroled from Alcatraz on November 16, 1939, and lived most of the rest of his life in Miami, Florida, suffering from late-stage syphilis. He never saw another Cubs game in person. He died in Miami on January 25, 1947. He is buried in a family plot in Mount Carmel Cemetery in Chicago.

John Dillinger Dillinger never made it to the Major Leagues as a player. He was released from prison in May 1933 and is alleged to have committed a dozen bank robberies over the next fourteen months. He once lamented, "I'd like to have enough money to enjoy life; be clear of everything—not worry; take care of my old man, and see a ball game every day."[17] Dillinger remained a loyal Cubs fan, attending games at Wrigley Field in the summers of 1933 and 1934. He often sat in the right-field bleachers, disguised as a mailman and using the alias Jimmy Lawrence. The last game he saw was on July 8, 1934. The Cubs blasted the Pirates that day, 12–3. Two weeks later, Dillinger was shot dead in Chicago outside the Biograph Theatre.

Harry "Snap" Hortman Snap Hortman died in the infirmary of the Anamosa Men's Reformatory in August 1934, fourteen months after the death of Warden Charlie Ireland, with whom he had traveled to Chicago to see Games Three and Four of the 1932 World Series. Hortman was buried in Cherokee, Iowa, next to his parents. His reputation lived on. Years later, a local newspaper columnist penned a short column of remembrance, noting that Anamosans missed seeing "Old Snap in the third base coach's box."[18]

THE COMMISSIONER AND THE PRESIDENTS:

Kenesaw Mountain Landis Judge Landis ruled the world of baseball for twenty-four years, from 1920 until his death in 1944. Two weeks after his death, a special committee voted Landis into the Hall of Fame.

Herbert Hoover After the Roosevelt landslide of 1932, Hoover moved back to Palo Alto, California, with his wife, Lou. When Lou died in 1944, Hoover returned to the East Coast and lived in New York City in Suite 31 A in the Waldorf Towers until his death on October 20, 1964, at the age of ninety. He had lived thirty-one years as an ex-president, a record at that time.[19] Hoover was a prolific writer in his retirement. In addition to writing books about history and international relations, he published his memoirs. He maintained an interest in baseball, watching games on a black–and–white television in his apartment. On the occasion of his eighty-seventh birthday, Hoover declared that he was "the oldest living baseball fan."

Franklin Delano Roosevelt In February 1933, a few weeks before his inauguration, Governor Roosevelt survived an assassination attempt in Miami when Giuseppe Zangara, an unemployed bricklayer, fired five shots at the president-elect. Roosevelt escaped injury, but Anton Cermak, the mayor of Chicago, who was standing nearby, was struck and mortally wounded. Roosevelt was inaugurated on March 4, Cermak died on March 6, and two weeks after Cermak's death, Zangara was executed in Florida's electric chair.

Roosevelt steered the country through the Great Depression and World War II. He never lost his love of baseball or his belief in the game as an essential part of American life. From his first year in office through 1941, he made it a point to attend opening day ceremonies at Griffith Stadium and throw out the first ball to commemorate the beginning of each new season. As president, Roosevelt threw out the first ball 9 consecutive seasons.

On January 14, 1942, just five weeks after Pearl Harbor, Judge Kenesaw Landis sent a handwritten letter to President Roosevelt, asking whether or not Major League Baseball should go ahead with the scheduled season, in light of the national emergency and the country's entry into World War II. Roosevelt wrote back the next day, dictating the response to his secretary, Dorothy Brady. Noting that the ultimate decision was up to Landis and the baseball team owners, Roosevelt stated his personal opinion: "I honestly feel it would be best for the country to keep baseball going."[20]

Roosevelt's response, dubbed the "Green Light Letter," prompted Landis to go ahead with the season. Four years of wartime baseball followed.

AUTHOR'S NOTE ON SOURCES

I began this project with the desire to tell the story of the 1932 baseball season in the context of what was happening in that chaotic and pivotal year in America—as the Great Depression threatened to crush the spirit of the country; as World War I veterans camped out within view of the White House; as Congress struggled to deal with the nation's anguish and discontent. It was also a presidential election year, and the choices made by the Republicans and Democrats at their summer conventions, and later by citizens voting in November, would shape the nation's future.

The books and other materials I relied on for historical background are cited in the Bibliography.

The 1932 season was, first and foremost for baseball fans, an extraordinary year of baseball, featuring record-setting achievements by players, tight pennant races, dramatic on-field and off-field events, and a memorable and historic World Series.

Much of my research into the season was done by reading daily newspapers, both online and on microfilm. Because the Cubs and Yankees would face off in the World Series, I spent most of my time focused on source material related to Chicago and New York. Stories and news reports from the *Chicago Daily Tribune* and the *New York Times* were particularly helpful and guided my research.

Box scores, historical information, and additional statistical data were available from a variety of online sources, including Baseball -Research.com; Baseball-Almanac.com; SABR.org; WrigleyIvy.com; baseballhall.org; and Retrosheet.org.

For biographies and information about players, managers, umpires, and others directly involved in the game, I consulted files at the National Baseball Hall of Fame, published player biographies, and oral histories, as well as biographical articles available on the SABR BioProject site.

For the stories of fans—especially the "boys of summer," who appear throughout the book and connect to the events of that summer in various ways—I looked at both published and unpublished material.

Two significant events anchor this story. The shooting of Billy Jurges, which occurred in the middle of the season, is the climax of the first part of this book. Babe Ruth's fifth inning home run in Game Three of the World Series—the called shot—is the narrative highlight of the second half of the book. Each of these events—brief moments, really, in the time span of a season—will be familiar to readers.

For the shooting of Billy Jurges: the basic facts of this incident are well-known and have been reported and written about extensively. The best source materials I found relating to the event are in "The Shooting of Billy Jurges and Eddie Waitkus," published at the WrigleyIvy.com website; and in Robert Ehrgott's *Mr. Wrigley's Ball Club*, published by the University of Nebraska Press. I read everything I could about the event and attempted in this book to provide the reader with a factual narrative account based on all that is known about what happened in room 509 of the Hotel Carlos—and the aftermath, much of which took place in public in a Chicago courtroom.

For the called shot: I read the first-hand newspaper accounts and as many books and articles as I could find that speculated or commented on that single historic at bat—the episode that cemented the importance of the relationship between Babe Ruth and the Chicago Cubs. The fact that there is still mystery and excitement about those few minutes suggests how a solitary moment can grow into something compelling and iconic for future generations.

NOTES

INTRODUCTION

1. Leuchtenburg, *The Perils of Prosperity*, 9.
2. Watkins, *The Hungry Years*, 41–49.
3. Statistics on Major League attendance figures at http://wwwballparksofbaseball.com/1930-1939-mlb-attendance/ and http://www.ballparksofbaseball.com/1920-1929-mlb-attendance/.

PROLOGUE: A BROKEN UMBRELLA IN A RAINSTORM

1. Ruth's early years are well documented in biographies by Creamer and Montville, *Babe*, 24–52; Montville, *The Big Bam*, 7–46.
2. Creamer, *Babe*, 169–70; Montville, *The Big Bam*, 75–76.
3. Creamer, *Babe*, 161.
4. Creamer, *Babe*, 162–65.
5. Eig, *Luckiest Man*, 82.
6. "Harry Hochstadter, Sports Scribe, Dies," *Decatur Herald*, January 3, 1931.
7. "Bomb Kills 4; Wounds 30," *Chicago Daily Tribune*, September 5, 1918.
8. Gabler, *Walt Disney*, 35. Disney, destined to become one of America's greatest marketers of mass entertainment, was working that day at the post office for forty cents an hour, sorting and delivering mail.
9. "I. W.W. Bomb Kills Four in Chicago," *New York Times*, September 5, 1918.
10. "Latest News of Hunt for Bomb Placer," *Chicago Daily Tribune*, September 5, 1918.
11. Fowler, *Skyline*, 108.
12. Fowler, *Skyline*, 108.
13. Fowler, *Skyline*, 107.
14. Fowler, *Skyline*, 109.
15. Fowler, *Skyline*, 109.
16. Wood, *Babe Ruth and the 1918 Red Sox*, 267.
17. Montville, *The Big Bam*, 77.
18. Creamer, *Babe*, 174.

19. Wood, *Babe Ruth and the 1918 Red Sox*, 278.

20. Montville, *The Big Bam*, 69.

21. Quoted in Wood, *Babe Ruth and the 1918 Red Sox*, 275.

1. ROGERS HORNSBY

1. Alexander, *Rogers Hornsby*, 44–47. Hornsby didn't like or trust college-educated players or managers; he once referred to Hendricks as a "bush leaguer."

2. Alexander, *Rogers Hornsby*, 47. Hornsby's salary in 1918, with the Cardinals, was $4,000. Alexander, *Rogers Hornsby*, page 42.

3. Leuchtenburg, *The Perils of Prosperity*, 37. More than seven million soldiers from Europe and Russia died in the war. By comparison, American losses were considerably lighter. Over one hundred thousand Americans died—roughly half from disease; half from combat.

4. For life in Fort Worth in its early years, see http://en.wikipedia.org/wiki/Fort_Worth_Texas.

5. For more about J. Frank Norris, see Hankins, *God's Rascal*.

6. Hornsby, *My Kind of Baseball*, 29.

7. Alexander, *Rogers Hornsby*, 18–20.

8. D. Amore, *Rogers Hornsby*, 8.

9. Alexander, *Rogers Hornsby*, 41, 32. This was Weeghman's second attempt to pry Hornsby away from the Cardinals and bring him to Chicago. In August of 1916, Weeghman had made a similar offer.

10. Lowenfish, *Branch Rickey*, 115–17.

11. Alexander, *Rogers Hornsby*, 78–86. During this time, Hornsby was separated from his wife. He was carrying on an affair with a married woman and was dragged into court by his lover's husband.

12. Alexander, *Rogers Hornsby*, 82.

13. Alexander, *Rogers Hornsby*, 84–85. The Cardinals were willing to trade Hornsby, but they wanted cash and players from the Cubs. Veeck's offer fell short of what the Cardinals wanted.

14. Alexander, *Rogers Hornsby*, 101. Rickey was not happy about being replaced. Upset at being dismissed by Breadon, he choose to sell his stake in the team. Hornsby, thanks to a loan arranged by Breadon, bought Rickey's 12.5 percent interest in the team, thus becoming both the manager and a minority shareholder. See also Lowenfish, *Branch Rickey*, 150–51.

15. Golenbock, *The Spirit of St. Louis*, 100.

16. Lowenfish, 162.

17. Lowenfish, 161–62. See also: Alexander, *Rogers Hornsby*, 114; and Doutrich, *Cardinals and the Yankees*, 147–49.

18. Ruth's numbers in 1926 were outstanding. In addition to the 47 home runs and 145 RBIS, both of which led the league, Ruth also led the league in runs scored, bases on balls, and slugging average. He hit .372, second to Heinie Manush of Detroit, who batted .378.

19. The Johnnie Sylvester story is well told in Poekel's *Babe and the Kid*. In the summer of 1926, Sylvester had been thrown from a horse and kicked in the head. A series of medical complications followed, and he was hospitalized. His parents requested a signed ball from the World Series as a way to cheer him up. Sylvester's father, a bank vice president, used his connections to get word to the Yankees and Cardinals about his son's request, and that resulted in the balls being taken to the opposing dugouts during the rain delay in Game Three.

20. Haines was not a good hitting pitcher. The homer in the 1926 World Series was an aberration. Over the course of his career, in more than 1,100 regular-season at bats, Haines hit only 3 home runs and batted a measly .186.

21. Various accounts suggest that Rhem and Alexander were sipping whiskey from a flask in the bullpen. It has also been said that Alexander might have been hung over from celebratory drinking the night before. Both men were known for drinking too much. Like so many baseball stories of the era, there is the possibility of embellishment or pure invention. About the flask and the drinking in the bullpen: I doubt that Alexander was outright drunk or recovering from a hangover in the bullpen. But it makes a good story. See Alexander, *Rogers Hornsby*, 119; and Doutrich, *The Cardinals and the Yankees*, 184.

22. On Ruth's decision to try to steal second: Ruth explained that the Yankees had been having trouble getting base hits off Alexander, so getting a runner in scoring position was critical—a reasonable strategy, all things considered—but a stunning failure. No other World Series has ended on a failed stolen base attempt.

23. Hornsby and Surface, *My War with Baseball*, 193.

24. There were two issues: money and the length of the contract. Breadon made a generous offer but hoped that Hornsby would turn it down. Breadon wanted to get rid of Hornsby. See Alexander, *Rogers Hornsby*, 124–25.

25. Lowenfish, 171. Breadon insisted on the trade; Rickey always maintained that he would not have traded Hornsby, simply because Hornsby was in the prime years of his career and had so much to offer as a player.

26. At the urging of Branch Rickey, the Giants were also enticed to include pitcher Jimmy Ring in the deal, though Ring never won a game for the Cardinals. Lowenfish, 173.

27. Hornsby was actually in charge of the team for roughly half the season. McGraw had hinted that when he was ready to step down permanently as

manager he thought Hornsby would be an excellent replacement. Alexander, *Rogers Hornsby*, 140–44.

28. Alexander, *Rogers Hornsby*, 136–44; quote from Arthur Daley, "He Who Gets Slapped," *New York Times*, September 18, 1953.

29. Arthur Daley, "He Who Gets Slapped," *New York Times*, September 18, 1953.

30. Alexander, *Rogers Hornsby*, 141; Alexander, *John McGraw*, 281; "Hornsby is Traded for 'Good' of Giants," *New York Times*, January 11, 1928

31. Alexander, *Rogers Hornsby*, 148–49.

32. It was the largest amount of cash ever paid in a player transaction. The five players acquired by the Braves were: Socks Seibold, Percy Jones, Lou Leggett, Freddie Maguire, and Bruce Cunningham. Seibold pitched for five years with the Braves, winning 41 games and losing 65. Maguire hit .257 in his career, with 1 home run. Jones had a lifetime record of 53-57, but won only 7 games for the Braves. Leggett and Cunningham had short-lived careers in the Majors.

2. WILLIAM WRIGLEY

1. Wrigley's net worth in 1932 would be roughly equivalent to half-a-billion dollars in 2019.

2. Golenbock, *Wrigleyville*, 174.

3. For Wrigley's early life and history, see: Golenbock, *Wrigleyville*, 173–75. See also: Zimmerman, *William Wrigley, Jr.* For the relationship between Weeghman and Wrigley, see "Weeghman and Wrigley" at WrigleyIvy.Com/

4. Weeghman was a successful businessman who had made his fortune with a chain of restaurants. Other investors at the time included J. Ogden Armour, the meat packing mogul, and Albert D. Lasker, who owned an advertising firm and is sometimes referred to as "the father of modern advertising."

5. Approached about making a small donation to the Roosevelt campaign, Wrigley wrote a check for $25,000. Zimmerman, *William Wrigley, Jr.*, 194.

6. Leuchtenburg, *The American Presidency*, 113.

7. Leuchtenburg, *The American Presidency*, 113.

8. Spatz and Steinberg, *1921*, 123–24.

9. Mead and Dickson, *The Presidents Game*, 44.

10. Leuchtenburg, *The American Presidency*, 118.

11. Leuchtenburg, *The American Presidency*, 126.

12. Of course, this is speculation. Others in the leadership of the Republican Party would have had a say in who became Harding's running mate, but Wrigley was an immensely popular figure, highly respected; and the convention in 1920 was held in Wrigley's hometown of Chicago. Strictly in terms of charisma and personal charm, it's safe to say that Wrigley would have been a far more attractive and dynamic candidate and eventual president than Calvin Coolidge.

13. Charles Weeghman later reported that he'd been tipped off, in August of 1919, that the series would be fixed. His contact was a Chicago gambler named Jacob "Mont" Tennes. But apparently Weeghman did not pass this information along to anyone in professional baseball—or anyone in law enforcement. See Pietrusza, *Judge and Jury*, 102–4, 160.

14. Rothstein, of course, was more than just a gambler with a passing interest in sports. He was the head of a major criminal organization in New York and the mentor to future crime boss Lucky Luciano. He has been immortalized in literature as a character in the short stories of Damon Runyon and as the character Meyer Wolfsheim, in F. Scott Fitzgerald's novel *The Great Gatsby*.

15. Asinof, *Eight Men Out*, 148.

16. Pietrusza, *Judge and Jury*, 159: Cub management received six telegrams and two phone calls warning of the fix.

17. Asinof, *Eight Men Out*, 226. Asinof explains that the confessions were later removed from the court files.

18. Contemporary historians have connected Rothstein to the plot, but he claimed to know nothing when called before the grand jury, and he was ably represented by a lawyer known as William "The Great Mouthpiece" Fallon.

19. Jack Bales "Baseball's First Bill Veeck." See also, Pietrusza, *Judge and Jury*, 153–72.

20. Bruce Watson, "The Judge Who Rules Baseball," *Smithsonian Magazine*, September 2000.

21. Bruce Watson, "The Judge Who Rules Baseball," *Smithsonian Magazine*, September 2000.

22. Asinof, *Eight Men Out*, 272–73.

23. "All Black Sox Acquitted On Single Ballot," *Chicago Tribune*, August 3, 1921.

24. Asinof, *Eight Men Out*, 273. See also, "White Sox Players are All Acquitted by Chicago Jury," *New York Times*, August 3, 1921; and "All Black Sox Acquitted on Single Ballot," *Chicago Tribune*, August 3, 1921.

25. Asinof, *Eight Men Out*, 273.

26. Asinof, *Eight Men Out*, 273.

27. "Black Sox Acquitted, But Out," *Chicago Tribune*, August 4, 1921.

28. Golenbock, *Wrigleyville*, 225.

29. Golenbock, *Wrigleyville*, 191.

30. Designed by the architect Earl Heitschmidt of Los Angeles, the building is now on the National Register of Historic Places. See www.https//npgallery.nps;gov/AssetDetail/NRIS89001045 (accessed March 25, 2019).

31. For facts about the history of Wrigley Field, see Shea, *Wrigley Field*; and Golenbock, *Wrigleyville*. See also https://www.WrigleyIvy.com/.

32. Golenbock, *Wrigleyville*, 203.

33. Shea, *Wrigley Field*, 143.
34. "William Wrigley Dies at Age 70," *New York Times*, January 27, 1932. The obituary cited the cause of death as "acute indigestion, complicated by apoplexy and heart disease."
35. Comiskey died October 26, 1931; Dreyfus died February 5, 1932.
36. *Chicago Tribune*, "Sports World Loses True Friend in Death of Wrigley," January 27, 1932.
37. *Chicago Tribune*, "Sports World Loses True Friend in Death of Wrigley," January 27, 1932.
38. Tribute quotes from the *Chicago Tribune's* "Sports World Loses True Friend in Death of Wrigley," January 27, 1932.

3. SPRING TRAINING

1. This list of legal cases only covers the period from 1921 to 1930. There were more to come.
2. The Frank Moore situation: see Alexander, *Rogers Hornsby*, 132–43; see also D'Amore, *Rogers Hornsby*, 89–90.
3. Stoneham liked to gamble. His dissatisfaction with Hornsby stemmed from the fact that he didn't like people who wouldn't pay off their debts.
4. Louis Norman "Bobo" Newsom recovered from his broken leg and pitched one inning for the Cubs in June 1932. He later found success in the Majors, pitching for nine different teams; retiring in 1953 at the age of forty-six. He won 211 games and lost 221 in his long career. In 1982 he was quoted as saying, "I played for Washington five different times. That beat Franklin Delano Roosevelt's record. He was only elected four times."
5. Alexander, *McGraw*, 302–6. McGraw and New York Giants owner Horace Stoneham thought they'd have bigger crowds and collect more revenue in Los Angeles, but the players didn't like the long commute to the ballpark from their hotel, and the crowds were smaller than hoped for. The McQuade legal decision was another irritant.
6. In the summer of 1941, Ruth played a series of charity golf matches with Ty Cobb. Both men were good golfers and notoriously competitive. Cobb won 2 of the 3 matches. See Stanton's *Ty and the Babe*.
7. Leavy, *Big Bam*, 449–50. Leavy quotes Ruth saying that he considered himself responsible for the increase in player salaries. The owners certainly benefited as well from Ruth's rise to fame and prominence.
8. Westbrook Pegler had been a World War I correspondent, and later he became well known as a conservative columnist who especially hated Franklin Roosevelt and the New Deal.

9. Westbrook Pegler, "Magnates Foot Bill; Players Get Sympathy," *Chicago Tribune*, February 3, 1932.

10. Pegler, "Magnates Foot Bill."

11. For more on the Reserve Clause, see Lowenfish, *The Imperfect Diamond*; and Miller, *A Whole Different Ball Game*.

12. Steve Wilstein, "Memories of the Babe: Mark Koenig, Who Once Had Fight with Ruth, Remembers Him as Being More than a Slugger," *Los Angeles Times*, September 27, 1987.

13. Ruth accused Durocher of stealing money and a watch from him. The incident may or may not have happened. Elden Auker describes what he remembers in his memoir *Sleeper Cars and Flannel Uniforms,* 21–23. It's clear from this book that Auker had nothing but disdain for Durocher. In his biography of Durocher, Paul Dickson downplays the incident. See Dickson, *Leo Durocher*, 3, 49.

14. "Ruth and Rupert Spar for Time," *New York Times*, March 14, 1932.

15. William Brandt, "Home-Run Ace Takes $5,000 Salary Cut," *New York Times*, March 17, 1932. Also see Montville, *The Big Bam*, 307–8; and Creamer, *Babe*, 355–56. Manville also reports that Ruth was to get a 25 percent cut of the gate receipts for all exhibition games, a provision that carried over from his previous contracts.

16. Brandt, "Home-Run Ace Takes $5,000 Salary Cut," *New York Times*, March 17, 1932.

17. "Statements by Ruth, Ruppert after Babe Signed Contract," *New York Times*, March 17, 1932.

18. "Mack Fears the Yankees' Speed and Punch Will Wrest League Title from Athletics," *New York Times*, March 19, 1932.

19. "Mack Fears the Yankees' Speed."

20. "Reds Will Keep Herman," *New York Times*, March 16, 1932.

21. Irving Vaughn, "Cubs Polish Their Party Manners for Giant Visit," *Chicago Tribune*, March 5, 1932.

22. Irving Vaughn, "Giants Pound Rookie Pitcher in Tenth; Defeat Cubs, 6 to 3," *Chicago Tribune*, March 7, 1932.

23. Irving Vaughn, "Hornsby Gives Barton Special Batting Lesson," *Chicago Tribune*, February 22, 1932.

24. "Yankees' Two Runs in Eighth Top Reds," *New York Times*, March 30, 1932.

25. Irving Vaughn, "Help! Police! Bold Burglar in Cubs' Camp," *Chicago Tribune*, March 11, 1932.

4. OPENING DAY

1. "Washington and Philadelphia Open Baseball Season Here Today," *Washington Post*, April 14, 1910.

2. "Some Who Saw the Game," *Washington Post*, April 15, 1910.

3. "Washington and Philadelphia Open Baseball Season Here Today," *Washington Post*, April 14, 1910.

4. Thomas, *Walter Johnson*, 75.

5. Mead and Dickson, *Baseball: The President's Game*, 3–4.

6. Mead and Dickson, *Baseball: The President's Game*, 9.

7. Shirley Povich, "Altrock and Schacht Cloak Enmity as Show Goes On," *Washington Post*, April 10, 1932. See also, Peter Gordon, "Nick Altrock," SABR BioProject, accessed August 24, 2019, https://sabr.org/bioproj/person/aea7c461; Ralph Berger, "Al Schacht," SABR BioProject, accessed August 24, 2019, https://sabr.org/bioproj/person/04d01542. Both Altrock and Schacht pitched in the Major Leagues. Altrock was the better hurler, compiling a career record of 82-75, including two 20-game win seasons. Schacht's career record was 14-10. While coaching together with the Washington Senators, the 2 formed a highly successful comedy act, performing at games and on the vaudeville circuit in the off-season. The duo performed together from 1922 to 1934, earning as much as $180,000 a year. Schacht continued as a solo act for 2 more decades and became known as the "Clown Prince of Baseball."

8. Mead and Dickson, *Baseball: The President's Game*, 60.

9. Shirley Povich, "Nats Defeat Red Sox, 1–0, in 10 Innings," *Washington Post*, April 12, 1932.

10. Shirley Povich, "Nats Defeat Red Sox."

11. Walter Waters, a World War I veteran, was living in Portland, Oregon in the spring of 1932, when he decided to lead a contingent of veterans to Washington DC to lobby for an early payment of the bonuses that had been promised to the veterans. In early May, he and a small group began heading east, traveling on freight trains and picking up supporters along the way. They named themselves The Bonus Expeditionary Force, a phrase that was later shortened to the BEF. The group joined other protestors in the nation's capital.

5. THE MATH WIZARD

1. Shirley Povich, "Club Boasts Added Punch, Great Infield, Effective Pitchers for Coming Race," *Washington Post*, March 27, 1932.

2. Ralph Berger, "Moe Berg," SABR BioProject, accessed August 24, 2019, https://sabr.org/bioproj/person/e1e65b3b.

3. Shirley Povich, "Club Boasts Added Punch, Great Infield, Effective Pitchers for Coming Race," *Washington Post*, March 27, 1932.

4. Shirley Povich, "This Morning with Shirley L. Povich," *Washington Post*, April 5, 1932.

5. Shirley Povich, "Form Shown Pleasing to Manager," *Washington Post*, March 31, 1932.
6. Charles Sydnor, "Monte Morton Weaver." Unpublished essay. In possession of the author. Note: Charles Sydnor was a former baseball player at Emory and Henry College, as well as president of the college from 1984 to 1992.
7. Warren Corbett, "Monte Weaver," SABR BioProject, accessed August 24, 2019, https://sabr.org/bioproj/person/537bd12a.
8. Corbett, "Monte Weaver." See also, Sydnor, "Monte Morton Weaver."

7. ROOKIE PITCHERS

1. Joseph Wancho, "Dizzy Dean." SABR BioProject. Accessed August 24, 2019, https://sabr.org/bioproj/person/40bc224d See also, Gregory, *Diz*.
2. Gregory, *Diz*, 41. Dizzy's younger brother, Paul, also a successful Major League pitcher, agreed with Rickey, saying "Diz is wonderful. There's nobody like him and there ain't been in years. He's as great as Mathewson, Alexander and Johnson were in their day." Quoted in Feldman, *Dizzy and the Gashouse Gang*, 140.
3. Gregory, *Diz*, 64.
4. Gregory, *Diz*, 64–65.
5. Gregory, *Diz*, 65.
6. Gregory, *Diz*, 79.
7. Nancy Snell Griffith, "Flint Rhem," SABR BioProject, accessed August 20, 2019, https://sabr.org/bioproj/person/97c73ab1.
8. "'Imagine Me, of All People,' Wails Flint Rhem as He Tells of Booze Seduction," *Atlanta Constitution*, September 19, 1930. See also, Heidenry, *The Gashouse Gang*, 47. See also, Griffith, "Flint Rhem."
9. Dan Duren, "Lon Warneke," SABR BioProject, accessed August 19, 2019, https://sabr.org/bioproj/person/5a2fe3c9.
10. Lowenfish, *Branch Rickey*, 266. Rickey regretted losing Warneke to the Cubs organization, but St. Louis reacquired Warneke in October 1937. Warneke won 83 games for the Cardinals between 1937 and 1942; then he was traded back to the Cubs.
11. Duren, "Lon Warneke."
12. Golenbock, *Wrigleyville*, 226.
13. Golenbock, *Wrigleyville*, 254; Duren, "Lon Warneke." In *Wrigleyville*, Phil Cavarretta notes how Warneke had a ukulele in his locker and that he liked to play while he sang or hummed. Duren describes how Warneke played various jokes on teammates: once with a dead snake; another time with a five dollar bill that had a string attached. For a guy who was supposedly quiet and

reserved—and who later became a county judge—Warneke exhibited some propensity for sly trickery and odd humor.

8. BRAWLS

1. Leuchtenburg , *The Perils of Prosperity*, 253.
2. Watkins, *The Hungry Years*, 70–78, 214–15, 423–24. Watkins notes that artists such as James Agee and Walker Evans—creators of *Let Us Now Praise Famous Men*—as well as others, like Eric Sevareid, Malcolm Cowley, Mary Heaton Vorse, and Theodore Dreiser observed and wrote about the plight of Americans impacted by the hard economic times.
3. Watkins, *The Hungry Years*, 215; Garrison, *Mary Heaton Vorse*, 241–48.
4. Dickson and Allen, *The Bonus Army*, 56–105.
5. Patman served forty-seven years in the House of Representatives and was known not just for his early advocacy of the payment of bonuses to World War I veterans, but also for his role in the investigation into the Watergate scandal. In 1972 Patman's banking committee looked into the payment of money to the Watergate burglars; and the committee's discovery eventually led to the formation of the Senate Select Committee on Watergate, headed by Sen. Sam Ervin.
6. Dickson and Allen, *The Bonus Army*, 103.
7. Ty Cobb and Hack Wilson both jumped into the stands to confront or chase hecklers. In 1928 Wilson punched a milkman who had been harassing him verbally. See Alexander, *Rogers Hornsby*, 159. In a particularly ugly incident in 1912, Cobb attacked a taunting fan, a partially disabled man named Claude Lueker. According to Cobb, Lueker had been calling him vile names and insulting his family. Cobb punched and kicked Lueker, sending him to the hospital. Cobb was suspended, though his teammates supported Cobb's story and understood Cobb's reaction. See Stump, *Cobb*, 206–8. See also, "A Beating in the Stands, Followed by One on the Field," *New York Times*, April 28, 2012.
8. Stump, *Cobb*, 296–97. Among the players watching the fight: Walter Johnson and Rogers Hornsby.
9. Stump, *Cobb*, 329–30.
10. Ruth was called "N–– Lips" at St. Mary's. Cobb was not the first, and would not be the last, to employ some variation of that racially coded remark within earshot of Ruth. It was an insult that incensed Ruth. See Creamer, *Babe*, 38, 185. See Montville, *The Big Bam*, 21, 43–44.
11. Montville, *The Big Bam*, 190–91. Stump, *Cobb*, 356–58.
12. Montville, *The Big Bam*, 154. Creamer, *Babe*, 264–65.
13. Montville, *The Big Bam*, 155.

14. Montville, *The Big Bam*, 231, 309.

15. Montville, *The Big Bam*, 150.

16. Creamer, *Babe*, 138–39. Initially credited with a perfect game, Shore's master-piece has remained controversial. Purists regard it as a combined no-hitter, not a perfect game.

17. Durocher's abrasive and combative personality has been well documented. See Dickson, *Leo Durocher*, and Marlett, "Leo Durocher." As for the Durocher/Bartell fight, ironically, Bartell later played on a team that Durocher managed.

18. The series was a best-of-nine competition, which Boston won 5 games to 3. Dineen pitched 4 times, winning 3 of the games, with a 2.06 ERA over 35 innings. The winner of the other 2 games was thirty-six-year-old Cy Young, in his only World Series.

19. "Stealing Home Base Records," *Baseball Almanac*, accessed August 24, 2019, https://www.baseball-almanac.com/recbooks/rb_stbah.shtml. The site notes that "Stealing home plate is NOT an officially recorded statistic so research into this unusual feat is still considered ongoing." *Baseball Almanac* credits Ty Cobb as the leader with 54 documented steals of home in his career. Moriarty is not listed among players with 10 or more steals of home, but Moriarty's biographer, Eric Enders, claims that Moriarty had at least 11 documented steals of home, "although the actual number is certainly larger." See Eric Enders, "George Moriarty," SABR BioProject, accessed August 24, 2019, https://sabr.org/bioproj/person/44c82f26. While the exact number of Moriarty's steals of home may be unknown, or unknowable, it was a feat for which he was renowned. By comparison, Babe Ruth is credited with 10 steals of home in his career.

20. Creamer, *Babe*, 261–62; Montville, *The Big Bam*, 152.

21. Enders, "George Moriarty."

22. Enders, "George Moriarty." Over the years, Barrow developed his own reputation as something of a brawler, having challenged Babe Ruth to a locker room fight in the spring of 1919. Barrow had boxed in his younger days and knew how to handle himself in a fist fight.

23. "Donnie Bush and Umpire Moriarty Renew Old Feud," *Chicago Daily Tribune*, July 6, 1931.

24. Mike Lynch, "The Memorial Day Brawl of 1932," May 29, 2011, at https://www.seamheads.com/2011/05/29/the-memorial-day-brawl-of-1932/.

25. Edward Burns, "Pitcher Handed 10 Day Layoff, Assessed $500," *Chicago Tribune*, June 1, 1932.

26. Evans had been known as "The Boy Umpire," having assumed the position of Major League umpire at the age of twenty-two. He is the youngest umpire to work a World Series game—at the age of twenty-five.

27. Edward Burns, "Pitcher Handed 10 Day Layoff, Assessed $500," *Chicago Tribune*, June 1, 1932.
28. Burns, "Pitcher Handed."
29. Burns, "Pitcher Handed."
30. Burns, "Pitcher Handed."
31. Burns, "Pitcher Handed."
32. Worst career record, based on how many fewer wins he had than losses. But Gaston was not nearly as bad a pitcher as his record indicates. He pitched for eleven years in the Majors, started 271 games, and completed 127. He pitched for some awful teams: mostly for the St. Louis Browns, the Boston Red Sox, and the Chicago White Sox; only once did his team finish in the first division. Gaston died at age one hundred, in 1996, one of the few Major Leaguers to reach that age. Reportedly, he stood and sang "Take Me Out to the Ballgame" at his one hundredth birthday party on January 27, 1996. See Bill Nowlin, "Milt Gaston," SABR BioProject, accessed Augusts 24, 2019, https://sabr.org/bioproj/person/239d1bf7. See also: *Boston Herald*, April 27, 1996.
33. The oldest living former Major Leaguer at the time of Gaston's death was Red Hoff, who pitched for the New York Highlanders and St. Louis Browns. Hoff, born on May 8, 1891, died on September 17, 1998, at the age of 107 years and 132 days. No former Major Leaguer has lived longer.

9. HORNSBY AND CUYLER

1. Alexander, *Rogers Hornsby*, 174.
2. Richbourg's main claim to fame was that he was once traded for Casey Stengel in a six-player transaction.
3. Barton played some years in the Carolina League, one of baseball's "outlaw leagues," so-called because the teams in the league signed players who were under contract with Major League clubs. Barton's potential as a power hitter was legitimate. On August 26, 1938, while playing for the Hickory Rebels, Barton homered 5 times in a nine-inning game against the Kannapolis Towelers. Despite Barton's one-time five-homer game, he was never able to hit consistently enough to get back to the Major Leagues.
4. "Pirates Great Young Hitter," *The Sporting News*, August 21, 1924.
5. Gregory H. Wolf, "Kiki Cuyler," SABR BioProject, accessed August 24, 2019, https://sabr.org/bioproj/person/7107706b.
6. In the twentieth century, 14 pitchers threw perfect games: 13 in regular-season play, plus Don Larsen's World Series perfect game. In the same century, ten players hit 4 home runs in a game: three American League players accomplished the feat, seven National League players.

10. BROOKLYN

1. Paul Geisler, "Billy Jurges," SABR BioProject, accessed August 20, 2019, https://sabr.org/bioproj/person/aada6293.

2. It is not known for certain when Popovich met, or dated, Lopez and Durocher. Popovich had been raised in Chicago but moved to New York in the late 1920s to pursue her entertainment career, so it's likely she met those two players in New York. Lopez played for the Dodgers as their regular catcher from 1928 to 1935. Durocher was with the Yankees in 1928 and 1929, before being traded to the Cincinnati Reds.

3. The history of Ebbets Field is described in a variety of books. See Lowry, *Green Cathedrals*, 117–20; D'Antonio, *Forever Blue*, 34–36; Ward and Burns, *Baseball*, 120; Shapiro, *The Last Good Season*, 34–36; Sandalow and Sutton, *Ballparks*, 227–30.

4. Malamud's mother, Bertha, died in a private mental hospital in Queens, in May 1929. The grocery store was featured in Malamud's novel, *The Assistant*. See Davis, *Bernard Malamud: A Writer's Life*.

5. Pollitt, "Creators on Creating.". The interview also appears in Lasher, *Conversations with Bernard Malamud*, 96–102.

6. Heller, "Malamud's Long View of Short Stories," in Lasher, *Conversations with Bernard Malamud*, 125. In Heller's interview, Malamud discusses the inspiration for his classic baseball novel *The Natural*, which he described as a book about "the experience of being a kid in Brooklyn," 125.

7. David W. Anderson, "Bill Klem," SABR BioProject, accessed August 19, 2019, https://sabr.org/bioproj/person/31461b94.

8. Bob LeMoine, "Beans Reardon," SABR BioProject, accessed August 24, 2019, https://sabr.org/bioproj/person/6d874f02. See also Dick Wagner, "Umpire's Widow Cherishes Memories of Beans, Baseball," *Los Angeles Times*, January 21, 1988. Late in his life Reardon married an artist named Eugenia Green. The Reardons mingled socially with Hollywood celebrities like Frank Sinatra and Ronald Reagan. Beans was close friends with Mae West and appeared in several of her films. Every Christmas, West would send Reardon a nude photo of herself. Reardon is also the subject of the Norman Rockwell painting "Bottom of the Sixth," a portrait of three umpires standing in the rain at home plate in Ebbets Field.

9. See *The Ballplayers*, edited by Mike Shatzkin, for Mickey Finn entry, 337. John Walter Mails, aka Duster "The Great" Mails, was a colorful character who pitched in the 1920s, winning 7 straight games for the Cleveland Indians late in the 1920 season. He was called Duster for his lack of control. The additional nickname "The Great" was self-proclaimed by Mails. See *The Ballplayers*, 656.

10. Mickey Finn died on July 7, 1933. His death was attributed to complications following surgery to repair a duodenal ulcer.

11. Mungo won 120 games in the Majors and was a mainstay of the Dodgers pitching staff during the 1930s. He twice led the league in starts, once in innings pitched, once in strikeouts, and 3 times in walks allowed. He was also the inspiration for a song titled "Van Lingle Mungo," written by jazz pianist Dave Frishberg. The song appeared on Frishberg's album *Oklahoma Toad*, in 1969. The song's lyrics are simply a recitation of the names of thirty-seven Major League ballplayers, rhymed to a bossa nova rhythm.

12. Durocher, *Nice Guys Finish Last*, 170–77.

13. Durocher, *Nice Guys Finish Last*, 176–77. See also Creamer, *Summer of '41*, 113–15.

11. ROAD TRIPS

1. Auker, *Sleeper Cars and Flannel Uniforms*, 41–42.

2. Halberstam, *Summer of '49*, 105.

3. Halberstam, *Summer of '49*, 105.

4. Betts is now remembered as giving up one of Ruth's most famous home runs: a nearly six-hundred-foot blast in an exhibition game at Waterfront Park— now known as Al Lang Field—in St. Petersburg, in 1934. Although the exact distance the ball traveled in the air cannot be proven, this particular homer is part of the Ruth legend. See Peter Kerasotis, "Home, at the Other House that Ruth Built," *New York Times*, March 10, 2014. See also Adminneje, "Babe Ruth's Longest Home Run," in *Northeast Journal* at http://northeastjournal.org /babe-ruths-longest-home-run.

5. Gregory H. Wolf, "Freddie Fitzsimmons," sabr BioProject, accessed August 24, 2019, https://sabr.org/bioproj/person/5a7df0b9. Casey Stengel referred to Fitzsimmons as "The Seal" for his short arms and fielding prowess.

6. John Kieran, Sports of the Times, "A Couple of Stout Fellows," *New York Times*, July 16, 1935. Fitzsimmons said "Some games say I throw a hundred balls up there [and] maybe fifty of 'em would be a knuckler."

7. Durocher, *Nice Guys Finish Last*, 145.

8. Gregory, *Diz*, 85.

9. Rickey quoted in Gregory, *Diz*, 86; Street quoted in "Dean, Disgruntled, Quits the Cardinals," *New York Times*, June 16, 1932.

10. Gregory, *Diz*, 88. The $225 had been advanced to Dean as a loan to his father when Dean signed his contract with the Cardinals, or so the Cardinals claimed. The money was later deducted from Dean's paycheck, which left him feeling he'd been cheated out of part of his salary. Once Rickey gave Dean the money, he was mollified and willing to resume his career.

12. CHICAGO CONVENTIONS

1. Barnhart and Schlickman, *John Paul Stevens*, 25. The purchase of land for the hotel was made possible by an investment in the project by James Stevens, the father of Ernest, and the founder of Illinois Life Insurance Company.

2. Barnhart and Schlickman, *John Paul Stevens*, 26–27.

3. Stephan, "A Justice for All," *Northwestern Magazine*, spring 2009 at https:// www.northwestern.edu/magazine/spring2009/cover/stevens.html.

4. The Sad Sam Jones on the 1932 White Sox is not to be confused with the Sad Sam Jones—also known as Toothpick Sam—who toiled for six Major League teams in the 1950s and 1960s, compiling a 21-15 record with a league-leading 2.83 ERA in 1959 for the San Francisco Giants.

5. Two teams had worse attendance in 1932: the St. Louis Browns who drew only 112,558 to their games, and the Boston Red Sox who drew 182,150.

6. "Diehard Cubs Fan," *Northwestern Magazine*, Spring 2009 at https://www .northwestern.edu/magazine/spring2009/cover/stevens_sidebar/cubs.html.

7. Starting in 1993, a young announcer named Ronald Reagan was hired to do the games for station WHO in Des Moines, Iowa, but the Chicago-based announcers—Totten, Elson, and Flanagan—were most likely the ones that Johnny Stevens would have listened to in his Chicago home.

8. Barnhart and Schlickman, *John Paul Stevens*, 28–30.

9. AZ Quotes, "Anton Cermak," accessed August 24, 2019. https://www.azquotes .com/author/23798-Anton_Cermak. Cermak was elected on April 6, 1931. He earned 58 percent of the vote from Chicagoans who had tired of the administration of Big Bill Thompson. Thompson had ridiculed Cermak for his surname and birth in Eastern Europe. For many of Chicago's ethnic minorities, Cermak was an appealing and refreshing change.

10. Baltimore had hosted the second most presidential nominating conventions: nine Democratic events and one Republican affair.

11. Bryson, *One Summer*, 79–81.

12. Neal, *Happy Days Are Here Again*, 211.

13. Levinsky was a modestly talented heavyweight boxer with a strong fan base in Chicago. Born Harris Krakow, he fought under the name Kingfish Levinsky because his family was known as fish sellers, on Maxwell Street in Chicago. Levinsky had 117 fights in his professional career, winning 75 of those bouts, including 40 by knockout. He fought most of the era's top heavyweights but never secured a title fight.

14. Dempsey's nickname came about because he'd been raised in the small Mormon town of Manassa, Colorado.

15. Kahn, *A Flame of Pure Fire*, 431–32.

16. Noted in Burner, *Herbert Hoover*, 308.

17. Smith, *An Uncommon Man*, 140–41.

18. Burner, *Herbert Hoover*, 307.

19. Smith, *An Uncommon Man*, 141.

20. Mencken quote from Smith, *An Uncommon Man*, 141.

21. Neal, *Happy Days Are Here Again*, 306.

22. Neal, *Happy Days Are Here Again*, 307.

23. Neal, *Happy Days Are Here Again*, 310.

24. Neal, *Happy Days Are Here Again*, 313; from Roosevelt, *Public Papers and Addresses: Volume One: The Genesis of the New Deal*, 647–59.

13. INDEPENDENCE DAY

1. "Six Youths Killed in Blast of Holiday Dynamite Caps," *Washington Post*, July 5, 1932. The three-day Fourth of July holiday produced multiple tragedies. More than a hundred people died in auto accidents. Over two dozen people drowned, including at least nine in floodwaters in Texas. In Mississippi, one man died when struck by lightning and another was gored to death by a bull. According to an article titled "NEARLY 200 ARE KILLED" in the *Indianapolis Star* on July 5: "There were more than two score drownings, and nearly as many miscellaneous deaths, including murders, suicides, airplane accidents and household accidents. The latter included three scalded to death by boiling lard in Iowa."

2. Ireland, "Conversation between Warden Thalacker and Charles Ireland." Unpublished. Also see: "Darrell Meredith," *Des Moines Register*, October 14, 2011. Meredith pitched for eight years in the Minor League organizations of the Chicago White Sox and the Brooklyn Dodgers, then returned to Iowa where he farmed for nearly seventy years. He died at the age of ninety-nine in Monticello.

3. See Leuchtenburg, *Franklin D. Roosevelt and the New Deal*, 14. Also see Dickson and Allen, *The Bonus Army*, 112. John Dos Passos and others commented in their news reports that the baseball field at the Anacostia site was often used for pickup games, with some of Glassford's men participating with the bonus marchers.

4. "Roundy Says," *The Wisconsin State Journal*, July 5, 1932.

5. "Griffith Asks Maximum Penalty for Dickey in Wire to Harridge," *Washington Post*, July 5, 1932.

6. "Levinsky v Walker," *Time*, May 9, 1932.

7. It is reasonable to assume that Levinsky received around 30 percent of the gate for his fights in 1931 and 1932, meaning that he would have earned close to $80,000 in that period. For more about the economics of boxing, see D'O'Brian, "The Business of Boxing," *American Heritage*, October 1991.

8. Although the fire inspector officially declared the fire to be "accidental," three years later, the arsonist Robert Driscoll admitted setting the blaze. Driscoll is believed to have set at least 115 fires in the Seattle area, perhaps as many as 140. See Eskenazi and Rudman, "Wayback Machine: A Fire That Changed Our Sports," at http://www.sportspressnw.com/2124688/2011/wayback -machine-a-fire-that-changed-our-sports.

14. DOUBLE X

1. John Kieran, Sports of the Times, "All Over the Field," *New York Times*, July 4, 1932.
2. After the trade of Mark Koenig during the 1928 off-season, the Yankees employed Leo Durocher, Lyn Lary, and Frank Crosetti at shortstop. Durocher was waived in the winter of 1930. Neither Lary nor Crosetti proved to be very reliable at the plate, though Crosetti was a good fielder.
3. John Bennett, "Jimmie Foxx," SABR BioProject, accessed August 24, 2019, https://sabr.org/bioproj/person/e34a045d; and Milliken, *Jimmie Foxx: The Pride of Sudlersville*, 1–18.
4. Frank Baker started his career with the Philadelphia Athletics, where he won his home run titles. He never hit more than 12 homers in a single season, but during the dead-ball era, he was considered the game's premier home run hitter. After seven seasons with the Athletics, he was traded to the New York Yankees, where he spent the last six years of his Major League career. He played on the 1921 and 1922 Yankees with the up-and-coming young slugger, Babe Ruth.
5. Milliken, *Jimmie Foxx*, 129. See also, Leaves from a Fan's Notebook, "James Emory 'Jimmy' Foxx," *The Sporting News*, July 7, 1932.
6. Milliken, *Jimmie Foxx*, 128.
7. Gomez and Goldstone, *Lefty*, 118. About another homer that Foxx hit off Gomez, the Yankee pitcher commented, in 1969, that a white object found by Neil Armstrong on the moon "was the home run Jimmie Foxx hit off me in 1937."
8. Milliken, *Jimmie Foxx*, 128.

15. WICKED CHICAGO

1. Ernie Fuhr, "Hal Carlson," SABR BioProject, accessed August 24, 2019, https://sabr.org/bioproj/person/b9c3739f. Cubs in the Hotel Carlos on the night that Carlson died: clubhouse attendant Ed Froelich, players Kiki Cuyler, Riggs Stevenson, and Cliff Heathcote. All four were with Carlson when he died. Froelich had called Cubs team physician, John Davis, but he arrived too late to do anything to save Carlson.

2. Fuhr, "Hal Carlson."

3. Abbott, *Sin in the Second City*, 24. For an expansive and entertaining history of the brothel run by Everleigh sisters, see Abbott's *Sin in the Second City*.

4. Mitgang, "With Bellow in Chicago," July 6, 1980, at https://archive.newyork-times.com/books/00/04/23/specials/bellow-chicago80.html.

5. Leuchtenburg, *Perils of Prosperity*, 247.

6. Watkins, *The Hungry Years*, 87.

7. Eig, *Get Capone*, 371. See also "Chicagoans Eat Tons of Turkey on Thanksgiving," *Chicago Daily Tribune*, November 27, 1931.

8. Bergreen, *Capone*, 493–509.

9. Kobler, *Capone*, 327.

10. Bergreen, *Capone*, 505.

11. Bergreen, *Capone*, 510.

12. Capone was not very good at hitting a pitched ball, but in one of the uglier and more gruesome moments in his murderous career, he is alleged to have beaten three of his henchmen—who supposedly were plotting against him—with a baseball bat, before he had the victims shot and killed. See Eig, Get *Capone*, 315–16; and Bergreen, *Capone*, 329–31.

13. Kobler, *Capone*, 333.

14. Machine Gun Jack McGurn was one of the more colorful—and dangerous—characters in Chicago during the era. He once slit the throat and cut off part of the tongue of singer/comedian Joe E. Lewis, in an effort to dissuade Lewis from entertaining at a rival club. Lewis survived, but his singing voice was never quite the same. McGurn is also widely believed to be the organizer and one of the gunmen involved in the St. Valentine's Day Massacre. He was investigated but never arrested because he claimed to have spent the day with his girlfriend, Louise Rolfe, who became known as "the blonde alibi."

15. Dickson, *Bill Veeck*, 42–43.

16. Bergreen, *Capone*, 232.

17. See pages 51–78 in Jean Hastings Ardell's excellent book *Breaking Into Baseball* for a history and analysis of so-called "Baseball Annies." For more on women in baseball, see Debra A. Shattuck's *Bloomer Girls: Women Baseball Pioneers* and Jennifer Ring's *A Game of Their Own: Voices of Contemporary Women in Baseball.*

18. Many writers focusing on the Cubs and this era have told the story of Violet Popovich and the shooting incident in the Hotel Carlos. For Violet's back-story, I have relied on legal records and newspaper stories. For the moment-to-moment events in the Hotel Carlos on July 5 and 6, 1932, I've looked at the newspaper accounts and various first person accounts of people who witnessed or were involved in the events. The best and most accurate published

accounts are Bales, "The Shootings of Billy Jurges and Eddie Waitkus" at https://www.wrigleyivy.com/the-shootings-of-billy-jurges-and-eddie-waitkus/; and Ehrgott, *Mr. Wrigley's Ball Club*, 283–91.

19. "Letter Solves the Shooting of Bill Jurges," *Chicago Daily Tribune*, July 7, 1932.

20. Holtzman and Vass, *Baseball, Chicago Style*, 53–55. The note that Violet allegedly left in Cuyler's room is based on an interview with Billy Jurges that took place in 1988—fifty-six years after the shooting at the Hotel Carlos. Readers might well be skeptical of Jurges's account—or memory—so many years after the event. Jurges suggests in this interview that Violet might have had a romantic interest in Cuyler—saying Cuyler was "a big ladies man." But Cuyler died in 1950, many years before the Jurges interview, so he wasn't around to confirm or rebut the account by Jurges. Another theory, also many years after the fact: on page 164 in Bill Veeck's *The Hustler's Handbook*, Veeck suggests that Violet was looking for someone other than Jurges—a married player (Veeck doesn't say whom)—when she entered room 509. But Veeck gets several facts wrong about the incident, so readers should be wary of this account. I think the suicide note Violet left is very clear: she meant to kill Jurges and then herself. A relative of Popovich's later confirmed this, based on what she had told him. See Bales, "The Shootings of Billy Jurges and Eddie Waitkus" at https://www.wrigleyivy.com/the-shootings-of-billy-jurges-and -eddie-waitkus/.

21. "Bill Jurges Wounded by Girl He Rejected," *New York Times*, July 7, 1932.

22. "Bill Jurges Wounded by Girl He Rejected," *New York Times*, July 7, 1932.

16. HARRY HORTMAN AND CHARLIE IRELAND

1. Portions of this chapter have been previously published, in slightly different forms, as essays in *The Cooperstown Symposium on Baseball and American Culture, 2005–2006* and *The Cooperstown Symposium on Baseball and American Culture, 2017–2018*, edited by William M. Simons.

2. The name of the institution had changed in the years that Hortman spent in prison. When he was sentenced in 1902, the facility was called the Anamosa State Penitentiary. The name was changed to the Iowa State Men's Reformatory in 1907. For the purpose of simplicity, I refer to the institution simply as the Men's Reformatory or the reformatory.

3. The origin of Hortman's nickname is unknown, but he was widely referred to at the prison and in the town of Anamosa as Snap Hortman.

4. Hortman also coached the reformatory's football team for several years.

5. Information in this chapter concerning Charlie Ireland, his family, and his tenure as warden of the Men's Reformatory comes from a variety of sources, including: the Anamosa Penitentiary Museum website; letters in possession

of the author from two of Ireland's grandchildren, Nancy Tschorn and John Schweitzer; interviews with Ms. Tschorn and Mr. Schweitzer; the unpublished memoir "An Account of the Term of C. H. Ireland as Warden of the Iowa State Men's Reformatory," by Charles Arthur Ireland; and "Conversation Between Warden Thalacker and Charles Ireland of Santa Barbara CA (son of Warden Ireland)," dated October 3, 1989.

6. In fact, baseball had been played in institutional settings—prisoner of war camps, penitentiaries, and reformatories for many years. For example: "A nineteenth century lithograph by Otto Boettichen depicts a casual game of baseball being played at the Salisbury Confederate Prison in North Carolina, with Union soldiers on the field—a baserunner breaking for second—as fellow prisoners and Confederate guards stand in clumps around the field as attentive spectators. The year was 1862." Quote from Wolf, "The Golden Era of Prison Baseball," 116–26.

7. See Seymour, *Baseball: The People's Game*, 396–412. The book was originally published with Harold Seymour as sole author, but Dorothy Seymour Mills has subsequently received recognition as coauthor.

8. Toland, *The Dillinger Days*, 13–25.

9. Toland, *The Dillinger Days*, 23.

10. Golenbock, *Wrigleyville*, 220. See also "Today's Cubs Birthday (June 22)" at www.justonebadcentury.com/todays-cubs-birthday-june-22/.

11. Robert Boyle, "Fight On, Old Sing Sing U," accessed August 24, 2019, https://www.si.com/vault/1967/01/23/543318/fight-on-old-sing-sing-u.

12. Sands played for the Indianapolis Clowns from 1950–1955. His original position with the Clowns was shortstop, but on November 20, 1951, the Clowns signed a seventeen-year-old prospect named Henry Aaron. Sands was moved to catcher. Aaron took over at shortstop.

13. Quoted by Hank Utley and Josh Davlin in "Alabama Pitts," accessed August 24, 2019, at https://sabr.org/bioproj/person/d7db6951.

14. Utley and Davlin, "Alabama Pitts."

15. While organized baseball waited for a final decision on whether or not Pitts would be allowed to play, he was offered a contract by the House of David, a barnstorming team noted for the beards its players wore. But Pitts turned down the offer, reportedly because he didn't want to grow a beard.

16. Pietrusza, *Judge and Jury*, 375–77.

17. With a name like Casey Coburn, it was probably inevitable that a clever inmate would come up with a poem that parodied "Casey at the Bat." In 1932 the *Men's Reformatory Press* published "Casey Coburn's Revenge," which ends with Casey becoming the hero, not the goat, of a clash between the Anamosa

prison team and a visiting team. For more about Coburn, the Snappers, and the poem, see Wolf, "The Golden Era of Prison Baseball," 116–26.

18. The Anamosa town team played in the newly formed Wapsie Valley League with Viola, Martelle, Morley, Mount Vernon, Olin, Onslow, and Monmouth. All teams had fifteen-man rosters. League play began on May 15, 1932. Anamosa residents also supported and attended games inside the walls of the reformatory, where they could cheer on the Snappers from the bleachers

19. Charles had two sisters: eighteen-year-old Maisie and eight-year-old Dorothy.

20. Ireland, "An Account of the Term of C. H. Ireland." Unpublished.

21. Ireland, "An Account of the Term of C. H. Ireland." Unpublished. Also: "Conversation between Warden Thalacker and Charles Ireland." Unpublished.

22. Ireland, "An Account of the Term of C.H. Ireland." Unpublished.

17. SBARBARO'S COURTROOM

1. Eig, *Get Capone*, 135; Kobler, *Capone*, 206–7; Bergreen, *Capone*, 276–78.

2. At this time, Capone was just beginning to take over the business of Johnny Torrio, who was retiring and in the process of moving to New York. O'Banion was both an associate and a rival. After O'Banion's death and Torrio's retirement, Capone was very much in control of the Chicago gangs.

3. Kobler, *Capone*, 75.

4. Bergreen, *Capone*, 128–35; Kobler, *Capone*, 118–26. O'Banion, an Irishman and practicing Catholic, didn't have much respect for Torrio and Capone and the Italian gangsters with whom they were allied. In particular, O'Banion didn't approve of Capone's prostitution business. Torrio and Capone decided to kill O'Banion when they believed he had stolen barrels of whiskey from them and then set them up to be arrested by federal agents.

5. Bergreen, *Capone*, 136–38.

6. Bergreen, *Capone*, 136–38.

7. Crowe attended Yale Law School and served as a judge of the circuit court in Chicago from 1916 to 1921. He became state's attorney for Cook County in 1921 and is most well known as the prosecutor in the Leopold and Loeb case.

8. Lesy, *Murder City*, 121–49.

9. Baatz, *For the Thrill of It*, 10–12, 86. The stains were caused by hydrochloric acid. The murderers believed that the substance would erode the skin and make the body harder to identify. But in the process of stuffing the body in the culvert and dousing it with the chemical, one of the killers inadvertently lost his glasses, leaving behind crucial evidence.

10. Baatz, *For the Thrill of It*, 127.

11. Higdon, *Leopold and Loeb*, 91–92.

12. Lesy, *Murder City*, 195–206.
13. Sbarbaro would have known that it was extremely difficult to get a conviction of a white woman accused of assaulting a man. See "Afterword" in Lesy, *Murder City*, 308. In Chicago, between 1905 and 1918, no white woman tried for the murder of a husband or boyfriend was convicted. See also, Jeffrey Adler, *First in Violence, Deepest in Dirt*, 85–120.
14. Ehrgott, *Mr. Wrigley's Ball Club*, 335; "Police Hold Chief of Jurges Blackmail Plot," *Chicago Tribune*, August 14, 1932.
15. Ehrgott, *Mr. Wrigley's Ball Club*, 289–90.
16. "Girl Who Shot Cubs' Player Goes Free," *Chicago Tribune*, July 16, 1932.
17. Bales, "The Shootings of Billy Jurges and Eddie Waitkus," accessed August 24, 2019, https://wrigleyivy.com/the-shootings-of-billy-jurges-and-eddie -waitkus/.

18. LEGS OF GLASS

1. "Reynolds Heir Commits Suicide," *New York Times*, July 7, 1932. The mysterious death of Smith Reynolds captivated the public for months. The story of the death, the investigation, and the trial of Libby Holman is well told in *Dreams That Money Can Buy: The Tragic Life of Libby Holman*.
2. "Thousands Forget New 3-Cent Letter Rate," *New York Times*, July 7, 1932.
3. Guido Enderis, "World Fliers Speed on to Moscow After Swift Trip to Berlin," *New York Times*, July 7, 1932.
4. A handful of BEF marchers took the tickets and left the city. A few sold their tickets, pocketed the cash, and returned to either Camp Marks or Camp Anacostia.
5. Paul Dickson and Thomas Allen, *The Bonus Army*, 144.
6. Dickson and Allen, *The Bonus Army*, 137.
7. Dickson and Allen, *The Bonus Army*, 144.
8. Anderson played from 1894 to 1908; Wiggs played from 1903 to 1906.
9. John Drebinger, "Ruth May Be Lost for about Three Weeks," *New York Times*, July 19, 1932.
10. Babe and Claire had the entire seventh floor of the building. They lived there from 1929 to 1940. A few years later, the apartment was divided into two units. In 2015 one of the units went up for sale. See Jennifer Gould Kile and C. J. Sullivan, "You Can Own Babe Ruth's Two-Bedroom UWS Apartment for $1.6M," *New York Post*, August 31, 2015.
11. "Ruth Hopes to Don Uniform in a Week, *New York Times*, July 20, 1932. McGovern was a former flyweight boxer and owned a gym in New York City, where he helped train and recondition athletes and celebrities. Jack Dempsey, the boxing champion, and Gene Sarazen, the professional golfer, were two of

his more notable clients, but McGovern is most famous as being the person credited with getting Ruth back in shape after his disastrous 1925 "bellyache heard 'round the world." As Ruth aged, he continued to rely on McGovern and his facilities to work himself into playing shape before the start of each season.

12. "Ruth Hopes to Don Uniform in a Week," *New York Times*, July 20, 1932.

13. Wood, *Babe Ruth*.

14. Robert Creamer, *Babe*, 197.

15. League leaders: George Sisler at .407, Tris Speaker at .388, Joe Jackson at .380, and Ruth at .376.

16. Ruth's numbers in 1921, arguably the best year of his career: 59 home runs, 177 runs scored, 171 runs batted in, a .378 batting average, and a slugging average of .846. He also led the league in walks with 144. Think about those bases on balls for a moment. Imagine what his statistics would have been if he hadn't been walked in 21 percent of his plate appearances.

17. Montville, *The Big Bam*, 139–41; Appel, *Pinstripe Empire*, 116–17; Creamer, *Babe*, 241–43.

18. Creamer, *Babe*, 281–92, 324. Montville, *The Big Bam*, 202–3. The phrase "the bellyache heard 'round the world" was coined by *New York Tribune* writer W. O. McGeehan.

19. Montville, *The Big Bam*, 291–92.

20. Creamer, *Babe*, 323.

21. Hugh Fullerton, "Why Babe Ruth is Greatest Home-Run Hitter," *New York Times*, Sept 11, 1921.

22. Hugh Fullerton, "Why Babe Ruth is Greatest Home-Run Hitter," *Popular Science Monthly*, October 1921.

19. THE END OF THE HORNSBY ERA

1. Dickson and Allen, *The Bonus Army*, 136–37.

2. Dickson and Allen, *The Bonus Army*, 150. At the behest of his advisors, Hoover left the city for a few days at the height of the crisis. It was feared that the marchers might try to storm the White House.

3. Richard Norton Smith, *An Uncommon Man*, 140.

4. Alexander, *Rogers Hornsby*, 176–78. See also, Ehrgott, *Mr. Wrigley's Ball Club*, 303–6, 324.

5. Burns, "Hornsby Removed by Cubs," *Chicago Tribune*, August 3, 1932.

6. Vaughn, "Hornsby Tells of Incidents in Ouster by Cubs," *Chicago Tribune*, August 6, 1932. Although Hornsby supposedly "laughed at" the notion that his betting and gambling habits had anything to do with his dismissal—and although Veeck contended the decision to fire Hornsby was strictly a base-

ball matter—it's simply not believable that Hornsby's gambling addiction and need to borrow money from players to cover his debts played no role in Veeck's decision.

7. Burns, "Cubs Open Grimm's Regime with 12–1 Victory," *Chicago Tribune*, August 5, 1932

8. Lowry, *Green Cathedrals*, 208–9. The field was built on top of a railroad tunnel that ran under center field. On two occasions—once in 1903, again in 1927—portions of the stands collapsed. The 1903 collapse caused the death of twelve fans during the second game of a doubleheader with the Boston Red Sox. In 1935 a bolt of lightning struck and damaged the flagpole.

9. Cramer, *Joe DiMaggio*, 40.

10. Cramer, *Joe DiMaggio*, 33–35.

11. Cramer, *Joe DiMaggio*, 38–56.

12. Cramer, *Joe DiMaggio*, 44–52. Cramer tells the story of DiMaggio's first season with the Seals.

13. Daniel Shirley, "Mark Koenig." SABR BioProject, accessed August 24, 2019, https://sabr.org/bioproj/person/560d9b03.

14. The Yankees were playing musical chairs at the shortstop position. Koenig had been the starting shortstop beginning in 1926. Leo Durocher played both second and short in 1928; then more games at shortstop in 1929. But Durocher was traded after the 1929 season, and Lyn Lary had taken over at shortstop in 1930, which made Koenig expendable.

15. The Cubs scout Jack Doyle deserves credit, too. Doyle had a high regard for Koenig and thought he would be a productive addition to the Cubs' team.

20. THE BOYS OF SUMMER

1. Robert Gold, "Searching Sing Sing for My Father," accessed August 24, 2019, http://www.correctionhistory.org/html/chronicl/state/singsing/sonsearching/html/gold08.html.
See also, Gary Sarnoff, "The Day Babe Ruth Came to Sing Sing," accessed August 24, 2019, https://sabr.org/research/day-babe-ruth-came-sing-sing.

2. In addition to a reporters from the *New York Times* and the *Sporting News*, the game was observed and written about by Frank Graham of the *New York Sun*, Don Skene of the *Herald Tribune*, Clifford Bloodgood of *Baseball Magazine*, and Ford Frick of *The Evening Journal*.

3. "Huggins Prepares to Renovate Yanks," *Sporting News*, September 12, 1929.

4. It is worth noting, however, in Gehrig's defense, that he did bat .300 during 1929, hit 35 home runs, and collect 125 runs batted in. Those numbers were a drop off from his production in previous years, but they were hardly the statistics of a marginal player.

5. Creamer, *Babe*, 346–47.

6. In 1953 Ethel and Julius Rosenberg, who were accused and convicted of giving atomic secrets to the Russians, were put to death in the Sing Sing electric chair. They went to their deaths proclaiming their innocence. Pleas to spare their lives came from around the world. The Rosenberg case has also been fictionalized: in E. L. Doctorow's *The Book of Daniel* and in Robert Coover's *The Public Burning*.

7. James Cain based two novels on the crime—*Double Indemnity* and *The Postman Always Rings Twice*—both of which have been made into films. The case was also the basis for Ron Hansen's novel *A Wild Surge of Guilty Passion*.

8. "Ruth Hits Three Homers in Sing Sing Game," *New York Times*, September 6, 1929.

9. Ruth also pitched in this game.

10. Willie Morris, *North Toward Home*, 107–8.

11. Ireland, "Conversation between Warden Thalacker and Charles Ireland." Unpublished.

21. JUDGE LANDIS INTERVENES

1. The Pirate infielders were especially shaky in the field. First baseman Gus Suhr, shortstop Arky Vaughn, and third baseman Pie Traylor all led the league in errors at their positions.

2. Ehrgott, *Mr. Wrigley's Ball Club*, 312–32. In chapters fifteen and sixteen of *Mr. Wrigley's Ball Club*, Ehrgott details the Landis investigation and the reactions of Grimm, Hornsby, and the Cubs players.

3. Ehrgott, *Mr. Wrigley's Ball Club*, 313.

4. Handbooks are off-site betting establishments: illegal, but highly popular at that time in Chicago. The one referenced in the *Chicago Daily News* article was located at Broadway and Belmont.

5. Veeck's rant sounds a little like a line of dialogue from a movie that was still ten years in future. In *Casablanca*, Captain Renault famously says to Rick Blaine, the casino owner, "I'm shocked, shocked to discover gambling is going on in here."

6. Montville, *The Big Bam*, 143.

7. Pietrusza, *Judge and Jury*, 102–6. Landis presided over the trial of a bookie named Mont Tennes, a pre-Capone crime lord in Chicago; Tennes was represented in court by Clarence Darrow. Pietrusza suggests that the Tennes case, in which Darrow advised his client to plead the fifth to all questions, resulted in Darrow getting many more cases from Chicago crime and underworld figures—a boon to his law practice and reputation in Chicago. See also Allan May, "The History of the Race Wire Service" at https://www.allenmay.com/Race_Wire_Service.html.

8. Hornsby, *My War with Baseball*, 24–25. See also, Grimm, *Grimm's Baseball Tales*, 84–86, and Pietrusza, *Judge and Jury*, 316–19.
9. Leslie O'Connor was a Chicago lawyer who had been Landis's assistant ever since Landis was appointed commissioner. See also Pietrusza, *Judge and Jury*, 176.
10. Ehrgott, *Mr. Wrigley's Ball Club*, 323.
11. Ehrgott, *Mr. Wrigley's Ball Club*, 324.

22. STRETCH RUN

1. Ehrgott, *Mr. Wrigley's Ball Club*, 337–38.
2. "Notes of the Cubs," *Chicago Tribune*, August 17, 1932; Ehrgott, *Mr. Wrigley's Ball Club*, 338.
3. Edward Burns, "Four Runs in Ninth!" *Chicago Tribune*, August 17, 1932,
4. Koenig and Jurges were both in the lineup because Woody English was out of action for a week with a bruised hand. When English returned, Jurges went to the bench.
5. Barnett later claimed that some of the letters were from Cuyler to Popovich. If true, that would explain why Cuyler's wife was somehow involved in Barnett's blackmail scheme.
6. "Police Hold Chief of Jurges Blackmail Plot," *Chicago Tribune*, August 14, 1932. Ehrgott, *Mr. Wrigley's Ball Club*, 334–37.
7. "Girl Regains Jurges Notes; Continue Case," *Chicago Tribune*, August 19, 1932.
8. "Girl Regains Jurges Notes."
9. Veeck, *Veeck as in Wreck*, 28. The younger Bill Veeck tells the story of how he and a friend, Marsh Samuel, climbed out of a window at school and raced to the ballpark in time to see the game. While Veeck doesn't accurately recall the details of the game, he does describe the delirium of the fans when the Cubs won in extra innings. Years later, the younger Veeck would proclaim that this was the best baseball game—of the thousands that he saw in person—that he had ever seen. See also, Ehrgott, *Mr. Wrigley's Ball Club*, 356.
10. Zach Taylor was in the game due to several lineup changes Grimm made in the late innings. For the season, Taylor collected just 6 base hits.
11. Veeck, *Veeck as in Wreck*, 28.
12. In Cubs lore, the Cuyler game would rank with the Merkle Game, the Homer in the Gloaming Game, the Sandberg Game, the Bartman Game—all arguably the most significant or memorable games in franchise history, at least until Game Seven of the 2016 World Series when the Cubs clinched their first championship since 1908, beating the Cleveland Indians 8–7 in 10 innings.
13. Ehrgott, *Mr. Wrigley's Ball Club*, 363.

14. Charlie Grimm, as manager, did not participate, and neither did the three ballplayers who had joined the team during the season: the pitcher Leroy Herrmann, the outfielder Frank Demaree, and the newest Cub, Mark Koenig.

15. Ehrgott, *Mr. Wrigley's Ball Club*, 363.

16. Paul Mickelson, "Chicago is Agog," *Washington Post*, September 22, 1932.

17. "Ticket Sales Boom as Cubs Clinch Crown," *Chicago Tribune*, September 21, 1932.

18. "Champion Cubs Go On Parade as 100,000 Cheer," *Chicago Tribune*, September 23, 1932.

23. YANKEES COAST

1. "Ruth Assures Cubs He Will Be in World Series," *Chicago Daily Tribune*, September 21, 1932.

2. Crosetti hit .241 for the season; Lary hit .232. Their combined home run total was 8.

3. Westbrook Pegler, "Crosetti's Just One of Yankees' Shortstop Crew," *Chicago Daily Tribune*, September 22, 1932.

4. Byrd achieved most of his success during the war years. A complete list of wins on the PGA tour: victories in the Greater Greensboro Open (1942), the Chicago Victory National Open (1943), the New Orleans Open (1944), the Philadelphia Inquirer Open Invitational (1944), the Texas Open (1945), and the Azalea Open (1945). He also won several Open and PGA state-wide tournaments in Pennsylvania and Michigan between 1939 and 1945. In addition to his two top-four finishes at the Masters, he also finished second in the U.S. Open, losing in match play to Byron Nelson.

5. The Yankees played 3 consecutive doubleheaders in Detroit: Friday, Saturday, and Sunday. The Yankees won 3 times, lost twice, and played to a 7–7 tie, in a game that was stopped after 7 innings. Edward King was the Yankees' team doctor.

6. Creamer, *Babe*, 358.

7. Creamer, *Babe*, 358.

8. Pennsylvania did not allow professional baseball games to be played on Sunday, which explains the scheduling quirk that required the Sunday game of the Senators/A's series to be played at Griffith Stadium in Washington.

9. Average time to play a Major League baseball game in 2018: https://www.baseball-reference.com/leagues/MLB/misc.shtml.

10. "39 Shares Named by Yanks in Series," *New York Times*, September 24, 1932.

11. Gomez and Goldstone, *Lefty*, 153–54.

12. "39 Shares Named By Yanks in Series," *New York Times*, September 24, 1932. MacFayden and Moore were both acquired from the Red Sox: MacFayden on June 5; Moore on August 1.

13. "39 Shares Named by Yanks in Series," *New York Times*, September 24, 1932.

24. THE WORLD SERIES BEGINS

1. See Haskins and Mitgang, *Mr. Bojangles*, 166–67, 234–35. See also, Ray Robinson, "When Bojangles Came to the Yankees' Defense," *New York Times*, August 23, 2009.

2. Robinson had appeared as a dancer in two early movies: *Hello Bill* (1929) and *Dixiana* (1930). His most well-known roles were opposite Shirley Temple, most notably in *The Little Colonel* (1934) and *Rebecca of Sunnybrook Farm* (1937). Robinson and Temple were the first interracial dance couple to appear in Hollywood films. Several of their scenes together were deleted for audiences in the South.

3. Bill Robinson's time at the Los Angeles Olympic trials—the 100 yard dash, run backward—was 14.2 seconds.

4. Notably, Bill Robinson was fifty-three years old when he set the record, well past his prime. His *Guinness Book of World Records* time for the 100 yards was 13.5 seconds.

5. "Richer by $12,000," *Chicago Defender*, October 8, 1932.

6. "Shower Disperses Fans," *New York Times*, September 28, 1932.

7. William E. Brandt, "Yankees Hold Drill at Series Scene," *New York Times*, September 27, 1932.

8. "McCarthy Banks on Ruth to Lead to Victory; Grimm Confident, but Sees Hard Fight Ahead," *New York Times*, September 28, 1932.

9. "McCarthy's Mother Certain Yanks Will Win," *New York Times*, September 27, 1932.

10. John Drebinger, "M'Carthy's Shrewd Experience Gives Yanks Managerial Edge Over Cubs," *New York Times*, September 27, 1932.

11. "Cubs Speeding East for Opening Clash," *New York Times*, September 27, 1932.

12. "Cubs Speeding East for Opening Clash," *New York Times*, September 27, 1932.

13. William Brandt, "Rival Clubs Relax on Eve of Battle," *New York Times*, September, 28, 1932.

14. John Drebinger, "Yankees Rout Cubs by 12 to 6 as 42,000 See Series Opener," *New York Times*, September 29, 1932.

15. John Drebinger, "Yankees Rout Cubs by 12 to 6 as 42,000 See Series Opener," *New York Times*, September 29, 1932. McKee had become acting mayor just four weeks earlier when the elected mayor, James Walker, had resigned in the midst of a scandal and fled to Europe.

16. Gregory H. Wolf, "Guy Bush," SABR BioProject, accessed August 24, 2019, https://sabr.org/bioproj/person/9c9bf76f.

17. Wayne Corbett, "Red Ruffing," SABR BioProject, accessed August 19, 2019, https://sabr.org/bioproj/person/7111866b. See also Appel, *Pinstripe Empire*, 170–71.

18. Ruffing's record with the Red Sox: 39-96. During those five seasons, the Red Sox finished last every year. With the Yankees, he won 234 games and lost 129.

19. Among pitchers (and not counting Babe Ruth) Ruffing is fourth all-time in home runs, behind Wes Farrell, Bob Lemon, and Warren Spahn. Ruffing also is credited with 2 pinch-hit home runs.

20. Ruffing homered once every 50 at bats, thus with greater frequency than Crosetti, Sewell, Chapman, and Combs. Of course, with Ruth, Gehrig, Lazzeri, and Dickey in the lineup, the Yankees didn't need more home run hitters.

21. John Drebinger, "Yankees Rout Cubs by 12–6 as 42,000 See Series Opener," *New York Times*, September 29, 1932.

22. "Yanks Exuberant Over Easy Victory," *New York Times*, September 29, 1932.

23. William Brandt, "Pitching of Gomez Impresses Grimm," *New York Times*, September 30, 1932.

24. William Brandt, "Pitching of Gomez Impresses Grimm, *New York Times*, September 30, 1932.

25. William Brandt, "McCarthy Advises Yanks to be Calm," *New York Times*, October 1, 1932.

26. John Drebinger, "Yankees and Cubs Ready for 3rd Game," *New York Times*, October 1, 1932.

27. William Brandt, "McCarthy Advises Yanks to be Calm," *New York Times*, October 1, 1932.

28. The party was at the home of Kitty McHie, whose husband was a newspaper editor. At the party, Gehrig met his future wife, Eleanor Twitchell. She was not the kind of woman one might have expected Gehrig to be attracted to. She had been a bit of a party girl who smoked and drank and played poker regularly with girlfriends. One of those girlfriends was Anna Torrio, the wife of Johnny Torrio, a powerful gangster. As Eleanor said, "I was well-known in speakeasy society." See Eig, *Luckiest Man*, 161–69. See also Eleanor Gehrig's memoir *My Luke and I*.

25. THE CROWD GATHERS

1. The bombing suspect was a man who felt he had been mistreated in court by the judge.

2. Story of Koepper's injuries in "All Chicago Stirred By a Bomb Outrage," *New York Times*, September 21; "Ruth Visits Youth Injured in Bombing: Presents

Autographed Baseball to 16-year-old Victim in Chicago Hospital," *New York Times*, October 2, 1932; AP story on October 1, datelined October 1. As for Ruth's promise to hit a home run that afternoon, see the Joe Sewell chapter in Donald Honig's oral history, *A Donald Honig Reader*, 525.

3. Jack Curry, "One Fan Makes His Point: Ruth Called That Shot," *New York Times*, August 30, 2008.

4. Irving "Pro" Boim, "Pro Boim Describes Babe Ruth's Called Shot," Part I, accessed August 24, 2019, https://www.youtube.com/watch?v=K9oUAvx-3bZs; and "Pro Boim Describes Babe Ruth's Called Shot, Part II, accessed August 24, 2019, Part II, https://www.youtube.com/watch?v=OfItDNUcL5A.

5. Boim, "Pro Boim Describes Babe Ruth's Called Shot." Boim says the first sighting of the players was at noon.

6. Gerald Bazer and Steven Culbertson, "When FDR Said 'Play Ball,'" accessed August 24, 2019, https://www.archives.gov/publications/prologue/2002/spring/greenlight.html. See also Collier and Horowitz, *The Roosevelts*, 105.

7. The Yankees played home games at the Polo Grounds until 1923.

26. THE CALLED SHOT

1. Inmates at Folsom Prison in California, were allowed to listen to Sunday's Game Four on loudspeakers set up in the prison yard, but they missed hearing the live call of Game Three. For many of the long-imprisoned Folsom inmates, it was the first time they had heard a radio broadcast. *Chicago American*, October 3, 1932.

2. Ruth's previous at bats in Chicago against the Cubs in the 1918 World Series had taken place at Comiskey Park.

3. Richards Vidmer, "Yankee Home Runs Crush Cubs, 7 to 5, Ruth and Gehrig Smashing Two Apiece in Third Straight World Series Victory," *New York Herald-Tribune*, October 2, 1932.

4. John Drebinger, *New York Times*, October 2, 1932.

5. At St. Mary's, Ruth was called "n–– lips." Ruth's biographers—Creamer, Montville, Leavy—have all reflected on Ruth's background, physical characteristics, and encounters with players who assumed or believed that Ruth had Negro blood. In particular, see Leavy, The Big Fella, 169–84, and Michael Wilbon, "Still Seeing Things in Black or White," *Washington Post*, May 12, 2006, www.washingtonpost.com/wp-dyn/content/article2006/05/11/AR2006051101901.html?noredirect=on.

6. Honig, *A Donald Honig Reader*, 525.

7. William Brandt, "Cub Fans Faithful in Spite of Defeat," *New York Times*, October 2, 1932

8. "Yankees Going Home Tonight, They Declare," *Chicago Tribune*, October 2, 1932.
9. "Yankees Going Home Tonight."
10. Ward and Burns, *Baseball*, 210.

27. THE WORLD SERIES ENDS

1. "Roosevelt Cheered by Fans at World Series," New York Times, October 1, 1932.
2. New York Times, October 2, 1932.
3. New York Times, October 3, 1932.
4. In 1932 the seating capacity for Wrigley Field was forty thousand, but because of the extra seating—bleachers and scaffolding—more than fifty thousand were squeezed into the park for the World Series games. See Lowry, *Green Cathedrals*, 27–32.
5. At the armory in Detroit, Roosevelt addressed a full-house crowd of six thousand supporters, while five thousand waited outside, hoping to hear him speak. The speech, called a "sermon" by one reporter, was dedicated to the notion of "social justice" and "a more equitable distribution of wealth," according to the *New York Times*.
6. Honig, *A Donald Honig* Reader, 526,
7. Honig, *A Donald Honig* Reader, 526.
8. Bill Corum, "Sports," *Chicago American*, October 3, 1932.
9. Hitting grand slam home runs was something Gehrig was known for. When he retired in 1939, Gehrig held the Major League record for most grand slams in a career—23—but that record was eclipsed by Alex Rodriquez in 2013. Gehrig had the record for seventy-five years, considerably longer than the number of years that Babe Ruth held the single-season home run record.
10. "Injuries Bring Downfall of Bush, Warneke," *Chicago Daily Tribune*, October 3, 1932.
11. "So the Yanks Took the Title and Sang a Bit," *Chicago Daily Tribune*, October 3, 1932.
12. "So the Yanks Took the Title and Sang a Bit."
13. "So the Yanks Took the Title and Sang a Bit."

28. POSTGAME

1. Walker, *Crack of the Bat*, 40.
2. "Sale of 3 Players Explained by Mack," *New York Times*, October 5, 1932.
3. "Sale of 3 Players Explained by Mack," *New York Times*, October 5, 1932.

4. Cochrane was traded for Johnny Pasek and $100,000. Grove was traded for Bob Kline, Rabbit Warstler, and $125,000.

5. In this deal, Mack also received a journeyman pitcher named Gordon Rhodes, who won 2 games for the A's in 1936, and a Minor League catcher named George Savino.

6. Mack continued to manage the team, retiring after the 1950 season at the age of eighty-seven. His teams never again challenged for a pennant. Jimmy Dykes, the third baseman from the glory years, took over as manager in 1951.

7. After being dismissed as manager of the Senators, Johnson was hired to manage the Cleveland Indians. He managed the Indians in 1933 and 1934, then was fired in midseason of 1935. A year later, on the basis of his outstanding career as a player, Johnson was inducted into the National Baseball Hall of Fame.

8. Cronin led the Senators to the World Series in 1933, losing in 5 games to the New York Giants. But the Senators slumped badly in Cronin's second year as manager, slipping to seventh place in 1934.

9. Yankee salary figures from 1932 at: https://www.baseball-reference.com/teams/NYY/1932.shtml.

10. Cub salary figures from 1930 at: https://www.baseball-reference.com/teams/CHC/1930.shtml. Hornsby was the highest paid at $40,000. Hack Wilson earned $22,500. Most of the regulars were paid between $11,000 and $18,000. Baseball-Reference only lists salaries for two Cubs for the 1932 season: Hornsby, still earning $40,000, and Mark Koenig, who was paid $6,000. A full World Series share for Koenig would have boosted his income from the Cubs by 70 percent.

11. Alexander, *Rogers Hornsby*, 180.

12. Alexander, *Rogers Hornsby*, 181.

13. Actually the fairness of Koenig's half-share had first been raised by the media shortly after the Cubs vote was made public.

14. Grimm, *Grimm's Baseball Tales*, 87–88.

15. Golenbock, *Wrigleyville*, 233.

16. Pietrusza, *Judge and Jury*, 337–38; Murdock, *Baseball Players and Their Times*, 289–92.

17. Pietrusza, *Judge and Jury*, 337–38; Murdock, *Baseball Players and Their Times*, 289–92.

29. FANS RETURN HOME

1. Schweider, *Iowa: The Middle Land*, 255–73; Schweider, *Patterns and Perspectives*, 361–77; Wall, *Iowa*, 174. The 1920s and early 1930s were devastating for

Iowa—and Midwestern farm families. Agricultural products dropped sharply in price and the value of farmland was reduced by nearly half.

2. "Herring Charges Iowa Warden Took Convicts to World Series," *Des Moines Register*, October 7, 1932.

3. "Herring Charges Iowa Warden."

4. "Warden Says His Trip With Convicts Was Humanitarian Act," *Des Moines Register*, October 7, 1932.

5. Herring's election as governor marked the beginning of a successful political career. He was reelected as governor in 1934 and elected as a senator in 1936. Herring was on the Roosevelt's short list of potential vice presidential candidates in 1940, but instead Herring's fellow Iowan, Henry Wallace, the secretary of agriculture, was chosen to run with Roosevelt.

6. Verlyn Klinkenborg, "The Conscience of Place: Highway 75, Iowa," accessed August 24, 2019, https://www.motherjones.com/politics/2001/03/conscience -place-highway-75-iowa/.

7. Rodney D Karr, "Farmer Rebels in Plymouth County, Iowa, 1932–1933," *The Annals of Iowa* 47 (1985), 637–45. Thirty-eight of the men involved in the kidnapping of Judge Bradley were eventually arrested. Although the state government accused them of being "outside agitators" and "communist sympathizers," all of the men were either farmers or farm laborers in the county.

8. Stout, *The Cubs*, 151. Herman performed adequately in 1933, batting .287 with 16 homers and 93 RBIs. Although his numbers didn't match his previous performances with Brooklyn and Cincinnati, he was a valuable addition to the club because Kiki Cuyler, age thirty-four, went down with a broken ankle and missed half the season, and Riggs Stevenson, age thirty-five, played only 70 games, due to injuries.

9. "Eternity," *Men's Reformatory Press*, July 1, 1933.

10. "'Snap' Hortman Dead," *Anamosa Journal*, August 9, 1934.

11. "'Snap' Hortman Dead"; *Cherokee Chief*, August 9, 1934.

30. RUTH'S LEGACY WITH THE CUBS

1. Ruth is the model in Malamud's *The Natural* for events related to both the Whammer and Roy Hobbs. It is, perhaps, in literature where Ruth's larger-than-real-life persona resides most impressively. See also, Carino, "History and Myth," 67–77.

2. Ruth appeared in 7 games in those two World Series. He also played in 5 regular-season games against the Cubs, in 1935, when he was a member of the Boston Braves. In his 12 at bats against the Cubs in those regular-season games, he delivered only 1 hit, just weeks before he retired, a home run at Wrigley Field on May 21, 1935, number 711 in his career.

3. Montville, *The Big Bam*, 312. Montville notes several instances where Ruth predicted he'd hit a home run: when Lindbergh came to Yankee Stadium to see a game; when he told the Yankees' traveling secretary that he'd hit a home run to end a game so the team could catch a train; when he told Ford Frick's father at an exhibition game in Fort Wayne, Indiana, that he'd homer—just to name a few from Montville's book. Not to mention Richards Vidmer's story in the *New York Times* that Ruth had predicted his first inning home run against the Cubs in the same game where he'd hit the called shot. Richards Vidmer, "Yankee Home Runs Crush Cubs."

4. Montville, *The Big Bam*, 312.

5. Creamer, *Babe*, 363.

6. Most observers credit Ruth with the longest home run hit at Wrigley Field, a distinction Ruth holds for many other ballparks as well.

7. Ward and Burns, *Baseball*, 231.

8. Sherman, *Babe Ruth's Called Shot*, 115.

9. Sherman, *Babe Ruth's Called Shot*, 116.

10. Sherman, *Babe Ruth's Called Shot*, 121.

11. Sherman, *Babe Ruth's Called Shot*, 84.

12. Sherman, *Babe Ruth's Called Shot*, 120.

13. Walsh, "Babe Ruth," 242–63.

14. All direct quotes in this paragraph from Walsh, "Babe Ruth," 242–63.

15. Patterson, *The Golden Voices of Radio*, Disc 1, Track 13. Garner, *And the Crowd Goes Wild*, Disc 1, Track 2.

16. Patterson, *The Golden Years of Radio*, Disc 1, Track 13.

17. Smith, *Voices of the Game*, 41–42. Curt Smith is the author of multiple books on baseball announcers and the history of broadcasters. In an email exchange with Mr. Smith, I asked about the authenticity of the Manning call as it was printed in Smith's book. On April 2, 2017, Mr. Smith responded "It has been a long time since I wrote *Voices of the Game*. . . . However, I am virtually certain that the Manning call is the real McCoy. . . . Bob Costas and I agree that the voice is Manning's." I made an effort to reach Mr. Costas to confirm his judgement, but he did not respond to my requests. Manning died in 1969. If he had recreated the broadcast, it would have been before that date, but no record that I can find suggests that the recording is not authentic. On the other hand, unless the original tape of the broadcast appears, it is impossible to say with certainty whether or not the Manning, or the Ryan, calls were recorded contemporaneously with the event. If those are the actual calls, the preponderance of this eyewitness evidence suggests that Ruth did, indeed, call his shot.

18. Handwritten note from Guy Bush, dated August 8, 1964. From Cooperstown Expert website, accessed May 5, 2019, https://www.cooperstownexpert.com

/player/guy-bush/ . Bush is also quoted in Sherman, *Babe Ruth's Called Shot*, 108: "I believe Ruth meant to call the home run."

19. Jack Curry, "One Fan Makes His Point: Ruth Called That Shot," *New York Times*, August 30, 2008.

20. Sherman, *Babe Ruth's Called Shot*, xxv–xxvi.

21. "Out of a Job," *Chicago Daily Tribune*, June 3, 1935.

EPILOGUE: THE BABE CALLS HIS LAST SHOT

1. Ruth did have one memorable moment in the 1933 season: playing and starring in the first All-Star Game. He hit the first home run in All-Star game history and even made a fine running catch in the outfield.

2. Ruth's daughter, Julia Stevens, commented on what a good manager Ruth might have been, but felt that one reason her father was shunned and not offered a Major League managerial job was because it would have been his desire to have African Americans on the team. Ruth, Stevens believed, would have demanded integration. After years of barnstorming with the greatest players of the Negro Leagues, Ruth harbored no prejudice against African Americans and would have welcomed them into the white Major Leagues. This is, perhaps, to put it generously, unrealistic, considering that in the years prior to World War II, Judge Landis and Major League owners strongly opposed integration. See Peter Kerasotis, "Home, at the Other House that Ruth Built," *New York Times*, March 10, 2014.

3. The contract also made Ruth an executive vice president of the team, a position with no real power, and permitted Ruth the option of buying shares of the franchise. This was also worth little since the franchise was in terrible shape financially.

4. For the 1935 season, Whitney would hit a respectable .273. Betts compiled a record of 2-9. Cantwell won 4 games and lost 25.

5. Creamer, *Babe*, 392. Creamer asserts this was the largest crowd ever to witness an exhibition game in Florida.

6. "Swift of Pirates Downs Braves, 7–1," *New York Times*, May 24, 1932.

7. Maranville played the 1921 through 1924 seasons with the Pirates, during the years that Ruth was establishing himself in New York as the biggest star in baseball.

8. Rick Shrum, "Parting Shots," *Pittsburg Post-Gazette*, May 10, 2006.

9. Andy (born Andrew) Warhola dropped the final "a" in his name in 1949 when he was beginning his career in the arts.

10. This ball is often on display at the National Baseball Hall of Fame.

11. Creamer, *Babe*, 397. Bush would surrender 152 home runs in his career, including the 2 that Ruth hit in Pittsburgh on May 25, 1932.

12. Creamer, *Babe*, 397.
13. Rick Shrum, "Parting Shots," *Pittsburgh Post-Gazette*, May 10, 2006.
14. Rick Shrum, "Parting Shots."
15. Cantwell's single-season record is arguably the worst win-loss performance in baseball history, though some Hall of Fame pitchers—Walter Johnson and Cy Young, to name two—had twenty-loss seasons. Some of the other worst-ever single-season records since 1903: Happy Townsend who went 5-26 with the 1904 Boston Braves; Kaiser Wilhelm who posted a 3-23 record with the 1905 Boston Braves; Jack Nabors whose 1916 record with the Philadelphia Athletics was a dismal 1-20; Don Larsen who compiled a 3-21 record with the 1954 Baltimore Orioles; Rodger Craig who went 5-22 with the 1962 New York Mets.
16. Paul Adomites and Saul Wisnia, "Babe Ruth," accessed August 24, 2019, https://entertainment.howstuffworks.com/babe-ruth41.htm.
17. Gehrig died twenty-three months later, on June 2, 1941.
18. Ruth's biographers have explored and theorized about the root causes of the estrangement between Gehrig and Ruth. One theory holds that Ruth's then-wife, Claire, was annoyed by comments made by Gehrig's mother about how Ruth's daughter Dorothy was dressed. Another theory holds that Gehrig thought his wife, Eleanor, had been too friendly with Ruth in his room during a cruise the couples took together. See Montville, *The Big Bam*, 331–32. See Creamer, *Babe*, 379–80.
19. Gary Cooper played Gehrig. In addition to Ruth playing himself, the film also cast Mark Koenig and Bill Dickey as themselves. See "Losing 47 pounds," in Montville, *The Big Bam*, 355.
20. The golf events were organized by Fred Corcoran. The book *Ty and the Babe* by Tom Stanton recounts the story of the matches. Cobb won 2 out of the 3 matches; delighting the competitive Cobb who felt his own stardom in the game had been surpassed by Ruth.
21. Elias, *The Empire Strikes Out*, 137.
22. Shirley Povich, "Sailors Beat Nats, 4–3," *Washington Post*, May 25, 1943.
23. Keene, *The Cloudbuster Nine*, 195–203. Keene's book tells the story of the navy training school at the University of North Carolina in Chapel Hill, where Williams, Johnny Pesky, Johnny Sain, and others—Gerald Ford, George H. W. Bush, John Glenn—received instruction as navy fighter pilots. Williams, Pesky, and Sain played on the Cloudbusters, the camp's baseball team.
24. Montville, *The Big Bam*, 357–59. Ruth had cancer, an inoperable tumor in the air passages behind his nose.
25. Max Kase, founder and organizer of the Hearst Sandlot game, was a newspaper reporter and editor for the *New York Journal-American*, one of the Hearst

papers. See also, Alan Cohen, "The Hearst Sandlot Classic: More than a Doorway to the Big Leagues," accessed August 24, 2019, https://sabr.org/research/hearst-sandlot-classic-more-doorway-big-leagues.

26. Alan Cohen, "The Hearst Sandlot Classic," accessed August 24, 2019, https://sabr.org/research/hearst-sandlot-classic-more-doorway-big-leagues.

EXTRA INNINGS

1. Twelve players in the 1928 series between the Yankees and Cardinals were eventually honored with Hall of Fame plaques. This series had the second most future Hall of Famers.

2. The other notable stars during the 1936–1939 run by the Yankees were Bill Dickey, Red Ruffing, and Lefty Gomez, all still in the prime years of their careers. Lou Gehrig was a productive member of the 1936, 1937, and 1938 teams, but then he was stricken, suddenly and eventually fatally, by ALS. In 1939 though Gehrig was just thirty-five, he was forced out of the game due to his illness. By that time, it was clear that the Ruth/Gehrig era had passed, and the new Yankee era was to be led by DiMaggio.

3. Fields, "Woody English," SABR BioProject, accessed August 19, 2019, https://sabr.org/bioproj/person/5b780054. For more about women in baseball and the All-American Girls League, see Jean Hastings Ardell, *Breaking Into Baseball*.

4. Dickson, *Bill Veeck*, 331.

5. O'Doul had a lifetime average of .349, but played in only 970 Major League games, so his career has been considered too short to merit serious consideration for Hall of Fame inclusion. Shoeless Joe Jackson, with a lifetime average of .356, is now ineligible for the Hall of Fame due to his alleged participation in the Black Sox scandal. All other modern era players with a higher lifetime batting average than Riggs Stevenson have been elected to the Hall.

6. Geisler, "Billy Jurges," SABR BioProject, accessed August 24, 2019, https://sabr.org/bioproj/person/aada6293.

7. Members of the Baseball Writers Association of America (BBWAA) did the voting. Ruth was named on 215 out of 226 ballots, but he was not the top vote getter. Ty Cobb was named on 98.2 percent of the ballots, being selected by 222 voters. At the time, both active and retired players, as well as players banned from baseball, such as Shoeless Joe Jackson, were considered eligible for selection.

8. The original painting is part of the Hall of Fame collection of artwork and is on display at the museum. Notably, the painting has one significant historical inaccuracy: the painting shows the right-field wall at Wrigley covered in ivy. The ivy was not introduced to the ballpark until 1937.

9. Ireland, "Conversation between Warden Thalacker and Charles Ireland." Unpublished.

10. Much literary criticism has been written about Malamud's classic work of fiction with reference to the historical incidents that inspired or played a role in Malamud's creation. See Carino, "History and Myth," 67–77; and DeMotte, "Baseball Heroes and Femme Fatales," 315–18.

11. Barnhart and Schlickman, *John Paul Stevens*, 88–98. Due to Stevens's understanding of baseball, he was chosen to interrogate Ty Cobb, who was called before Cellar's committee as its first witness. Stevens also conducted the questioning of Cubs owner Philip K. Wrigley. Years later, Stevens served as an informal advisor to Charles O. Finley, when the cantankerous and idiosyncratic owner wanted to move his team from Kansas City to Oakland. Although Stevens's area of legal expertise was antitrust, he put his substantial knowledge of baseball to good use in his legal practice.

12. Barnhart and Schlickman, *John Paul Stevens*, 128 (photo).

13. Judge Sbarbaro's involvement in the Leopold and Loeb case quietly continued for several decades. Richard Loeb was murdered in prison, in January of 1936. Nathan Leopold became a model prisoner, doing volunteer work in the prison, teaching and participating in medical studies. In 1954 Leopold wrote directly to John Sbarbaro, asking for his help in gaining a parole. Sbarbaro's public support of Leopold's freedom was instrumental in Leopold's eventual release, and Sbarbaro remained in contact with the parolee after Leopold settled in Puerto Rico and married. In a letter dated March 31, 1958, Leopold thanked Sbarbaro for sending him a transistor radio, and writes "Thank you again, Judge Sbarbaro, for all your kindness. I will never forget you or cease to be grateful."

14. Veeck, *Veeck as in Wreck*, 35–36. William Veeck's son, Bill, relates how he approached Ralph Capone—Al was in prison at the time—and requested the favor. Ralph Capone's boys delivered cases of expensive bootleg champagne to the William Veeck residence during Veeck's last days. Bill Veeck wrote: "The last nourishment that passed between my daddy's lips on this earth was Al Capone's champagne." The story also appears in Golenbock, *Wrigleyville*, 242–43.

15. Sherman, *Babe Ruth's Called Shot*, 168–85.

16. Sherman, *Babe Ruth's Called Shot*, 186–88.

17. Girardin and Helmer, *Dillinger*, 165.

18. Drivel by Davenport, "Charley Ireland, Man of Many Talents," *Anamosa Eureka*.

19. Hoover's record was eclipsed by Jimmy Carter.

20. Ward and Burns, *Baseball*, 276.

BIBLIOGRAPHY

ARCHIVES AND UNPUBLISHED

Ireland, Charles Arthur. "An Account of the Term of C. H. Ireland as Warden of the Iowa State Men's Reformatory." Unpublished memoir.

———. "Conversation between Warden Thalacker and Charles Ireland of Santa Barbara CA (son of Warden Ireland), October 3, 1989." Unpublished manuscript.

Letters of Charles H. Ireland. Private collection.

Sydnor, Charles. "Monte Morton Weaver." Unpublished tribute. Archives of the Emory and Henry College Library, Emory VA.

Vranicar, Greg. "The Bonus March: An Examination of the Rationale for the Use of Federal Power in Response to Protest." Senior history project. Grinnell College, Grinnell IA, January 1972.

PUBLISHED WORKS

Abbott, Karen. *Sin in the Second City: Madams, Ministers, Playboys, and the Battle for America's Soul*. New York: Random House, 2007.

Adler, Jeffrey. First in Violence, Deepest in Dirt: Homicide in Chicago, 1875–1920. Cambridge MA: Harvard University Press, 2006.

Adminneje. "Babe Ruth's Longest Home Run." Northeast Journal. August 24, 2019. http://northeastjournal.org/babe-ruths-longest-home-run/.

Adomites, Paul, and Saul Wisnia. "Babe Ruth Retires." HowStuffWorks. August 24, 2019. https://entertainment.howstuffworks.com/babe-ruth41.htm.

Alexander, Charles C. *Breaking the Slump: Baseball in the Depression Era*. New York: Columbia University Press, 2002.

———. *John McGraw*. New York: Viking, 1998.

———. *Rogers Hornsby*. New York: Henry Holt, 1995.

Allen, Frederick Lewis. *Only Yesterday: An Informal History of the 1920s*. New York: Harper & Row, 1931.

Anderson, David W. "Bill Klem." SABR BioProject. August 19, 2019. https://sabr.org/bioproj/person/31461b94.

Appel, Marty. *Pinstripe Empire: The New York Yankees from Before the Babe to After the Boss*. New York: Bloomsbury Publishing, 2012.

Ardell, Jean Hastings. *Breaking Into Baseball: Women and the National Pastime*. Carbondale: Southern Illinois University Press, 2005.

Asinof, Eliot. *Eight Men Out: The Black Sox and the 1919 World Series*. New York: Owl Books, 1987.

Auker, Elden, and Tom Keegan. *Sleeper Cars and Flannel Uniforms: A Lifetime of Memories from Striking Out the Babe to Teeing it Up with the President*. Chicago: Triumph, 2001.

AZ Quotes. "Anton Cermak Quotes." August 24, 2019. https://www.azquotes.com/author/23798-Anton_Cermak.

Baatz, Simon. *For the Thrill of It: Leopold, Loeb, and the Murder That Shocked Chicago*. New York: HarperCollins, 2008.

Bales, Jack. "Baseball's First Bill Veeck." *Baseball Research Journal*, (Fall 2013): 7–17.

Bales, Jack. *Before They Were Cubs: The Early Years of Chicago's First Professional Baseball Team*. Jefferson NC: McFarland, 2019.

——— . "The Shootings of Billy Jurges and Eddie Waitkus," WrigleyIvy. August 24, 2019. http://wrigleyivy.com/the-shootings-of-billy-jurges-and-eddie-waitkus/.

——— . "The Showgirl and the Shortstop: The Strange Saga of Violet Popovich and Billy Jurges." *Baseball Research Journal* (Fall 2016). https://sabr.org/research/show-girl-and-shortstop-strange-saga-violet-popovich-and-her-shooting-cub-billy-jurges.

Barnhart, Bill, and Gene Schlickman. *John Paul Stevens: An Independent Life*. DeKalb: Northern Illinois University Press, 2010.

Barthel, Thomas. *Babe Ruth Is Coming to Your Town*. Self-published, 2018.

Baseball Almanac. "Stealing Home Base Records." August 24, 2019. https://www.baseball-almanac.com/recbooks/rb_stbah.shtml.

Baseball Reference. "1932 New York Yankee Statistics." August 24, 2019. https://www.baseball-reference.com/teams/NYY/1932.shtml.

Baseball Reference. "1932 Chicago Cubs Statistics." August 24, 2019. https://www.baseball-reference.com/teams/CHC/1932.shtml.

Baseball Reference. "1930 Chicago Cubs Statistics." August 24, 2019. https://www.baseball-reference.com/teams/CHC/1930.shtml.

Baseball Reference. "Major League Baseball Miscellaneous Year-by-Year Averages and Totals." August 24, 2019. https://www.baseball-reference.com/leagues/MLB/misc.shtml.

Bazer, Gerald, and Steven Culbertson. "When FDR Said 'Play Ball.'" *Prologue Magazine* 34, no. 1 (Spring 2002). https://www.archives.gov/publications/prologue/2002/spring/greenlight.html.

Bennett, John. "Jimmie Foxx," SABR BioProject. August 24, 2019. https://sabr.org/bioproj/person/e34a045d.

Berger, Ralph. "Al Schacht," SABR BioProject. August 24, 2019. https://sabr.org/bioproj/person/04d01542.

———. "Moe Berg," SABR BioProject. August 24, 2019. https://sabr.org/bioproj/person/e1e65b3b.

Bergreen, Lawrence. *Capone: The Man and the Era*. New York: Simon & Schuster, 1996.

Blaisdell, Lowell. "Remembering the Babe: October 1, 1932." *Nine* 12, no. 1 (Fall 2003).

Big Six Sports. "Guy Bush." August 24, 2019. https://www.cooperstownexpert.com/player/guy-bush/.

Boim, Irving "Pro." "Pro Boim Describes Babe Ruth's Called Shot, Part 1." August 24, 2019. https://www.youtube.com/watch?v=K9oUAvx3bZs.

———. "Pro Boim Describes Babe Ruth's Called Shot, Part 2." August 24, 2019. https://www.youtube.com/watch?v=OfItDNUcL5A.

———. "Pro Boim on Babe Ruth's Called Shot, Striking Out Ted Williams, Playing in the Minors." August 24, 2019. https://www.youtube.com/watch?v=3KCyo_dWFp0

Boyle, Robert. "Fight On, Old Sing Sing U." *Sports Illustrated*. January 23, 1967. https://www.si.com/vault/1967/01/23/543318/fight-on-old-sing-sing-u.

Bradshaw, Jon. *Dreams That Money Can Buy: The Tragic Life of Libby Holman*. New York: William Morrow, 1985.

Brown, Warren. *The Chicago Cubs*. New York: G. P. Putnam's Sons, 1946.

Bryan, Patricia L., and Thomas Wolf. "On the Brink: Babe Ruth in Dennis Lehane's *The Given Day*." In *The Cooperstown Symposium on Baseball and American Culture, 2009–2010*, edited by William M. Simon, 42–57. Jefferson NC: McFarland, 2011.

Bryson, Bill. *One Summer: America, 1927*. New York: Doubleday, 2013.

Burner, David. *Herbert Hoover: A Public Life*. New York: Knopf, 1979.

Cain, James. *Double Indemnity*. New York: Vintage, 1989 (reprint edition).

———. *The Postman Always Rings Twice*. New York: Vintage, 1989 (reprint edition).

Carino, Peter. "History and Myth in Bernard Malamud's *The Natural*." *Nine: A Journal of Baseball History and Culture* 14, no. 1 (Fall 2005): 67–77.

Cieradkowski, Gary. With illustrations by the author. *The League of Outsider Baseball: An Illustrated History of Baseball's Forgotten Heroes*. New York: Touchstone, 2015.

Cohen, Alan. "The Hearst Sandlot Classic: More Than a Doorway to the Big Leagues." August 24, 2019. https://sabr.org/research/hearst-sandlot-classic-more-doorway-big-leagues.

———. "Van Lingle Mungo," SABR BioProject. August 24, 2019. https://sabr.org/bioproj/person/e4f05449.

Cohen, Rich. *The Chicago Cubs: Story of a Curse*. New York: Farrar, Straus and Giroux, 2017.

Collier, Peter, and David Horowitz. *The Roosevelts: An American Saga*. New York: Simon & Schuster, 1994.

Cook, William A. *Waite Hoyt: A Biography of the Yankees' Schoolboy Wonder*. Jefferson NC: McFarland, 2004.

Coover, Robert. *The Public Burning*. New York: Viking Press, 1977.

Corbett, Warren. "Monte Weaver," SABR BioProject. August 24, 2019, https://sabr.org/bioproj/person/537bd12a.

———. "Red Ruffing," SABR BioProject. August 19, 2019. https://sabr.org/bioproj/person/7111866b

Corcoran, Cliff. "99 Cool Facts about Babe Ruth," *Sports Illustrated*. July 11, 2013. https://www.si.com/mlb/strike-zone/2013/07/12/99-cool-facts-about-babe-ruth.

Cramer, Richard Ben. *Joe DiMaggio: The Hero's Life*. New York: Simon and Schuster, 2000.

Creamer, Robert W. *Babe: The Legend Comes to Life*. New York: Simon and Schuster, 1974.

———. *Baseball in '41*. New York: Viking Penguin, 1991.

D'Amore, Jonathan. *Rogers Hornsby: A Biography*. Westport CT: Greenwood Press, 2004.

Daniel, Harrison W. *Jimmie Foxx: The Life and Times of a Baseball Hall of Famer, 1907–1967*. Jefferson NC: McFarland, 1996.

D'Antonio, Michael. *Forever Blue: The True Story of Walter O'Malley, Baseball's Most Controversial Owner, and the Dodgers of Brooklyn and Los Angeles*. New York: Riverhead, 2009.

Davis, Philip. *Bernard Malamud: A Writer's Life*. New York: Oxford University Press, 2007.

DeMotte, Charles. "Baseball Heroes and Femmes Fatale." In *The Cooperstown Symposium on Baseball and American Culture*, edited by William M. Simons, 315–18. Jefferson, NC: McFarland, 2003.

———. *James T. Farrell and Baseball: Dreams and Realism on Chicago's South Side*. Lincoln: University of Nebraska Press, 2019.

Dickson, Paul. *Bill Veeck: Baseball's Greatest Maverick*. New York: Walker Publishing Company, 2012.

———. *Leo Durocher: Baseball's Prodigal Son*. New York: Bloomsbury Publishing, 2017.

Dickson, Paul, and Thomas B. Allen. *The Bonus Army: An American Epic*. New York: Walker, 2004.

"Diehard Cubs Fan." *Northwestern Magazine* (Spring 2009). https://www.northwestern.edu/magazine/spring2009/cover/stevens.html.

D'O'brian, Joseph. "The Business of Boxing." *American Heritage*, (October 1991): 69–81.

Doctorow, E. L. *The Book of Daniel*. New York: Random House, 1971.

Doutrich, Paul E. *The Cardinals and the Yankees, 1926*. Jefferson NC: McFarland, 2011.

Drivel by Davenport. "Charley Ireland, Man of Many Talents." *Anamosa Eureka*.

Duren, Don. "Lon Warneke," SABR BioProject. August 19, 2019. https://sabr.org /bioproj/person/5a2fe3c9.

Durocher, Leo. *Nice Guys Finish Last*. New York: Simon and Schuster, 1975.

Ehrgott, Roberts. *Mr. Wrigley's Ball Club: Chicago and the Cubs During the Jazz Age*. Lincoln: University of Nebraska Press, 2013.

Eig, Jonathan. *Get Capone: The Secret Plot That Captured America's Most Wanted Gangster*. New York: Simon and Schuster, 2010.

——— . *Luckiest Man: The Life and Death of Lou Gehrig*. New York: Simon and Schuster, 2005.

Elias, Robert. *The Empire Strikes Out: How Baseball Sold U.S. Foreign Policy and Promoted the American Way Abroad*. New York: New Press, 2010.

Enders, Eric. "George Moriarty." SABR BioProject. August 24, 2019. https://sabr .org/bioproj/person/44c82f26.

Enss, Chris. *Playing for Time: The Death Row All Stars*. Charlestown SC: Arcadia, 2004.

Eskenazi, David, and Steve Rudman. "Wayback Machine: A Fire that Changed our Sports." SportsPressNW. August 24, 2019. http://sportspressnw.com/2124688 /2011/wayback-machine-a-fire-that-changed-our-sports.

Fak, Michael. *Portions of a Life: Recollections and Reflections*. Booklocker.com, 2005.

Feldman, Doug. *Dizzy and the Gashouse Gang*. Jefferson NC: McFarland, 2000.

Fields, Dan. "Charlie Grimm." SABR BioProject. August 23, 2019. https://sabr.org /bioproj/person/c008379d.

——— . "Woody English," SABR BioProject. August 19, 2019. https://sabr.org/bio-proj/person/5b780054.

Fimrite, Ron. "The Raging Rajah Rogers Hornsby, One of this Century's Best Ballplayers, was Also One of its Biggest Boors." *Sports Illustrated*, October 1995.

Fowler, Gene. *Skyline: A Reporter's Reminiscence of the 1920s*. New York: Viking, 1961.

Freidel, Frank. *Franklin D. Roosevelt: A Rendezvous with Destiny*. New York: Little Brown, 1990.

Fuhr, Ernie. "Hal Carlson," SABR BioProject. August 24, 2019. https://sabr.org/bio-proj/person/b9c3739f.

Fullerton, Hugh. "Why Babe Ruth is the Greatest Home-Run Hitter." Popular Science Monthly, October 1921.

Gabler, Neal. *Walt Disney: The Triumph of the American Imagination*. New York: Vintage, 2007.

Garner, Joe. *And the Crowd Goes Wild: Relive the Most Celebrated Sporting Events Ever Broadcast*. Naperville IL: Sourcebooks, 1999.

Garrison, Dee. *Mary Heaton Vorse: The Life of an American Insurgent*. Philadelphia: Temple University Press, 1989.

Gehrig, Eleanor, and Joseph Durso. *My Luke and I*. New York: Thomas V. Crowell, 1976.

Geisler, Paul. "Billy Jurges," SABR BioProject. August 20, 2019. https://sabr.org/bioproj/person/aada6293.

Genoways, Ted, ed. *Hard Time: Voices from a State Prison, 1849–1914*. St. Paul: Minnesota Historical Society Press, 2002.

Giamatti, A. Bartlett. *A Great and Glorious Game: Baseball Writings of A. Bartlett Giamatti*. Edited by Kenneth S. Robson. Chapel Hill NC: Algonquin, 1998.

Ginsberg, Daniel. "Ty Cobb," SABR BioProject. August 20, 2019. https://sabr.org/bioproj/person/7551754a.

Girardin, Russell G., and William Helmer. *Dillinger: The Untold Story*. Bloomington: University of Indiana Press, 1994.

Gold, Robert. "Searching Sing Sing for My Father." New York Correction History Society. August 24, 2019. http://www.correctionhistory.org/html/chronicl/state/singsing/sonsearching/html/gold08.html.

Golenbock, Peter. *The Spirit of St. Louis: A History of the St. Louis Cardinals and Browns*. New York: William Morrow, 2000.

———. *Wrigleyville: A Magical Mystery Tour of the Chicago Cubs*. New York: St. Martin's, 1998.

Gomez, Veronica, and Lawrence Goldstone. *Lefty: An American Odyssey*. New York: Random House, 2012.

Gordon, Peter. "Nick Altrock," SABR BioProject. August 24, 2019. https://sabr.org/bioproj/person/aea7c461.

Gould, Stephen Jay. *Triumph and Tragedy in Mudville: A Lifelong Passion for Baseball*. New York: W. W. Norton, 2003.

Gregory, Robert. *Diz: The Story of Dizzy Dean and Baseball During the Great Depression*. New York: Penguin, 1992.

Griffin, Nancy Snell. "Flint Rhem," SABR BioProject. August 20, 2019. https://sabr.org/bioproj/person/97c73ab1.

Grimm, Charlie and Ed Press. *Jolly Cholly's Story: Grimm's Baseball Tales*. Notre Dame IN: Diamond Communications, 1983.

Halberstam, David. *Summer of '49*. New York: William Morrow, 1989.

Hankins, Barry. *God's Rascal: J. Frank Norris and the Beginnings of Southern Fundamentalism*. Lexington: University of Kentucky Press, 2010.

Hansen, Ron. *A Wild Surge of Guilty Passion: A Novel*. New York: Scribner's, 2011.

Haskins, Jim, and N. R. Mitgang. *Mr. Bojangles: The Biography of Bill Robinson*. New York: William Morrow, 1988.

Hawkins, Joel, and Terry Bertolino. *The House of David Baseball Team.* Chicago: Arcadia, 2000.

Heidenry, John. *The Gashouse Gang: How Dizzy Dean, Leo Durocher, Branch Rickey, Pepper Martin, and Their Colorful, Come-from-Behind Ball Club Won the World Series—and America's Heart—During the Great Depression.* New York: Public Affairs, 2007.

Heilbron, W.C. *Convict Life at the Minnesota State Prison.* Stillwater MN: Valley History Press, 1996.

Heller, Karen. "Malamud's Long View of Short Stories." In *Conversations with Bernard Malamud*, edited by Lawrence M. Lasher, 123–27. Jackson: University Press of Mississippi, 1991.

Higdon, Hal. *Leopold and Loeb: the Crime of the Century.* Champaign: University of Illinois Press, 1999.

Holtzman, Jerome. *No Cheering in the Press Box.* New York: Holt, Rinehart, and Winston, 1974.

Holtzman, Jerome, and George Vass. *Baseball, Chicago Style: A Tale of Two Teams, One City.* Chicago: Bonus, 2001.

Honig, Donald. *A Donald Honig Reader.* Simon & Schuster, 1988.

Hornsby, Rogers. *My Kind of Baseball.* Edited by J. Roy Stockton. New York: David McKay, 1953.

Hornsby, Rogers, and Bill Surface. *My War with Baseball.* New York: Coward-McCann, 1962.

Jenkinson, Bill. *The Year Babe Ruth Hit 104 Home Runs: Recrowning Baseball's Greatest Slugger.* New York: Carroll & Graf, 2007.

Johnson, Bill. "Gabby Hartnett." SABR BioProject. August 20, 2019. https://sabr .org/bioproj/person/ab6d173e.

——— . "Joe Sewell." SABR BioProject. August 22, 2019. https://sabr.org/bioproj/ person/94842ba3.

Kahn, Roger. *A Flame of Pure Fire: Jack Dempsey and the Roaring '20s.* New York: Harcourt, Inc., 1999.

Kaempfer, Rick. "Today's Cubs Birthday (June 22)." Just One Bad Century. June 22, 2019. http://www.justonebadcentury.com/todays-cubs-birthday-june-22/.

Karr, Rodney D. "Farmer Rebels in Plymouth County, Iowa, 1932–1933." *The Annals of Iowa* 47 (1985): 637–45.

Keene, Anne R. *The Cloudbuster Nine: The Untold Story of Ted Williams and the Baseball Team that Helped Win World War II.* New York: Sports Publishing, 2018.

Klinkenborg, Verlyn. "The Conscience of Place: Highway 75, Iowa." *Mother Jones*, March/April 2001, https://www.motherjones.com/politics/2001/03/conscience-place-highway-75-iowa/.

Kobler, John. *Capone: the Life and World of Al Capone.* Da Capo. Reprint Edition. 2003.

Lasher, Lawrence M., ed. *Conversations with Bernard Malamud.* Jackson: University of Mississippi Press, 1991.

Leavy, Jane. *The Big Fella: Babe Ruth and the World He Created.* New York: Harper-Collins, 2018.

LeMoine, Bob. "Beans Reardon." SABR BioProject. August 22, 2019. https://sabr .org/bioproj/person/6d874f02.

Lerner, Michael A. *Dry Manhattan: Prohibition in New York City.* Cambridge MA: Harvard University Press, 2007.

Lesy, Michael. *Murder City: The Bloody History of Chicago in the Twenties.* New York: W. W. Norton, 2007.

Leuchtenburg, William E., editor. *American Places: Encounters with History.* New York: Oxford University Press, 2000.

——— . *The American Presidency: From Teddy Roosevelt to Bill Clinton.* New York: Oxford University Press, 2015.

——— . *Franklin D. Roosevelt and the New Deal: 1932–1940.* Harper Perennial, 2009.

——— . *The Perils of Prosperity 1914–32.* Chicago: University of Chicago Press, 1958.

Levy, Alan H. *Joe McCarthy: Architect of the Yankee Dynasty.* Jefferson NC: McFarland, 2005.

Leyden, Dick. "Rabbit Maranville." SABR BioProject. August 19, 2019. https://sabr .org/bioproj/person/ba80106d.

Lieb, Fred. *Baseball As I Have Known It.* New York: Grosset and Dunlap, 1977.

Lowenfish, Lee. *Branch Rickey: Baseball's Ferocious Gentleman.* Lincoln: University of Nebraska Press, 2009. Introduction by the author.

Lowry, Philip J. *Green Cathedrals: The Ultimate Celebrations of All 273 Major League and Negro League Ballparks Past and Present.* Addison and Wesley (Reprint Edition), 1993.

Lynch, Mike. "The Memorial Day Brawl of 1932." SABR BioProject. August 24, 2019. https://sabr.org/latest/memorial-day-brawl-1932.

Marlett, Jeffrey. "Leo Durocher." SABR BioProject. August 24, 2019. https://sabr .org/bioproj/person/35d925c7.

May, Allan. "The History of the Race Wire Service." Allan R. May. 1999. http:// www.allanrmay.com/Race_Wire_Service.html.

McMurray, John. "Joe McCarthy." SABR BioProject. August 24, 2019. https://sabr .org/bioproj/person/2c77f933.

McNeil, William F. *Gabby Hartnett: The Life and Times of the Cubs' Greatest Catcher.* Jefferson NC: McFarland, 2004.

Mead, William B., and Paul Dickson. *Baseball: The President's Game.* Washington DC: Farragut, 1993.

Miller, Marvin. *A Whole Different Ball Game: The Inside Story of the Baseball Revolution.* Chicago: Ivan R. Dee, 2004.

Milliken, Mark R. *Jimmie Foxx: The Pride of Sudlersville*. Lanham MD: Scarecrow, 2005.

Mitgang, Herbert. "With Bellow in Chicago." *New York Times*. July 6, 1980. Web edition. Books section. http://movies2.nytimes.com/books/00/04/23/specials /bellow-chicago80.html.

Montville, Leigh. *The Big Bam: The Life and Times of Babe Ruth*. New York: Doubleday, 2006.

Moore, April. *Folsom's 93: The Lives and Crimes of Folsom Prison's Executed Men*. Fresno CA: Craven Street, 2013.

Morris, Willie. *North Toward Home*. New York: Random House, 1967.

Murdock, Eugene. *Baseball Players and Their Times: Oral Histories of the Game, 1920–1940*. Westport CT: Meckler, 1991.

Neal, Steve. *Happy Days Are Here Again: The 1932 Democratic Convention, the Emergence of FDR—and How America was Changed Forever*. New York: William Morrow, 2004.

Nowlin, Mike. "Milt Gaston." SABR BioProject. August 24, 2019. https://sabr.org /bioproj/person/239d1bf7.

Okrent, Daniel. *Last Call: The Rise and Fall of Prohibition*. New York: Scribner, 2010.

Patterson, Ted. *The Golden Voices of Baseball*. Oak Brook IL: Sports Publishing, 2002.

Pietrusza, David. *Judge and Jury: The Life and Times of Judge Kenesaw Mountain Landis*. South Bend IN: Diamond Communications, 1998.

——. *Rothstein: The Life, Times, and Murder of the Criminal Genius Who Fixed the 1919 World Series*. New York: Carroll and Graf, 2003.

Poekel, Charlie. *Babe and the Kid: The Legendary Story of Babe Ruth and Johnny Sylvester*. Charleston SC: History Press, 2007.

Pollitt, Katha. "Creators and Creating: Bernard Malamud." *Saturday Review*, February 1981.

Reisler, Jim. *Babe Ruth: Launching the Legend*. New York: McGraw-Hill, 2004.

Ring, Jennifer. *A Game of Their Own: Voices of Contemporary Women in Baseball*. Lincoln: University of Nebraska Press, 2015.

Ritter, Lawrence S. *The Glory of Their Times: The Story of the Early Days of Baseball Told by the Men Who Played It*. New York: HarperCollins, 2002.

Roberts, Randy, and Carson Cunningham, eds. *Before the Curse: The Chicago Cubs' Glory Years 1870–1945*. Urbana: University of Illinois Press.

Roessner, Amber. *Inventing Baseball Heroes: Ty Cobb, Christy Mathewson, and the Sporting Press in America*. Baton Rouge: Louisiana State University Press, 2014.

Roosevelt, Franklin D. *The Public Papers and Addresses of Franklin D. Roosevelt: Volume One: The Genesis of the New Deal*. New York: Random House, 1938.

Ruth, Babe. *Babe Ruth's Own Book of Baseball*. Lincoln: University of Nebraska Press, 1992. First published 1928 by G. P. Putnam's Sons (New York).

Sandalow, Marc, and Jim Sutton. *Ballparks: A Panoramic History*. New York: Chartwell Books, 2014.

Sarnoff, Gary. "The Day Babe Ruth Came to Sing Sing." SABR BioProject. August 24, 2019. https://sabr.org/research/day-babe-ruth-came-sing-sing.

Schweider, Dorothy. *Iowa: The Middle Land*. Iowa City: University of Iowa Press, 1996.

——. *Patterns and Perspectives in Iowa History*. Ames: Iowa State University Press, 1973.

Seymour, Harold. *Baseball: The Early Years*. New York: Oxford University Press, 1960.

——. *Baseball: The Golden Age*. New York: Oxford University Press, 1989.

——. *Baseball: The People's Game*. New York: Oxford University Press, 1990.

Shapiro, Michael. *The Last Good Season: Brooklyn, the Dodgers, and Their Final Pennant Race Together*. New York: Doubleday, 2003.

Shattuck, Debra A. *Bloomer Girls: Women Baseball Pioneers*. Champaign: University of Illinois Press, 2017.

Shatzkin, Mike, ed. *The Ballplayers: Baseball's Ultimate Biographical Reference*. New York: William Morrow, 1990.

Shea, Stuart. *Calling the Game: Baseball Broadcasting from 1920 to the Present*. Phoenix AZ: Society for American Baseball Research, 2015.

——. *Wrigley Field: The Unauthorized Biography*. Potomac Books, 2006.

Sherman, Ed. *Babe Ruth's Called Shot: The Myth and Mystery of Baseball's Greatest Home Run*. Guilford CT: Lyons, 2014.

Shirley, Daniel. "Mark Koenig," SABR BioProject. August 24, 2019. https://sabr.org/bioproj/person/560d9b03.

Shrum, Rick. "Parting Shots: Two Local Men Recall Being Witness to Babe Ruth's Final Three Home Runs." *Pittsburg Post-Gazette*, May 10, 2006.

Skipper, Doug. "Connie Mack." SABR BioProject. August 21, 2019. https://sabr.org/bioproj/person/3462e06e.

Smith, Curt. *Voices of Summer: Ranking Baseball's 101 All-Time Best Announcers*. New York: Carroll & Graf, 2005.

——. *Voices of the Game: The Acclaimed Chronicle of Baseball Radio and Television Broadcasting—from 1921 to the Present*. New York: Simon and Schuster, 1992.

Smith, Richard Norton. *An Uncommon Man: The Triumph of Herbert Hoover*. New York: Simon and Schuster, 1984.

Snavely, Richard, and Steve Wendl. *Images of America: Anamosa Penitentiary*. Chicago: Arcadia, 2010.

Spatz, Lyle, and Steve Steinberg. *1921: The Yankees, the Giants, and the Battle for Baseball Supremacy in New York*. Lincoln: University of Nebraska Press, 2010.

Stanton, Tom. *Ty and the Babe: Baseball's Fiercest Rivals: A Surprising Friendship and the 1941 Has-Beens Golf Championship.* New York: Thomas Dunne Books, 2007.

Steele, William. *A Member of the Local Nine: Baseball Identity in the Fiction of W. P. Kinsella.* Jefferson NC: McFarland, 2012.

Steinberg, Steve, and Lyle Spatz. *The Colonel and Hug: The Partnership that Transformed the New York Yankees.* Lincoln: University of Nebraska Press, 2015.

Stephan, Terry. "A Justice for All." *Northwestern Magazine* (Spring 2009). https://www.northwestern.edu/magazine/spring2009/cover/stevens.html.

Stout, Glenn. *The Cubs: The Complete Story of Chicago Cubs Baseball.* With photographs selected and edited by Richard A. Johnson. Boston: Houghton Mifflin Company, 2007.

———. *Yankees Century: 100 Years of New York Yankees Baseball.* With photographs selected and edited by Richard A. Johnson. Boston: Houghton Mifflin, 2002.

Stump, Al. *Cobb: A Biography.* Chapel Hill NC: Algonquin, 1996.

Theodore, John. *Baseball's Natural: The Story of Eddie Waitkus.* Carbondale: Southern Illinois University Press, 2002.

Thomas, Henry W. *Walter Johnson: Baseball's Big Train.* Lincoln NE: Bison Books, 1998.

Thorn, John. *Baseball: Our Game.* New York: Penguin, 1995.

Toland, John. *The Dillinger Days.* New York: Da Capo, 1995.

Utley, Hank and Josh Devlin. "Alabama Pitts." SABR BioProject. August 24, 2019. https://sabr.org/bioproj/person/d7db6951

Vecsey, George. *Baseball: A History of America's Favorite Game.* New York: Modern Library, 2008.

Veeck, Bill, and Ed Linn. *The Hustler's Handbook.* Chicago: Ivan R. Dee, 1965.

———. *Veeck as in Wreck: The Autobiography of Bill Veeck.* Chicago: University of Chicago Press, 2001.

Vitti, Jim. *Chicago Cubs: Baseball on Catalina Island.* Charlestown SC: Arcadia, 2010.

Wagenheim, Kal. *Babe Ruth: His Life and Legend.* Chicago: Olmstead, 2001.

Wagner, William J. *Wrigley Blues: The Year the Cubs Played Hardball with the Curse (but Lost Anyway).* Lanham MD: Taylor, 2005.

Waldo, Ronald T. *Hazen "Kiki" Cuyler: A Baseball Biography.* Jefferson NC: McFarland, 2012.

Walker, James. *Crack of the Bat: A History of Baseball on the Radio.* Lincoln: University of Nebraska Press, 2015.

Wall, Joseph Frazier. *Iowa: A Bicentennial History.* New York: Norton, 1978.

Walsh, John Evangelist. "Babe Ruth and the Legend of the Called Shot." *Wisconsin Magazine of History* 77, no. 4 (Summer 1994): 242–63.

Wancho, Joseph. "Bill Dickey," SABR BioProject. August 20, 2019. https://sabr.org
/bioproj/person/25ce33d8.

――――. "Dizzy Dean," SABR BioProject. August 24, 2019. https://sabr.org/bioproj
/person/40bc224d.

Ward, Geoffrey C., and Ken Burns. *Baseball: An Illustrated History*. New York:
Alfred A. Knopf, 1994.

Waters, Walter W., and William C. White. *B.E.F.: The Whole Story of the Bonus
Army*. New York: AMS, 1970.

Watkins, T. H. *The Hungry Years: A Narrative History of the Great Depression in
America*. New York: Henry Holt, 1999.

Watson, Bruce. "The Judge Who Ruled Baseball." *Smithsonian Magazine*, September 2000.

Weintraub, Robert. *The House That Ruth Built: A New Stadium, the First Yankees
Championship, and the Redemption of 1923*. New York: Little, Brown, 2011.

Wendl, Steve. "From the Hangman's Noose to the World Series." Voice of Jones
County Podcast Radio. September 10, 2019. https://www.voiceofjonescounty
.com/stories-from-the-anamosa-penitentiary.html.

Wolf, Gregory H. "Charlie Root," SABR BioProject. August 20, 2019. https://sabr
.org/bioproj/person/22e9a7e7.

――――. "Freddie Fitzsimmons," SABR BioProject. August 24, 2019. https://sabr.org
/bioproj/person/5a7df0b9.

――――. "Guy Bush," SABR BioProject. August 24, 2019. https://sabr.org/bioproj
/person/9c9bf76f.

――――. "Kiki Cuyler," SABR BioProject. August 24, 2019. https://sabr.org/bioproj
/person/7107706b.

Wolf, Thomas. "The Golden Era of Prison Baseball and the Revenge of Casey
Coburn." In *The Cooperstown Symposium on Baseball and American Culture,
2017–2018*, edited by William M. Simons, 116–26. Jefferson NC: McFarland,
2019.

――――. "The Warden Takes a Murderer to the World Series: A Tale of Depression-
Era Compassion." In *The Cooperstown Symposium on Baseball and American
Culture, 2005–2006*, edited by William M. Simons, 201–14. Jefferson NC:
McFarland, 2007.

Wood, Allan. "Babe Ruth." SABR BioProject. August 24, 2019. https://sabr.org/bio-
proj/person/9dcdd01c.

――――. *Babe Ruth and the 1918 Red Sox*. Lincoln NE: Writer's Club Press, 2000.

Zimmerman, William. *William Wrigley, Jr.: The Man and His Business, 1861–1932*. R.
R. Donnelley. Private Edition. 1935.

INDEX